UNITED STATES ARMY IN WORLD WAR II

The War Department

THE ARMY AND INDUSTRIAL MANPOWER

by

Byron Fairchild

and

Jonathan Grossman

OFFICE OF THE CHIEF OF MILITARY HISTORY

DEPARTMENT OF THE ARMY

WASHINGTON, D. C., 1959

This volume, one of the series UNITED STATES ARMY IN WORLD WAR II, is the seventh to be published in the subseries THE WAR DEPARTMENT. All the volumes will be closely related, and the series will present a comprehensive account of the activities of the Military Establishment during World War II. A tentative list of subseries is appended at the end of this volume.

Library of Congress Catalog Card Number: 59—60000

For sale by the Superintendent of Documents, U.S. Government Printing Office
Washington 25, D.C.—Price of this volume $2.75 (Cloth)

UNITED STATES ARMY IN WORLD WAR II

Kent Roberts Greenfield, General Editor

Advisory Committee

(As of 30 May 1958)

Elmer Ellis
University of Missouri

Samuel Flagg Bemis
Yale University

Gordon A. Craig
Princeton University

Oron J. Hale
University of Virginia

W. Stull Holt
University of Washington

Brig Gen. John B. Sullivan
U.S. Continental Army Command

Brig. Gen. Edgar C. Doleman
Army War College

Brig. Gen. Frederick R. Zierath
Command and General Staff College

Brig. Gen. Kenneth F. Zitzman
Industrial College of the Armed Forces

Col. Vincent J. Esposito
United States Military Academy

T. Harry Williams
Louisiana State University

Office of the Chief of Military History

Maj. Gen. Richard W. Stephens, Chief

Chief Historian	Kent Roberts Greenfield
Chief, Histories Division	Col. Seneca W. Foote
Chief, Editorial and Publication Division	Lt. Col. E. E. Steck
Editor in Chief	Joseph R. Friedman
Chief, Cartographic Branch	Elliot Dunay
Chief, Photographic Branch	Margaret E. Tackley

iii

The History of

THE WAR DEPARTMENT

Chief of Staff: Prewar Plans and Preparations
Washington Command Post: The Operations Division
Strategic Planning for Coalition Warfare: 1941–1942
Strategic Planning for Coalition Warfare: 1943–1944
Global Logistics and Strategy: 1940–1943
Global Logistics and Strategy: 1943–1945
Buying Air Power: Procurement of Matériel
The Army and Economic Mobilization
The Army and Industrial Manpower

. . . to Those Who Served

Foreword

This book is one of a number in the present series that describe what happened to the U.S. Army in World War II as the result of two prevailing circumstances. One was that the War Department had a vital interest and a leading role in maintaining the production of supplies needed to win the war. The other was that, once organized for war, the War Department and the Army comprised an administrative machine incomparably more efficient for getting things done than any other at the disposal of the President. In both connections Army officers found themselves drawn into the realm of industrial management—one surely remote from the field of battle. A companion volume, *The Army and Economic Mobilization,* shows how extensively and deeply the War Department became involved in business relationships. The authors of the present volume examine and illustrate the ways in which the Army and its officers dealt with the problems into which they were drawn in dealing with organized labor. Since World War II the Army has become even more deeply involved in relations, present and potential, with industry and industrial management. No officer can therefore afford to overlook the instructive experience that this book recounts.

Washington, D. C.
30 May 1958

R. W. STEPHENS
Maj. Gen., U. S. A.
Chief of Military History

The Authors

Byron Fairchild received the Ph.D. degree in history from Princeton University and has taught at the University of Maine, Amherst College, and Munson Institute of Maritime History. He is the author of *Messrs. William Pepperrell,* which received the Carnegie Revolving Fund Award of the American Historical Association for the outstanding manuscript in any field of history in 1954, and has contributed a number of articles and reviews to historical journals. As a civilian professional historian with the Army since 1949, Dr. Fairchild has been coauthor of two other volumes scheduled to appear in the Army's official World War II series: *The Framework of Hemisphere Defense* and *Guarding the United States and Its Outposts.*

Jonathan Grossman has his Ph.D. degree from Columbia University and has taught at City College of New York and Rutgers University. Author of the biography, *William Sylvis, Pioneer of American Labor,* Dr. Grossman has also worked on projects with the National Industrial Conference Board, prepared sections of a history of the Metropolitan Life Insurance Company, and worked as a historian on the Morgenthau Diary. He joined the staff of the Army's Office of the Chief of Military History in 1949, leaving in 1953 to become Historian for the Office, Chief of Finance, where he is currently writing a history of fiscal activities during World War II.

Preface

Over the years the Army in peacetime has become accustomed to performing tasks that have had only remote if any bearing on its role as a defender of the country and guardian of law and order, while in time of war its energies have been concentrated on fighting the enemy. But as war has changed in character and has come to be more "total," more mechanized, so the role of the Army has broadened. Activities that in former times were extraneous have become inherently part of the conduct of war. Statecraft, diplomacy, scientific research, and business management have become part of the soldier's stock in trade, and now the labor expert-in-uniform has taken his place alongside the soldier-diplomat and the military scientist.

As a result of its World War I experience, the War Department in 1920 was given responsibility for planning the mobilization of industry. As the full scope of responsibility gradually developed, the mobilization planners brought industrial labor within the range of their endeavors, but when World War II placed unprecedented demands on American industry the Army finally found itself drawn into a position with respect to labor that was not precisely according to plan. The nature of the problems that the Army then faced and the major steps taken to deal with them make up the substance of the story told in the following pages.

To write a comprehensive and complete history of the Army's activities in the field of industrial labor problems would mean treating the subject thoroughly on a number of levels—the service commands, the various technical services, Army Service Forces headquarters, the Bureau of Public Relations of the War Department, and the Under Secretary's office—and it would lead outside the War Department as well. It would mean dealing systematically with each of the capacities in which the War Department became involved in labor matters, namely, as the agency principally responsible for the procurement of military matériel, as the direct employer of civilian labor in government-owned and government-operated plants, as the chief military claimant for the use of the nation's manpower, as the agency responsible for internal security and for custody of prisoners of war, and as one of the agencies called upon to enforce labor and manpower policies for which the laws failed to provide adequate sanctions. A history on so vast a scale could be produced only if time and space were unlimited. In any case, large segments of the story at these different levels can be found in other volumes of the UNITED STATES ARMY IN WORLD WAR II. The histories of the respective technical services and those dealing with procurement, supply, and economic mobilization place labor matters within the setting of the organization or activity that comprises the subject of the particular volume.

In this volume we have told the story principally from the vantage point of the Office of the Under Secretary of War and the Industrial Personnel Division, ASF, with only brief and very general excursions into the field. It is an account not so much of operations as of relationships, policies, and interests. The problems connected with the utilization of industrial manpower into which the Army was drawn are illustrated, rather than traced, by discussing successively the principal elements that affected the productivity and size of the industrial labor force, the major efforts to counteract adverse factors, and the ways and means of enforcing manpower policies. The approach is topical, but the topics are not treated as case studies. We have presented the facts chronologically and according to their causal relationship, without the plastic surgery so often required for proving a point or general principle.

We have been saved from pitfalls at every turn by the advice and aid of our colleagues and of many of the people who helped to make the history that we were writing. For their assistance we are grateful. Our debt to Kent Roberts Greenfield, Chief Historian of the Army, is large. The brute facts that we have failed to tame in spite of Dr. Greenfield's good shepherding are evidence of what the book would have been like without his help. Although an associate only in the early stages of the work, Albert A. Blum, at present a member of the faculty of New York University, has contributed much to the final product. His assistance lightened the drudgery of research and his ground-breaking studies on selective service provided the basis for the sections on that subject that appear in the book. Helen McShane Bailey, editor of this volume, her colleague, Mary Ann Bacon, Loretto Carroll Stevens, copy editor, and Joseph R. Friedman, editor in chief, have rescued us from infelicities, inconsistencies, and disorder on nearly every page. Finally we wish to express our special indebtedness to all those who, in addition to Dr. Greenfield, have read the manuscript and generously given us the benefit of their comments and suggestions. We particularly thank W. G. Flinn, Col. S. W. Foote, U.S. Army, John P. Hall, John H. Ohly, Albert F. Sanderson, Jr., and Lt. Col. T. H. Swan, U.S. Army, as well as Leonard P. Adams, Leo P. Brophy, Goldthwaite H. Dorr, Ralph F. Gow, Edward S. Greenbaum, Maj. Gen. R. P. Hollis, U.S. Army, Albert Kay, John D. Millett, Samuel Silver, and Sidney C. Sufrin. It seems almost superfluous to add that for any error of fact or interpretation the authors alone are responsible.

Washington, D. C.   BYRON FAIRCHILD
30 May 1958   JONATHAN GROSSMAN

Contents

Tables

Charts

THE ARMY AND INDUSTRIAL MANPOWER

CHAPTER I

War Department Labor Planning: 1920–40

For centuries, Mars made his public appearances clad in his one and only suit of armor, wearing the same old helmet and bearing the same sword and shield. But World War I demonstrated that if he were to keep up with the times he would have to have an extra suit of clothes. He would need a pair of overalls and a workman's cap and he would have to learn to wield a wrench as well as a sword. What was more, he would be expected to wear both suits at the same time. Thus the War Department, by Armistice Day, 1918, had found it necessary to go beyond the raising of an army and beyond the conduct of military operations into the field of industrial manpower and labor relations. The War Department, to quote its report on these activities, had become "a dominant factor in the industrial and labor situation." It had become involved in adjusting labor disputes, in fixing wages and hours of work, and in providing war workers with a host of community services. In order to function in these new fields, the War Department had created a number of emergency boards, commissions, and offices under the general direction of an Assistant Secretary, Benedict Crowell, a former Cleve - land industrialist.[1]

Statutory recognition of the War Department's new role and the basis for its subsequent activities in the field of industrial mobilization were given in the National Defense Act of 1920, which charged the Assistant Secretary of War "with supervision of the procurement of all military supplies and other business of the War Department pertaining thereto and the assurance of adequate provision for mobilization of matériel and industrial organiza- tions essential to wartime needs."[2] In the field of industrial mobilization, the authority vested in the Assistant Secretary was sweeping and potentially enormous, for his peacetime planning responsibilities extended beyond the confines of the War Department almost as far as he chose to go.

[1] *A Report of the Activities of the War Department in the Field of Industrial Relations During the War* (Washington: Government Printing Office, 1919), pp. 7, 11–26, 28–44.
[2] 41 Stat. 764, National Defense Act, June 4, 1920, Sec. 5a.

To carry out these tasks, a Procurement Division consisting of a Planning Branch and a Current Supply Branch was established on 25 October 1921 in the Office of the Assistant Secretary. The Planning Branch was assigned the function of planning for industrial mobilization and procurement in time of war. For some time it was for all practical purposes the only agency of the government engaged in planning for industrial mobilization. Later, its work in this field was supplemented by that of the Army Industrial College, and still later the "nominal sponsorship" of industrial mobilization plans passed into the hands of the Joint Army and Navy Munitions Board (ANMB). Nevertheless, the Planning Branch continued to do the major share of work until as late as 1940.[3]

The First Decade of Planning

During the decade of the 1920's emphasis was almost entirely on procurement planning. In 1922, 1924, and 1928 the Planning Branch submitted to the Assistant Secretary three basic plans, which, whether entitled "War Plan for Industrial Mobilization" or "Basic Procurement Plan," dealt almost exclusively with wartime procurement. The Army Industrial College, established in February 1924 for the purpose of training officers in the procurement duties and industrial mobilization planning functions laid down in the National Defense Act, likewise focused its attention on procurement. The problems and exercises assigned to the students were "intended to orient [them] in the field of procurement planning . . . ," and in 1927 Assistant Secretary Hanford MacNider pointed with pride to the fact that "in the supply branches more and more of the graduates of the college are being employed upon work connected with procurement planning."[4] Procurement received the greater emphasis partly because procurement policies and requirements were considered the necessary foundation for a program of industrial mobilization and partly because a legislative framework in the field of labor, wage, and price control had to be built up.

Only a few halting steps were taken in the direction of industrial mobilization planning. The War Department's responsibility for determining the transportation load that a future war might impose upon any particular locality had been noted in the 1922 plan. As for control of railroad facilities

---

[3] Harold W. Thatcher, *Planning for Industrial Mobilization, 1920–1940,* QMC Historical Studies, 4 (Washington, 1943, reprinted 1948), pp. 15–18, 59–60. For a more comprehensive account of planning in the interval between World War I and World War II, see R. Elberton Smith. *The Army and Economic Mobilization,* UNITED STATES ARMY IN WORLD WAR II (Washington: Government Printing Office, 1959), Part Two.

[4] Thatcher, *op. cit.,* quoted on pp. 30, 33.

and operations in an emergency, the War Department steadfastly maintained a hands-off policy. The 1922 plan also had made mention of the War Department's responsibility for estimating and analyzing labor requirements of industrial facilities that might be allocated to war production. In the 1924 plan, no attempt was made to cope with the labor problem. This plan contained one important new feature related to industrial mobilization planning, namely, a list of "superagencies" to be established by act of Congress or by the President, under Congressional authority, "for the purposes of coordinating, adjusting and conserving the available agencies and resources so as to promptly and adequately meet the maximum requirements of the military forces and the essential needs of the civilian population." [5] An administrative organization for labor was included in the list. The 1928 plan went somewhat further and in certain provisions envisaged a measure of control, even coercion, of workers and employers alike. Specifically, the plan proposed that industrial establishments assigned to war production be required to recruit labor only through federal employment agencies. Workers who left their jobs in war plants were to be required to obtain a certificate of discharge, on which it was to be noted whether the employee left as a result of a wage dispute, and if this were the case both his wage and the wage demanded were to be shown.[6]

Some progress was made toward providing the necessary legislative framework. The temper of the times—the period was one of "Red" scares, of disillusionment over the "war to end wars," and of ruthless, lawless industrial strife—spawned a number of proposals for a universal draft of manpower and for controlling prices, labor, and industrial resources in time of war. At least ten bills to this general end were introduced in Congress during the 1920's, but none passed. One of them, sponsored by the American Legion in 1922, had been prepared with the assistance of the War Department and remained the "real core of the [War Department's] whole legislative program" at least until 1931.[7] This bill would have authorized the President, in the event of a national emergency, "to draft into the service of the United States such members of the Unorganized Militia as he may deem necessary . . . without exemption on account of industrial occupation," and, in case of war or whenever he considered war to be imminent, he was authorized and required "to determine and proclaim the material resources, industrial organizations and services over which Government control is necessary . . .," to exercise such

[5] *Ibid.*, quoted on pp. 67–68.
[6] *Ibid.*, pp. 78–79.
[7] *Ibid.*, pp. 104, 124.

control through existing agencies or ones created for that purpose, and "to take such steps as may be necessary to stabilize prices of services and of all commodities declared to be essential, whether such services and commodities are required by the government or by the civilian population." [8] The term "services" was understood to include labor. In full agreement with the principles of the bill, the Secretary of War wrote the chairman of the House Committee on Military Affairs that it would provide "for the first time in our history a legal basis on which to formulate plans in time of peace for mobilizing all of our resources as contemplated in the National Defense Act." [9] Samuel Gompers, president of the American Federation of Labor (AFL) was now taking "more than ordinary interest"—as he himself expressed it—in the subject of industrial mobilization planning, and he urged the War Department to consult union officials, as it had during World War I, on labor's vital role in war production. [10] Although the bill was rejected by Congress, it was incorporated in the legislative appendix to the 1924 Industrial Mobilization Plan.

The Planning Branch of the Assistant Secretary's office, with the help of the Judge Advocate General's office had prepared drafts of several other bills, which were likewise annexed to the early plans. The more important of these authorized, upon declaration of war, the creation of nine superagencies, the suspension of certain laws that might have restricted procurement, and the acquisition of private property of all kinds. In 1924 the War Department favored the enactment in peacetime of legislation that would be needed for its wartime program, but by 1930 it had shifted its position. The failure of Congress to pass such legislation, recognition that constant revision would be needed to meet changing conditions, and the rise of an unfavorable climate of opinion persuaded the War Department not to seek the enactment of specific legislation. Drafts of appropriate bills were to be prepared, as the Planning Branch had been doing, and then filed for discussion, revision, and presentation to Congress as soon as an emergency arose. [11]

Beginning in the summer of 1929, the Planning Branch turned its attention to drafting a genuine plan for industrial mobilization. By the end of the following year it had produced such a plan, the first one that was more than either a procurement plan or a bare skeleton of industrial mobilization. From the vantage point of 1930, the War Department viewed the problem

---

[8] *Ibid.* For the text of the bill, see pages 107–08.

[9] *Ibid.*, quoted on p. 109.

[10] Ltr, Gompers to SW, 26 May 24, quoted in Memo, 3 Jan 35, sub: Notes on Relationship Between OASW and the AFL, OUSW Res and Prod Div 175, Labor 1935–39.

[11] Thatcher, *op. cit..* pp. 118–21, 127–28.

as one that involved stabilizing the peacetime economy rather than transforming it for purposes of war. The role of the federal government would be, in the words of the plan, "to minimize damaging effects of sudden changes in industrial activity and to use its influence to maintain an approximate economic equilibrium throughout the Nation. No radical changes in normal economic relationships . . . ," the War Department asserted, "should be instituted. The methods and customs of peace must be employed as far as practicable, . . ." [12]

Throughout the history of the United States, manpower had never been one of the more abundant resources of the nation. Nevertheless, the War Department planners proceeded on the assumption that it would be adequate for any war effort the United States might be called upon to make. "It is almost impossible," the 1930 plan stated, "to assume a situation where our population would be in danger of suffering actual hardships in war due to a lack of personnel to produce the necessaries of life." The approach, therefore, was that "of determining how many men we believe it necessary to organize into military and naval units under a given situation, rather than how many we could safely so organize." [13] The labor problem, so the War Department planners thought, resolved itself into "the minimizing of excessive migration of labor by an equitable distribution of war orders, the prevention of unethical competition for labor by war industries, compilations for the information of the President of lists of industrial deferments required for efficient operation of war industries, the avoidance and settlement of industrial disputes, and the coordination of employment services." [14] It was not considered necessary in 1930 to devote much attention to the problem of recruiting, training, or mobilizing additional workers for war industry in wartime.

Criticisms and Revisions: 1931–37

The 1930 plan was the first of the industrial mobilization plans to be subjected to public scrutiny. Growing resentment over the great stock market crash of 1929 and the impact of economic depression led to a widespread belief that huge fortunes had been made in World War I, and this in turn impelled Congress to create, in June 1930, a joint Congressional and Cabinet commission specifically charged with investigating the expropriation of pri-

---

[12] *Ibid.,* quoted on pp. 157–58.

[13] *Ibid.,* quoted on p. 155.

[14] *Ibid.,* quoted on pp. 160–61. The passage quoted represents a slight revision (1931) of the original text.

vate property for public use in time of war.[15]   As one of its first acts, the War Policies Commission obtained a copy of the 1930 Industrial Mobilization Plan for each member.   During public hearings in the spring of 1931 a measure of suspicion and criticism of the plan became evident.

Nearly fifty witnesses appeared, presented their views, and were questioned by the commission.   The great bulk of testimony and interrogation dealt with matters of price control, excess profits, and government operation of industrial establishments.   Under the terms of the resolution creating it, the commission was expressly forbidden to entertain any suggestion for conscripting labor, but one of the members, Representative Ross A. Collins of Mississippi, seemed determined to show that industrial mobilization planning meant just that.   It was a ticklish question.   Even representatives of veterans' associations, who advocated a universal draft law, hesitated to go on record as favoring more than merely "controlling" labor.[16]   Bernard M. Baruch, who had been the head of the War Industries Board in 1918–19, testified that he had not thoroughly "digested" the complete industrial mobilization plan, and, when Representative Collins asserted that it seemed to him as though "the War Department's mobilization plan has in mind the conscription of labor," Mr. Baruch replied, "If it does, I am opposed to it." [17]   Representatives of organized labor who appeared before the commission were, as might be expected, unalterably opposed to conscripting labor.   They were joined by others besides Baruch: by former Secretary of War Newton D. Baker, by Brig. Gen. Palmer E. Pierce, wartime member of the General Munitions Board and War Industries Board, and even by industrialists.   In attempting to maneuver witnesses into committing themselves on the question, and perhaps to raise the bogy of militarism, Representative Collins gave to the War Department's plan an aspect that spokesmen for the War Department categorically rejected.   The chairman of the commission, Secretary of War Patrick J. Hurley, sought to make clear the position of the War Department, and, in answer to one of his questions, Maj. Gen. George Van Horn Moseley, then Deputy Chief of Staff, stated explicitly: "The policy of the War Department is that we can never in time of emergency draft labor.   There is no plan in the War Department based on that principle." [18]   The Chief of Staff,

[15] Public Resolution 98, 71st Congress, reprinted in House Document 271, 72d Congress, 1st Session, *Documents By War Policies Commission* (Washington: Government Printing Office, 1932), pp. 892–93.

[16] See Statement of Thomas Kirby, National Legislative Chairman Disabled American Veterans, and of Ralph T. O'Neil, National Commander the American Legion, in House Document 271, 72d Congress, 1st Session, *Documents By War Policies Commission,* Part 1, pp. 2–6; 7–29.

[17] *Ibid.,* Part 1, p. 71.

[18] *Ibid.,* Part 2, p. 389.

General Douglas MacArthur, in the course of a thorough exposition, likewise assured the commission that the War Department counted only upon the voluntary support of labor.

The early draft of the plan, which had been furnished to members of the commission, had been somewhat vague on the question of labor, and the legislative annex contained drafts of bills that, if broadly construed, might have provided authority for conscripting labor. Some time before the commission hearing opened, Lt. Col. Clarence B. Ross of the Planning Branch had begun a thoroughgoing overhaul of the labor sections of the plan. Revisions were made throughout 1931, with the result that the plan annexed to the War Policies Commission's report late in 1931 was a different version from the one that had been made available to the commission.[19]

The plan provided for an organization based on the draft bills drawn up over the preceding years. Four superagencies—selective service, war industry, public relations, and war labor—were provided for, each headed by a civilian who together with the Secretaries of War and the Navy would constitute the President's advisory war council. As head of war labor, an administrative agency, the labor administrator's primary function would be to insure that war industries and essential civil industries had an adequate labor supply. The plan had this to say:

The administrator of labor must develop policies designed to get men through their voluntary cooperation into the proper places in industry and keep them there. He must supervise relationships between labor and its employers; he must act as a mediator in disputes; he must collect and analyze statistics. He must at one and the same time be labor's advocate and representative in the highest executive circles, while serving as the agent of the Federal Government, guiding its employment for the common cause.[20]

Further comment on the tasks of the administrator would appear to be superfluous. To assist him in his Herculean labors there was to be an advisory council appointed by the President and consisting of ten members, five of whom were to be nominated by the AFL. Organized labor, that is to say the AFL, was to be specifically represented on all levels of the war labor administration as well as in the Office of the Assistant Secretary of War and in the office of the director of war industry. President William Green of the AFL, to whom Colonel Ross sent a copy of the revisions, wrote that the executive committee of the federation found "nothing objectionable in the plan as submitted."[21]

[19] Thatcher, *op. cit.*, pp. 146n, 177–78. All extant copies of the 1930–31 plan are the revised version.

[20] Plan for Industrial Mobilization, 1931, in House Document 271, 72d Congress, 1st Session, *Documents By War Policies Commission*, pp. 395–470.

[21] Ltr, Green to Ross, 11 Feb 32. OUSW Res and Prod Div 175, Labor 1935–39.

Within the War Department itself, the 1931 revisions met with bitter criticism. G–1, the General Staff division responsible for Army personnel policies, objected strenuously to the labor sections. Brig. Gen. Andrew Moses, chief of the division, insisted that the primary mission of the proposed labor administration was "to assist industry." [22]   As it seemed to G–1, the plan disregarded this end in favor of making organized labor "the controlling factor."   Instead of being designed to supply industry with the necessary manpower, it was aimed, so the criticism went, at protecting the interests of labor in time of war.   The organization should be revised, G–1 suggested, to make the labor administrator subordinate to the administrator of war industry.   Furthermore, G–1 objected to the relationship between the labor administration and the selective service system.   Under the revisions made by Colonel Ross, the local labor boards, which were responsible to the central labor administration in Washington, were to advise and make recommendations to the local selective service boards in the matter of occupational deferments.   G–1 objected on the ground that labor, specifically the AFL, was put in a position where it could bring pressure to bear on the local draft boards.   With a war labor administration paralleling the selective service system "from top to bottom," G–1 envisaged a situation arising in which selective service chose the men who would fight at the front while the war labor administration selected those who would stay comfortably at home. The slightest suspicion that a special group was in a favored position would undermine public confidence in the selective service system, G–1 asserted. World War I experience, when the needs of industry required the deferment of less than 3 percent of all registrants, indicated to G–1 that plans for wide-scale industrial deferments would, in any event, be unnecessary.[23]

Although the bulk of the objections fell on the labor sections of the plan, other deficiencies were found by other critics.   Both the Navy Department and the War Plans Division of the War Department criticized the 1930–31 plan for its failure to make mention of the Army and Navy Munitions Board. The ANMB had been established for the purpose, among other things, of co-ordinating industrial mobilization plans and policies with the requirements of Army-Navy joint war plans, but it had been moribund almost from the

[22] Memo, G–1 for ASW, 24 June 32, OUSW Res and Prod Div 116.6, Plan for Industrial Mobilization (Labor Adm and Labor Sec).

[23] Memo, Lt Col R. D. Coombs, 22 Apr 32, sub: Comments on Mobilization Plan, Labor Adm OASW, Memo, Comdr R. W. Wurt, USN, 11 Jun 32, sub: Comments on the Labor Plan, Memo, Lt Col W. S. Fulton for G–1, 20 Jun 32, sub: IMP—Labor, and Memo, G–1 for ASW, 24 Jun 32, sub: IMP—1930, Labor Sec, all in OUSW Res and Prod Div 116.6, Plan for QM (Labor Adm and Labor Sec); Memo, The Labor Adm Plan of Lt Col C. B. Ross . . . Compared, 1 Mar 33, OUSW Res and Prod Div 175, Labor 1935–39.

start and was ignored in the 1930-31 plan.   Now the ANMB was showing signs of reviving.   Secretary of War Hurley, in reply to the Navy criticism, agreed that "any plans . . . that affect national resources, must of necessity be drawn with the fullest cooperation of the Navy Department," and he assured Secretary of the Navy Charles F. Adams that "the War Department is in thorough accord with the Navy Department that the two services should proceed without delay to the joint development of such plans . . . ."   As a result, a reconstruction of the ANMB took place during the last half of 1931, just in time for it to play a role in drafting a new industrial mobilization plan.[24]

The new plan, the Industrial Mobilization Plan of 1933, took heed of most of the criticism.   After studying the objections that had been raised against the 1931 edition, Assistant Secretary of War Frederick H. Payne had rejected the suggestion that the labor administration be subordinate to the director of war industries, but he had instructed the Planning Branch to modify "some of the details of the labor section of the industrial mobilization plan to overcome the objections of G-1." [25]   This the Planning Branch did, to such an extent that the 1933 plan was made vulnerable to attack from the opposite direction.   The provisions of the 1931 version assuring labor of representation by "its natural leaders" in the war industries administration and providing for labor representatives in the other government agencies that would deal with industrial matters were eliminated in the 1933 plan.   The members of the labor administrator's advisory council, who in the 1931 plan were to have been "nominated by the American Federation of Labor," were referred to in the 1933 plan merely as "representing labor."   The labor administrator himself, for whom no specific qualifications had been established in the 1931 plan, was required by the 1933 edition to be "an outstanding industrial leader."   In addition, the labor administration organization was divorced from selective service operations by the elimination of that part of the 1931 plan which had authorized the local labor boards to participate in setting up occupational deferments.[26]   The organization and functions of the reinvigorated ANMB were set forth in one of the appendixes to the plan, while in the foreword the fact was noted that "the Navy Department also is vitally interested . . . and has collaborated in the preparation of this revision.

---

[24] Thatcher, *op. cit.*, pp. 46–49.   The quotations are from pages 47–48.

[25] Memo, ASW for Dir Planning Br, 8 Jul 32, OUSW Res and Prod Div, 116.6, Plan for QM (Labor Adm and Labor Sec).

[26] *Industrial Mobilization Plan, Revised 1933* (Washington: Government Printing Office, 1933).   See also Thatcher, *op. cit.*, pp. 203–04, 206.   Thatcher's detailed account of the 1930–33 planning is obscure.

The labors of the two Departments have been coordinated by the Army and Navy Munitions Board, which is charged with this responsibility by administrative directives." [27]   As yet this responsibility was far from onerous, for the Navy Department had nothing at all similar to the Army industrial mobilization plan, and the 1933 plan was in no sense a joint plan.[28]   But the fact that the ANMB's existence was recognized was a step forward.

The 1933 plan soon became something of a whipping boy at the hands of a special Senate committee headed by Senator Gerald P. Nye of North Dakota and charged with investigating the munitions industry.   Unlike the earlier War Policies Commission, which had chiefly concentrated upon the effectiveness and purposes of the 1930 plan as a means of industrial mobilization, the Nye Committee chose to probe into the social and economic effects of the proposed wartime controls.   An inquiry of this sort, had it been conceived in sincerity and conducted impartially, would have been most desirable, but the Nye Committee's interest in industrial mobilization planning was only tangential to its primary aim of exposing the "merchants of death" whom it held responsible for the United States' entry into World War I. Convinced that a conspiracy of munitions makers and Wall Street bankers had dragged the nation into war, the Nye Committee sought to twist the industrial mobilization plan into evidence of an alliance between the Army and the group that had been the "plotters" of 1917.   After nearly two years of hearings, the committee, thoroughly primed with sensationalism, issued a report that even at the time was viewed by many Americans as being important only as a striking example of extreme isolationism and political demagoguery.   The committee, stressing the theme that the plan favored capital over labor, charged that the proposed selective service system would be in effect an instrument for setting up a military dictatorship in time of war and that the proposed labor administration was a club that could be used for beating labor into submission.[29]   Scrutinizing the draft bills appended to the industrial mobilization plan, the Nye Committee saw fit to issue the following warning:

In view of the growth of dictatorships in the world using labor under military control, it is very important that the people weigh the grave dangers to our democracy involved in the draft of manpower and labor under the conditions proposed.   The price of a war may be actual operating dictatorship, under military control, in this country.[30]

[27] *Industrial Mobilization Plan, Revised 1933*, p. v.

[28] Robert H. Connery, *The Navy and the Industrial Mobilization in World War II* (Princeton: Princeton University Press, 1951), pp. 38–39.

[29] Senate Special Committee Investigating the Munitions Industry, 73d Congress, Hearings on Senate Resolution 206, *Munitions Industry*, pp. 4296–99, 4303; Senate Report 944, 74th Congress, 2d Session, June 1, 1936, Part 4, p. 50.

[30] Senate Report 944, Part 4, p. 5.

The exaggerated findings of the Nye Committee were eagerly seized upon by radicals of the labor movement and by groups that had no other concern for labor than as a wedge to be insidiously used for splintering American loyalties, as had been the case with the War Policies Commission report several years earlier. Such critics as these were able to capitalize on the widespread interest aroused by the Nye Committee's sensational plunge into the reasons for American participation in World War I, an opportunity not presented by the comparatively apathetic reception of the War Policies Commission report. Moreover, the Nye Committee provided more fuel; the 1933 plan was more susceptible to distortion than the 1930–31 plan had been; and, finally, in the intervening years the chorus of deceptive criticsm had grown more strident.[31]

A new industrial mobilization plan, a preliminary draft of which was ready early in 1936, had been in preparation while the Nye Committee hearings were in progress. It was the first to appear under the sponsorship of the ANMB. As the next to final stage in the evolutionary process that culminated in the Industrial Mobilization Plan of 1939, the revision of 1936 is of interest in three respects: in its recognition of a transition period between peace and war, in its treatment of the legislative basis for industrial mobilization, and in its attempts to make the labor provisions more satisfactory to legitimate critics. Perhaps most important of the changes relating to labor was the stipulation that the war labor adminisrator must be an "outstanding citizen" instead of an "outstanding industrial leader," as provided in the preceding plan. Under the 1936 plan, the mediation board and other agencies engaged in adjusting labor disputes were to remain in the Department of Labor, instead of being transferred to the war labor administration. A section of the early plan that dealt with "assigning" jobs to the unemployed was deleted. A potential stalemate was eliminated by revising the composition of the war labor administrator's advisory council, which under the 1936 plan was now to consist of four labor representatives, four management representatives, and two members representing the general public. Finally, instead of the regional labor boards provided in the 1933 plan, the Industrial Mobilization Plan of 1936 reverted to the earlier proposal for a decentralized system of state boards to cope with local problems.[32]

---

[31] See Seymour Waldman, *Death and Profits: A Study of the War Policies Commission* (New York: Brewer, Warren, and Putnam, 1932) and Rose M. Stein, *M-Day, The First Day of War* (New York: Harcourt, Brace and Company, 1936). Thatcher, *op. cit.*, pp. 213–15, discusses the attack on the 1933 plan.

[32] *Industrial Mobilization Plan, Revised 1936* (Washington: Government Printing Office, 1936), pp. 14, 19, 34–44.

Pacifist organizations and the working man's self-styled friends whose roots went back to Marx rather than to Samuel Gompers continued their attacks on the industrial mobilization plan. From both pacifists and Marxists, the criticism took much the same line: that the plan was a "blueprint for fascism," that it was directed against labor, and that its basic purpose was to perpetuate high profits for the big industrialists who would be placed in control of industrial mobilization.[33] However spurious they were, allegations like these played upon and heightened a basic American aversion to regimentation.

All critics, including the most thoughtful and responsible, opposed the conscription of labor, and some were persuaded that the Army counted on drafting labor. Bernard Baruch, commenting on the 1936 plan, expressed himself vigorously in opposition to military control over civilian activities. Certain features of the plan relating to procurement, plant expansion studies, and the organization of the ANMB were, in Baruch's opinion, lacking in the necessary civilian control.[34] Other responsible critics, including spokesmen for the AFL, news commentators, and officers of the American Legion, seemed to take it for granted that the Army proposed to draft workers for wartime jobs.

Efforts by the War Department to correct this widely held misconception were not altogether successful. Except for the brief period from 1929 to 1931, when Reserve officers who were union members participated in the planning and the opinion of the AFL was sought, organized labor had been given no role in the preparation of the industrial mobilization plans. Thus it was easy to persuade the working man that discrimination, even coercion, was in store for him and difficult to convince him that the War Department based its plans on labor's voluntary co-operation. The elimination of objectionable provisions from the plans did not dispel labor's suspicions that the War Department had incorporated these provisions in some secret plans.

The Last of the Industrial Mobilization Plans

From the spring of 1930 to the summer of 1937 the position of Assistant Secretary of War had been held first by a Massachusetts industrialist and

[33] Labor Department of the National Council for the Prevention of War, Industrial Mobilization Plan (1 October 1936), mimeographed pamphlet in OUSW Res and Prod Div 175, Labor 1935-39; Frank B. Blumenfield, A Blueprint for Fascism, an Analysis of the Industrial Mobilization Plan, pamphlet published by the American League Against War and Fascism (February, 1937), reprinted in Senate Committee on Military Affairs, 75th Congress, 1st Session, Hearings on S. 25, Part II, pp. 175-86. See also Thatcher, op. cit., p. 259.
[34] Thatcher, op. cit., pp. 248-50.

then by a Kansas banker. On 28 June 1937 it was turned over to a West Virginia lawyer, Louis Johnson. Johnson, a former national commander of the American Legion, was an unremitting advocate of all-out preparedness. Calling attention to the deteriorating international scene, the new Assistant Secretary in his first annual report declared that "effective industrial planning is an indispensable element in the adequate national defense and the War Department is making marked progress in the development of such plans." [35] Johnson plunged energetically into the task of expanding and spurring on the Planning Branch.

A revision of the 1936 plan was begun in February 1938, the same month in which Hitler's mailed fist started to descend on Austria. By May 1939 the Planning Branch, in co-ordination with the ANMB, had completed a tentative draft, which was circulated among the armed services and sent to some selected civilians in industry for comment and criticism. [36] On 28 October 1939, eight weeks after the war in Europe had begun, the new industrial mobilization plan was released to the public. In form, it differed radically from the preceding plans. All the appendixes, in which were to be found the real meat of the plan and which heretofore had been part of the public release, were now relegated to a secret document. A veil of secrecy was necessary, in the opinion of the Planning Branch, in order to permit the constant revision required by rapidly changing conditions and to avoid duplicating the work of other government agencies. [37] As a reason for not making the labor provisions public, the secret labor annex pointed to the danger that premature action might "place in the hands of the pacifistic bloc and of other groups . . . material which may be dangerous to the national interests if misrepresented." [38]

Although perhaps not intended as such, the secret labor provisions of the 1939 plan represented a compromise between the 1933 and 1936 versions. Nothing was said about the war labor administrator being an industrialist or a labor leader. The 1939 plan stipulated that he must "enjoy the complete confidence" of industry, labor, and the public. Instead of one deputy, two were provided for in the 1939 plan, and one of them was to be "chosen from organized labor." On the labor administrator's advisory council, the AFL,

---

[35] *Annual Report of the Secretary of War to the President, 1937* (Washington: Government Printing Office, 1937), p. 21.

[36] Thatcher, *op. cit.,* p. 268.

[37] Col Charles Hines to ASW, 3 Oct 39, from Thatcher, *op. cit.,* p. 269.

[38] Labor Annex to Industrial Mobilization Plan 1939, p. 12, OUSW Res and Prod Div 116.7, Plan for Industrial Mobilization and Labor Sec (also in National Archives, War Records Div 865 IX, Industrial Mobilization Plan 1938, ANMB Part I).

the Congress of Industrial Organizations (CIO), and the Railway Brotherhoods were all to have representation.   Occupational deferments from selective service were provided for, and a modification of draft regulations was recommended with a view to making available to draft boards industrial advisers who would provide information on essential industries and occupations.   A committee for promoting co-operation between local draft boards and the U.S. Employment Service in matters of deferment and transfer of workers was to be established, and labor agencies were to be represented on the committee.   The machinery was intended to provide for "the equitable and voluntary distribution of labor."   On the other hand, the plan called upon labor to make certain sacrifices.   It contemplated the suspension in wartime of legislation that labor regarded as protective but which the Army considered restrictive of production.   It envisaged a limited application of the "work or fight" principle.   Strikes and lockouts were declared to be in conflict with the public interest.   Should the machinery that was set up to insure the fair, prompt, and uniform adjustment of disputes fail, the plan then called for compulsory and public investigation of the issue and a "delay in calling strikes or lockouts until a reasonable time has elapsed after a decision has been rendered by a War Labor Arbitration Commission or by an umpire designated by that body." [39]   The labor annex rejected "direct legal restrictions" on labor in favor of "indirect means, such as the use of priority assignment, withdrawal of industrial deferments, or withholding of jobs in war industries. . . ." [40]

Recognizing that such regimentation was "contrary to our traditions," the annex stressed that control should not be exercised "by any body composed of military men." [41]

The organization provided for in the Industrial Mobilization Plan of 1939 was built upon the possibility, first recognized in the 1936 plan, that mobilization measures might have to be started before the actual outbreak of hostilities.   A war resources administration was to be created "promptly when war is imminent."   This was the superagency that until 1936 had been designated as the war industries administration, which now became a super-superagency for co-ordinating the activities of the labor administration and the other temporary emergency agencies.   Since it was contemplated that the war resources administration would come into being in advance of the other agencies, the labor section of the war resources administration was to exer-

[39] *Ibid.*, pp. 13, 15, 31, 33, 36, 39, 49, 50, 58.   The passage quoted immediately above is from pages 33–34.

[40] *Ibid.*, p. 46, as quoted in Thatcher, *op. cit.*, p. 283.

[41] Labor Annex to Industrial Mobilization Plan 1939, p. 15.

cise the functions of the labor administration until the latter agency was organized. It was likewise contemplated that, should there be any delay in creating the war resources administration, the Army and Navy Munitions Board would for the time being assume responsibility for guiding the mobilization of manpower and industry. In this event, the supervision of labor affairs would be exercised through the Labor Section of the ANMB Liaison Division. Since the industrial mobilization plan explicitly barred military agencies from imposing controls over labor, the ANMB could assume only a limited measure of responsibility, as the plan was careful to point out.[42]

The 1939 plan was the culmination of nearly two decades of planning. Although the mobilization of industrial manpower was an important element in the plans, it was not the principal one. The War Department was chiefly interested in procurement and production. It approached the labor problem as a production factor, one that did not promise to be overly critical. To seek the support and co-operation of production men, industrialists rather than labor leaders, was entirely in keeping with the focus on production and with the traditional organization of American business. Whenever the Army planners deferred to criticism by the guardians—actual or self-styled—of labor, the result was in turn criticized as an unnecessary deviation or extension in the scope of the plans. The planners during the 1930's veered back and forth, attempting to satisfy their critics on both sides. In the absence of a convincing explanation of the intent and scope of the industrial mobilization plans, labor and the public were either confused or indifferent.

By the time the 1939 plan appeared, Europe had plunged into the whirlpool of war and the immediate reaction of the United States was to avoid being dragged along. Those, including President Roosevelt, who believed that the United States could best stay out by helping France and Great Britain to win found that the restrictions imposed by the "neutrality" legislation of 1937 would prevent effective support of the democracies. Congress, called into special session to consider repeal or revision of the neutrality laws, was the object of the pulls and pressures that otherwise might have been directed upon the new industrial mobilization plan. Neutrality, not military dictatorship, was the catchword in October 1939.

Organizing for Industrial Mobilization

While pushing the 1939 plan through to completion, Assistant Secretary Johnson had taken what he hoped would be a step toward putting it into

---

[42] *Ibid.*, pp. 8, 11, 18, 44; Thatcher, *op. cit.*, pp. 274–75.

effect.   During 1937 and 1938 both Johnson and President Roosevelt had given thought to the appointment of a board of prominent citizens that would review industrial mobilization plans and advise the planning agencies on the subject, but no action had been taken.   The following summer, at a Cabinet meeting on 4 August 1939, Johnson again proposed the appointment of a civilian board of review and received the President's approval.   To head the board, the President chose Edward R. Stettinius, Jr., chairman of the board of directors of the U.S. Steel Corporation.   The other members were John L. Pratt, a member of the board of directors of General Motors Corporation; Walter S. Gifford, president of the American Telephone and Telegraph Company; Robert E. Wood, board chairman of Sears, Roebuck and Company; Dr. Harold G. Moulton, president of the Brookings Institution; and Dr. Karl T. Compton, president of the Massachusetts Institute of Technology.   John M. Hancock, a friend of Bernard Baruch and a partner in the New York investment firm of Lehman Brothers, was added to the board a few weeks later.   The press release in which Assistant Secretary Johnson and the Assistant Secretary of the Navy jointly announced the creation of the board and Johnson's remarks at the first meeting, on 17 August 1939, revealed that Johnson was considering a much larger role for the board than that of merely reviewing industrial mobilization plans.   It was perhaps no coincidence that the name War Resources Board had been given to it, for Johnson announced that in the event of an emergency the board "would become the War Resources Administration visualized in the . . . Industrial Mobilization Plan." [43]

It soon appeared that President Roosevelt, who had given approval to a board of review only, had other ideas.   He was not opposed to setting up an organization to direct economic mobilization, but only to setting it up according to the industrial mobilization plan blueprint.   In planning the reorganization of his Executive Office, President Roosevelt had been considering the possibility of constituting the Secretaries of War, Navy, Interior, Agriculture, Commerce, and Labor as a Council of National Defense, as provided for in an act of 1916, and of creating an Advisory Commission to the council to be placed in the Executive Office of the President.   At a meeting with the members of the War Resources Board on 30 August, President Roosevelt outlined his views on where the board might be fitted into the organization he had in mind.   It would not be as a super-co-ordinating agency, but as one of the six or seven divisions of the Advisory Commission over which he, the

[43] WD Press Release, 17 Aug 39, quoted in Civilian Production Administration, *Industrial Mobilization for War: History of the War Production Board and Predecessor Agencies, 1940–1945,* I, *Program and Administration* (Washington: Government Printing Office, 1947), 8.

President, would exercise co-ordination. This much only was clear: the problem of precisely defining its own functions and of drafting a detailed organizational plan was something for the board itself to solve.

The problem was insoluble. The composition of the board evoked much criticism from journalists, labor leaders, and even from members of the President's Cabinet. Its creation and the role of Assistant Secretary Johnson had aroused the wrath of Secretary of War Harry H. Woodring, who had been away when the board was formed and who considered his Assistant Secretary a "war hawk." Furthermore, the President, without waiting for the board to report, had proceeded with the reorganization of the Executive Office, including provision for emergency agencies whose functions would be similar to those of agencies proposed in the industrial mobilization plan. The report of the War Resources Board was completed in October 1939 and was similar in tone and approach to the 1939 plan. Although it divested the war resources administration of co-ordinating functions, the report proposed to keep that agency as the central operating agency for industrial mobilization. The substance of co-ordination would be achieved by having a representative of the war resources administration on each of the other emergency boards.[44]

The War Resources Board submitted its report to the President early in November 1939. He thanked the board, expressed his appreciation of its task, and quickly tabled the report. On 24 November he wrote to each of the members, saying that with the completion of the report the board had finished the job that it had been created to do. Thus ended the first and only conscious attempt to implement the Army's prewar industrial mobilization plan.[45]

A number of reasons have been advanced as the explanation for the President's course of action. Perhaps he was of the opinion, as some have said, that the proposed war resources administration, even as modified in the War Resources Board report, represented an abdication of his emergency powers. Perhaps he acted in response to the criticism that the board represented Wall Street. It is more likely that he rejected the report and the whole industrial mobilization plan concept as being an acknowledgement that the United States soon would be involved in the war. With the public temper as it

[44] A text of the report is given in Special Senate Committee Investigating the National Defense Program, 80th Congress, 1st Session, Hearings, *Investigation of the National Defense Program,* Part 42, Exhibit 2673, p. 25957.

[45] On the vicissitudes of the War Resources Board and its report, see Troyer S. Anderson, Introduction to the History of the Under Secretary of War's Office (1947), Ch. IV, pp. 9–16, MS, OCMH.

was, there would have been little chance of the American people's accepting any part of a plan that by its very provisions was not intended to be put into effect until war was imminent. When, in the spring of 1940, the European war burst its bounds and threatened to spread to the Western Hemisphere, the President called into being the Advisory Commission to the Council of National Defense (NDAC). The function of NDAC was to advise the President on economic mobilization policies.

Although the Army's industrial mobilization plan was never put into effect, it does not follow that the years of planning were entirely fruitless. It is true that the wartime organization was not built from the Army's prewar blueprints, but the structure that was raised by the end of the war had certain resemblances to the blueprints. By May 1943 there had evolved from the Advisory Commission to the Council of National Defense a super-coordinating agency—the Office of War Mobilization—which was similar in some respects to the war resources administration of the prewar industrial mobilization plans. But the operating agencies through which industrial mobilization was to have been carried out had not similarly developed. Operating functions were taken on by agencies of the War Department, the Navy Department, and other executive departments, and were assigned and redistributed among a host of new temporary agencies, all of which had only tenuous ties with each other and with the co-ordinating agency, although, indeed, certain of the civilian agencies such as the War Production Board, National War Labor Board, and War Manpower Commission corresponded in many respects to those contemplated by the industrial mobilization plans. Because the wartime organization evolved piece by piece, it was not a centralized structure tied together by neat lines of co-ordination and control. Perhaps the most striking departure from the industrial mobilization plan concept was the extent to which the Army came to participate directly in matters of production and industrial manpower. The explanation again lies in the fact that the organizational development was an evolutionary process starting from an agency, the NDAC, that appeared to be clothed with inadequate authority. Forced by circumstances to assume a role for which no plans had been made, the Army developed its own organization by trial and error.

CHAPTER II

Organizational Problems: 1940–45

In June 1940 President Roosevelt announced the appointment of a distinguished elder statesman, Henry L. Stimson, as Secretary of War. The friends and associates to whom Stimson turned for help were men whose views had been shaped by the problems they had encountered in mobilizing the nation for World War I. Among the first whom he consulted was Benedict Crowell, who had kept in close touch through the years with the work of his successors in the War Department. Among them also were Grenville Clark, one of the founders of the Military Training Camps Association ("the Plattsburg Idea"), and Goldthwaite H. Dorr, who had been an assistant to Stimson when the latter was U.S. Attorney for the Southern District of New York and afterward had been Crowell's assistant on the General Munitions Board during World War I. Harvey H. Bundy, who had devotedly served as Stimson's Assistant Secretary of State during the Hoover Administration, and John J. McCloy had long stood high in Stimson's regard. The new Assistant Secretary of War, Judge Robert P. Patterson of New York, although not a close acquaintance of Mr. Stimson, was well known to Goldthwaite Dorr and an intimate friend of Grenville Clark, in whose law firm he had begun his career and at whose suggestion his name had been presented for the appointment. Like the others, Patterson had an abiding zeal for preparedness. He had been a gallant combat soldier in World War I. Forthright, direct in manner, with a singleness of purpose and a sense of urgency that stood in contrast to the complacency of those who talked of "business [or labor] as usual," Judge Patterson knew the needs of an army in action, but his successful career as a lawyer and jurist had included no experience with labor and production problems. When he accepted the appointment he had, in fact, been unaware of the Assistant Secretary's responsibilities in the field of industrial mobilization. A conversation with Crowell on the eve of his departure for Washington gave Patterson his first insight into the specialized nature of the task he had been called upon to undertake.[1]

[1] Anderson, Introduction to the History of the Under Secretary of War's Office, Ch. V, p. 13, Ch. VI, pp. 16–18.

Revamping the Labor Section

The rising tide of procurement orders, the growth of strikes in defense industries, the passage of the Selective Service Act, and a variety of other problems that faced the new Assistant Secretary indicated the need for appointing special advisers with special talents. One of the first to be brought in was Maj. Sidney P. Simpson, a Reserve officer called to active duty from the faculty of the Harvard University Law School. Major Simpson and his two assistants—John H. Ohly and Huntington Thom—were soon given the task of looking after labor relations and personnel matters that might affect the procurement program. They viewed the problem as one of developing contract clauses for the protection of labor, of collecting information on strikes, and of helping the NDAC and other agencies to settle labor disputes in defense industries. A few weeks after he came to Washington Major Simpson, at the request of the NDAC, undertook to mediate a serious dispute that had arisen at the Seattle plant of the Boeing Aircraft Company. The success of his efforts made it seem likely that the War Department would be called upon for similar intervention in the future.[2] At the same time the War Department was becoming increasingly involved in the question whether and to what extent compliance with federal labor legislation should be stipulated in War Department contracts.[3] To handle these and other pressing problems, Major Simpson on 18 October 1940 suggested to Assistant Secretary Patterson that a labor section be established. Patterson agreed, and on the following day designated Major Simpson (in addition to his other duties) as chief of the Labor Section in the Office of the Assistant Secretary. After this action had been taken, Patterson and Simpson discovered for the first time that in the Contributory Division of the Planning Branch a Labor Section already existed. This was the section that for years had been engaged in drawing up the labor annexes of the various industrial mobilization plans. Now under Lt. Col. William H. Sadler, it had lately been dealing with current labor problems. A delineation of functions was soon worked out, in accordance with which Colonel Sadler relinquished all matters of current bearing.[4]

The arrangement was short-lived. Major Simpson's next venture as mediator in a labor dispute turned out most unfortunately.[5] He left the War De-

---

[2] Further details may be found below, page 158.

[3] See below, pp. 35–45.

[4] H. M. Somers and John H. Ohly, War Department Organization for the Handling of Labor Problems in World War II, ASF IPD Monograph 2, Part I, pp. 7–8, copy in OCMH.

[5] For an account of these mediation attempts, see Chapter IV, below.

partment at the end of November and his office was then combined with Colonel Sadler's under the latter as chief.   Edward F. McGrady, a former Assistant Secretary of Labor, sometime union official, and in 1940 an executive of the Radio Corporation of America, was appointed as special adviser to Patterson and consultant to Colonel Sadler's office.   The appointment of McGrady coincided with a major alteration in the status of the Assistant Secretary's office.   Secretaries of War in the years after 1920 had occasionally had difficulties with their Assistant Secretaries because of the fact that the responsibility of the Assistant Secretary in the field of procurement and industrial mobilization planning was a matter of statutory, and not delegated, authority.   For this reason Secretary Stimson had insisted on the appointment of Patterson as a condition to his own acceptance of the Cabinet post, and later, in August, he had suggested to the President that a new office, that of Under Secretary, be created in the War Department to exercise by delegation the functions assigned to the Assistant Secretary by law.[6]   As soon as Congress passed the necessary legislation in December 1940, Patterson was named Under Secretary of War.   With the appointment of McGrady as special assistant, it seemed desirable to all those concerned that Colonel Sadler's Labor Section be raised in status and given broader scope.

A directive to this effect was issued on 25 February 1941.   It created a Labor Section in the Office of the Under Secretary, separate from any other component of the office.   Colonel Sadler was designated chief of the section, under the direction of McGrady.   The duties of the Labor Section were described as follows:

a. The formulation, under policies promulgated by higher authority, of basic War Department labor policy and the coordination thereof with the Navy Department, the U.S. Maritime Commission, the Department of Labor, the Office of Production Management and any of its sub-divisions, the Advisory Commission to the Council of National Defense, the Federal Security Administration, and any other governmental department or agency, now existing or hereafter created, which is directly or indirectly concerned with labor matters.

b. The supervision of the administration of War Department labor policy and the coordination of all activities of the various branches of the War Department in all matters pertaining to labor.

c. The study of all problems relating to labor and industrial relations for the purpose of preparing, and recommending or putting into effect, approved solutions.

d. The collection and organization of information pertaining to all labor matters, including information concerning current industrial disputes, and the transmittal of pertinent information to the government agencies charged with the administration of such matters.

[6] Henry L. Stimson and McGeorge Bundy, *On Active Service in Peace and War* (New York: Harper & Brothers, 1948), pp. 323–24; Rudolph A. Winnacker, The Office of the Secretary of War Under Henry L. Stimson, Part I, p. 7, a preliminary draft MS in OCMH.

e. The representation of the War Department in its dealings with other governmental agencies on matters of labor policy.

f. Advising the Secretary and Under Secretary of War on all labor matters.[7]

The supply arms and services, and all other Army agencies concerned with labor matters, were directed to appoint labor officers whose responsibility it would be to co-operate with the Labor Section and to keep it informed of the activities of their components. The directive further set forth as a general policy that no War Department representative would participate in the arbitration, conciliation, or mediation of labor disputes, or take part in any negotiations pertaining to such disputes.

During the year following the promulgation of the February 1941 directive, the Labor Section was shunted back and forth between its former place in the Planning Branch and its more recent position as a separate unit, but its basic functions and responsibilities remained much the same regardless of its organizational status. Attention continued to focus on labor relations, but a growing interest in the supply of labor led to a corresponding expansion of the responsibilities assigned to the Labor Section. After the Office of Production Management (OPM) established a Labor Supply Branch with regional labor supply committees, the Labor Section of the Under Secretary's office was designated the War Department representative to deal with the OPM Labor Supply Branch. Responsibility for representing the War Department on the OPM regional labor supply committees was assigned to the field officers of the Labor Section who were serving as advisers to the selective service boards. At the same time all the Army agencies that had been directed in February to appoint labor officers were now instructed to designate labor supply representatives. For the most part, both functions were assigned to the same men.[8] These changes were embodied in two directives issued on 28 August 1941. No further changes were made before the United States entered the war.

A long-contemplated reorganization, designed to centralize the Office of the Under Secretary, was announced on 14 February 1942. Three branches—Administration, Procurement, and Resources—were created, into which all the existing components of the Office of Under Secretary were fitted. The labor functions were turned over to the Resources Branch. The old Labor Section thus became the Manpower Section, Manpower and Liaison Division, Resources Branch, of the Office of the Under Secretary. Col. Joseph F. Battley, who had succeeded Colonel Sadler as chief of the Labor Section in June 1941 and had moved up to head the old Contributory Division, was

---

[7] Quoted in Somers and Ohly, *op. cit.,* Part I, pp. 11–12.

[8] *Ibid.,* Part I, pp. 21–24.

continued as chief of the new Manpower and Liaison Division.   Organizationally, the arrangement was similar to that of 1940 when the Labor Section had been part of the Contributory Division of the Planning Branch.   Functionally, labor activities had been moved up a notch.   The new setup lasted less than·a month, for on 9 March 1942 a major reorganization of the War Department was announced.[9]

For at least the fourth time in less than two years a new organizational chart had to be drawn up.   The reorganization of March 1942 created a Services of Supply or, to give it its later name, the Army Service Forces (ASF), under Lt. Gen. Brehon B. Somervell, into which was dumped a variety of service and administrative functions including the procurement, production, and labor functions previously exercised by the Under Secretary's office.[10] The statutory role of the Under Secretary himself was preserved by making the commanding general of the Army Service Forces responsible to him in matters relating to procurement, but most of the office staff of the Under Secretary and its administrative duties were absorbed by the new organization.[11]

The Labor Section Under the Army Service Forces

The directive creating the Army Service Forces established nine staff divisions: Resources (taken entirely from the Office of the Under Secretary), Requirements, Procurement, Distribution, Defense Aid, Operations, Budget and Financial Administration, Training, and Personnel.   The Personnel Division, composed mainly of officers from the G–1 Division of the War Department General Staff, was intended by Col. Wilhelm D. Styer, Chief of Staff, ASF, to be the home of Under Secretary Patterson's old Labor Section.   Although Patterson acquiesced in the general scheme, he did not at first approve of placing the Labor Section in the Personnel Division.   He would have preferred that it be in the Resources Division.   After much discussion between the Under Secretary, Colonel Styer, and General Somervell, it was decided to split the Personnel Division into two divisions—a Military Personnel Division and a Civilian Personnel Division (later and more appropriately named

[9] *Ibid.,* Part I, pp. 43–44.   For detailed accounts of the reorganization of March 1942 and its significance, see the following volumes in the series UNITED STATES ARMY IN WORLD WAR II: Ray S. Cline, *Washington Command Post: The Operations Division* (Washington: Government Printing Office, 1951), Ch. VI; Kent Roberts Greenfield, Robert R. Palmer, and Bell I. Wiley, *The Organization of Ground Combat Troops* (Washington: Government Printing Office, 1947), pp. 148–55; and John D. Millett, *The Organization and Role of the Army Service Forces* (Washington: Government Printing Office, 1954), Ch. II.

[10] The Services of Supply was renamed Army Service Forces in March 1943.

[11] Millett, *The Organization and Role of the Army Service Forces,* pp. 37, 338–39.

Industrial Personnel Division). The Industrial Personnel Division (IPD), as it seems best to call it from the start, was to be headed by James P. Mitchell, who for some years had been adviser on labor matters to General Somervell. Mr. Patterson accepted the plan, and the Labor Section on 21 March was officially absorbed by the Industrial Personnel Division.[12] The IPD comprised three branches: Civilian Personnel, Labor Relations, and Manpower. The Civilian Personnel Branch was assigned all matters relating to the civilian employees of the War Department who came under jurisdiction of the ASF. The Labor Relations Branch, as its name indicated, was given responsibility over labor-management relations. The Manpower Branch was assigned all matters pertaining to the supply of labor.[13] The staff taken over from Under Secretary Patterson's office was augmented by recruits from two sources—from Sidney Hillman's group in the War Production Board and later from the War Manpower Commission. It was unlikely that the newcomers would be content to stay on the sideline when industrial disputes and labor problems arose.

Writing at the end of the war, an officer then assigned to the IPD expressed an opinion that "at least until the fall of 1942" the Labor Relations Branch and the Manpower Branch performed "only a very limited portion of the functions which had been set down on paper for them."[14] The explanation lies partly in the fact that the two branches, although intended to work closely together, for a long time had neither regular nor close contact with each other, and partly in the fact that an immediate and extensive build-up in the staffs of the two branches had seemed necessary. A third factor, and like the first two probably a minor one, was the frequency with which the internal organization of the two branches changed during the first six months of their existence. But apart from these factors the explanation must undoubtedly be sought in the difficulties experienced by the IPD in setting up a field organization and in establishing satisfactory working relationships with the technical services and the Army Air Forces.

Although the field organization that had evolved under the Labor Section of the Under Secretary's office had started with the officers assigned to selective service duties, labor relations—not the supply of labor—had accounted for much of the field activity throughout 1941. The primary interest of the Labor Section was in the problem of industrial relations; the supply of labor

---

[12] Memo, USW for Styer, 11 Mar 42, Memo, Styer for USW, 16 Mar 42, and Memo, USW for Ohly, 16 Mar 42, all in Ohly file, Labor Br IPD, Organization; Millett, *The Organization and Role of the Army Service Forces,* p. 352.

[13] Ohly and Somers, *op. cit.,* Part II, p. 3.

[14] *Ibid.,* Part II, pp. 3–4.

had not been considered a pressing problem. After the War Department reorganization of March 1942, the selective service liaison officers reported to an agency—the Manpower Branch—whose responsibility was specifically the supply of labor and which was charged with the supervision of occupational deferment policies. The Manpower Branch also began to augment the field organization with such rapidity that to members of the Labor Relations Branch it appeared that most of the men commissioned as field representatives were unqualified.[15] Although the intent seems to have been for the Labor Relations Branch to appoint its own field representatives, in actual practice the branch did not do so and preferred to rely on the field personnel of the Manpower Branch. The result was that the field personnel were confused and uncertain as to their responsibilities.

The organizational difficulties with the Army Air Forces and the technical services were likewise partly inherited and partly a result of the March reorganization. They were not confined to labor matters. In accordance with the directives of February and August 1941, the Air Corps and the technical services had established labor agencies that ranged from mere skeletons to fully formed and efficient establishments like that of the Quartermaster Corps. Over these agencies the Labor Section of the Under Secretary's office had exercised only limited supervision. The reorganization of March 1942, which should have brought about a closer control of the labor sections of the Air Forces and the technical services, resulted in a wider parting of the ways. The Air Forces, having achieved an autonomous position in the War Department, felt the need of gaining adequate recognition of its status and continued its efforts for a self-contained air arm. The technical services, having lost their autonomy, were restive, and to some of Somervell's associates it seemed that the technical services spent the war quietly fighting to regain their former status. In any event, the distribution of procurement functions and responsibilities under the terms of the March reorganization made a certain amount of conflict in the field of labor responsibilities inevitable. Although ASF was vested with the administration of all procurement, supply, and services, "Army-wide in scope," including "mobilization of industrial manpower, and labor relations," the Army Air Forces was at the same time given responsibility for procurement of all equipment "peculiar to the Army Air Forces."[16] During 1941 the Air Corps had assigned responsibility for handling labor problems to its procurement division, and thereafter attempts by

[15] *Ibid.*, Part II, p. 6.
[16] WD Circular 59, 2 Mar 42, par. 7, Sec. e(7), from Ohly and Somers, *op. cit.*, Part II, p. 9; Millett, *The Organization and Role of the Army Service Forces*, pp. 38, 124, 168–71, 298, 308–11, 331, 418.

the Industrial Personnel Division, ASF, to supervise and control Air Forces labor matters were frequently ignored as being encroachments upon Air Forces procurement responsibilities.[17] The Quartermaster Corps, during 1941, had moved even more rapidly than the Air Corps to establish a labor organi-zation, and like the Air Corps it viewed many manpower problems as being "inextricably interwoven with the procurement mission." After the War Department reorganization, the Office of The Quartermaster General (OQMG) transferred its labor section from the OQMG Procurement Division to the Personnel Division in accordance with a recommendation of the Industrial Personnel Division, ASF, but the shift was not welcome. The Quartermaster depots "had come to look to the Procurement Division for guidance with regard to their suppliers' production problems . . .," and the transfer "came to be looked upon as an encroachment on the Procurement Division's contract control prerogatives."[18]

Never considered as something permanent and sacrosanct, the ASF head-quarters organization itself underwent a series of changes. During the first year of its existence and continuing throughout 1943, offices were added, abolished, or shifted here and there in a pattern reminiscent of "musical chairs."[19] Within the Industrial Personnel Division, the sharp distinction between labor supply and labor relations came under criticism. There was an opinion that the distinction was artificial and gave rise to a duplication of effort. Moreover, at the end of 1942 the question of labor supply was be-ginning to assume importance for the first time. Therefore, in January 1943 it was decided to combine the two branches—Manpower and Labor Rela-tions—into a single Labor Branch organized in four sections, three of which were primarily concerned with policy questions, information, and research. The fourth section—Labor Operations—acted as an agency of communication between field personnel on the one hand and ASF headquarters, the War Manpower Commission, and the War Production Board on the other. The Labor Operations Section was organized geographically. Two officers, desig-nated area co-ordinators, were assigned responsibility for each of three large regions of the continental United States. These area co-ordinators were the sole channel through which industrial manpower problems, whether of sup-ply and utilization of labor or of labor-management relations, reached ASF

    [17] Memo, Col William F. Volandt for Air Corps Proc Dist, 13 Nov 41, AAF 004.06, Labor Conditions; Army Air Forces, Air Technical Service Command, History of AAF Activities During World War II in the Field of Industrial Manpower, pp. 1–21, *passim,* copy in OCMH.
    [18] Harry B. Yoshpe, *Labor Problems in Quartermaster Procurement,* QMC Historical Studies, 11 (Washington, 1945), pp. 14–19. The quoted passages are from page 17.
    [19] See Millett, *The Organization and Role of the Army Service Forces,* Ch. XXII.

headquarters.   The function of the area co-ordinators was to pass the problems on to the War Manpower Commission or the National War Labor Board for handling.[20]

Simultaneously with the changes in the organization of the Industrial Personnel Division, the field organization was also overhauled.   Heretofore labor officers in the field had been attached, as representatives of the IPD, directly to ASF headquarters.   But manpower difficulties were a local problem, and it seemed best to reorganize the field structure along regional lines. Accordingly, in January 1943, ASF assigned all its labor activities in the field to the service commands, which under the War Department reorganization of March 1942 had replaced the corps areas.   A labor branch was established in each service command as a staff agency reporting directly to the commanding general of the service command, and the existing field personnel were transferred to the labor branches.   They, the labor branches of the service commands, were made responsible for supervising the activities of the labor officers of the technical services and for maintaining liaison with the field representatives of other agencies dealing with labor problems.[21]

By the end of 1943 both arrangements—the reorganization of the Industrial Personnel Division and the establishment of the service command labor branches—were proving unsatisfactory.   The Labor Operations Section of the IPD Labor Branch and the area co-ordinators had been misnamed.   The section was not an operating agency.   It relied on the War Manpower Commission and on National War Labor Board representatives in the field for the actual measures to be taken.   Likewise, the area co-ordinators found themselves co-ordinating not action but only requests for action.   The result was that when a crisis developed there was little the IPD could do.   The failure of the system was made evident in the summer of 1943 when a critical shortage of labor at the Boeing Aircraft plant in Seattle threatened to cut production.   The War Manpower Commission seemed unable to remedy the situation.   The War Department thereupon decided to take direct measures, and the Industrial Personnel Division sent a special project team to the plant.

[20] Ohly and Somers, *op. cit.,* Part III, pp. 16–18; Annual Reports Assistant Chief for Operations, Labor Branch, and Assistant Chief for Labor Supply, Labor Branch, IPD, for Year Ending 30 June 1943, Ohly file, Labor Br IPD, Organization.

[21] Memo, Mitchell for Chief Chemical Warfare Sv *et al.,* 8 Feb 43, sub: Reorganization of the Civilian Pers Div and the Establishment of Labor Brs in the Sv Comds, Ohly file, Labor Br IPD, Organization.   See also Millett, *The Organization and Role of the Army Service Forces,* p. 329, and Ohly and Somers, *op. cit.,* Part III, pp. 23–24.   Ohly and Somers give Somervell's 1943 proposal to "streamline" the ASF as a factor in establishing the service command labor branches.   According to Millett (page 409), Director Mitchell was completely unaware of the Somervell proposals, which in any case do not seem to have jelled before the summer of 1943.

The success of the new technique spelled the end of the area co-ordinators.[22] In the meantime the service command labor branches and the labor officers of the technical services had been unable to reach a satisfactory working arrangement. The labor officers of the technical services were not accountable to the service commands, and how the labor branches were to exercise supervision over personnel in a completely separate chain of command was never clarified in spite of further instructions issued in December 1943. The new instructions by explicitly designating the labor branches as the exclusive representatives for dealing with the other government agencies concerned in labor matters only aggravated the situation. The technical services continued to view labor problems as procurement factors, and since the service commands had no procurement responsibilities the labor officers of the technical services considered it necessary to have the right of dealing with labor agencies of the federal, state, or local governments.[23]

The final months of 1943 and the early months of the next year were marked by a growing recognition on the part of the ASF that the labor factor had to be dealt with as an element of procurement and production. The continuing pinch of manpower shortages on the west coast coupled with a jurisdictional conflict between the War Manpower Commission and the War Production Board over the assignment of manpower urgency ratings had resulted in the establishment of a new program. In accordance with a directive from Director of War Mobilization James F. Byrnes, the so-called west coast manpower program was put into effect on 15 September 1943 in five areas of the Pacific coast. In each area two interagency committees were constituted: an Area Production Urgency Committee, headed by a representative of the War Production Board, and a Manpower Priorities Committee, headed by a representative of the War Manpower Commission. One of the primary functions of the Area Production Urgency Committee was to assign priority to the various production activities in the area, and on the basis of these "urgency ratings" the Manpower Priorities Committee established manpower needs, set employment ceilings, and assigned labor priorities for all the industrial plants.[24]

---

[22] See Chapter VII, below, for a detailed account of the special project teams and the west coast manpower program.

[23] Manpower—the Second Phase, 20 August 1943, draft MS in Ohly file, Labor Br IPD, Organization; Ohly and Somers, *op. cit.,* Part III, pp. 22–24; Millett, *The Organization and Role of the Army Service Forces,* p. 329.

[24] CPA, *Industrial Mobilization for War,* I, 707–08; Ohly and Somers, *op. cit.,* Part IV, pp. 29–30. For a discussion of the role of the Area Production Urgency Committee in the placement of contracts, see Chapter IV, below.

The Army was represented on both committees, and generally the same individuals who served on one committee served also on the other. Instructions sent out by the War Manpower Commission to its field representatives directed them to handle the matter of Army representation on the Manpower Priorities Committees with the chiefs of the service command labor branches.[25] On the other hand, the ASF channel for liaison with the War Production Board ran through the Production Division, ASF, which was one of Maj. Gen. Lucius D. Clay's responsibilities as Director of Matériel. Up to this time the Production Division had not greatly concerned itself with the labor problem, since shortages of goods, equipment, and facilities had been the major bottlenecks in production. During 1943, however, the blame was shifted to the growing shortage of labor. This development, according to General Clay, brought the labor problem within the field of his responsibility, and he insisted on the right of controlling Army appointments to the Area Production Urgency Committees and the Manpower Priorities Committees. The acceptance by Somervell of Clay's point of view and the extension of the west coast program to the rest of the United States early in 1944 necessitated a rearrangement of the ASF field organization. The plan that was worked out represented something of a compromise between the IPD and General Clay's Production Division, one in which the role of the service commands was considerably reduced and that of the technical services correspondingly enlarged.[26]

The result served to confuse further an already complicated organizational structure. A new regional organization, corresponding to the thirteen regions into which the country had been divided for War Production Board purposes, was drawn up. Each ASF region was headed by a regional representative designated by General Clay. An alternate regional representative and a labor adviser to the regional representative were to be chosen by the director of the IPD. Responsibility for designating the Army member of the Area Production Urgency and Manpower Priorities Committees was placed in the hands of the regional representative. As regional representative, Clay chose the officer in command of an important technical service activity in each area. The New England regional representative was, for example, the commanding general of the Springfield Ordnance District; at Philadelphia,

[25] War Manpower Commission, Bureau of Placement, Handbook on the Establishment, Organization, and Functions of Manpower Priorities Committees, 10 January 1944.
[26] Statement of Maj. Gen. L. D. Clay Before Truman (Mead) Committee, 16 Aug 44, Production Problems Confronting the ASF, OUSW Amberg files, Mead Committee Inquiry; Ohly and Somers, op. cit., pp. 30–32.

he was the commanding general of the Philadelphia Signal Depot; at Atlanta, the Division Engineer was designated the ASF regional representative. Since all of them had important administrative duties to perform in their own technical service, the regional representatives tended to regard their labor responsibilities as secondary and subordinate. Consequently, their labor advisers played an important part. In six of the thirteen regions, IPD director Mitchell named the chief of one of the service command labor branches as labor adviser; in six of the remaining regions, he chose a technical service officer. But General Clay had consented to the appointment of service command officers only on condition that they have no accountability to the service commands in all matters pertaining to their new duties. Since the field of labor relations was not covered by the new regional committee system and continued to be a function of the service commands, the labor advisers had to serve two masters who exercised authority side by side but not hand in hand. In two cases the seats of authority were literally miles apart. The chief of the Third Service Command labor branch had to shuttle back and forth between Baltimore and Philadelphia, while the chief of the labor branch at the Ninth Service Command headquarters in Salt Lake City had to go considerably farther to advise the ASF regional representative in San Francisco.[27]

The service commands severely criticized the new regional organization, and the Industrial Personnel Division was inclined to agree with them. The commanding generals of the service commands argued that the problems of labor supply and of labor relations were inseparable. They objected to the anomaly of having to assign service command personnel to duties, the responsibility for which had been stripped from the service commands, and, in a round-robin letter addressed to Somervell by the commanding generals of all but one of the service commands, they proposed that the entire labor field be returned to service command control. The Industrial Personnel Division agreed with the criticism but not with the remedy proposed by the service commands. The Labor Branch, IPD, had hoped to be the capstone of a line of command organization for all labor functions that would parallel the ASF procurement and production organization. Having failed to achieve this, the IPD suggested that the Labor Branch be placed under General Clay, and only as a last resort did it recommend returning all labor functions to the service commands. General Somervell himself admitted that the arrangement did "some violence to the theory of good organization." Nevertheless,

---

[27] Minutes of Staff Meetings, Labor Br IPD, 19 Sep 44, ASF IPD, Minutes of Staff Meetings; Millett, *The Organization and Role of the Army Service Forces,* pp. 330–31.

he considered it a "going" concern and the war too far advanced to permit the radical readjustment that might be required.[28]

The question who should control the field personnel was a major issue, one that went beyond the mere desire for authority as an end in itself. On one level the issue lay between the Industrial Personnel Division, on the one hand, and the technical services and service commands, on the other. Confronted with immediate, day-to-day problems, the technical services and the service commands first looked for the most expedient and opportune means of solution. They therefore wanted a decentralized field organization, and for this reason also each wanted to exercise control over the field personnel. The Industrial Personnel Division was interested in seeing to it that policies were carried out, and for this purpose it also wanted to control the field personnel. On another level the issue lay between the technical services and the service commands. In this regard, one of General Somervell's staff officers wrote some years after the war as follows:

> It remains a fact that the Army Service Forces never solved the problem of a unified field structure for handling labor supply problems. On this subject the interests of the technical services and the service commands clashed. The technical services would not leave supervision of an important procurement matter, whether it pertained to manpower or supply, to the service commands. In consequence the ASF never had an effective field organization for labor supply questions.[29]

The organization that finally developed was a compromise, which, like all compromises, failed to please everyone and did not completely please anyone.

---

[28] Ohly and Somers, *op. cit.,* Part IV, pp. 42–43. Somervell's comments are from Memo, Somervell for CG First Sv Comd, 18 Jul 44, Ohly file, Labor Br IPD, Organization.

[29] Millett, *The Organization and Role of the Army Service Forces,* p. 331.

CHAPTER III

Wartime Limitations on the Size and Utilization of the Civilian Labor Force

During the prewar period, in fact from the beginning of industrial mobilization planning, the War Department had anticipated difficulties from the various statutory regulations governing hours, wages, and conditions of labor. The War Department believed that legislation such as the Wagner Act, the Walsh-Healey Act, and the like would seriously limit the maximum utilization of the labor force in time of war. As a consequence, the draft of a bill to suspend such restrictive regulations in wartime had been appended to the several industrial mobilization plans.

In some contrast to its concern over legal limitations on the utilization of the labor force, the War Department did not foresee a general shortage of manpower. The manpower requirements of the armed forces were not expected to act as a limitation on the size of the civilian labor force, and, conversely, the needs of industry were disregarded as a factor in determining the size of the Army. War Department planners considered the size of the Army to be a matter of military decision, dictated by strategic needs. After the personnel requirements of the armed forces were thus taken care of, the remaining manpower would, it was believed, be more than adequate for all other purposes. This approach was sound as long as War Department planning went no further than an initial mobilization force of 1,000,00 men. It was probably still sound when the War Department began to think in terms of an eventual Army strength of 4,000,000 men.

Neither question—the statutory limitations on the maximum use of the labor force and the relation of the size of the Army to the nation's total manpower—worked out exactly as the War Department had anticipated. The first question arose months before the United States entered the war, and instead of showing itself in the form of restricted production it began, developed, and ended as a problem of policy. The second question, which labor experts brought to the attention of military experts as soon as the Army's manpower requirements began to skyrocket, had policy overtones, but it ended with the gradual acceptance of the view that the size of the Army was a real limitation on the size of the civilian labor force.

Labor Laws and Defense Contracts

Most of the legislation that the War Department believed might inhibit war production dated from the attempt to redress the balance of labor and management in the mid-thirties. Of particular interest to the War Department were the National Labor Relations Act (Wagner Act), the Davis-Bacon Act, the Walsh-Healey Act, and the Fair Labor Standards Act. Both the Davis-Bacon Act and the Walsh-Healey Act established minimum wages, maximum hours, and certain other conditions of employment for work performed on government contract, and both laws stipulated that government contracts must contain clauses binding the contractor to comply with the law. On the other hand, neither the Wagner Act nor the Fair Labor Standards Act, both of which applied to industry in general, made any provision for compliance clauses in public contracts. The Wagner Act, which established the right of employees to participate in union activities, to bargain collectively through representatives of their own choosing, and to engage in concerted activity for bargaining purposes, and which prohibited certain "unfair labor practices" on the part of employers, had been hailed by organized labor as its Magna Charta and met by employers with considerably less enthusiasm. The War Department soon discovered that the major problem was not the direct effect on production of this legislation but what to do about contractors who refused to comply with the Wagner Act. The problem does not seem to have arisen to any great extent in connection with the Fair Labor Standards Act, probably because its provisions were largely duplicated in the Walsh-Healey Act, which applied specifically to public contracts.

The question was settled for the time being by a ruling of the Comptroller General of the United States in July 1937 to the effect that the National Labor Relations Board and the courts were responsible for enforcing the Wagner Act and that the withholding of government contracts from violators was not one of the sanctions provided by Congress.[1] This established War Department policy. It also defined the issue, for labor leaders imme-

---

[1] House Special Committee to Investigate National Labor Relations Board, 76th Congress, 3d Session, Pursuant to House Resolution 258, Hearings, *National Labor Relations Act,* Vol. 28, p. 7426, Exhibit 1795, Decisions of Comptroller General, A–86908, 17 Comptroller General 37.

diately sought, unsuccessfully, to have the ruling set aside either by legislation or by executive order.

In midsummer of 1940, with defense contracts multiplying sharply and labor attempting to consolidate its position in new and expanding industries, John L. Lewis, president of the CIO, renewed the struggle against the Comptroller General's decision. He sought to enlist the support of Sidney Hillman, chief of the Labor Division of the National Defense Advisory Commission, in obtaining an executive order, but, convinced of the futility of this approach, Hillman could only assure Lewis that a labor policy for defense industry was being worked out.[2]

By the end of August the NDAC had agreed upon a statement of principles. Its primary objective was to further the expansion of defense production with a minimum of disturbance to the normal peacetime production of civilian goods and without upsetting the social gains of labor. The labor principles adopted by the NDAC were announced, appropriately, on Labor Day, 1940. The general factors to be considered in the choice of plant locations should include, the commission asserted, the availability of labor, and those to be taken into account in letting defense contracts should include an adequate consideration of the labor standards that prevailed in the plant of the bidder. To implement these principles, the commission held that "all work carried on as part of the defense program should comply with federal statutory provisions affecting labor wherever such provisions are applicable," and that defense contractors should be further required to comply with state and local laws in the matter of labor relations, wages, hours, workmen's compensation, safety, and the like.[3]

Questions of interpretation, of the legality of compliance clauses in various types of contracts, and of practicality soon arose and proved to be a source of confusion for several months. On 27 September, three weeks after the NDAC issued its statement of principles, Assistant Secretary Patterson directed the chiefs of the supply arms and services to accept it as a guide in awarding contracts.[4] It was quite another matter to require contractors to comply with the labor laws by incorporating an appropriate clause in their contracts, which was the very thing that labor unions desired. This problem

---

[2] *Ibid.,* p. 7273, Exhibit 1791, Ltr, Hillman to Lewis, 30 Jul 40. Hillman, a respected labor leader, was a former president of the Amalgamated Clothing Workers of America.

[3] House Document 950, 76th Congress, 3d Session, *National Defense Contracts.* pp. 2–3; Yoshpe, *Labor Problems in Quartermaster Procurement,* QMC Historical Studies, 11, pp. 9–10; CPA, *Industrial Mobilization for War,* I, 58, 82.

[4] Memo, ASW for Chiefs Supply Arms and Svs, 27 Sep 40, and Ltr, ASW to Hillman, 27 Sep 40, both in OUSW Amberg files, Labor 1941–42.

was not merely an abstract legal issue, for several companies with substantial defense contracts were being charged by union leaders with violating the Wagner Act. The Ford Motor Company had been cited repeatedly for failure to comply with the act, and a particularly important Air Corps contract with that company was then pending. The Attorney General, to the immediate and violent dismay of American industrialists, supported the NDAC with a statement on 2 October 1940 that National Labor Relations Board findings of a Wagner Act violation on the part of an employer were "binding and conclusive upon other agencies of the executive branch of the government" until overturned by the courts.[5] All that the statement meant, the Attorney General testified before a House committee a few days later, was that, if a firm was found by the board to be violating the Wagner Act, other executive departments could not say that the company was not guilty. It was not intended to establish contract policy, the Attorney General said. If the War Department wished to award a contract to a company that was violating the Wagner Act, it could do so.[6]

Testifying before the same House committee, Assistant Secretary of War Patterson elaborated on the policy of the War Department. The War Department, he stated, could not reject low bids in awarding advertised, competitive contracts, but as for negotiated contracts the War Department was permitted to consider various elements. A rapid rate of production was, Patterson pointed out, one of the most important of these elements. The labor record of a company was related to its production rate, but a dozen or so other factors were also involved. In placing a negotiated contract, the War Department would not be guided, he continued, solely by a company's labor relations or by the mere fact of an alleged violation of the Wagner Act. Whether a violation would bar a company from an award would depend upon the seriousness of the violation, its relation to production, the importance of the company's facilities, the existence of an alternative source of supply, and similar considerations.[7] Leaders of organized labor on the one hand interpreted Patterson's statement as a retreat and on the other charged that he had "blitzkrieged" the policy announced by the NDAC. The Comptroller General, noting the distinction drawn by Assistant Secretary Patterson between negotiated and bid contracts, further complicated the picture by asserting on 9 October 1940 that the military agencies could reject all bids and

[5] Hearings, *National Labor Relations Act,* Vol. 28, p. 7413, Exhibit 1788, Ltr, Attorney Gen to Hillman, 2 Oct 40.

[6] *Ibid.,* pp. 7263–71, Testimony of Attorney Gen, 8 Oct 40.

[7] *Ibid.,* pp. 7246–53, Testimony of ASW, 8 Oct 40.

could insist upon contractors complying with the Wagner Act whether the contract was awarded through competitive bids or was negotiated.[8]   But as far as the War Department was concerned, the labor relations factor was only one element in determining the ability of a company to execute a contract. The prime factor, according to Patterson, was the expeditious accomplishment of the defense program.[9]

Meanwhile, complaints about the War Department dealing with the Ford Motor Company and other companies against whom labor had a grievance continued to mount.   In addition to the pending Air Corps contract, which involved the construction of additional plant facilities for the manufacture of aircraft engines, the Ford Motor Company received an order in November for 1,500 light reconnaissance cars.   On 14 November 1940 President Roosevelt wrote to the NDAC calling attention to the complaints.   Forwarding the President's letter to Assistant Secretary Patterson, the NDAC requested information on the amount involved in contracts awarded to violators of the Wagner Act.   The specific information desired by the NDAC was not readily available, but Patterson discussed the President's letter with members of the commission and all agreed that a clear-cut policy was needed.   They were unable to agree on what the policy should be.[10]   Much of the discussion turned on the question of the Ford contracts.   Commissioners Hillman and Harriet Elliott and Donald M. Nelson, Co-ordinator of National Defense Purchases, asserted that they had originally approved the contracts, but only conditionally, on the basis that Wagner Act compliance clauses would be inserted later.   Patterson held that the Ford facilities were essential to the aircraft production program, that the basic emergency plant facilities contract had not included compliance clauses, and that it was unfair to require new and additional contractual obligations.[11]   At this point, in order to prevent Army contracting officers from falling into hopeless confusion, the Army Chief of Staff issued instructions that the NDAC statement of labor prin-

---

[8] *CIO News,* October 14, 1940; Ltr, Comptroller Gen to SW, 9 Oct 40, OUSW Amberg files, Labor 1941–42; Richard J. Purcell, *Labor Policies of the National Defense Advisory Commission and the Office of Production Management, May 1940 to April 1942,* Civilian Production Administration Study 23 (1946), p. 51.

[9] Hearings, *National Labor Relations Act,* Vol. 28, pp. 7246–53, Testimony of ASW, 8 Oct 40.

[10] Purcell, *Labor Policies,* pp. 52–53; Civilian Production Administration, *Minutes of the Advisory Commission to the Council of National Defense, June 12, 1940, to October 22, 1941,* Documentary Publication 1 (Washington: Government Printing Office, 1946) (hereafter cited as CPA, *NDAC Minutes*), 29 Nov 40, pp. 116–18.

[11] Memo, ASW for Nelson, 17 Sep 40, sub: Proposed Projects . . . for Production of Aircraft Engines . . ., Memo, Nelson for ASW, 17 Sep 40, Draft Ltr [not sent], and Memo, ASW for Nelson, 7 Dec 40, all in OUSW Ford, Dearborn (No. 1) (AF) (DPC); Connery, *The Navy and the Industrial Mobilization in World War II,* pp. 96–97.

ciples was to be used as a guide in awarding contracts under competitive bids. In this particular respect, the instructions (issued in Procurement Circular 43, 4 December 1940) did little more than extend to competitive bids the policy previously announced by Patterson with respect to negotiated contracts. Procurement Circular 43 went further, however, and required that compliance with federal, state, and local labor laws be specified in every invitation for bids. Although Procurement Circular 43 gave added fuel to those who argued that the Army should withhold contracts from firms that refused to conduct their labor relations within the framework of the Wagner Act, Hillman reluctantly approved the Ford aircraft engine contracts on the basis of the War Department's assertion of national need. The case for the reconnaissance car contract was not so clear, since it was not well established that only Ford and no other company could fill the order. Patterson took much the same position as he had toward the other contracts: that the cars were needed for military purposes and that because the contract had been drawn up before Procurement Circular 43 was issued it would be unfair to insist on the new conditions. Rejecting Hillman's protests, the War Department announced toward the end of December that the contract had been awarded.[12]

The award once more brought to a boil the simmering conflict between the War Department, union leaders, and labor spokesmen in the NDAC. Union spokesmen again protested that the War Department was tearing the labor policy of the government to shreds, that the Ford contract gave a green light to "union enemy No. 1," that it would seriously undermine the morale of defense workers, and that the Army was not to be trusted in matters of labor policy.[13] The War Department abruptly halted negotiations that were in progress on another Ford contract. New invitations for bids were sent out to more than a hundred and fifty companies, including Ford, with the stipulation that the award would be subject to Procurement Circular 43, requiring compliance with the Wagner Act. The Ford Motor Company offered the lowest bid and the earliest delivery date but would not agree to the labor terms. A Chrysler subsidiary, whose bid was about $250,000 higher, was awarded the contract.[14] Rejection of the Ford bid created as much uproar as the previous awards had produced. Spokesmen for the

[12] *The New York Times,* December 14 and 28, 1940, and January 5, 1941; CPA, *NDAC Minutes,* 6 Dec 40, pp. 120–23.

[13] *CIO News,* January 6, 1941; *The New York Times,* December 29 and 30, 1940, and January 1, 1941.

[14] *The New York Times,* January 31, 1941.

company charged the War Department with wasting time and money in order to throw a "sop to labor." They claimed that Ford was being black-listed out of the defense program, and several congressmen demanded an investigation. The CIO unions were delighted at the turn of events and urged the War Department to extend the compliance provisions of Procurement Circular 43 to negotiated contracts.[15]

The War Department in the meantime was seeking a way out of the the dilemma. Patterson's advisers on labor matters attempted to draft a compliance clause for contracts that would be satisfactory to organized labor as well as to bidders. At least eight different versions were drawn up, not one of which proved acceptable to all concerned. To suspend competitive bidding in favor of negotiated contracts, which were not subject to Procurement Circular 43, offered no lasting solution. Patterson did adopt this procedure in February 1941 in the case of contracts for motor vehicles, but it was only a rather dubious expedient, certain to arouse as much protest from union spokesmen as would the outright repeal of the circular. The latter course had its proponents, notably The Quartermaster General and Julius H. Amberg, special assistant to Secretary Stimson. They recognized, on the other hand, that repeal of the circular would provoke a tremendous outcry from organized labor. It seemed better, and to Amberg possible, to work out a formula.[16] Patterson, now Under Secretary, encouraged Amberg to try his hand at drafting a satisfactory clause for insertion in procurement contracts, but his efforts were no more successful than those of others.

Apart from the fundamental issue of how much discretion was to be permitted in awarding contracts to firms that did not comply with the Wagner Act, the principal stumbling block was the question whether contracts should be withheld from derelict firms until the long process of judicial review had been completed. The Wagner Act permitted a firm that had been cited for violations to appeal to the courts, without any time limit within which the appeal had to be made. The result was that the average length of time between the National Labor Relations Board order and the final decree of the U.S. Circuit Court amounted to 353 days, and in some cases the process took two years. If the War Department were to place contracts with firms that had appealed a board decision, the possibility of almost endless evasion lay open.

---

[15] *Ibid.*, January 31, and February 1, 9, and 21, 1941; *CIO News,* February 3, 1941.
[16] Memo, Amberg for USW, 11 Apr 41, sub: Proc Circular 43, Memos, Amberg for USW, 18 and 21 Jan, and 17 Feb 41, all in OUSW Amberg files, Labor 1941–42.

Secretary Stimson discussed the problem with Justice Felix Frankfurter. What Justice Frankfurter advised does not appear in the records, but shortly afterward Stimson suggested that the War Department stipulate that a contractor had either to comply with a board order or to appeal within thirty days. This, like Amberg's efforts, was discussed by a special interagency committee consisting of Amberg for the War Department, James D. Wise for the Navy Department, and Isador Lubin for the Office of Production Management (the successor agency to NDAC). They were unable to agree on the proposal, and Amberg reluctantly concluded that "the NLRA subject presents an irreconcilable conflict of views." [17]

While the spate of strikes and labor disputes that struck defense industry in the winter of 1940–41 was making a solution even more imperative than before, Army procurement officials were beginning to think themselves stymied by Circular 43. The Quartermaster General, Maj. Gen. Edmund B. Gregory, noted on 1 April 1941 that the Ford Motor Company was the only source of certain types of trucks, but that under Circular 43 it was impossible to make use of the company's productive capacity even though it was urgently needed in the interest of national defense. He requested that either the circular be rescinded or the chiefs of supply services be authorized to dispense with it whenever in their opinion it was impeding the defense program. The Chief of Engineers likewise inquired about the possibility of waiving Circular 43, since the Bethlehem Steel Company, whose facilities were of vital importance, was refusing to accept contracts embodying the NDAC statement of principles.[18] Amberg was sympathetic but counseled patience, possibly because the issue had again been taken to the White House. On 5 April 1941 Roosevelt discussed the question of government contracts and labor laws with the Secretary of the Treasury, Henry Morgenthau, Jr. Morgenthau aligned himself with the critics of the War Department by proposing that firms cited for noncompliance with the Wagner Act be barred from contracts and that any legal doubt in the matter of negotiated contracts be

---

[17] Memo, Amberg for Stimson, 15 Feb 41, sub: Time Consumed in Appeals . . ., Memo, Amberg for Patterson, 17 Feb 41, sub: Status of NLRA and Compliance Situation, Memo, Patterson for Amberg, 18 Jan 41, Memo, Amberg for Patterson, 3 Mar 41, sub: . . . Lubin-Wise-Amberg-OPM Committee . . . Concerning the NLRA, and Ltr, Amberg to OPM, 17 Mar 41, all in OUSW Amberg files, Labor 1941–42; Statement of Negotiations of the Special OPM Committee Concerning NLRA, 1 Mar 41, OUSW 160, Contracts.

[18] Memo, Amberg for Ohly, 31 May 41, sub: CofEngrs Request for Exclusion of Statement of Labor Policy, Memo, TQMG for USW, 1 Apr 41, sub: Proc Circular 43, Memos, McGrady for USW, 11 and 26 Apr 41, sub: Proc Circular 43, Memos, Amberg for USW, 11 and 24 Apr 41, sub: Proc Circular 43, all in OUSW 160, Contracts, Proc Circular 43.

cleared up by appropriate legislation.   The President referred Secretary Morgenthau's proposal to Donald Nelson, Director of Purchases in OPM, and
asked Nelson and Morgenthau for a joint recommendation.   Although Nelson seems to have believed that a contract clearance system that OPM had
instituted would be more effective than a compliance clause in contracts, he
concurred with Morgenthau in recommending what was virtually the latter.
Their recommendation—that a contractor receiving a defense order be required to certify that he was complying and would continue to comply with
all federal labor laws—encountered opposition in the OPM Council.[19]   The
Morgenthau-Nelson proposal was rejected, and a substitute suggested by
Secretary Stimson, who represented the War Department on the council,
was likewise rejected.   Stimson then informed the other members of the
council that the War Department would repeal Procurement Circular 43.[20]
Hillman decided to accept the verdict.   He and Knudsen drafted a letter to
the President on 1 May 1941 which recognized the War Department's position.   Although OPM would not give clearance to contracts entered into
with "habitual violators" of the labor laws, Hillman and Knudsen stated, exceptions would be made in particular cases if the refusal to clear would result
in "undue interference" with the defense program.   Secretary Stimson noted
his approval as follows: "I approve—I understand from Patterson that the letter does not compel the insertion of the objectionable labor clause of last
autumn into the contracts."[21]   On 5 June 1941 there appeared, buried near
the end of a ten-page procurement circular, an inconspicuous item officially
rescinding Circular 43.   The Army had won its point.

The circular had a quiet burial.   Not even on the part of organized labor
was there much wailing and gnashing of teeth, for by this time the issue was
of minor importance.   The German U-boat assault along the North Atlantic
sea lanes, the *Bismarck* episode, rumors and portents of a German drive toward the South Atlantic—all gave force to President Roosevelt's declaration
of an unlimited national emergency.   The war, he asserted, was "approaching

[19] The OPM Council was the policy making group for OPM.   It consisted of the Secretary of
War, the Secretary of the Navy, the Director General, OPM (William S. Knudsen), and the
Associate Director General, OPM (Sidney Hillman).
[20] Covering Ltr and Memo, Morgenthau to President, 6 Apr 41, with sample certificate of com-
pliance and draft of legislation (H. R. 4499, 23 Apr 41, 77th Congress, 1st Session), Draft Ltr
[not sent], Nelson to President [mid-April 1941], and Joint Memo, Nelson and Morgenthau for
President, 24 Apr 41, all in OUSW Amberg files, Labor 1941–42; Memo, Amberg for USW, 29
Apr 41, OUSW 160, Contracts.
[21] Ltr, Knudsen and Hillman to President, 1 May 41, Ltr, Amberg to J. L. O'Brian, Gen
Counsel OPM, 1 May 41, and Note, H. L. S. [Stimson] to O'Brian, 1 May 41, all in OUSW
Amberg files, Labor 1941–42.

the brink of the Western Hemisphere itself." Furthermore, labor's traditional weapon—the strike—was proving more effective than its efforts to obtain legal or administrative sanctions against recalcitrant employers. The
rising record of strikes in 1941 is a measure of the trend.[22] The unionizing
campaign in the expanding aircraft industry and against such holdouts as the
Ford Motor Company and Bethlehem Steel was making headway. On 20
June 1941 Ford signed a contract with the United Automobile Workers, CIO,
which among other things provided for a union shop and a wage scale equal
to the highest in the industry. While the industrial giants were capitulating,
smaller business firms were becoming increasingly dependent on government
contracts and were showing an increasing disposition to adjust their labor
relations accordingly.

So far as the War Department was concerned the issue had never been
one of prolabor versus antilabor interests, nor had the problem for the War
Department been one of clarifying or working out a policy of its own.
Secretary Stimson, Patterson, and their advisers on labor matters had from
the beginning maintained a clear and consistent position: that their interest
was in production, that the War Department was not an appropriate instrument for enforcing labor laws, that the labor relations record of a firm was
only one of many factors to be taken into account in awarding contracts, and
that the weight to be given the labor relations factor should depend upon
the relationship of the particular case to the defense program. The pulls and
pressures that had been exerted on the War Department had created the
problem. With the proclamation of a national emergency on 27 May 1941,
and to a much greater extent after the United States entered the war, this
problem gradually became inconsequential. The OPM and its contract clearance policies gave way to the War Production Board and to a different, wartime emphasis that more closely corresponded to the position of the War
Department.

The question whether, in the absence of specific statutory direction, the
War Department should enforce the labor policy of the government by withholding contracts arose also in connection with decisions of the National
Defense Mediation Board and later of the National War Labor Board and
the War Manpower Commission. The War Department consistently,
though not always successfully, opposed this extension of responsibility. Its
position remained as Amberg expressed it in the fall of 1941: "I doubt that
we should adopt the theory of enforcing Mediation Board recommendations

[22] See Ch. IV, below.

by withholding orders from non-compliant companies. Such precedent would be reminiscent of Circular 43. I think you should withhold orders solely for the reason that production is stopped . . . ."[23]

As the Wagner Act issue subsided, certain provisions of the Walsh-Healey Act began to cause a measure of concern. The overtime provisions complicated the procurement of canned fruits and vegetables and hindered the use of railroad machine shops for work done under defense contracts. The child and female labor provisions limited the expansion of cotton textile contracts. The definition, in the act, of "manufacturers" seemed to prohibit contracts with jobbers and manufacturing associations. A remedy, however, was provided in the act itself. If the conduct of government business would be seriously impaired by including the stipulations of the act in a contract, and if the head of the contracting agency submitted a written finding to this effect to the Secretary of Labor, the latter was authorized to grant an exemption. Only four exemptions had been requested by the War and Navy Departments in the three and a half years before December 1940, but in 1941 at least half a dozen exemptions were requested and obtained by the War Department.[24] The objections of labor leaders, who feared a breakdown of standards, made the process of obtaining exemptions a rather slow one. The merits of each individual case were difficult to determine. The result was a strong reluctance on the part of the War Department to apply for exemptions and a careful scrutiny by the Labor Department of each application. Probably for similar reasons the authority to suspend the stipulations of the Walsh-Healey Act that was granted the President in Public Law 671, 76th Congress (Act of 28 June 1940), was never invoked.

Even after the United States entered the war the number of exemptions remained small. When exemptions were made, employers frequently asked that employees be "disexempted" so that overtime wages could be paid as an incentive for staying on the job.[25] From 1 January 1942 to 1 July 1944, the Labor Department granted at the request of the War Department a total of about eighteen exemptions. At least two additional requests, and probably several others, were withdrawn by the War Department when it appeared

---

[23] Note, J. H. A. [Julius H. Amberg] for USW, 1 Oct 41, OUSW Miscellaneous and Subject, Labor 1941–42.

[24] Ltr, L. M. Walling, Administrator Div of Public Contracts Dept of Labor, to Rear Adm Ray Spear, Chief Bureau of Supplies and Accounts Navy Dept, 10 Dec 40, and Dept of Labor Order, 5 Dec 41 (Federal Register Document 41–9207), enclosed with Ltr, JAG (USN) to All Bureaus and Offices Navy Dept, 27 Nov 42, all in Ohly file, Statutes, Walsh-Healey Act. See also Yoshpe, *op. cit.*, pp. 23–26.

[25] Annual Report of the Wage and Hour and Public Contracts Division, Department of Labor, for Fiscal Year Ended June 30, 1943.

that they would not be granted, and perhaps an equal number were adjusted without a formal exemption order.[26]   The exemptions ranged from those covering an entire industry, such as the canning industry, or an entire category of employees, such as females under eighteen years of age, to those that applied to a single company.   Since the effect of the restrictions of the act was, as in the case of so many of the wartime labor problems, not general in scope or incidence, the remedies were likewise specific.   The regulations and the growing list of firms blacklisted for violations put a strain on contracting officers, but nothing in the records indicates that war production suffered as a result of the Walsh-Healey Act or that without the act production could have been greater.

The effect of prewar labor legislation upon the full utilization of labor was not that which had been anticipated.   As an impediment to full production, statutory safeguards of labor standards turned out to be of considerably less concern than the size of the labor force and the limitations on output that might result from work stoppages.

The Strength of the Army and the Size of the Labor Force

An Army that might perhaps be of such size as to tax the manpower resources of the nation was first suggested in the summer of 1941.   A year earlier, in June 1940, the President had promised that the United States not only would rearm at home, but would also serve as the "arsenal of democracy."   Now, in order to formulate a long-range production program that would satisfy the demands of both foreign aid and American rearmament, President Roosevelt, on 9 July 1941, requested the Army and Navy to explore "the overall production requirements" necessary for the defeat of "our potential enemies."[27]   The Army planning staff was not at all reluctant to raise its sights beyond the limited objectives of the current emergency, but it rejected the President's implication that a production program would set the pattern of victory.   The proper approach, according to Brig Gen. Leonard T. Gerow, head of the War Plans Division, would be to "first evolve a strategic concept . . . and then determine the major military units (Air, Navy and

[26] The exemptions granted in 1942 are given in the Department of Labor orders attached to the letter from JAG (USN) to All Bureaus and Offices, Navy Department, 27 November 1942, and a list of all Walsh-Healy Act cases and action taken thereon for 1943 and January–August 1944 is attached to Table, Incidence of Walsh-Healy Cases By Months, Ohly file, Statutes, Walsh-Healey Act.

[27] President Roosevelt's letter is given *in extenso* in Mark Skinner Watson, *Chief of Staff: Prewar Plans and Preparations*, UNITED STATES ARMY IN WORLD WAR II (Washington: Government Printing Office, 1950), pp. 338–39.

Gound) required to carry out the strategic operations . . . ."[28] From this determination could be computed the ultimate requirements in munitions and matériel.

Lt. Col. Albert C. Wedemeyer of the War Plans Division, who had been working for some weeks on a strategic estimate of more limited scope, was assigned the task of making the exploration requested by the President. Instead of following the formula suggested by the President, Colonel Wedemeyer took as his point of departure the manpower that would be available for the armed forces. The components were tailored to fit the total, and a basis for calculating production requirements was thus provided. The production requirements that thus became the "Victory Program," were based upon an Army of 8,795,658 men—double the size of any force suggested in previous planning. Apart from its relation to Army plans and logistical preparations, the story of which is told elsewhere in this series, the figure that Colonel Wedemeyer arrived at for the ultimate strength of the Army is notable in two respects: first, although at best only an enlightened guess, it exceeded by no more than 500,000 the actual peak strength of the Army reached on 31 May 1945; and second, it was computed by methods more reminiscent of those employed by labor and production experts than of those of the military expert.[29] Although some confusion now exists as to the precise method of calculation, it is clear that, in computing the figure he used, Colonel Wedemeyer did not follow the approach suggested by General Gerow, the approach customarily taken by the War Department planners. Instead, Wedemeyer made an estimate of the total able-bodied manpower of the nation, from which he deducted the estimated number of men that would be required by industry, the Navy, and other agencies. The remainder was the number of men that would be available to the Army.[30] From the traditional point of view of the military planner, this was working backward.

The Wedemeyer estimate did not inject a disturbing factor into manpower calculations since it was simply a basis for supply and production planning. It was not the figure accepted as that necessary for the execution of the Army's strategic plans or as that on which mobilization planning was based. In the summer of 1941 the approved estimate of strength, determined by the number and types of units that might be required, was less than half as large as Wedemeyer's Victory Program estimate.

[28] *Ibid.*, p. 342.
[29] *Ibid.*, Ch. XI; Richard M. Leighton and Robert W. Coakley, *Global Logistics and Strategy: 1940–1943*, UNITED STATES ARMY IN WORLD WAR II (Washington: Government Printing Office, 1955), Ch. V.
[30] *Ibid.*

The first troop basis—the Army's official manpower budget—to approach the Victory Program estimate was drawn up during the late summer of 1942. At that time G–3 proposed an Army of 7,500,000 enlisted men, which would mean a total, including officers, of about 8,200,000. Navy, Marine Corps, and Coast Guard requirements brought the aggregate for all the armed forces up to 10,894,000 officers and men. The War Department set 31 December 1943 as the date for attaining the proposed strength.[31]

This troop basis came under attack almost immediately. The War Production Board and the War Manpower Commission objected on the grounds that an Army of the size proposed would throw the national economy out of balance and would prove too large for efficient use. The Bureau of the Budget insisted that the Combined Chiefs of Staff and the Combined Production and Resources Board should have been consulted, and the Navy believed that shipping requirements had not been given due consideration.[32]

The War Manpower Commission, headed by Paul V. McNutt, and the Selective Service System, directed by Maj. Gen. Lewis B. Hershey, had not completed their studies of the maximum manpower available for the armed services when the Joint Chiefs of Staff, in early September 1942, asked both agencies for data on the subject.[33] Pending completion of the War Manpower Commission study, McNutt estimated that no more than 9,000,000 men would be available for the armed forces by 31 December 1943 and that "mobilization of the nation to the ultimate degree" would make only 10,500,000 men available "without regard to any given year." He stated his belief that accurate estimates could not be made without a "thoroughgoing study of military requirements, civilian requirements, production programs, and manpower resources," and to this end he proposed that representatives of the Army and Navy confer periodically with the War Manpower Commission

[31] Greenfield, Palmer, and Wiley, *The Organization of Ground Combat Troops,* pp. 212–17.

[32] The Combined Chiefs of Staff committee was the organization of service representatives of the United Kingdom and the United States established at the end of 1941 to carry out the strategic direction of the war. The Combined Production and Resources Board, the creation of which was announced by President Roosevelt on 9 June 1942, was organized to direct the most effective use of the combined resources of the United Kingdom and the United States in the prosecution of the war. Canada later was given representation on the Combined Production and Resources Board.

[33] The Joint Chiefs of Staff, a committee that held its first meeting on 9 February 1942, was composed at first of General George C. Marshall, Army Chief of Staff; Admiral Harold R. Stark, Chief of Naval Operations; Lt. Gen. Henry H. Arnold, Chief of the Army Air Forces; and Admiral Ernest J. King, Commander in Chief, U.S. Fleet. After attending only a few meetings, Stark left Washington, and King assumed the duties of Chief of Naval Operations in addition to those of Commander in Chief, U.S. Fleet. In July 1942 Admiral William D. Leahy, who became Chief of Staff to the President, was added.

and the War Production Board.[34]   General Hershey, in his reply to the request of the Joint Chiefs of Staff, enclosed a study made by the Social Security Board in June 1942, which also estimated that a maximum of 9,000,000 men would be under arms at the end of 1943.[35]   Since these figures seemed no more reliable than those of the services themselves, the subcommittee of the Joint Staff Planners that had been charged with making a report on the troop basis accepted the figures presented by each of the armed services.[36] On 21 September 1942 it recommended for the approval of the Joint Chiefs of Staff an aggregate of 10,894,623 for all the armed services as the troop basis for 31 December 1943.[37]

The Joint Chiefs of Staff on 29 September 1942 approved the subcommittee's report and at the same time discussed McNutt's proposal for interagency conferences on the subject.   Secretary Stimson had been informed by his adviser on manpower, Goldthwaite Dorr, that conferences with the War Manpower Commission and the War Production Board were advisable.   General George C. Marshall, the Chief of Staff of the Army, and Admiral Ernest J. King, Commander in Chief, U.S. Fleet, and Chief of Naval Operations, agreed, but they insisted that the determination of military requirements was the responsibility solely of the respective services.   They decided to inform McNutt that the Joint Chiefs of Staff heartily concurred in his suggestion, but that any conclusions reached in the conferences could not be considered an expression of the views of the armed services until they were approved by the Joint Chiefs of Staff.   In their letter to McNutt, the Joint Chiefs explained that the 1943 requirements of the Army and Navy, totaling "approximately 10,900,000," had already been submitted to the President, that studies to determine the ultimate manpower requirements of the armed forces were in preparation, and that as soon as Army and Navy representatives could be appointed they would get in touch with McNutt for the purpose of arranging the conferences.[38]

President Roosevelt at first gave only conditional approval to the troop basis approved by the Joint Chiefs of Staff.   When Admiral William D. Leahy, who acted as chairman of the Joint Chiefs of Staff, submitted the rec-

---

[34] Ltr, McNutt to Brig Gen J. R. Deane, Secy JCS, 16 Sep 42, in History of the Joint Chiefs of Staff, Sec. IIC, Ch. V, "The JCS Begin Manpower Mobilization Planning," by Maj Margaret A. Bacchus, pp. 18–19.

[35] Ltr, Hershey to Brig Gen W. B. Smith, Secy JCS, 10 Sep 42, in History of the Joint Chiefs of Staff, Sec. IIC, Ch. V, p. 17.

[36] The Joint Staff Planners was a planning committee of the Joint Chiefs of Staff.

[37] History of the Joint Chiefs of Staff, Sec. IIC, Ch. V, pp. 21–24.

[38] Ibid., pp. 26–28; Memo, Dorr for Stimson, 24 Sep 42, and Memo, SW for Dorr, 25 Sep 42, both in Stimson files, Manpower.

ommendations, the President noted that he approved them only for "allocation of material and equipment and for planning of personnel." Additional funds for the increases in personnel would be approved later, from time to time, "if" they were needed.[39]   Telling of his interview with the President, Admiral Leahy subsequently wrote:

> When the President returned on October 1 from an inspection of war plants in the Northwest, the Pacific Coast, and the Southeastern states, I laid the JCS recommendations before him. He objected to such a radical increase in the authorized strength at one time but said he would be willing to approve limited additions from time to time. I did not insist too much on getting the 10,000,000-man authorization. We were getting along all right. Besides, it would probably have wrecked the labor market.[40]

Not long afterward, on 3 November 1942, the Joint Chiefs of Staff met with the heads of the interested agencies. The War Production Board, which had geared its production studies to a 7,600,000-man Army and Navy, viewed any higher figure as unrealistic and impracticable. The chief of the War Production Board Planning Committee, Robert R. Nathan, had characterized the Joint Chiefs of Staff recommendation as a "highly injudicious allocation of the nation's manpower," and he repeated the charge even after the 10,000,000-man troop basis became official. Nathan, it should be noted, took a leading role in the concurrent "feasibility dispute" between the War Production Board and the War Department, the sharp controversy over how large a procurement and facilities expansion program the nation's resources could support. An analysis of shipping space made by the War Production Board Planning Committee convinced that agency that the Army would be unable to deploy troops to the combat zone in numbers anything like those it was planning for, and that the result would be "a stagnant pool of manpower, contributing neither to the defense of the country . . . nor to its productive capacity."[41]   At the meeting of 3 November, General Marshall discussed the difficulties the Army faced in economizing on manpower. "We cannot," he said, "make any cuts in our requirements for combat units if we expect to win the war." No formal decisions were made at the meeting, but the discussion revealed the necessity for providing the War Manpower Commission with the estimated rate of inductions to December 1943, in order to permit better planning for withdrawing men from industry.[42]

[39] History of the Joint Chiefs of Staff, Sec. IIC, Ch. VI, "Manpower Becomes a Problem: Conflict Between JCS and Civilian War Agencies, September–December 1942," by Maj. William P. Moody, p. 13.

[40] William D. Leahy, *I Was There* (New York: Whittlesey House, 1950), p. 129.

[41] CPA, *Industrial Mobilization for War,* I, 414; History of the Joint Chiefs of Staff, Sec. IIC, Ch. VI, p. 18. The feasibility dispute referred to above is discussed in Smith, *The Army and Economic Mobilization,* Ch. VII.

[42] History of the Joint Chiefs of Staff, Sec. IIC, Ch. VI, pp. 15–17.

The next day the War Department was astonished to receive a letter from the Director of the Bureau of the Budget stating that the size of the Army was set at 7,553,000 enlisted men for fiscal year 1944. This was the exact figure, exclusive of officers, that the President had approved for planning purposes for calendar year 1943. General Marshall strongly urged the President to revoke the latest instructions, but the President at first refused. He was convinced that there was no conflict in the figures and that if the Army and the Bureau of the Budget followed his instructions there would be no argument between them. Nevertheless, after "much correspondence and many conferences" over the next two weeks, Roosevelt was persuaded to approve the 7,500,000-man Army for the calendar year 1943.[43]

The question who should decide the size of the Army and what factors should determine it had been officially settled in favor of the Army, but this was only the first round of the struggle. It had been waged mostly on technical questions involving production goals, shipping requirements, and combat needs, and a decision on these grounds did not preclude a continuation of the fight on other grounds. The War Production Board and the War Manpower Commission, the latter reinforced by an executive order requiring the War and Navy Departments to consult with the War Manpower Commission chairman on the armed forces' monthly quotas, continued to press for a larger share of responsibility. More dangerous to the War Department was the criticism that involved matters of attitude, the basic ingredient of which was an amalgam of isolationism, politics, material self-interest, and misguided amateur strategy.

Several Congressional committees interested themselves in one aspect or another of the question. The Senate Special Committee Investigating the National Defense Program (Truman Committee) reported that the armed services had not consulted manpower or production authorities in establishing requirements and objected to the size of the Army being determined "solely by the number of males of military age who can pass the physical fitness tests . . . ."[44] The House Select Committee Investigating National Defense Migration (Tolan Committee) urged the President to create a central authority to fix the size of the Army and allocate manpower among the armed services, industry, and agriculture.[45] A number of senators and other

[43] Ibid., pp. 21–22.

[44] Senate Report 480, 77th Congress, 2d Session, Investigation of the National Defense Program, Part 11, Manpower, November 12, 1942. The preliminary report on manpower was transmitted to the President by Ltr, Senator Harry S. Truman to President, 23 Oct 42.

[45] House Report 2589, 77th Congress, 2d Session, National Defense Migration, Sixth Interim Report of House Select Committee Investigating National Defense Migration, October 20, 1942, Changes Needed for Effective Mobilization of Manpower.

individuals vigorously opposed a large Army.   Secretary of Agriculture Claude R. Wickard pointed to the shortage of farm labor and the danger of food shortages, while William Green, president of the AFL, protested that industrial production would suffer if the Army continued to take skilled workers. The most eminent critic was former President Herbert Hoover.   Testifying before the Senate Committee on Appropriations subcommittee on manpower in February 1943, the former President noted three important factors in the manpower situation: first, the home front, where there were great strains in agriculture and industrial production; second, the war front, where the United States was growing stronger and the enemy weaker; and third, the "shipping bottleneck," which Hoover believed made it unfeasible to mobilize so many men.

If we put all three factors together [Hoover concluded] . . . it would seem at least warranted to study a revision of our whole program of national production and supply based on the bottleneck limitation.   It is possible that this would reduce the financial as well as the mineral, the agricultural, the food and other home front strains.   In any event, we must have more labor in those fields if we are to maintain our national strength. Such a program might not meet the views of the generals or admirals, who of necessity look only to the maximum military activity, but it is a serious consideration that we might break the back of our people on the home front and start internal degeneration.[46]

In defense of its own estimates, the War Department pointed out that the Army Air Forces alone required nearly 1,500,000 men for installations in the United States, 50 percent more than the War Production Board estimated for Army and Air Forces combined.   General Marshall pointed out also that large numbers of men in the continental United States were in training and could not therefore be considered "a stagnant pool."   Its estimates, the War Department was convinced, were "based upon its best judgment as to requirements to fulfill the important mission of supplying and training troops to be transported overseas to defeat the enemy and to maintain support for the overseas Army and defend the United States." [47]   Further analyzing the War Production Board's estimates, Brig. Gen. Edwin S. Greenbaum of Under Secretary Patterson's office wrote:

War Production Board's sphere of interest in the subject should necessarily be limited to a study of the ability of the country to support and supply the Armed Forces.   In the absence of very clear proof that this country cannot support an Armed Force of 10,800,000 (and so far WPB has not even attempted such proof) a difference of opinion relating to

[46] Testimony of Herbert Hoover, 8 February 1943, Senate Subcommittee of Committee on Appropriations, 78th Congress, 1st Session, Hearings, *Investigation of Manpower*, Part 1, pp. 223–44, and Part 3, Report of Senator Theodore Francis Green, Member of the Subcommittee.

[47] Memo, Greenbaum for USW, 24 February 43, sub: WPB's Office Memos . . . in Reference to Size of the Army, copy in OCMH, Selective Service; Memo, Greenbaum for USW, sub: Size of the Army, ASF Control Div, Manpower Problems.

1/70 of the total population would scarcely seem to justify WPB's attempt to advise the Army on this purely military subject.[48]

Throughout the winter of 1942–43 the debate went on.   Secretary Stimson, who had taken no active part as long as the argument stayed on the technical level, plunged into the fray against those who seemed to him to be looking for some easy way to win the war without too much trouble and sacrifice.   This attitude he characterized as a "subtle danger which, unless guarded against, may destroy our present bright hopes for a decisive victory." [49]   The theory "that the projected army would too greatly strain the nation's manpower resources . . .," to quote Stimson's biographer, "in Stimson's view embodied one of the most pertinacious fallacies of all, and he jumped on it with both feet." [50]   It was "wholly illogical," he claimed, to provide for industry and agriculture at the expense of the Army until industry and agriculture were really keyed to an all-out war.   The President supported the War Department.   At a press conference on 19 February 1943, Mr. Roosevelt called for 11,000,000 men for the armed forces by the end of the year, but he conceded that manpower was becoming a problem and that troops might have to be used to tide over a labor shortage at harvest time. Shortly afterward he appointed a special committee, consisting of Bernard Baruch, Harry Hopkins, Admiral Leahy, Judge Samuel I. Rosenman, and the Director of Economic Stabilization, James F. Byrnes, to investigate and report on the manpower problem.   After hearing the testimony of labor leaders and government experts, the committee reported that if measures to conserve manpower and to utilize more women in industry were taken the nation could support 11,160,000 men in the armed services.   The committee agreed that if the war continued much longer some form of national service act would be inevitable, but it also agreed that the country was not ready to accept one.[51]

The controversy had in the meantime complicated planning for the 1944 Troop Basis.   Estimates of personnel requirements for the year 1944, arrived at by each of the services separately, had been combined by a subcommittee of the Joint Staff Planners and presented to the Joint Planners on 22 October 1942.   The Army planned to have 10,572,000 under arms at the end of 1944; the Navy, Marine Corps, and Coast Guard placed their requirements at

---

[48] *Ibid.*
[49] Radio address of 9 March 1943, quoted in Stimson and Bundy, *On Active Service in Peace and War,* p. 477.
[50] *Ibid.,* p. 479.
[51] *The New York Times,* February 20, and March 7 and 17, 1943; Leahy, *op. cit.,* pp. 149–50; Samuel I. Rosenman, *Working With Roosevelt* (New York: Harper & Brothers, 1952), pp. 421–22.

3,514,556. The total of 14,086,557 men was more than 3,000,000 higher than the controversial 1943 Troop Basis. Because of the stir caused by the latter, the Joint Staff Planners did not even consider approving the subcommittee's estimates, much less releasing them to civilians.[52]

When the report of the Joint Staff Planners reached the Joint Chiefs of Staff, the strategic concept on which the estimates had been based was questioned by both General Marshall and Admiral King, and it was decided on 1 December 1942 to defer action on the 1944 Troop Basis until a revised strategic concept was agreed upon.[53] The Joint Chiefs of Staff further decided to inform the War Manpower Commission that the War and Navy Departments were restudying their personnel requirements with a view to reducing them. At the first of the long-postponed staff conferences with War Manpower Commission representatives, on 9 December, there was therefore a marked reversal of roles. The War Manpower Commission, which for weeks had been pressing the Joint Chiefs of Staff for information and data on military manpower planning, was now requested to submit an estimate of manpower available for 1944. The service representatives took the position that military requirements could not be finally determined until the commission furnished this information. At the beginning of January 1943, after preliminary estimates were received from the War Manpower Commission and a new strategic concept was approved by the Joint Chiefs of Staff, the Joint Staff Planners resumed its study of the 1944 Troop Basis. It proposed to give "due consideration" to the effect of the withdrawal of manpower from agriculture and industry and to keep the troop basis "in line with available manpower, the estimated production demands, and the estimated availability of shipping."[54]

The controversy over the 1943 Troop Basis continued to delay the preparation of the 1944 Troop Basis. The question whether shipping would be adequate had raised a difference of opinion between the War and Navy Departments lasting well into February 1943. Foreseeing a shortage of manpower, the Navy members of the Joint Staff Planners' subcommittee now insisted that the Army should reduce its 1943 estimates even though they had been approved by the President. The Army representatives believed it preferable to make economies, recall enlisted reservists, and reduce calls on

---

[52] History of the Joint Chiefs of Staff, Sec. IIC, Ch. VII, "Planning the Troop Bases for All Services for 1944 and Beyond," by Maj. William P. Moody, pp. 2–4.

[53] See Maurice Matloff and Edwin M. Snell, *Strategic Planning for Coalition Warfare, 1941–1942*, UNITED STATES ARMY IN WORLD WAR II (Washington: Government Printing Office, 1953), Chapters XVI–XVII, for strategic planning in December 1942 and January 1943.

[54] History of the Joint Chiefs of Staff, Sec. IIC, Ch. VII, pp. 6–10.

Selective Service during 1943 in order to make the savings available in 1944. This solution, in general, was finally recommended to the Joint Staff Planners on 24 April 1943 and approved by them on 5 May. For the 1944 Troop Basis, the Army was to be held at the 1943 figure; the Navy, Marine Corps, and Coast Guard were to be raised to 3,799,000, making a total for the armed services of 12,047,000. Again the Joint Chiefs of Staff decided to reject the recommendations of their planners.[55]

Again the delay was the result partly of the controversy over the 1943 Troop Basis and partly of the changing strategic plans. Concerned by public criticism and Congressional suspicion, the Army had embarked on an economy drive. Three committees—the Gasser Board, the Bessell Committee, and the Maddocks Committee—were appointed early in 1943 to study the strength of the Army in various aspects.[56] Their reports convinced General Marshall that the Army's 1943 Troop Basis could be cut by more than 500,000 men, to a total of approximately 7,686,000. The Maddocks Committee, pointing to the decision taken at the U.S.-British conference TRIDENT in Washington in May 1943 to have only fifty U.S. divisions in combat theaters on 1 October 1944 and hopeful that the combined bomber offensive would weaken Germany's will to resist while the Soviet Union continued to contain the German armies on the Eastern Front, had recommended that the 1943 Troop Basis be reduced. General Marshall gave his approval on 8 June 1943. The Navy, meanwhile, found it necessary to revise its enlisted strength upward. With the concurrence of Marshall, Admiral Leahy transmitted the Navy's request for additional personnel to President Roosevelt, who gave his approval on 3 August. The net change in the 1943 Troop Basis was slight, but until the revisions were decided upon and approved the detailed planning for the 1944 Troop Basis had to be postponed. Further delay resulted when the Army, now a stanch champion of retrenchment, urged the Navy to make economies for 1944. By diligent effort the Navy was able to make some reductions, and on 9 November 1943 the Joint Chiefs of Staff finally approved and dispatched to the President the 1944 Troop Basis. The strength

---

[55] Ibid., pp. 18–24.

[56] The Gasser Board, officially the War Department Manpower Board, was established in early 1943 as a War Department Special Staff Division. The Bessell Committee, an informal group headed by Col. William W. Bessell, Jr., was created by the Operations Division, War Department General Staff, in February 1943 for the purpose of studying the current military program and the effect of arming foreign forces on the manpower situation. The Maddocks Committee was an ad hoc committee comprised of Col. Ray T. Maddocks and Lt. Col. Marshall S. Carter of the Operations Division and Col. Edwin W. Chamberlain of the G–3 Division, War Department General Staff. For a discussion of the Maddocks Committee's recommendations, see Cline, Washington Command Post: The Operations Division, pp. 275–76.

of the Army was to be stabilized at approximately 7,700,000; the Navy, Marine Corps, and Coast Guard were to be reduced to 3,564,000, making a total of 11,264,000 men planned for the armed forces by the end of 1944. On 15 November 1943 the President returned the 1944 Troop Basis to the Joint Chiefs of Staff with his "O.K." [57]

The approval of the 1944 strength estimates marked the end of troop basis planning during World War II. Thereafter the problem was to implement the troop basis and to prevent "leaks" that might develop from the activation of units not called for in the troop basis, from the increasing number of men in the "pipeline," and from similar complications that arose when a constantly fluctuating organization such as the Army was fitted into a rigid framework. The only subsequent change in the Army's authorized ceiling strength came in May 1945, when the actual strength of approximately 8,291,000 men was approved as the total for the troop basis.[58] By April 1944 the Army had attained the 7,700,000-man strength established by the 1944 Troop Basis, but the process of growth had continued. Thereafter, the issue was not how many men the Army should have, but how many it really had.

Although General Marshall and the Army planners never abandoned their position that the size of the Army was a matter for the War Department to decide, by the fall of 1943 they had accepted the view that factors other than military contributed to shaping the decision. The reluctance of Marshall to approve an increase in the troop basis was no sign that the Army had all the men it needed. It rested on the belief that the armed forces could not be further enlarged without straining the national economy beyond the point of wisdom. At it was, the peak strength of 12,124,418, which the Army and Navy reached in May 1945, was somewhat higher than the figure that had been estimated in the spring of 1943 as the maximum the country could support. Fortunately perhaps for the prosecution of the war, but unfortunately for purposes of analysis, the peak strength was reached after the peak of industrial and agricultural requirements had passed. As a very broad generalization, it can be said only that the criticism and controversy over the 1943 Troop Basis served to bring home to the War Department planners some-

[57] History of the Joint Chiefs of Staff, Sec. IIC, Ch. VII, pp. 32–39; Walter G. Hermes, Manpower Limitations, Draft MS in Matloff files, OCMH; Maurice Matloff, *Strategic Planning for Coalition Warfare, 1943–1945,* UNITED STATES ARMY IN WORLD WAR II (Washington: Government Printing Office, 1959), Chs. VIII and XI.

[58] Lt. Col. Mervin A. Kreidberg and 1st Lt. Merton G. Henry, *History of Military Mobilization in the United States Army, 1775–1945,* Department of the Army Pamphlet 20–212 (Washington: Government Printing Office, 1955), Ch. XVIII; Minutes of WD General Council Meeting, 21 May 45; Greenfield, Palmer, and Wiley, *The Organization of Ground Combat Troops,* pp. 235–38.

thing they had not anticipated before the war—the possibility of an over-all manpower shortage and its inhibiting effect on the size of the Army. Whether a larger Army could have been raised and whether the Army that was raised acted as an inhibition on industrial and agricultural production are still debatable questions.

CHAPTER IV

Labor Disputes and the War Department

Maintaining the labor force at maximum size and revising the contractual limitations upon its utilization would not insure maximum production unless labor fully co-operated by putting out its maximum effort. From time to time American workingmen had set limits on their own output, generally in protest against unsatisfactory working conditions, frequently as a means of spreading the work, occasionally to provide themselves with a *quid pro quo* for collective bargaining. In the power politics of peacetime industry, labor was accustomed to having recourse to strikes, to slowdowns, and to other forms of curtailing production. That labor might hesitate to change its tactics during a national emergency is no less understandable than management's reluctance to abandon business as usual.

Strikes and the Defense Effort

In the twenty years before World War II, the Army's chief interest in strikes had stemmed from its role as defender of law and order. In this capacity, the Regular Army had dispersed bonus marchers and the National Guard had several times appeared on the scene of industrial disputes. After the outbreak of war in Europe in September 1939 and the birth of a United States preparedness program, strikes in defense industries became a matter of concern to the War Department primarily because of their effect on production. Nevertheless, it remained the settled policy of the War Department not to inject itself into labor disputes as a mediator or arbitrator, but instead to remain in the background and to work through the Department of Labor and other agencies for a settlement.

Although the year 1940 was one of comparative peace on the industrial front, there were a number of strikes that tested the policy of nonintervention. After the Advisory Commission to the Council of National Defense was established on 29 May 1940, the War Department enlisted the services of Sidney Hillman's Employment Division when labor disputes at Timken

Detroit Axle Corporation, Marathon Rubber Company, and Ford Instrument Company threatened to curtail production of military items. In the Ford Instrument Company dispute in September, the War Department made a direct appeal to national officials of the CIO to keep production going, but Army representatives would not meet with a union committee that came to Washington until Hillman took charge of the situation.[1] A short time later, when a truck drivers' strike in New York tied up Army shipments, the War Department made a direct approach to the union involved. The result was an arrangement under which the War Department identified the goods it needed and the strikers undertook to move them without delay.[2]

The most severe strains and stresses were in the aircraft industry. A new and rapidly expanding industry, it was not only suffering from a shortage of facilities but was also in the throes of being unionized. Production had been cut by strikes in several companies when in August 1940 the workers at Boeing—then the sole source of B-17 bombers—threatened to walk out in a dispute over the wage rate. With the fall of France the war in Europe had taken a most critical turn, while on the other side of the world Japan was on the brink of casting in its lot with the Axis. The moment was serious and every plane that the Boeing Company could produce would be needed. Assistant Secretary Patterson's special assistant on labor problems, Major Simpson, went to Seattle with a representative of the NDAC, Joseph D. Keenan, to see what could be done to keep production going. In consultation with union and company officials, they worked out a plan that provided for increasing the hiring rate to sixty-two and one-half cents per hour, which was acceptable to both parties. Major Simpson's warning that an invasion of the United States was not impossible and that Americans "must work as we have never worked before" to escape the fate that France had suffered was instrumental in bringing about the settlement.[3] There was no strike.

Another dispute in the aircraft industry flared up a few weeks later at Vultee Aircraft, Incorporated, in Los Angeles. The United Automobile Workers, CIO, had driven an entering wedge into the aircraft industry and was insisting on a wage scale comparable to that of the automobile industry. The trouble at the Vultee plant began when the union demanded a starting

---

[1] Memo, QMC for ASW, 29 May 40, sub: UAW . . . , Memo, Prod Br for TQMG, 26 Sep 40, sub: Request of Marathon Rubber Co. . . . , Memo, Sadler for Dir Prod Br, 27 Sep 40, and Telgm, United Electric Radio and Machine Workers Union to Sadler, 27 Sep 40, all in OUSW Res and Prod Div 175, Labor 1935–39.

[2] Memo, Sadler for Col Spalding, 9 Oct 40, and Telgms, Sadler to OQMG in NYPOE, 12–15 Oct 40, all in OUSW Res and Prod Div, Labor 1935–39.

[3] Seattle *Post Intelligencer,* September 5, 1940.

wage of seventy-five cents an hour instead of the fifty-cent rate then in effect. It claimed that while the company's profits were soaring sky-high its wage scale was more like that of a surrey factory.   The company denied that it was profiteering on defense and countered with the charge that the union was attempting to use Vultee as a guinea pig for the industry.   The fifty-cent rate, the company pointed out, was paid to beginners, most of whom were very young men who received training at company expense; the average rate was sixty-eight cents an hour, which was above that of most industries.   Since no headway was made in negotiating an agreement, the union in mid-November called out the men and threw picket lines around the plant.   More than five thousand men were made idle and eighty million dollars worth of military aircraft, vital to national defense, "tail-spinned to a crash." [4]

While Air Corps pilots hastily removed completed planes from the Vultee plant, Major Simpson, fresh from his success in Seattle, was rushed back to the west coast "to impress upon both sides . . . that the production of aircraft is a matter much bigger than the demands of labor or the generosity of employers."   He found what seemed to him a very bad situation, but he promised to "lick" it.   "My impression is," he reported to the War Department, "that Hillman's office is sissy on this one.   I am going to take drastic action if I have to." [5]   But after trying for several days to bring the negotiators together, Major Simpson was considerably less certain of the outcome. The settlement he proposed was in essence a compromise: the starting wage for men with practical shop experience would be sixty-two or sixty-two and one-half cents an hour; men without experience would start at fifty-five cents and receive the higher rate at the end of ninety days' employment.   The proposed contract, which would contain a no-strike clause and provide for compulsory arbitration of all disputes, was to run for two years.   At the end of one year either party might reopen the question of wage rates on thirty days' notice, and if no agreement was then reached the dispute would be submitted to arbitration.   The company, in Simpson's words, "grabbed the proposed contract" and adamantly opposed any further concessions.   The union, on the other hand, refused to accept it, principally because of the arbitration provisions.   Although these provisions were similar to those of the Boeing agreement and of certain CIO contracts in other industries, they were not typical of the contracts that the United Automobile Workers had with the automobile industry.   Moreover, the union took the position that if the

---

[4] Los Angeles *Times*, November 15–18, 1940; *CIO News*, November 25, 1940.
[5] Notes of Tel Conv Between Simpson and T. E. P., WD, n.d., Ohly file, Industrial Disputes of Particular Interest in World War II.

wage question could be reopened at the end of the year the contract would actually be a one year agreement, and that the union should then be free to use its customary methods to obtain an adjustment.[6]

The deadlock on this issue continued for three or four days. By this time Major Simpson had become *persona non grata* to the union. Complaints against his handling of the situation mounted. Charges were made, so it was reported, that his personal conduct hindered, instead of helped, the negotiations.[7] Whether or not the accusations had any basis in fact, Simpson's usefulness as a mediator was obviously at an end. He was immediately called back to Washington and a few days later, on 30 November, he was relieved from active duty.

Within a week after Simpson left Los Angeles the strike was settled. The agreement called for a beginning wage rate of fifty-five cents and sixty-two and one-half cents, the latter to be reached in sixty days instead of the ninety Simpson had proposed, and the union accepted compulsory arbitration for a period of sixteen months. On 26 November, after a twelve-day shutdown, the Vultee plant resumed production.[8]

To assess the more deep-seated effect of strikes on the defense effort in general is at best extremely difficult and for the most part impossible. When the War Department began to compile strike statistics in January 1941, it very soon found itself involved in a lengthy controversy with the Department of Labor, then with the Office of Production Management, and later with the War Production Board over the accuracy and interpretations of the statistics. Each agency not only questioned the validity of the other's statistics but also considered the other an interloper in the field. The principal difference between the War Department and the others was that whereas the civilian agencies viewed strikes as natural phenomena, as inevitable as thunderstorms, and considered strike statistics to be somewhat in the nature of weather maps, the War Department, on the other hand, believed that something ought to be done and could be done to prevent strikes in defense industries. To this end, it sought to use its strike statistics as a publicity weapon to bring home to the American people the effect of strikes on defense production. That idleness due to strikes was lost effort and represented lost production was the theory underlying the War Department's use of these statistics. By this theoretical yardstick it could be shown that the Vultee

---

[6] Notes of Tel Convs Between Simpson and WD Officials, 19 and 22 Nov 40, Ohly file, Industrial Disputes of Particular Interest in World War II.

[7] Los Angeles *Times*, November 19–27, 1940.

[8] *Ibid.; Facts on File*, November 26, 1940.

strike cost the nation the number of planes that could have been produced in the time the men were idle on strike. Notwithstanding the objections to this yardstick and the absence of any accurate measure of the deep-seated effect of the strike, it was generally agreed that the Vultee shutdown was one of the most serious and bitter disputes of the early defense period.

Its effect on the War Department's approach to the problem of strikes was more clearly marked. Major Simpson's intervention in the Boeing dispute had been a deviation from established policy. His success on that occasion appeared to call for similar measures in the Vultee dispute. But there the trend aborted. Simpson's attempts to mediate the Vultee strike produced a fiasco, as a result of which the War Department reaffirmed its policy of nonintervention. Army representatives were instructed not to mediate, conciliate, or even to suggest terms in a labor dispute, or to express any opinions on a controversy that could be construed as showing partiality. The War Department again was content to recognize the responsibility of the civilian agencies in this field.[9] In line with this policy the War Department played a major role in the creation of the National Defense Mediation Board in March 1941.

The settlement that ended the strike at Vultee touched off a chain reaction of union demands upon other aircraft manufacturers. The next victory won by the United Automobile Workers involved the Ryan Aeronautical Company in San Diego. The union then moved into the Inglewood, California, plant of North American Aviation, Incorporated, where it won an election as bargaining agent and began agitating for a general wage increase. Meanwhile, a faction of the AFL union in the Boeing plant had begun a movement for seceding from the AFL in favor of joining the CIO union. Although the situation remained delicate at both North American Aviation and Boeing, it actually flared up first at the Los Angeles plant of the Harvill Aircraft Die Casting Corporation, where on 14 March 1941 about four hundred United Automobile Workers men went on strike and brought production to an abrupt halt. The Harvill company, which had developed a new and superior method of making alloy castings, supplied practically every aircraft manufacturer on the west coast. Should the strike be a protracted one, the production of military aircraft would, the War Department feared, grind to a halt also. It was, in Hillman's opinion likewise, "the country's No. 1 strike." Nevertheless, despite the gravity of the strike, the bitterness and

9 Memo, Labor Sec for M. H. Pettitt, sub: Participation of Ord Officers . . . , 26 Jun 41, and Statement With Respect to Strikes, Lockouts, and Other Industrial Disputes, n.d., both in Ohly file, Industrial Disputes of Particular Interest in World War II.

violence that attended it, and the impasse that was soon reached, the War Department refused to intervene. Hillman, now Associate Director General of OPM, had dispatched a strong team of mediators and conciliators to Los Angeles. Their efforts were rewarded with a settlement on 24 March.[10] The union had won another substantial victory. About three weeks later, formal negotiations opened between the United Automobile Workers and the management of North American Aviation, Incorporated. Since no progress toward an agreement was made, negotiations were broken off in late May and the union prepared to go on strike.[11] The War Department was much concerned by the situation for North American Aviation was producing approximately 20 percent of all military planes in the United States. It held contracts aggregating about $200 million, and its output was essential to U.S. defense preparations.[12]

By this time it had become apparent that 1941 was going to be a turbulent year for American industry. The rash of strikes that had broken out in the last quarter of 1940 continued to spread, not only among the aircraft plants but also through industry in general. *(Chart 1)* The number of strikes affecting defense production jumped from twenty in the last quarter of 1940 to fifty-seven in the first quarter of 1941, and dropped only slightly— to fifty-four—in the second quarter of 1941. There were more than twice as many man-days of idleness in defense industries during the first quarter of 1941 as there had been in the final quarter of the previous year, and in the second quarter of 1941 the figure almost doubled again. The proportion of idleness to total working time rose from .54 percent in the last quarter of 1940 to .89 percent in the first quarter of 1941 and to 1.14 percent in the second quarter.[13] Nor did these figures include the month-long bituminous coal strike, which, although not classified as a defense strike, was accounted one of the most serious of the period. The roll call of only a few of the most important strikes in the first half of 1941 makes an impressive list— Allis-Chalmers Manufacturing Company, International Harvester Company, Ford, Bohn Aluminum, Aluminum Company of America, Northwest lum-

---

[10] Memo, J. W. Bishop, Jr., for USW, sub: Strike at Harvill Die Casting Co. . . . , 22 Mar 41, Ohly file, Industrial Disputes of Particular Interest in World War II; Winnacker, The Office of the Secretary of War Under Henry L. Stimson, Part I, p. 125.

[11] U.S. Bureau of Labor Statistics Bulletin 711, *Strikes in 1941 and Strikes Affecting Defense Production* (Washington: Government Printing Office, 1942), p. 25; R. B. Johnson, Government Seizure and Labor Disputes, Thesis, University of Pennsylvania, 1948, p. 55.

[12] John H. Ohly, History of Plant Seizures During World War II (Emergency Operation of Private Facilities by the War Department) [1947], I, 14, MS, OCMH.

[13] U.S. Bureau of Labor Statistics Bulletin 711, p. 29. These figures include only those strikes that the Labor Division, OPM, considered as having interfered with or delayed defense production.

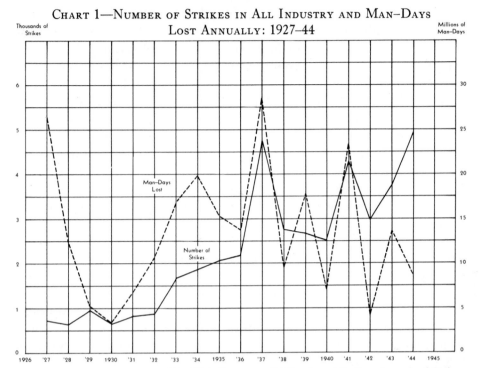

CHART 1—NUMBER OF STRIKES IN ALL INDUSTRY AND MAN-DAYS
LOST ANNUALLY: 1927–44

Source: Senate Document 136, 79th Congress, 2d Session, *Wartime Record of Strikes and Lock-Outs, 1940–1945,* a study by Rosa Lee Swafford (Washington: Government Printing Office, 1946) Table I, p. 4.

bermen, soft-coal miners, Vanadium Steel, Youngstown Sheet and Tube, Universal Cyclops, and San Francisco shipyards. All, except the Ford and bituminous-coal strikes, in some degree directly and adversely affected the rearmament program. The Ford strike and the coal strike offered potential threats. Production of machine tools, steel, rubber, lumber, electrical equipment, trucks and automobiles, chemicals, and small arms ammunition—all of them basic to the defense effort—suffered as a result.

As a consequence of the alarming increase of strikes in the early part of 1941, and of the Allis-Chalmers strike in particular, the Labor Section of Under Secretary Patterson's office began a study of what the government could do should the situation get out of hand. Serious consideration was given to the possibility of government seizure. The Labor Section accordingly directed its research into the War Department's experiences during World War I, but the research was "un-co-ordinated and somewhat superficial." [14]   Furthermore, the view was widely held—by Secretary Stimson and others in the Administration—that some of the most troublesome strikes were inspired and led by Communists for the purpose of scuttling the defense effort, that if measures were taken to deter Communist activities in key plants the situation would improve, and that drastic remedies such as seizing plants would not be needed.   As for the Allis-Chalmers strike, the Navy Department had primary interest and would have been the agency to carry out the seizure.   The War Department study of plant seizures and related measures was more in the nature of an academic exercise than of active planning, and the results of the study were not drafted until mid-June 1941, after the Army had been plunged into the North American Aviation seizure.[15]

The policy of the War Department meanwhile continued to be one of nonintervention, but this did not mean an attitude of aloofness.   The Labor Section of the Under Secretary's office kept close track of all trouble spots, actual or potential, that might affect defense production, kept the civilian agencies informed of its interest, and frequently made a direct appeal to the union and the employer to lay aside their differences so that the wheels of production would continue to move.   When, for example, trouble threatened at the Western Cartridge Company plant in East Alton, Illinois, as a result of the company's insisting upon its right to appeal a decision of the National Labor Relations Board, the War Department asked John Olin, one of the top executives of the company, to come to Washington to confer with Under Secretary Patterson.   Not wishing to be drawn into a discussion with the union, Olin demurred.   In a telephone conversation with Olin, Maj. Joseph F. Battley of Patterson's office made it clear that the War Department's only concern was to keep production going.   When Olin insisted that recognition of the union would cause "more trouble rather than less," Battley refused to take the union question into consideration.   "We cannot take sides in these controversies," he told Olin.   The role of the War Department was merely that of watchdog of production.[16]   There was at this time an extremely critical scarcity of small arms ammunition, of which the Western Cartridge Company was an important producer.   The shortage delayed Maj. Gen. Claire L. Chennault's efforts to get the American Volunteer Group into action in China; it delayed lend-lease shipments to the Netherlands Indies; it placed a limit on plans for setting up task forces; and it hindered the Army's training program.   The War Department could not sit idly by and

---

[14] Ohly, *op. cit.,* I, 1–2.
[15] *Ibid.,* I, 11; Stimson and Bundy, *On Active Service in Peace and War,* pp. 489–90.
[16] Tel Conv, Battley and Olin, 24 Jun 41, ASF IPD, Western Cartridge.

let the dispute at Western Cartridge Company, or for that matter at any vital defense plant, develop into a full-fledged strike. When the company remained adamant in its refusal to accept the National Labor Relations Board ruling, Under Secretary Patterson instructed the Chief of Ordnance, Maj. Gen. Charles M. Wesson, to be prepared to take over the operation of the plant. Finally, toward the end of July, the company made sufficient concessions to avert a strike.[17]

Equally important and of even more direct concern to the War Department was a fourteen-day strike of electrical workers at Wright Field, Ohio, in March 1941. Since a highly essential Air Corps installation was involved, Stimson sought President Roosevelt's permission for the War Department itself to negotiate a settlement, and in the meantime Patterson telegraphed the AFL local at Dayton that the Army's aviation program depended on the resumption of work at Wright Field. The telegram had its effect. The union, placing the burden of blame on a flank attack by CIO workers, assured the War Department that its men would "march back" immediately to "man the nation's home defenses." [18]

Shortly afterward the General Motors Corporation and the United Automobile Workers reached an impasse in the collective bargaining process, and a halt in production appeared likely to follow. As soon as the dispute was certified to the National Defense Mediation Board, the War Department informed the board that the offer made by the union not to call out workers actually engaged in defense production would avail little, since in all but three plants it appeared to be impossible to segregate defense workers from those engaged in normal production. The War Department also pointed out that a strike of any General Motors plant would have particularly serious effects upon the Ordnance Department.[19] An appeal to the union was drafted, in which it was noted that the War Department had no concern with the general terms of the agreement under negotiation but that "in the successful consummation of this agreement and in a following year of harmonious relationship between the parties thereto the War Department is deeply interested." The War Department hoped that the agreement would embody "some form of joint covenant under which both management and

[17] Memo, USW for Wesson, 3 Jul 41, Memo, J. H. O., 30 Jul 41, sub: Western Cartridge, Ltr, R. W. Houghton to T. Kheel, 28 Jul 41, and NDMB Case 44, Western Cartridge Co. and Chemical Workers Union, Local 22574 (AFL), all in ASF IPD, Western Cartridge.

[18] Exchange of Telgms Between USW and J. Breidenback, International Brotherhood of Electrical Workers, Dayton, Ohio, 19–21 Mar 41, ASF–IPD 230.1404, Strikes.

[19] Memo, Sadler, Chief Labor Sec, for NDMB, 28 Apr 41, sub: Effect on WD Proc of General Motors Strike, Ohly file, Industrial Disputes of Particular Interest in World War II.

labor, in recognition of the important public mission which they have been asked to carry out, would pledge themselves to refrain from any . . . interruption to production . . . and to adjust every grievance, of whatsoever character, through channels voluntarily agreed to . . . ."[20] At the last moment, the National Defense Mediation Board succeeded in averting a strike. The General Motors and Western Cartridge Company disputes and the strike at Wright Field were only three of about eleven hundred labor disputes during the first half of 1941 in which the War Department took the same approach and made its interest felt to one extent or another.[21]

After a brief midsummer lull, strike activity again began to increase. Although the number of workers involved and man-days idle did not quite reach the high peaks of the previous spring, the number of strikes rose to a new level and then rounded off at a level somewhat higher than the May peak. In August, the Bureau of Labor Statistics counted 698 strikes in progress; in September, 687; and in October, 644. The rise in defense strikes was even more marked. In the third quarter of 1941 the Office of Production Management recorded a total of 113 new strikes that interfered with or delayed defense production, which was more than double the number in the second quarter. October, in which 69 new defense strikes occurred, was the peak month of the year. In November, the number of defense strikes dropped to 23, the lowest figure since June. Idleness due to defense strikes amounted to 1,595,420 man-days in the third quarter of the year, compared with 2,153,655 man-days (the Ford strike accounted for about 1,000,000 man-days) in the second quarter and 1,383,212 in the first quarter.[22] Statistics compiled by the War Department, which included all strikes in plants engaged in War Department production and strikes on Army construction projects, confirmed the trend. The number of War Department strikes in the last six months of 1941 amounted to 326, compared with 187 in the first half of the year. Approximately 2,358,390 man-days of work were lost in the last half of the year, compared with 2,458,150 in the first half.[23]

The strikes in the so-called captive mines—the coal mines owned by steel companies—were the most serious of the period. They not only slowed production of steel and fomented "sympathy" walkouts, but they also proved to

[20] Draft Ltr to UAW, unsigned, n.d., attached to memo cited n. 19.

[21] Memo, Battley, Chief Labor Sec, for Col B. D. Edwards, 27 Aug 41, sub: Duties of Labor Sec of OUSW, OUSW Amberg files, Labor 1941–42.

[22] U.S. Bureau of Labor Statistics Bulletin 711, pp. 4, 29. The figures given for defense strikes represent the number of strikes beginning in each month.

[23] Report on Strikes for the Six Months Ended 31 December 1941, dated 20 Mar 42, Labor Br IPD, Analysis of Strikes 1939–44.

be the rock on which the National Defense Mediation Board foundered. The issue was the union shop, which the commercial bituminous operators had accepted after the soft-coal strike of April 1941, but which the steel companies refused to accept for their captive mines. The strike began on 15 September 1941. After five days of idleness, the United Mine Workers, CIO, agreed to reopen the mines for a period of thirty days while negotiations were in progress. When no settlement had been reached at the expiration of the truce, the National Defense Mediation Board recommended arbitration, but the union rejected the board's proposal and on 27 October called the miners out again. Three days later the union agreed to send the men back to work for two weeks with the understanding that the board would, in full session, consider the merits of the dispute and issue its final recommendations. On 10 November the board, by a vote of nine to two, decided against the miners. The CIO representatives on the board, who had registered the two dissenting votes, immediately resigned, and the coal miners for a third time went on strike. While the War Department debated the pros and cons of an elaborate plan for sending troops to the coal regions and taking over the operation of the mines, President Roosevelt succeeded in persuading the union and the operators to submit the dispute to arbitration. A three-man board, consisting of John L. Lewis, representing the miners, Benjamin F. Fairless, representing the operators, and John R. Steelman, director of the United States Conciliation Service, representing the public, was appointed. On 7 December it handed down its decision. The miners were awarded the union shop. Fairless, as the employer member of the board, had voted against the award, but as president of the U.S. Steel Corporation he accepted the decision, and the other operators did likewise.[24]

As far as the War Department was concerned, the most serious consequence of the captive-mine strikes was the collapse of the National Defense Mediation Board. The War Department had placed high hopes in the mediation board and had geared its policy to the effective functioning of the board. Although the board continued formally in existence for two months after the CIO members resigned, no further disputes were certified to it. The Japanese attack on Pearl Harbor caught the United States with its gov-

---

[24] U.S. Bureau of Labor Statistics Bulletin 711, p. 24; G-2 Rpts 1-13, Seventh Corps Area, 15-24 Nov 41, Memo, PMG for CofS and SW, 18 Nov 41, and Memo, USW for SW, 22 Nov 41, all in Stimson files, Labor, Coal Strikes; Proceedings of the 37th Constitutional Convention of the UMWA, 6-14 Oct 41, I, 63-87; Ohly, *op. cit.,* I, 75-78, and II, App. K-1 through K-4.

ernmental machinery for the settlement of industrial disputes almost at a standstill.[25]

Slowdowns and Similar Restraints on Production

The existence of a strike is at once, and all too clearly, apparent. It becomes an immediate matter of record, a statistic that can be weighed and balanced, and its particular effects on the operations of a plant can be measured and assessed. Workers could, on the other hand, slow down the production lines and conceal their slackened efforts, if they chose, in a fog of casuistry and argument that was fully as thick and obfuscating as the fog of battle. Unless the slowdown took the form of union rules specifying the number of men to a crew or machine, or prohibiting the use of laborsaving devices, or of any of a number of similar restrictions, there was seldom anything tangible about the slowdown except the decreasing output. Since even the existence of a slowdown was frequently a controversial point, it was difficult to bring the situation into focus and to place it in proper perspective especially as to cause, effect, and appropriate remedy.

Slowdowns, or alleged slowdowns, were sufficiently widespread during 1941—the United States' last year of peacetime production before entry into World War II—to be a matter of concern to the War Department. On the west coast, the Boeing Aircraft Company was building up a long record of labor trouble. The Air Corps representative at the Boeing plant reported to Maj. Gen. Henry H. Arnold in February 1941 that thousands of man-hours were being lost as a result of obstructive tactics on the part of the workers. There were instances, he reported, of workers taking advantage of the clause in the collective bargaining contract that provided for discussion of grievances on company time. The procedure was for the worker and shop representative to take an unsettled dispute to the foreman, and then, if it remained unsettled, to the grievance committee, all on company time. At each step of the procedure the argument and discussion were as lengthy and comprehensive as an Indian powwow. Since key personnel were involved, the Air Corps representative reported, supervision throughout the plant loosened up and production slowed down.[26]

A more serious situation was brought to the attention of the Air Corps in October by the Air Corps factory representative at the Continental Motors

[25] Allan R. Richards, *War Labor Boards in the Field* (Chapel Hill, N. C.: University of North Carolina Press, 1953), p. 22.

[26] Special Report of Air Corps Factory Representative for General Arnold's Personal Attention, 26 Feb 41, sub: Slowdown in Plant of Boeing Aircraft Co., AAF 230.44A, Labor Morale Rpts.

Corporation in Detroit, Michigan. Continental Motors, which manufactured aircraft parts, had, according to the Air Corps representative, more than a hundred instances in less than a month of workers deliberately slowing down production. One employee, who at the request of the management had devised a method of increasing the output of certain machines, found the clothes in his locker slashed and received a warning against any speed-up. Gear cutters were broken, hundreds of parts appeared to have been intentionally damaged, and the union shop stewards resisted every measure the company attempted to take to improve production. Although a number of men were discharged for conducting slowdowns, the company was reluctant to proceed vigorously against union members for fear of bringing on labor trouble and consequent intervention by the National Labor Relations Board.[27]

The sudden entry of the United States into the war brought a surge of patriotism from all sides. Union leaders hastened to pledge the support of organized labor to the war effort. Philip Murray, president of the CIO, no doubt expressed the general sentiment when he warned that the "lagging of talent or strength . . . must be regarded as criminal." Although strikes and slowdowns diminished noticeably, labor's no-strike pledge did not prevent wildcat strikes, nor did Murray's warning completely put an end to slowdowns. In a survey taken in the spring of 1942, 17 percent of the workers in the Detroit area and 4 percent in Pittsburgh admitted to slowing down production.[28] War Department inquiries into the extent of such restraints on output revealed specific instances of both union-inspired and spontaneous limitations. A particularly flagrant example of the former occurred at the National Stamping Company in Detroit, which was engaged in manufacturing metal belt links for machine gun ammunition. Not only was the question of the individual daily output in dispute between the union and the company, but it also happened that one of the girls in the plant was operating four production units against three for the others. When the company hesitated to comply with the union's demand that the girl be fired, three hundred workers—the full complement of one of the shifts—threatened to go on strike. The company quickly gave in and discharged the girl. There were other similar, although less obvious, cases in the Detroit area. At the Budd Wheel Company, which was producing 105-mm. shells, two workers who

---

[27] Memo, Air Corps Factory Representative to Continental Motors Corp. for Office Chief Air Corps, Matériel Div, 4 Oct 41, sub: Labor Morale, Continental Motors Corp., AAF 230.433A, Labor Morale Rpts.
[28] Office of Facts and Figures, Bureau of Intelligence, Workers and War, 28 Apr 42, Dorr classified files.

had been turning out 592 shells during their eight-hour shift were set upon outside the plant by several unidentified men who threatened them with a beating unless they cut production to 550 shells.   In another Detroit factory, where the workers consistently turned out the same number of pieces from day to day, the union committeemen appeared to be responsible for holding production down.[29]

A similar instance of a union failing to recognize that such practices as featherbedding ill-became a nation at war occurred at the American Car and Foundry plant in Berwick, Pennsylvania.   This plant, a pioneer in tank production, through experience and by improvements in machinery, in plant layout, in production methods, and in the flow of supplies, had been able to reduce the number of workers needed per unit of output.   Yet the union insisted that the old ratio of assembly-line employees to tanks, which had been established during an experimental stage of production, be maintained regardless of increased efficiency.[30]

In some cases the curtailment of output was traceable to a specific point at issue, and in these cases the remedy was simple.   A wage increase of seven cents an hour immediately brought the lagging output of a Cleveland company up to normal.   When the Regional War Labor Board disapproved a wage increase to workers in a Des Moines aircraft plant, production dropped as much as 35 to 38 percent.   But as soon as the wage rate was adjusted to the satisfaction of the men, production rose to its normal level.[31]   If union-inspired slowdowns and obstructive union policies were difficult problems because they were planned, purposeful, and policed, they nevertheless could be dealt with through the normal channels of collective bargaining.   Once the union was won over, production could be counted upon to improve.

In perhaps the majority of instances the roots of the problem were considerably more intricate.   One large corporation in the east, an arms manufacturer, found that the men on one of the eight-hour shifts were stopping their machines about half an hour before quitting time in spite of an incentive wage plan that the company had instituted.   There was no union in the plant.   Workers at the Lockheed Aircraft Corporation in Los Angeles, at Standard Parachute Corporation in San Diego, and at the Parker Appliance

[29] Memo, CofOrd for Labor Relations Sec ASF, 24 Mar 42, sub: Interference With Full Prod in Plants of Importance to Ord, and Memo, M. H. Pettitt, Personal Observations Upon the Case of Genevieve Samp, 11 Mar 42, both in ASF Prod Div, Union Restrictions on Maximum Prod.
[30] Memo, CofOrd for Labor Relations Sec ASF, 24 Mar 42, cited n. 29.
[31] Weekly Rpt, Defense Labor Morale, Cleveland, 15 Nov 41, AAF 230.433A, Labor Morale Rpts; AAF Technical Sv Comd, History of the AAF Activities During World War II in the Field of Industrial Manpower, pp. 267–68.

Company in Cleveland slowed down production during the early months of 1942. The action was apparently taken spontaneously, without union backing. The men merely decided, for one reason or another, that there was no great urgency.[32] Many a war worker going to his first job in a defense plant was amazed and shocked by this attitude of "take it easy . . . there's no hurry."

Of the many factors that had gone into the making of a climate favorable to the growth of labor-imposed limitations on output, the most important were the persistence of long-standing peacetime attitudes, blundering labor policies on the part of some companies, and unexpected changes in the War Department's procurement schedules. The first reaction of the War Department to this unfortunate climate was to accept Mark Twain's dictum: "If you don't like the weather, just wait a minute." Partly because the primary authority for dealing with manpower had been vested in civilian agencies, partly because many War Department production officials were skeptical of the handwriting on the wall that pointed toward a labor shortage, and partly because the Army refused to permit itself to be used as an instrument of social betterment, the War Department at first approached the problem only indirectly and in desultory fashion. When the Army, in late 1942 and early 1943, began a direct and systematic assault on the manpower problem, the attack was made on a broad front. The War Department then took steps to bring work to areas that had a labor surplus and to bring in new workers to swell the existing labor force. At the same time it began to intervene in labor disputes that were curtailing, or threatening to curtail, war production. Strikes and slowdowns of every description became direct objects of attack.

Strikes in Wartime: 1942–45

Encouraging prospects of peace between American labor and management had appeared in the weeks immediately following the attack on Pearl Harbor. Union officials promised that labor would "produce and produce without interruption." A new umpire—the National War Labor Board—took the field. Strikes continued to follow the downward trend that had begun in November 1941.

[32] Rpt, 20 Mar 42, sub: Limitation of Prod, ASF Prod Div, Prod, Labor Limitations; Weekly Rpts, Dist Air Plant Protection Officer, Western Dist, Matériel Div Air Corps, sub: Morale Improvement of Defense Labor, 10 Jan, 14, 16, and 21 Feb 42, AAF 230.44A, Labor Morale Rpts; Memo for Files, 21 Mar 42, sub: Restrictions on Prod—Limitations on Output by the Union, ASF Prod Div, Prod, Labor Limitations.

Judged by the strike record, labor-management relations ran more smoothly during the three months after 7 December 1941 than they had for nearly two years past. In December, there were 287 strikes in progress, involving 476,471 man-days of idleness, compared with 464 strikes and 1,396,585 man-days of idleness in the previous month. In January 1942, there were 239 strikes resulting in 330,567 man-days of idleness; in February, 255 strikes with 357,333 man-days of idleness. Not since the early spring of 1940 had there been two successive months in which idleness due to strikes dropped below 400,000 man-days. The War Department's list of strikes in defense plants and on defense construction showed corresponding improvement.[33] The job of eliminating work stoppages in war industry was, in the opinion of the National Labor Relations Board, almost completely accomplished in January and February 1942.[34]

Under Secretary Patterson agreed with the National Labor Relations Board to the extent of acknowledging that "relatively speaking" very few strikes had seriously delayed war production in these months. He nevertheless refused to adopt a complacent attitude. War Department procurement continued to be directly affected by strikes and other industrial disputes. In the three weeks after the attack on Pearl Harbor six new strikes, resulting in 9,760 man-days of idleness, broke out in war plants. In January 1942 a total of thirteen strikes, costing 7,945 man-days, were in progress; in February, the number had risen to twenty-five, costing 35,360 man-days of idleness; and in March, there were in progress in war plants a total of twenty-four strikes, involving 91,100 man-days of idleness. Although the record was a considerable improvement over that of the preceding year, Patterson insisted that "no partial or total interruption of work as a result of labor disputes is justified in time of war."[35] Nor did the statistics tell the whole story. A small strike in a vital, key plant could delay production as much as a strike involving thousands of men in some other plant. Slowdowns, which were bringing considerable concern to War Department procurement officials, seemed if anything to have been stimulated by the no-strike pledge, but slowdowns did not enter into the statistics.[36]

[33] U.S. Bureau of Labor Statistics Bulletin 711, p. 4, and Bulletin 741, *Strikes in 1942* (Washington: Government Printing Office, 1943), p. 4; Labor Br IPD, Analysis of Strikes, 1939–44.

[34] Memo, 16 Mar 42, sub: Interdepartmental Conference . . . , Ohly file, Labor, Strike Statistics, Gen.

[35] Ltr, Patterson to Representative Louis Ludlow, 30 Mar 42, Ohly file, Labor, Strike Statistics, Gen. The statistics cited above are from Labor Br IPD, Analysis of Strikes, 1939–44.

[36] See above, pp. 68–71.

The trend of strikes in plants engaged in War Department work fluctuated during the late spring and summer of 1942, and then fell off during the last three months of the year. The rise had been most pronounced in June and July, when the loss amounted to 132,110 and 143,780 man-days of idleness, respectively. In one two-week period in June there had been fifty-one strikes, resulting in a direct loss of War Department production to the extent of 60,000 man-days. The number of strikes in the entire month of June was the largest monthly total since the beginning of the defense period in June 1940. After an August lull, the loss of time and production due to strikes again rose in September, when 128,380 man-days of idleness were reported by the Industrial Personnel Division, ASF. The situation then began to improve, as it had in November 1941, and by the end of 1942 the amount of idleness due to strikes was reduced to less than 42,000 man-days.[37]

For industry as a whole, the picture was much the same. After reaching a midsummer peak, strike activity in general declined in the last quarter of 1942. November, with a total of 172 strikes in progress involving 128,164 man-days of idleness, had less idleness and, except for December, fewer strikes than any single month in the preceding three years.[38] When the year ended Army procurement officials could well heave a sigh of relief, for with the United States at war 1942 had been a year of relative peace and tranquility on the industrial front. Compared with 1941 there had been in 1942 a decline of 31 percent in the number of strikes, of 64 percent in the number of workers involved, and of 82 percent in strike idleness. At the same time industrial production was 16 percent higher and the number of employed workers averaged 7 percent greater than in the preceding year. The number of strikes in 1942 was slightly above the average for the decade past, but the number of man-days of idleness was the lowest, except for 1930, of any year on record.[39]

Except in the coal industry, strike activity increased only slightly in 1943. Idleness due to strikes (not including the coal strikes) rose about 12.5 percent over 1942. Indeed, in fifteen of the twenty-eight industry groups listed by the Bureau of Labor Statistics there was a decline. The exception, however, outweighed the rule, for the coal industry alone suffered more than 9,000,000 man-days of idleness due to strikes. Most of the time was lost as the result of four general, industry-wide stoppages, which by no stretch of imagination or terminology could have been called unauthorized or wildcat

---

[37] Labor Br IPD, Analysis of Strikes, 1939–44; Ltr, USW to Secy Labor, 14 June 42, Ohly file, Labor, Strike Statistics, Gen.

[38] U.S. Bureau of Labor Statistics Bulletin 741, p. 4.

[39] *Ibid.*, p. 1.

strikes.   The dispute began in January with a short strike in the anthracite field, was resumed in March when negotiations were entered into for a renewal of contract, reached an impasse in May and June, and continued intermittently through the remainder of the year.   It was characterized by the blasts of invective that United Mine Workers president, John L. Lewis, launched against the operators and the National War Labor Board, by mounting public indignation, and by rising antiunion sentiment.[40]

Although the coal strikes were the most serious ones of the year so far as the general economy was concerned, there were a number of others that were of more serious concern to the War Department since the Army procurement program was more directly affected by them.   During the week ending on 22 June 1943, some fifty-six strikes were in progress in plants engaged in War Department work.   The loss in productivity in that one week amounted to 340,000 man-days, five and a half times greater than the loss in June 1942. Twice in less than a month's time, there was a teamsters' strike in Chicago. The first strike caused a partial or complete shutdown of fifty-six plants working on Ordnance items, and only the use of Army trucks to move priority materials prevented the shutdown of fifty-two other plants.   During the second strike a division of troops had to be employed to man and protect the trucks.   At the same time 49,300 rubber workers in Akron, Ohio, and 51,400 automobile workers in Detroit and Hamtramck were on strike.   Production of bogie wheels for tanks at the Goodyear Tire and Rubber plant and of aircraft engines at the Packard Motor Company came to a halt.[41] Like practically all the wartime strikes, these 1943 strikes were short, seldom lasting more than a week.   The Packard Motor Company strike in June, for example, lasted only six days, and two earlier ones, in March and May, were of even briefer duration.   Yet they cost the Air Forces 240 engines.

Following what might appear to be a cyclical pattern, strike activity dropped off sharply after the midyear peak, but in 1943—unlike the previous year—the decline was reversed at the end of the year.   Principally because of the November coal strikes, which were followed in December by a short but widespread walkout of steel workers, idleness due to strikes rose to a total of 4,662,221 man-days in the last three months of 1943.[42]

[40] Joel I. Seidman, *American Labor From Defense to Reconversion* (Chicago: The University of Chicago Press, 1953), pp. 136–42.

[41] Rpt in Labor Br IPD, Analysis of Strikes, 1943–44; U.S. Bureau of Labor Statistics Bulletin 782, *Strikes in 1943* (Washington: Government Printing Office, 1944), p. 13.

[42] U.S. Bureau of Labor Statistics Bulletin 782, Table 2, p. 3.   Quarterly totals were as follows: first quarter, 748,564 man-days; second, 6,828,262 man-days; third, 1,261,482 man-days; and fourth, 4,662,221 man-days.

The year 1944 was one of comparative quiet in the mining industry, but in almost every other industry there was an increase in strike activity. There were more strikes than in any other year on record, and the number of workers involved had been exceeded only in 1919 and 1941. Idleness (not including that in the mining industry) rose almost 77 percent over 1943. The peak was reached in May, and for the next six months the strike record fluctuated at a fairly high level. Finally, in December, it dropped sharply. The year ended with fewer strikes in progress and fewer men on strike than in any month since September 1943.[43]

The attitude of the War Department toward strikes in wartime had been clearly stated by Patterson in March 1942, when he insisted that no such interruption of work could be justified. He and James Mitchell, Director of the Industrial Personnel Division, rejected the wildcat excuse and condemned all subterfuges such as mass resignations. As one of Patterson's assistants pointed out, labor had pledged that there would be no strikes, not simply that there would be no authorized strikes. The coal strikes of 1943, coinciding with the manpower crisis, were considered by Secretary Stimson to be evidence of "outrageous irresponsibility" on the part of the union leaders.[44] The soaring cost of living and the accumulated strains of the period often had more effect on the rank and file of labor than the warnings of public officials or even of labor's own leaders. The result was a series of measures—plant seizures, prohibitory legislation, morale campaigns, and the like—by means of which the government sought to prevent strikes and maintain war production.

The War Department and Antistrike Measures

Every wave of strikes had produced in Congress and the public at large the typically American reaction that "there ought to be a law against it." Antistrike bills by the score were introduced in Congress and at least a hundred of them were reviewed by the War Department during 1941. Some would have required a waiting, or cooling-off, period before a union could strike; others proposed to outlaw all strikes in defense industries, to curtail

---

[43] U.S. Bureau of Labor Statistics Bulletin 833, *Strikes and Lockouts in 1944* (Washington: Government Printing Office, 1945), *passim.*

[44] Ltr, Mitchell to J.P. Coyne, President of Building and Construction Trades Dept AFL, 29 Jul 42, Ohly file, Labor, Strike Statistics, Gen; Ltr, Patterson to R. J. Thomas, President UAW CIO, 10 Oct 42, ASF IPD, Miscellaneous, Strikes; Memo for Files, Ohly, 13 May 42, sub: Comment on Unauthorized Strikes, Ohly file, Labor Disputes, Plans to Prevent, Discussion; Stimson and Bundy, *op. cit.,* p. 489.

the bargaining rights of labor, or to overhaul completely the National Labor Relations Act.

The type that received most attention in Washington was illustrated by a bill introduced in Congress early in 1941 by Representative Carl Vinson of Georgia. It proposed a cooling-off period of twenty-five days during which the parties to the dispute were required to make an effort to adjust their grievances. The Vinson bill would have given statutory authority to the recently established National Defense Mediation Board and would have frozen union security provisions for the duration of the emergency. When strikes reached a new peak in June 1941, the House of Representatives promptly added to the Army appropriation bill several riders prohibiting strikes in defense industries, providing for compulsory arbitration, and denying compensation to any firm, person, or corporation that refused to comply with recommendations of the National Defense Mediation Board. At the same time Senator Tom Connally of Texas introduced an amendment to the Selective Service Act that would have explicitly empowered the President to seize any defense plant shut down by a strike or lockout.[45] The captive coal mine strikes and the scuttling of the National Defense Mediation Board by the miners' union in the late fall of 1941 resulted in the passage by the House of Representatives of the most extreme antistrike bill that had been under serious consideration. This bill, introduced by Representative Howard W. Smith of Virginia, prohibited strikes in defense industries until a thirty-day cooling-off period had expired. Strikes for a closed shop, jurisdictional strikes, and boycotts were declared illegal in defense industries. A majority vote by secret ballot, conducted by the U.S. Conciliation Service, was required before a union could issue any call for a strike. Among other provisions, the Smith bill required all unions to register annually with the National Labor Relations Board and denied the benefits of the Wagner Act to any union that permitted a member of a Communist or Fascist organization to hold office. Although labor unions protested violently, an equally aroused House of Representatives passed the bill by a sizable majority. Four days afterward came the attack on Pearl Harbor. With the nation at war and pledges of co-operation coming from every side, the Senate shelved the Smith bill. For almost a year and a half the moratorium on antistrike legislation continued.[46]

War Department reaction to the various antistrike bills was mixed. Although there appear to have been among staff officers some who thought that stringent antistrike measures were long overdue, Stimson and Patterson,

[45] Seidman, *op. cit.*, pp. 70–71; Johnson, *op. cit.*, p. 33n.
[46] Seidman, *op. cit.*, pp. 72–73; Richards, *op. cit.*, pp. 22–23.

with their labor advisers, took a dimmer view of such legislation. Their position was that legislation should be avoided if any other means of adjusting industrial disputes could be found. Voluntary mediation was preferable, they held, if it could be made to work.[47] Patterson's advisers feared that the Smith bill would promote discord instead of peace. Their appraisal of the bill ranged from a caustic comment that it represented "legislation by spleen rather than reason" to the view it was an omnibus measure in which good and bad features were haphazardly mixed.[48]

The legislatures of a number of states had enacted laws similar to the bills considered by Congress. These state laws were in varying measure designed to restrict collective bargaining and to curtail the gains of labor in such matters as overtime pay, Sunday work, and the maintenance of labor standards. The divergent points of view within the War Department, which extended to these laws as well, were reconciled, as they also were in the case of the bills before Congress, in favor of not disrupting unduly labor's gains.

The War Department's attitude in 1941 seems to have developed from two considerations: first, that antistrike legislation was a dubious solution of the labor problem, which was not in itself and in general one of the War Department's responsibilities; and second, that government seizure as a last resort was a more effective means of keeping production lines moving, the problem of primary concern to the War Department.

By the time the attack on Pearl Harbor took place, the War Department had been involved in the operation of two aircraft companies—North American Aviation, and Air Associates, Incorporated—whose production had been halted by labor troubles.[49] The roots of the troubles were, in one case, irresponsible union leadership that was believed by some to be Communist-inspired, and in the other an equally irresponsible management that persisted in flouting the recommendations of the National Defense Mediation Board. At both plants employment returned to normal and production was resumed within three days after the Army took over. In neither case did the Army withdraw until continued operation of the plants was assured. The North American Aviation company's facilities were returned to the company after three weeks, but a number of special problems prolonged the Air Associates

---

[47] Ltr, SW to Vinson, 11 Apr 41, Ltr [probably draft], SW to Senator E. D. Thomas, 21 Apr 41, and Ltr, USW to Vinson, 1 Apr 41, all in Ohly file, Labor Legislation Proposed 76th Congress.

[48] Memo, Ohly for USW, 9 Dec 41, App. A., sub: The Smith Bill, H. R. 6149, Memo for Maj Johnson, 5 Dec 41, sub: Hasty Comments on the Smith Bill, and Memo, Melvin Sims for Johnson, 5 Dec 41, sub: Comments on Smith Bill, all in Ohly file, Labor Legislation Prosposed 76th Congress.

[49] For an account of plant seizures as a means of enforcing manpower policies, see Chapter X, below.

seizure for almost nine weeks. The War Department's objective—to maintain the production of material needed for the defense effort—was achieved.[50]

Except for the brief three-day seizure of a small, belt-line railway in Ohio, the War Department did not find it necessary to take over any industrial facility in 1942 for the purpose of restoring and maintaining production. The War Department did take over, at the behest of the President, a Massachusetts manufacturing company that had refused to comply with a directive of the National War Labor Board, but this was purely and simply a case of using government seizure as a means of enforcing the directive of the board. Although there was a possibility that a strike might have occurred if the dispute had continued, the union had not issued a strike call and the company was in full production when the Army took possession.[51] Had labor-management relations been as turbulent in 1942 as in 1941, the plant seizure story might have been different.

The great coal strikes in the spring of 1943, the teamsters' strike, the automobile workers' strike, and other disputes in June 1943 revived Congressional sentiment for antistrike legislation. The result was the enactment, over President Roosevelt's veto, of the War Labor Disputes Act of 25 June 1943, popularly known as the Smith-Connally Act. It prohibited strikes for a period of thirty days after the union issued a strike notice, and at the expiration of this cooling-off period the National Labor Relations Board was required to conduct a strike vote by secret ballot. At the same time the act empowered the President to seize any plant that was shut down because of a strike and prohibited under penalty of fine or imprisonment any strike in a plant seized by the government. Other provisions gave statutory authority to the National War Labor Board and forbade unions to make contributions to political campaign funds in federal elections. At first, when the bill was under consideration in Congress, the War Department had taken the same position that it had officially held toward previous antistrike laws—that labor's voluntary co-operation, even if only partially effective, was preferable to compulsion. Assistant Secretary John J. McCloy, with the approval of Under Secretary Patterson, wrote to the Speaker of the House, Sam Rayburn, on 14 May 1943 that elaborate criminal penalties against strikes would upset the "no-strike agreement." By mid-June, however, the War Department had shifted its position. The conviction had developed that labor and management could not be relied upon to co-operate voluntarily and that government seizure was an unsatisfactory substitute. On 17 June 1943 Secretary Stimson

[50] Ohly, *op. cit.*, I, Chs. II and IV.
[51] *Ibid.*, I, Ch. VII, Parts 1 and 3, and Ch. VIII, Part 1.

joined the Secretary of the Navy in approving the Smith-Connally bill. "We feel strongly," they asserted, "that in view of the changed labor situation, and especially developments in the recent coal strike, the reasons for approving the bill far outweigh any objections to it." [52]

The spread of strikes in midsummer 1943 and the "widely prevalent view that the passage of the War Labor Disputes Act would invite takeovers" led to a revision of War Department procedures for handling plant seizures. The principal aim was to relieve the Under Secretary's office of responsibility for operational details. The Under Secretary's office, under the provisions of a directive issued on 9 August 1943, would continue to be responsible for plans and policies and would delegate responsibility for operating seized plants to either the Commanding General, Army Air Forces, or the Commanding General, Army Service Forces. At the same time a manual designed to clarify procedures was published for the guidance of officers conducting seizure operations. As it turned out, most of the operational details continued to be handled by the Office of the Under Secretary. [53]

The expected increase in the number of plant seizures did not immediately materialize. From 25 June, when the Smith-Connally Act was passed, to 1 November only one seizure was made, and that by another agency of the government. In the last two months of 1943, when idleness due to strikes increased sharply, there were four plant seizures, three of which were undertaken by the War Department. With strikes and labor unrest continuing to mount in 1944, the number of industrial establishments taken over by the government likewise increased. From 1 November 1943 to 31 July 1945 the War Department made twenty-five seizures, about half the total of all government seizures. In ten of the twenty-five cases the War Department objected, unsuccessfully, to being designated the seizing agency. It took the initiative in instituting seizure proceedings in eleven instances, and it concurred in its designation as the seizing agency in four cases instituted by other agencies of the government. Most of the plant seizures in this period were undertaken to enforce compliance with the labor policy of the government, but that policy included keeping essential workers at their jobs. [54] The technique was more successful in maintaining production in particular cases than in preventing the spread of strikes.

[52] Ltr, SW and Secy Navy to Dir Bureau of Budget, 17 Jan 43, Memo, USW for ASW, 14 May 43, and Ltr, McCloy to Rayburn, 14 May 43, all in Troyer Anderson file, OCMH. See also, Weekly Strike Report, n.d., Labor Br IPD, Analysis of Strikes, 1939–44, and Memo, USW for McCloy, 29 May 43, ASF IPD, Smith-Connally Bill.

[53] Ohly, *op. cit.*, I, pp. 144–52. The passage quoted above is from page 144.

[54] *Ibid.*, I, 159, and III, App. AA–1.

Neither restrictive legislation nor the threat of government seizure had
been sufficient to deter strikes and slowdowns.   Neither was designed for
this purpose.   When work stoppages and labor disputes rose precipitously
in midsummer of 1944, the War Department unleashed a powerful publicity
campaign.   Attributing the situation to "peace jitters," the War Department
aimed the program at creating a "proper sense of urgency" within industry.
Leading the attack, General Somervell, in a Fourth of July speech at Indianapolis, declared that he could detect a note of overoptimism, which was slowing
down war production.   Nine days later, on 13 July, Under Secretary Patterson
claimed that there was a "feeling abroad in the country that the war is about
over" and that this feeling was responsible for workers leaving their jobs.[55]
Whether anticipatory or not, this analysis of the situation was the basis for
the War Department's publicity campaign.

In speeches before various groups of labor leaders and industrialists, in
radio broadcasts, and in press releases, Patterson and Somervell tried to ham-
mer home the theme that the war was far from won.   In a news conference
on 1 August, Somervell outlined the strategy and his "estimate of the situation."   "What we have to get is a sense of the urgency of the matter," he
asserted.   "Manpower is the problem, and . . . if you ask some of those
doughboys who are battling it out on the front lines whether the war isn't
over, they'll tell you pretty quick what they think about it and how bad the
situation is for them.   The farther from the front you get, the better things
look." [56]   Later on he told the Sixth Service Command: "If you could get all
the people to absorb the sense of urgency which we all have, the winning
of the war would be a shorter and less difficult task . . . . Many people
seem to believe that this is the time for the seventh inning stretch, and while
they're stretching, the Nazis are digging in . . . ." [57]   Strikes and work stoppages were the result of this false optimism and shortages of ammunition at
the front were the result of the reduced production at home, so the argument
ran.   Now pleading for greater production, now praising industry for its past
efforts, War Department spokesmen carried the campaign to business groups
and labor organizations throughout the country.   To the AFL assembled in
convention, Somervell personally appealed for increased production "all the
way down the line."   The day after he addressed the AFL, he spoke at the
CIO convention and made the same appeal, which he reinforced with mes-
sages from General Marshall and General Dwight D. Eisenhower stressing

[55] Somervell's Speeches, Hq ASF files; *The New York Times,* July 14, 1944.
[56] Quoted in *The New York Times,* August 2, 1944.
[57] Somervell's Speeches, Hq ASF files.

the urgent need for more ammunition, tanks, and trucks. A week later Stimson spoke out in a similar vein, and he was followed shortly afterward by Patterson.[58] A motion picture showing the shifting pattern in matériel requirements and the vast amount of munitions and equipment used up in war was released to theaters, and traveling war shows of troops and equipment—"Fire for Eisenhower" caravans, they were named—toured the country to help bring home to the public the lessons of which Stimson, Patterson, and Somervell spoke. The War Department's morale-raising campaign thus brought the already complicated manpower problem squarely up against one of the still-unsolved questions of World War II—where should responsibility for front-line shortages be placed?

The campaign, moreover, had originated partly in one of the most vexing policy disputes of the wartime period, that between the War Department and the War Production Board over the reconversion of industry to peace-time production. The War Department had not objected to the relaxation of production controls on items intended for current civilian needs; it did object violently to steps being taken for postwar reconversion. When the War Production Board began to plan for reconversion, "all proposals for additional civilian supplies were beclouded with suspicion of carrying postwar intention." They were "met by a storm of protest from the military and almost as frequently from WMC." [59]

Apart from any procedural or jurisdictional matters, the principal bone of contention was manpower. Chairman Donald Nelson of the War Production Board held to the view that the labor force was not a fluid commodity which could readily be directed where most needed, that the creation of local pools of idle labor would force workers out of the labor market altogether and not into centers of war industry, and that the best way of boosting morale and softening the transition to a peacetime economy was to authorize manufacturers in these areas of idle labor (by so-called spot authorizations) to begin production of civilian goods from which War Production Board restrictions might be lifted in the near future.[60] Nelson believed that the placement of war contracts could be so controlled as to direct war work to areas of labor surplus and out of areas of labor shortage, but the Army's experience in this respect had revealed serious limitations to such an approach.[61] The War Department took the position that the War Production

---

[58] *Ibid.; The New York Times,* November 22 and 29, and December 1, 1944.

[59] Herman M. Somers, *Presidential Agency: OWMR, the Office of War Mobilization and Reconversion* (Cambridge, Mass.: Harvard University Press, 1950), p. 182.

[60] *Ibid.,* pp. 186–87; CPA, *Industrial Mobilization for War,* I, 718, 789–90.

[61] See Chs. VI and X, below.

Board reconversion policy would lessen the sense of urgency the Army was attempting to create, that by inducing workers to seek employment in jobs with peacetime prospects it would adversely affect war production, and that it was "incompatible with the new and more stringent manpower controls put into effect by WMC" on 1 July 1944.[62]   Strikes in war industry were, therefore, not the sole object of the War Department's publicity campaign. It was generated equally by the proposals of the War Production Board and the pressure of business and labor interests for reconversion.   General Somervell's remarks on several occasions leave no doubt on this score.   "I am concerned," he told a business group in New York, "that you in industry may be so deeply engrossed in postwar planning that you are not giving all the thought you should to current action."   Several days earlier, in Boston, he had warned another group of businessmen that the American armies were 40 percent short in items needed to carry on the war because thousands of war workers were leaving their jobs for nonessential industries and because manufacturers were turning to peacetime products.[63]

By this time, at the beginning of December, whatever cause for optimism there had been in midsummer had been dissipated by the hard, costly, and not altogether successful fighting before the Siegfried Line.   On 1 December the War Production Board agreed to suspend spot authorizations for a period of ninety days in areas where a critical shortage of manpower existed, where war production was behind schedule, or where a shortage of labor that could be employed in making munitions existed.[64]   The German counteroffensive in the Ardennes—the Battle of the Bulge—ended for the time being all thought of turning toward peacetime production.   To conserve manpower and prevent absenteeism, race tracks were closed, a midnight curfew for amusement places was established, a "brownout" of lighting displays was instituted, and allocations of critical metals for civilian products were further restricted.   On 18 January 1945 the suspension of spot reconversion authorizations was extended for an additional ninety days and made applicable to areas in which labor shortages might be expected in the future.   Not until 27 April 1945 were any further steps taken for the reconversion of industry.   By then the surrender of Germany was only ten days away, and the War Department interposed no objection to reconversion plans.

If the War Department's morale-boosting campaign was responsible for the sharp drop in strikes during December 1944, the effect was short-lived.

[62] Somers, *op. cit.,* p. 187.

[63] Somervell's Speeches, Hq ASF files; *The New York Times,* December 2 and 3, 1944; *Facts on File,* December 1, 1944.

[64] Manpower Report, December 1944, ASF IPD, Monthly Manpower Reports (1943–45).

In the early months of 1945 idleness due to strikes increased substantially. Although the number of strikes did not rise greatly, the disputes lasted longer and involved more workers than in the preceding year. By the end of September 1945 almost as many man-days had been lost as in the entire year of 1943, even including the coal strikes.

Having experimented briefly with direct mediation in late 1940, the War Department for the most part thereafter approached the strike problem indirectly—by attempting to impress upon the civilian agencies charged with responsibility for labor relations the seriousness of work stoppages, by attempting to eliminate subversive influences, and by embarking upon a publicity campaign aimed at raising the morale of war workers. The War Department did not, for the most part, favor punitive, antistrike legislation of the type illustrated by the Smith-Connally Act. It supported and relied upon the seizure and operation of industrial plants by the government as a means of preventing the curtailment of production due to strikes. Its role in plant seizures again brought the War Department directly into the field of industrial manpower when plant seizures became the means of enforcing the policies established by the National War Labor Board.

The effectiveness of these measures in keeping the workers at work cannot be assessed. A myriad of other factors—employment stabilization plans of the War Manpower Commission, price and wage trends, housing programs, and questions of personal motivation—exerted their influence in one direction or another. Indeed, the very question of labor's wartime strike record depends upon the observer's point of view. Certainly the 39,484,000 man-days lost because of strikes from 1 January 1942 to the end of September 1945 cannot easily be glossed over.[65] On the other hand, nearly twice as many man-days had been lost in a similar period of time during the mid-1930's, while in the last four months of 1945, after the war had ended, strikes accounted for 27,605,000 man-days of idleness. The picture is blurred also by the tremendous increase in U.S. production during the war years and by the not too dissimilar strike record of Great Britain, Canada, and Australia.[66] There is perhaps only enough evidence to suggest that cyclical trends exerted more influence than did antistrike controls, direct or indirect, voluntary or compulsory.

[65] The figure above is derived from House Document 136, 79th Congress, 2d Session, *Wartime Record of Strikes and Lock-Outs, 1940–1945,* a study by Rosa Lee Swafford (Washington: Government Printing Office, 1946), Table I, p. 4.

[66] See Seidman, *op. cit.,* pp. 150, 275.

CHAPTER V

Subversive Activity, Security, and Labor Supply

The strident yapping of Fascist-minded bunds, the Communist party's well-known tactics of infiltration, and the inclination of some of the more irresponsible and militant labor leaders to dally with communism had very early aroused a strong suspicion within the government as well as in the public at large that not all the strikes and slowdowns in defense industries were aimed at furthering the labor movement. The possibility that some of them were deliberate attempts to sabotage the rearmament program presented different problems from those created by bona fide labor disputes. The measures required for security against subversive activities likewise differed from those designed to prevent disputes between labor and management from curtailing production. Extreme care had to be taken that security measures did not impair the civil liberties of the workers. Finally, it was essential not to push security beyond the point where it became a serious obstacle to the effective utilization of labor.

The Army and Subversive Activity

The strike at Vultee Aircraft in November 1940 was one of the first to be suspect on this score. Newspaper accounts reported that the Department of Justice had evidence that several of the strike leaders were Communists, or were closely associated with the Communist party, but that the evidence was insufficient to bring charges against the men under existing laws.[1] Major Simpson, the Army representative, described the strike as having "something fishy" about it, and he suggested that the War Department call upon the Federal Bureau of Investigation (FBI).[2] When the plant reopened, the FBI made a careful check of each returning worker.[3] None of the men seems to have been rejected. A tinge of red was likewise thought to be

[1] *The New York Times,* November 24, 1940; Los Angeles *Times,* November 24, 1940.
[2] Tel Conv Between Simpson and T. E. B. [WD], 21 Nov 40, in Ohly file, Industrial Disputes of Particular Interest in World War II.
[3] Los Angeles *Times,* November 28, 1940.

visible in the slowdown at the Boeing Aircraft Company, in the strikes at Allis-Chalmers Manufacturing Company, Universal Cyclops Steel Company, ALCOA, and the Harvill Aircraft Die Casting Corporation, and in the storm that was brewing at the North American Aviation plant.

Spurred by Secretary Stimson, the War Department pressed the Department of Justice for a greater degree of attention than the latter considered it could give to the situation. The difficulty was partly procedural, or administrative. The FBI had been given charge of all investigations of espionage and sabotage and had undertaken a plant survey program. A system of co-ordinating the collection and dissemination of all information on the subject, through the medium of an interdepartmental intelligence committee, had been worked out, but there were areas in which the delineation of FBI and G–2 activities was not clearly marked. Brig. Gen. Sherman Miles, Assistant Chief of Staff, G–2, was extremely punctilious about not invading those fields he considered reserved to the FBI. When the latter, because of legal limitations, could not on every occasion call upon local police for assistance in collecting evidence of subversive activities in industry, General Miles though it would be "a great mistake" for G–2 "to get into this business." Although he was convinced that "foreign-fostered agencies are now directing in this country a well-organized effort" at sabotage through strikes and slowdowns, he was equally convinced that "the military forces ought not . . . to be drawn into investigational activities in the civilian industrial field." [4] On the other hand, the FBI was sometimes reluctant to exercise responsibility for fear of stepping into the field of labor relations. It required about three weeks and at least two letters from Under Secretary Patterson to persuade the Attorney General that the slowdown at the Boeing plant was a pertinent matter for investigation. [5] Here lay the crux of the problem.

The importance, to quote Stimson, of "drawing the line sharply between legitimate labor controversies and subversive action by men who have ulterior motives against our defense" goes without saying. [6] The real problem was where and from what bench marks the line of distinction should be drawn. The term subversive had come into use to describe acts falling outside the scope of treason or sabotage and lying just beyond the margin of seditious conspiracy. The act of 28 June 1940, entitled "An Act to prohibit certain subversive activities . . . ," which made it a crime to advocate know-

[4] Memo, Miles for ASW McCloy, 29 May 41, in G–2 10996–12y No. 51; Memo, Miles and Capt A. G. Kirk, USN, for SW and Secy Navy, 28 May 41, in G–2 2736–ZZ–56.

[5] Ltrs, USW to Attorney Gen, 5 and 11 Mar 41, and Memo, USW for Arnold, 20 Mar 41, all in AAF 230.433A, Labor Morale Rpts.

[6] Quoted in Stimson and Bundy, *On Active Service in Peace and War*, p. 490.

ingly or willfully the overthrow of the government by force, only served to emphasize the lack of any precise legal definition of the term. As matters stood, a Nazi or a Communist could openly advocate resistance to the government and the defense effort without fear of prosecution so long as he confined his advocacy and resistance to the use of passive measures like walkouts or slowdowns and avoided acts of sabotage.

To plug this loophole—a theoretical one at best—the Office of Production Management proposed, early in June 1941, that the Sabotage Act be amended to prohibit the willful "hindering, retarding or delaying" of defense production done "with the intent to injure, interfere with or obstruct the national defense of the United States."[7] This proposal would not have solved the basic problem, which was one of identification and definition. In considering the problem and the possible legal remedies, Julius Amberg, Stimson's special assistant on labor matters, suggested adding to the OPM proposal a provision that malicious intent "may be presumed upon a showing that the accused, knowing the purposes thereof, is, or at any time within the last five years has been, a member of or an affiliate with any society, group or assembly of persons who teach, advocate or encourage, or who have taught, advocated or encouraged, the overthrow or destruction of the United States by force or violence."[8] A provision of this sort might have ended strikes and slowdowns fomented by Communists for subversive purposes; it would also have interdicted a strike or slowdown aimed at unsatisfactory working conditions, if any of the leaders happened to have had Communist affiliations. Since a number of labor leaders were suspected of having flirted with communism at one time or another and since the effect on the defense effort of any halt in production was the same regardless of intent, there would have been real danger of the deed itself being considered as evidence of subversive intent. Other possible legislation, besides the proposed revision of the Sabotage Act, was studied during May and June, but the War Department refrained from advocating any new legislation except an amendment to the Selective Service Act that would broaden the President's authority to seize industrial establishments. The War Department's position rested perhaps on a realization of the dilemmas posed by the problem, on the fact that the Communist party line shifted after the USSR entered the war, and on the satisfactory outcome of seizing the North American Aviation plant.

[7] Proposed Amendment of Sabotage Act, OPM Draft, 4 Jun 41, OUSW Amberg files, Labor 1941–42.

[8] J. H. A. [Amberg], Redraft of OPM Draft, Proposed Amendment of Sabotage Act, 13 Jun 41, OUSW Amberg files, Labor 1941–42.

Actually, the objective of the War Department program, as it got under way, was not to take counteraction against acts already committed but to forestall any delays or disruption of defense production before they occurred.[9] To the extent that such disruption might arise as the result of a dispute over working conditions, the problem of prevention was one of labor relations; in every other respect it was a security problem.   Whereas in identifying and suppressing subversive activities the nature of the act and the question of intent must be essential considerations, in taking precautionary security measures, on the other hand, the measures must precede the act and proof of intent is not necessary.   Thus to label the War Department's industrial security program as a "removal of subversives program" or to approach it as essentially an antisubversive program is to becloud an already intricate picture by raising problems that did not belong to it.

The program aimed at weeding out all workers whose trustworthiness was subject to reasonable doubt.   The Army took its first step in this direction in May 1941 when Under Secretary Patterson instructed the chiefs of supply arms and services to organize an inspection service for the purpose of surveying measures taken by defense industries in the field of plant protection, including the investigation and control of employees.[10]   The Army inspections were not intended to supplant those which the FBI had been conducting at the request of the War Department and as a result of which the War Department had compiled 550 reports "on subversive individuals and suspected cases of sabotage" in the first six months of 1941.[11]   Since it was highly questionable how far, in peacetime, a democratic government could go in demanding implicit trust and confidence of any but its own employees and since private employers, however co-operative, were often hamstrung by union agreements and labor laws, the War Department, as the agency with the largest financial interest in defense contracts, took the initiative in studying the possibility of securing new legislation.   Nothing was decided and no action was taken by the Army to rid defense plants of undesirables until the situation was changed by the entry of the United States into the war.

An executive order, drafted in the Office of the Provost Marshal General and signed by the President on 12 December 1941, authorized the Secretary

[9] OPMG Monograph, Removal and Suspension of Subversives Program, as Administered by the Provost Marshal General, pp. 1–4, OCMH.

[10] Ibid., Tab 16, Memo, USW for Chiefs Supply Arms and Svs, 12 May 41, sub: Plant Protection Inspection Sv.

[11] Ibid., Tab 17, Memo, Maj H. G. Reynolds, Prod Br OUSW, for A. G. Cooke, OUSW, 5 Jul 41, sub: Statement in Answer to Sabotage Question in the House Military Affairs Committee Investigation, Special Committee 3.

of War and the Secretary of the Navy "to establish and maintain military guards and patrols, and to take other appropriate measures, to protect from injury or destruction," national defense material, premises, and utilities.[12] This order provided the basis for the Army's industrial security program.

A number of administrative procedures for putting the program into effect were discussed by representatives of the War, Navy, and Labor Departments, and union leaders. The Navy Department at first proposed a plan for handling the dismissal of undesirable workers through union-management committees in each plant. Ohly of Under Secretary Patterson's office took the position, on the other hand, that the procedure must be entirely divorced from the field of labor relations. The representatives of organized labor wanted assurances that legitimate union activities would not be interfered with and that adequate procedures for reviewing dismissals would be established. The result of the discussions and deliberations was a joint Army-Navy memorandum, dated 10 January 1942, which placed responsibility for the removal of undesirable employees on the naval inspectors and Army plant representatives. Subversive activity was broadly defined as "sabotage, espionage or any other willful activity intended to disrupt the National Defense Program." When investigation revealed good cause for suspecting such activity on the part of a worker, the Army or Navy field representative was authorized to request his immediate removal after first notifying the management of the plant and local union officials in order that the latter might have the option of handling the removal. Provision was made for a review, upon written request, if applied for within thirty days after the dismissal of the employee.[13] This memorandum was the procedural blueprint for the employee security program. Its major provisions remained unchanged for the duration of the war. Specific instructions were issued to plant protection inspectors on 5 February 1942 that they were to consult with representatives of the Military Intelligence Division and the FBI before requesting the removal of an employee. The plant protection inspectors were also notified that they were under no obligation to reveal any of the evidence for dismissal to labor representatives and that, if the latter did not remove the person under suspicion, the plant protection inspectors should submit the case to the Office of the Under Secretary (Plant Protection Division) for action through the chief of the supply arm or service concerned. The in-

---

[12] Ibid., Tab 22, EO 8972, 12 Dec 41.

[13] Ibid., Tab 26, Joint Memorandum on Removal of Subversives From National Defense Projects of Importance to Army or Navy Procurement, 10 January 1942, signed by Robert P. Patterson, Under Secretary of War, and Ralph A. Bard, Assistant Secretary of the Navy.

structions made it clear that "no employee shall be discharged as a result of idle rumor, normal labor activity, gossip, or anonymous communication," but they also indicated the real objective, namely, to get rid of workers against whom only "a reasonable suspicion" of subversive activity might be raised. It was "not necessary . . . that concrete evidence sufficient to justify an arrest for violating the National Sabotage or Espionage Acts be present prior to discharge." [14]

Although a procedure had thus been established for removing undesirable workers, there was none for uncovering them.   The forty or fifty employees removed by the Army from defense plants by 15 April 1942 were dismissed on the basis of information received from the FBI, Office of Naval Intelligence, G–2, and other sources.   On 22 April 1942 the War Department put into effect a screening and investigation program designed to establish the reliability and trustworthiness of certain "key personnel."   Questionnaires were to be distributed to all employees of defense plants who were suspected of disloyalty, to all employees who were in positions in which they could inflict damage that would curtail production or in which they could acquire and convey to the enemy information concerning production, and to all who were in the more important supervisory positions or positions of particular trust.[15]   The information obtained from the completed questionnaires was used by the Office of the Provost Marshal General to decide which employees should be investigated.

In the meantime, the question of establishing a definite procedure for reviewing dismissals had been raised by Patterson's office.   From the inception of the War Department program in January, union officials had insisted on the need of an adequate review procedure.   Philip Murray, president of the CIO, had assured all affiliated organizations that machinery would be set up for hearing appeals, and he anticipated that it would consist of local appeal boards with a board of final review in Washington.[16]   For the time being, the few appeals that had resulted from first dismissals under the program were reviewed informally by one of the officers in the Provost Marshal General's office.   Early in April Ohly, who was now in the headquarters of the Army Service Forces, suggested that the time had come to establish a more formal procedure and that a review board, composed of one Army and one Navy officer, one civilian from the War Department, and two members represent-

[14] *Ibid.,* Tab 32, WD Circular [unnumbered], 5 Feb 42, Discharge of Subversives From Private Plants and War Department Plants Privately Operated of Importance to Army Procurement.

[15] *Ibid.,* p. 15; OPMG Monograph, Key Personnel Program, pp. 6–7, OCMH.

[16] OPMG Monograph, Removal and Suspension of Subversives Program, Tab 28, Ltr, Philip Murray to All National and International Unions, 20 Jan 42.

ing the public at large should be created. Organized labor agreed to the plan in general, but it was not adopted. Instead, on 4 May 1942, a review committee consisting of four officers was created in the Internal Security Division of the Provost Marshal General's office.[17] The only real effect of this measure was to debar any officer who had taken part in the original proceedings from acting in an appellate capacity.

Neither labor nor the War Department was entirely satisfied with the early results of the removal program. Shortly after the review committee was established, Lee Pressman, general counsel for the CIO, entered a vigorous protest against the whole procedure. His principal complaints were that local unions were not receiving prior notification of dismissals, that individuals were not afforded a real opportunity to present their cases before a review board, and that no effort was being made to find work elsewhere for men who had been dismissed from war plants.[18] Later, after a meeting of the entire CIO legal staff at which Maj. Sidney C. Sufrin of the Industrial Personnel Division discussed the program, Pressman agreed to the procedures. There was no further difficulty with the CIO on this score.

Although the Provost Marshal General in early August 1942 instructed the service commands to take action when information of subversive activity came to their attention and to give dismissed employees written notification of their right of appeal, neither the number of dismissals made by Army field representatives nor the number of appeals showed a proportionate increase. The greater number of dismissals continued to be handled by the Office of the Provost Marshal General in Washington until early in 1943, and, except for a few special cases, all appeals were sent to Washington until late in 1943. Certain segments of organized labor continued to be unappeased. The Army refused to accept any charges that the program was antilabor or unfairly administered, but it was readily admitted, at least "within the family," that mistakes had been made and that during the first year the Office of the Provost Marshal General had had to feel its way slowly. Insufficient personnel, the demands of other aspects of the plant security program, and the lack of specific instructions in directives were cited as reasons for the slow start. Furthermore, it was soon recognized that placing emphasis on the im-

---

[17] OPMG Monograph, Industrial Employment Review Board, Tab 16, Memo, Ohly for Reynolds and Maj. Thomas A. Lane, 10 Apr 42, Tab 17, Memo for Files, Ohly, 22 Apr 42, and Tab 20, Br Memo, Lt. Col. Thomas A. Lane, Chief Facility Employee Br, Internal Security Div OPMG, 4 May 42.

[18] OPMG Monograph, Removal and Suspension of Subversives Program, Tab 51, Memo, Dir Civilian Pers Div SOS for PMG, 4 Jun 42, sub: Plant Protection—Removal of Subversives.

portance of a particular key job as the basis for investigating the employee was resulting in only those employees being investigated who were generally the most loyal and trustworthy.[19] In addition, the reports of investigation and the records of dismissal proceedings were sometimes incomplete. This was most frequently the reason for reversing dismissals that had been made in the field. Finally, considerable confusion over the proper procedures to be followed existed among service command field representatives throughout the first year.[20]

The machinery was put in better working order during 1943. A formal review board, the Industrial Employment Review Board, was created in the Office of the Provost Marshal General with Navy and Army Air Forces representation. Arrangements were made for holding local hearings and for giving dismissed employees the opportunity to appear in person before the review board. A procedure was established by which employees who had been dismissed without good cause and subsequently reinstated could recover their lost wages. Decentralization of the program to the service commands was carried out. Along with these administrative changes, further efforts were made to clarify the grounds for removing undesirable employees and to define more closely the conditions under which Army representatives could take action.[21]

The program reached the height of activity in late summer and early fall of 1943. August 1943 marked the peak month, when 137 civilian industrial employees were dismissed after a security investigation. Then, after dropping to 104 in the following month, dismissals leveled off in the neighborhood of 130 per month until the end of the year. The number of dismissals in the last six months of 1943 amounted to 707, which was almost exactly the total for the entire first year of operations.[22] The volume of appeals brought before the review board likewise rose. Early in the year, between 50 and 75 cases had been carried before the board each month. In July the

[19] OPMG Monograph, Key Personnel Program, Tab 26, Remarks by Maj Bradford Ross, OPMG, at ASF Internal Security Conference at St. Louis, Mo., 20–23 Apr 43.

[20] OPMG Monograph, Removal and Suspension of Subversives Program, Tab 83, Discussion of the Subversive Circular Delivered by Maj Bradford Ross, OPMG, at ASF Internal Security Conference at St. Louis, Mo., 20–23 Apr 43.

[21] Ibid., pp. 35–41; OPMG Monograph, Industrial Employment Review Board, Tab 81, Memo, Asst PMG for USW, 13 Sep 43.

[22] Monthly figures are given in OPMG Monograph, Removal and Suspension of Subversives Program, Tab 123. A slightly different figure for the first year (to the end of February 1943) is given in OPMG Monograph, Industrial Employment Review Board, Tab 46, Memo, Chief Pers Security Br OPMG for PMG, 23 Feb 43.

number reached about 125, in August about 90, and in each of the last three months of 1943 the board received between 150 and 165 appeals.[23]

At the very time when the program was moving into high gear the decision was made to revise and curtail it. Industries were then scraping the manpower barrel. Apart from the workers dismissed from war jobs, many of whom were not shifted to less sensitive employment, the security program drained off other employees and Army personnel whose services were required to keep the program moving. The War Department in early November 1943 accordingly decided to limit the removal program. The master list of plants to be inspected was reduced. The service commands were instructed to weigh the risk carefully against manpower needs and to help all removed employees to find other more appropriate employment.[24] In January 1944 the number of removals dropped 43 percent from the previous month's figure, and in February only twenty-five employees were removed from war plants. Throughout the rest of the war the program continued to operate at reduced pace: 465 removals were made during 1944, and only 56 in the first six months of 1945. From the beginning of the program in February 1942 to the end of July 1945, approximately 2,400 security risks were removed from employment in war plants.[25]

Practically every worker who was removed from his job as a result of the security program appealed his case. By the end of October 1945 the review board had received 2,380 appeals, of which 458 were decided in favor of the worker and a reinstatement order was issued.[26]

To assess the results of antecedent, preventive measures is a difficult task when that which is to be prevented fails to materialize. The original objective had been to prevent Nazi sympathizers and Communists from disrupting production by fomenting strikes and slowdowns. Communism, if not Communists, ceased to be a factor after the USSR's entry into the war in June 1941, but when the United States became a belligerent the possibility of Nazi-inspired labor disturbances increased. Perhaps the screening of employees and the dismissal of a questionable few prevented disturbances of this

[23] OPMG Monograph, Industrial Employment Review Board, Tab 154, Progress Report and Chart Industrial Employment Review Board.

[24] OPMG Monograph, Removal and Suspension of Subversives Program, pp. 25–26, Tab 98, Joint Army-Navy Circular 2, 3 Nov 43, and Tab 101, TAG Ltr to CGs AAF, Sv Comds, and Mil District of Washington, 8 Jan 44.

[25] *Ibid.*, Tab 123, Summary of Suspensions.

[26] OPMG Monograph, Industrial Employment Review Board, Tab 172, Progress Rpt, 26 Oct 45. Appeals heard by the New York and Chicago local panels in 1944–45 are apparently not included in these figures.

sort and succeeded in holding work stoppages to the minimum.   Certainly strikes and slowdowns did not cease when the United States entered the war, and the trend bore little relation to the progress of the industrial security program.   By the time the Army's antisubversive program got under way the objective had shifted, broadened perhaps, to encompass the prevention of sabotage and espionage.   Whether without the Army's program the war production effort would have been plagued with sabotage and breaches of military security is only a matter of conjecture.

The Alien Problem

Like its antisubversive program, the War Department's interest in the employment of aliens in industry was at first directed toward safeguarding the secrets of military production and protecting plants and materials against sabotage.   The policy, like that aimed at strikes or slowdowns of possible subversive origin, was precautionary and preventive.   In putting the policy into effect the War Department had to strike a balance between complete security and maximum production, for either one could be achieved only at the expense of the other.

In 1940, when defense production was getting under way, the balance was tipped in favor of security.   By a law of 2 July 1926 aliens had been barred from work on government aircraft contracts except by "written consent beforehand of the Secretary of the department concerned." [27]   This prohibition was extended, in June 1940, to cover all classified government contracts and was interpreted as applying even to such operations as stevedoring.[28]   One of the stumbling blocks in the way of obtaining the special consent of the Secretary of War, as required by law, was that the application had to come from the company or employer, not from the individual whose job was at stake.   Another hurdle was the widely inclusive basis laid down by Assistant Secretary Patterson for rejecting such applications.   Whether an alien had applied for first papers and whether citizens were available for the job were the principal criteria.   An alien would "probably" be rejected if he were a citizen of a country "concededly inimical" to the United States or had relatives or financial interests in such a country, if he were a member of any of certain organizations, or if his neighbors believed that he had shown sympathy toward an unfriendly nation.   An alien would "possibly" be rejected

[27] 44 U.S. Stat. 721, Public Law 446, 2 July 1926.
[28] Act of 28 June 1940, Public Law 671, 76th Congress, Sec. 11.

if he evaded questions, if he were not important to production, or if he had remote connections in a country hostile to democracy.[29]

The procedure itself and the failure of aliens and employers alike to understand it resulted in the exclusion of a number of loyal noncitizens. The process was time-consuming. The Army and the Navy had different regulations and in some cases a contractor had to obtain the consent of both. Application had to be made every time an alien changed his job. Rather than follow what seemed to be a cumbersome procedure, contractors tended to reject out of hand all aliens and even some foreign-born citizens who sought employment. Complaints on the subject began to flow into the War Department and Congress.

In the spring of 1941 the Labor Division of the Office of Production Management tried to cushion the impact of a rigid administration of the laws by suggesting to the War Department that contracting officers be allowed to make exemptions in subcontracts. The War Department rejected the proposal on the grounds that it might constitute an illegal delegation of authority and that it might open an unpluggable hole in the dike. Security risks in subcontracts, according to the War Department, could be just as dangerous as any in prime contracts.[30]

The role of minority groups in the defense effort had meanwhile become a cause of concern. An attack against discrimination based on race, creed, or color had been spearheaded by the National Defense Advisory Commission when that agency formulated its principles of labor policy in the late summer of 1940. After the creation of the OPM, two branches were established in that office to give attention to minority problems. The principal focus was on the integration of Negroes in defense work so as to assure them of a fair share of employment opportunities. Noting that complaints had been made in this matter, President Roosevelt on 12 June 1941 directed Knudsen and Hillman, as joint heads of OPM, to take immediate steps to facilitate the full utilization of American manpower. The doors of employment, the President stated, must be opened to "all loyal and qualified workers regardless of race, national origin, religion or color." The President on 25 June 1941 followed up his memorandum to OPM with an executive order to all departments and agencies in which the policy of nondiscrimination in de-

---

[29] Memo, ASW for ACof S G–2, 25 Nov 40, Internal Security Div OPMG Alien Program; Amberg Memo, 19 Jun 41.

[30] Memo, Asst to Dir Purchases and Contracts for Amberg, 29 Apr 41, sub: Employment of Aliens Clause, OUSW Amberg files, Employment of Aliens, Negroes, etc.

fense employment was reaffirmed.   All contracting agencies of the government were directed to include in defense contracts "a provision obligating the contractor not to discriminate against any worker because of race, creed, color, or national origin." [31]   By the same executive order a Committee on Fair Employment Practice was established in OPM to hear and investigate complaints, to redress valid grievances, and to recommend measures necessary or proper for carrying out the provisions of the order.

The inclusion of the phrase "national origin" in the President's memorandum to OPM and in his executive order of 25 June immediately raised the question of its applicability to the employment of aliens in defense industries.   It was agreed by members of Under Secretary Patterson's staff that a contract clause in the language of the executive order would not affect or modify the provisions of existing statutes, but beyond that there was a difference of opinion.   Ohly of the Labor Section held the view that the executive order covered aliens as well as citizens and that it extended equality of opportunity in employment to aliens except where they were barred by the Acts of July 1926 and June 1940.   Patterson and his special assistant, Amberg, took a contrary view.   They held that the order in no way applied to the hiring of aliens, that the phrase "national origin" referred merely to place of birth, not to citizenship.   Although Ohly feared that this interpretation might be criticized as condoning a general discrimination against aliens, the weight of opinion was against him.   In substance, the War Department's official position was, therefore, that a shift in the direction of a more positive policy of utilizing alien workers was not required. [32]   That the President's order prohibiting discrimination protected only United States citizens was accepted by the executive secretary of the Committee on Fair Employment Practice in a conference with members of Patterson's staff on 21 August. [33]

Instances of contractors arbitrarily rejecting all aliens instead of seeking permission to hire them continued to come to the attention of the War Department.   Since such practices were not considered a violation of the nondiscrimination clauses that had been inserted in contracts after the President issued the executive order of 25 June 1941, there was little to be done except

[31] EO 8802, 25 Jun 41.

[32] Memos, Asst to Dir Purchases and Contracts for Chief Air Corps and Chiefs Supply Arms and Svs, 27 Jun and 2 Jul 41, Memo, Ohly for Dir Purchases and Contracts, 10 Jul 41, Memo, Amberg for Brig Gen J. W. N. Schulz, 11 Jul 41, Memo, Schulz for Ohly, 17 Jul 41, and Memo, Ohly for Dir Purchases and Contracts, 19 Jul 41, all in OUSW Amberg files, Employment of Aliens, Negroes, etc.

[33] Ltr, L. W. Cramer, Exec Secy Committee on Fair Employment Practices, to USW, 22 Aug 41, OUSW Amberg files, Employment of Aliens, Negroes, etc.

to reply that the contractor had not applied for permission to hire the individual concerned and that any application would be given prompt attention when it was received.[34]   In the hyperemotionalism engendered by the attack on Pearl Harbor, the lot of an alien of German, Italian, or Japanese extraction became very difficult.   Even noncitizens from countries friendly to the United States did not escape the wave of antipathy.   In the San Francisco area the CIO Council Against Discrimination reported that eleven hundred thoroughly experienced longshoremen who came from friendly nations were barred from working on government ships.   Three hundred friendly aliens belonging to one local who had worked on the waterfront for periods ranging from fifteen to forty-two years were replaced by inexperienced men brought in from outside the area.   In New York a committee of the State Council of Defense declared that existing federal procedures were "almost inoperable in the case of aliens seeking employment."[35]

President Roosevelt in a public statement on 2 January 1942 lashed out against the misguided patriotism that was depriving the country of the services of loyal workers.   It was, he said, as "stupid" as it was "unjust."[36]   Less than a week later the OPM Council agreed that a public announcement should be made that "there is no legal barrier to the employment of aliens in general war work and that plants producing secret items may employ aliens after obtaining specific permission from the War and/or Navy Department."[37]

Neither pronouncement got to the root of the matter, which, as the committee of the New York State Council of Defense had noted, was simply that the procedural machinery was not designed to facilitate the hiring of aliens but to permit the granting of clearance in exceptional cases.   Finally, on 25 March 1942, the President wrote to the Secretaries of War and the Navy, the Attorney General, and the chairman of the Committee on Fair Employment Practice asking them to study a procedure that would give blanket consent to aliens from friendly nations for work in war industry.

[34] Ltrs, Stimson to Representative A. J. Engel, 24 Jun 41, to Senator Prentiss Brown, 6 Nov 41, to Senator Sheridan Downey, 27 Dec 41, to Attorney Gen, 24 Feb 42, and to Actg Secy State, 24 Mar 42, all in OSW Aliens No. 1000.

[35] Copy of Resolution Passed Unanimously by the Committee on Discrimination in Employment, New York State Council of Defense, 27 Feb 42, and Rpt on the Effect of Recent Army and Navy Regulations on the Employment of Aliens in San Francisco, CIO Bay Area Council Against Discrimination, forwarded 13 Apr 42, both in OUSW Miscellaneous and Subject, Aliens.

[36] Samuel I. Rosenman (compiler), *The Public Papers and Addresses of Franklin D. Roosevelt, 1942 Volume: Humanity on the Defensive* (New York: Harper & Brothers, 1950), p. 5.

[37] OPM Council Meeting, 7 Jan 42, Excerpt From Minutes, copy in OUSW Amberg files, Employment of Aliens, Negroes, etc.

The President suggested that enemy aliens be classified along lines followed in Great Britain.   He believed that in this way alien manpower would best be utilized.[38]

Sharp differences of opinion appeared during the interdepartmental discussions that ensued from the President's letter.   The War and Navy Departments took a narrower view of the suggested remedies than that adopted by the Department of Justice and the Committee on Fair Employment Practice, but a minimum program was agreed upon and submitted to the President.   Although a blanket clearance for any group of aliens was rejected, it was agreed that individual applications for certain aliens, such as those from friendly countries or with long residence in the United States, would be expedited.   The U.S. Employment Service was to help aliens fill out forms, which would be acted upon in a matter of a few days.   An intensive public relations program was begun, in which a number of departments and agencies joined.   The campaign hammered away on the theme that aliens were eligible for all jobs except those on classified or aircraft contracts, and to this old theme a new and stronger note was added, that even for the restricted jobs a loyal alien could now obtain the necessary special dispensation easily and without red tape.   Although there was no letup in the publicity campaign, it failed to produce any great results.[39]

The differences of opinion that had arisen from time to time between the various agencies concerned in the alien problem became acute during the summer and fall of 1942.   The section of the 1940 statute that prohibited the employment of aliens in classified contract jobs (Public Law 671, Section 11, 76th Congress) expired on 28 June 1942, and a bill continuing that section in effect was vetoed.   Since the bill had been vetoed because of provisions unrelated to the employment of aliens, the War Department assumed that the alien restrictions would be acceptable if divorced from the other provisions and presented by themselves.   A draft of a new bill was therefore submitted by the War Department to the Bureau of the Budget, which in turn referred it to Paul McNutt, chairman of the newly established War Manpower Commission.   McNutt opposed the War Department's bill.   The 1940 statute, he observed, had resulted in "wholesale discrimination" by pro-

---

[38] Ltr, Roosevelt to Stimson, 25 Mar 42, OUSW Miscellaneous and Subject, Aliens.

[39] Ltrs, Patterson to Asst Secy Navy and to Attorney Gen, 27 Mar 42, Ltr, Patterson, Francis Biddle, Frank Knox, and Malcolm S. McLean to Roosevelt, 19 Jun 42, and Press Release, 11 Jul 42, Employment of Aliens in National War Industries, all in OUSW Miscellaneous and Subject, Aliens; Memo, Col J. N. Dalton for Chiefs Supply Arms and Svs, Matériel Comd AAF, and Others, 18 Jun 42, with Presidential statement attached, sub: Employment of Aliens, in Hq ASF SPGC–L, SPAD 014.31.

viding employers with support for their existing prejudices.[40]   Within the
War Department, James Mitchell, Director of the Industrial Personnel Division, ASF, was inclined to agree with McNutt.   Mitchell considered that the
1940 law had had an adverse effect because of the criminal penalties levied
against contractors for putting aliens to work on classified jobs without obtaining clearance, since in order to protect themselves employers refused to
hire aliens for any work.   Without these particular penalties, there would
still be, according to Mitchell, adequate means of enforcing security.[41]
Although Mitchell's opinion was generally highly regarded in the War Department, in this instance it was bluntly rejected.   In reply to Mitchell,
Patterson expressed himself clearly and unmistakably: "I am still of the opinion that Section 11 of Public 671 should be re-enacted."[42]   Stimson said the
same thing at considerably greater length in a letter to the Director of the
Bureau of the Budget, who favored a watered-down version of the act.
Stimson's argument followed the same line as that of the War Department
a year and a half earlier when OPM had suggested changes in administering
the law.   A single alien employee by a single act of sabotage to one of the
larger plants could, Stimson warned, create damage resulting in the loss of
man-hours "comparable to the employment of all the technically trained
aliens in the United States for a considerable period of time."   The dangers
of espionage and sabotage were so great, he continued, that the War Department considered the re-enactment of the alien section of the 1940 law
"essential and urgent."[43]

The Bureau of the Budget nevertheless remained firmly opposed to stern
measures and drafted a bill that purported to achieve the security objectives
of the War Department without jeopardizing the production program.
Adopting the approach that had been rejected earlier in the year, the Bureau
of the Budget proposed that various groups of aliens be exempted from the
regulations and that penalties be reduced.   The bill met with a mixed reception when it was circulated among the War Department offices and
agencies.[44]   Heaviest opposition came from the Internal Security Division of

[40] Ltr, Stimson to Senator R. R. Reynolds, Chairman Committee on Mil Affairs, 6 Jul 42,
OSW Aliens No. 1000; Ltr, McNutt to F. J. Bailey, Asst Dir Legislative Reference Div, Bureau of
Budget, 19 Aug 42, copy in OUSW Amberg files, Employment of Aliens, Negroes, etc.

[41] Memo, Mitchell for Amberg, 6 Sep 42, OUSW Amberg files, Employment of Aliens, Negroes,
etc.

[42] Memo, Patterson for Amberg, 16 Sep 42, OUSW Amberg files, Employment of Aliens,
Negroes, etc.

[43] Ltr, Stimson to Harold D. Smith, 24 Sep 42, OSW Aliens No. 1000.

[44] Draft Bill on Employment of Aliens, and Memo, Maj. John B. Hill, Legal Br, Purchases Div
SOS, for Amberg, 19 Dec 42, both in OUSW Amberg files, Employment of Aliens, Negroes, etc.

the Office of the Provost Marshal General.   Col. Marion S. Battle, in charge of alien employment controls, expressed the views of the division when he declared that he could not understand the type of thinking that led to the opening of the barriers protecting war industry.   "Are we at war to employ a few aliens?" he asked.   Security and production were Siamese twins, he said, and security could not be neglected without destroying production.[45] The top policy-makers in the War Department were in substantial agreement with Colonel Battle's views.   Patterson was thoroughly opposed to the drafted bill, and Amberg believed that no bill would probably be better than the one proposed by the Bureau of the Budget.   Stimson, writing to Budget Director Harold D. Smith, argued that the proposed bill would not afford adequate protection, that it would upset existing internal security procedures, and that it would unduly endanger war production.   He predicted serious difficulties if the original regulations were not re-enacted.[46]

The bill drafted by the Bureau of the Budget was not enacted, nor were the original statutory provisions restored.   An effort to revive the provisions of the 1940 act was made early in 1945, but in view of the previous controversy the attempt was dropped.   As a result, from June 1942 to the end of the war the control of alien employment rested on the Air Corps Act of 1926 and on the contract provisions set forth in War Department regulations.[47]

As the controversy over legislation receded, the administration of the program was decentralized, procedures were simplified, and policy was redefined. In the early spring of 1943 responsibility for administering the alien employment program had been consolidated in the Personnel Security Branch, Internal Security Division, Office of the Provost Marshal General.   During the next two years, increasing authority to handle applications for clearance was delegated to local officers.   Suggested by the OPM in the spring of 1941 and at that time rejected by the War Department, the step was gradually put into effect after the spring of 1943, until by the end of the war alien employment applications were for the most part being handled by the service com-

---

[45] Memo, Battle, Chief Pers Security Br Internal Security Div, for Col H. G. Reynolds, Deputy Chief Internal Security Div, 29 Dec 42, sub: Employment of Enemy Aliens, and Memo, Reynolds for Amberg, 19 Dec 42, sub: Bureau of the Budget's Proposed Substitute . . ., both in OUSW Amberg files, Employment of Aliens, Negroes, etc.

[46] Memo, Amberg for Hill, Legal Br, Purchases Div SOS, 21 Dec 42, OUSW Amberg files, Employment of Aliens, Negroes, etc.; Ltr, Stimson to Smith, 28 Dec 42, OSW Aliens No. 1000.

[47] Memo, Maj E. F. Ghalagher for JAG, 19 Feb 45, sub: Proposed Legislation to Restrict Access by Aliens . . ., Memo, Lt Col J. W. Brebner-Smith, Chief Legal Office OPMG, for Ghalagher, 15 Feb 45, sub: Proposed Legislation . . . with incls including, Proposed Memo for Speaker of the House of Representatives, and Memo, Amberg for Brebner-Smith, 15 Mar 45, sub: Proposed Legislation . . ., all in OUSW Amberg files, Employment of Aliens, Negroes, etc.; AR 380–5.

mands and the Air Forces procurement districts, under the supervision of the Provost Marshal General. Security checks of aliens by the FBI and special investigations by G–2 became less frequent. Applicants were screened and only those who seemed suspicious were investigated. Service commands and procurement districts developed ground rules for the temporary approval of aliens under which decisions were usually made within twenty-four hours. When investigations were necessary, the time lag was reduced from two or more months to an average of three weeks.[48] Despite dire predictions by internal security officers that the floodgates would be opened to espionage and sabotage, the alien employment policy of the War Department took a new turn in June 1943, when Ohly's interpretation of the President's executive order of 25 June 1941 was finally accepted. In a joint statement on 7 June 1943, the Secretary of War, Secretary of the Navy, Attorney General, and Chairman of the U.S. Maritime Commission took the position that the executive order had been "intended to apply equally to citizens and noncitizens." Stressing the need to make full use of manpower, the statement warned contractors that failure to comply with the executive order would be a breach of contract and contrary to national policy.[49]

The effect on employment of the reversed policy as well as the effect of the original War Department policy cannot be adequately measured. During the war 201,000 applications for the employment of aliens were approved and 5,400 were rejected. Without considering duplications, the number of aliens thus made available to war industry was fairly small. On the other hand, it was likewise only a small percentage of the total alien population, and many aliens were employed in jobs not classed as war jobs or in which clearance was not required.[50] Presumably some of them released native-born Americans for work in aircraft plants or on classified government contracts. Whether the absence of any substantial instance of enemy-inspired sabotage during the war is the true measure of success of the War Department's alien employment policy is equally incalculable.

[48] Hist Monograph 408, Alien Employment Program, pp. 7–11, OCMH; TAG Ltr, 12 Sep 42, sub: Alien Employment Program, SPX 014.31(9 Sep 44)OB–S–SPMGP–M; Memo, Patterson, Actg SW, for CG AAF, PMG, CGs All Sv Comds, CG Mil Dist of Washington, CofOrd, Chief CWS, and CofEngrs, 18 Mar 43, sub: Alien Employment Program, OUSW 014.31(3–18–43) Alien Employment Program; Memo, Patterson for PMG, 30 Jun 43, OUSW 014.31(7–1–43)(1); TAG Ltr, 27 Jun 44, sub: Alien Employment Program, SPX 014.31(27 Jun 44)OB–S–SPMGP–M.

[49] Joint Statement by SW, Secy Navy, Attorney Gen, and Chairman of U.S. Maritime Commission on the Employment of Aliens, 7 Jun 43, OUSW 014.31(4–24–43)(1).

[50] A study by Leifur Magnusson and Michael S. Poluhoff, Manpower in Industrial Mobilization, Industrial College of the Armed Forces, R29, June 1946, pages 67–68, gives the total number of aliens in the United States in 1941 as 4,921,452, of whom "nearly three million" were in the labor force.

CHAPTER VI

Bringing Work to the Worker

The defense effort, coming at the end of a depression, set in motion large numbers of men who left their old homes and poured into the new defense centers in search of work. Many found jobs, but others were caught in a vacuum created by reduced civilian production and lagging war employment. The less fortunate were forced to join the ranks of those already out of work by reason of "technological unemployment." While some towns and cities boomed, others, of which New York City was perhaps the most striking example, suffered from unemployment. In both cases serious economic and social problems arose which, in turn, hampered defense production.

The obvious answer to glut and famine in labor supply was to bring work to the worker. Housing, transportation, and community facilities could be saved and large amounts of labor and materials released for defense purposes if workers were not compelled to travel far afield to find jobs. As the largest single consumer of military goods, the War Department could go a long way toward providing a solution by placing contracts with companies in localities where a labor surplus existed, by exercising care in cutting back its orders, and by locating new plants and installations to take advantage of labor supply. The third of these—location of facilities—was the most important one. Not only did the original construction absorb workers, but once a facility had been built the War Department could scarcely let it remain idle. The flow of contracts and the progress of cutbacks were to a large measure determined by the location of facilities.

The Location of Facilities

In the early defense period—1940 and 1941—the supply of labor was only one of several factors that determined the site of a plant or an airfield. Great emphasis was placed on the physical nature of the site, its proximity to transportation and power facilities, its vulnerability to possible enemy attack, and the availability of raw materials. Also important was its proximity to existing plants that could produce military items. Other factors—geographic distribution, the pressure of local interests and their representatives in Congress—entered into the choice of sites, and sometimes labor supply was an important consideration.

The technical service or the Air Forces, as the interested procurement or using agency, and the Corps of Engineers or the Construction Division, OQMG, as the constructing agency, were responsible for making the preliminary choice of a site. The proposal was then reviewed by a War Department board and given final approval by the National Defense Advisory Commission or its successor, the Office of Production Management. When the OPM in the spring of 1941 became the chief agency directing the defense effort, it appointed a committee which recommended that civilian officials work closely with the Army and Navy at all stages of site planning and that, after due consideration of military factors, plants should be located according to a policy of "wide geographic decentralization of defense industries and full employment of all available labor." On 13 May 1941 OPM established the Plant Site Board, and the War Department in turn established the Facilities Board, which screened the recommendations of the technical services before they were reviewed by the Plant Site Board.[1]

The labor factor had already entered into the choice of locations for early Ordnance and Air Forces facilities. The Indiana Ordnance Works, the first smokeless powder plant built during the defense period, was placed in a rural area, but it was only sixteen miles from Louisville, Kentucky, the population center for about two million people living within a radius of seventy-five miles. The location of the second smokeless powder plant at Radford, Virginia, was criticized because of an insufficient labor supply in the immediate neighborhood. In defense of the site, Ordnance officers reported that there were 23,000 employables within ten miles of the plant. At the time the site was chosen there was sufficient labor, but Radford later faced acute labor shortages. Among the considerations taken into account in locating the Elwood Ordnance Plant was the fact that it was within commuting distance of Joliet, Illinois, a city of 70,000, while skilled technicians could be brought in from Chicago, only seventy miles away. An expansion of small arms production at East Alton, Illinois, was transferred to St. Louis because a manpower study showed a probable labor shortage at East Alton.[2] The Chief of

---

[1] Expansion of Industrial Facilities Under Army Air Forces Auspices, 1940–1945, MS, AAF Hist Studies 40 (hereafter cited as Expansion of Industrial Facilities Under AAF), pp. 40–42.

[2] Basic History of Elwood Ordnance Plant, MS, I, Part I, pp. 6–7; History of Indiana Ordnance Works, MS, I, 9; Maj J. F. Joorfetz, Site-Report, Mar 44, pp. 8–9, and Apps. on Indiana Ordnance Works and Radford Ordnance Works, filed as Industrial Sv Ammunition Div OCO Hist, Vol. I, Ord Hist files; Ammunition Br Small Arms Div OCofOrd, Small Arms Ammunition: A History of an Industry, 1918–1944, 2 vols., Philadelphia, Pa., Frankford Arsenal [1946], copy in OCMH.

Ordnance reported in March 1941 that thirty-two plants under construction would ultimately employ about 90,000 workers, nearly all of whom lived near the sites, and that plants were located only after a survey of labor in the area.[3] New sites for aviation plants had been chosen with a view to the labor factor. The original centers of airplane production on the west coast showed early signs of potential manpower shortage. Air officers planned to build two plants in the area between the Mississippi River and the Rocky Mountains but feared that there were no communities that could furnish enough workers for the size of plant necessary. Instead they selected four sites—at Tulsa, Forth Worth, Kansas City, and Omaha—where there was sufficient labor and where future demand for other war products would not be likely.[4]

The Plant Site Board did not promulgate any general rules, but its decisions in individual cases created a pattern. Soon after the board was established the Ordnance Department submitted a list of six cities as possible locations for three small arms ammunition plants. The board objected to Omaha since a plant there would compete for labor with existing aircraft plants. It decided that Milwaukee should be reserved for facilities that required more highly skilled labor than was needed for the production of small arms ammunition. It objected to Atlanta on the ground that plans to locate Quartermaster and Air Forces depots there would exhaust the supply of labor. In this case the board erred; the Atlanta area continued to have a surplus of labor. Instead of Omaha, Milwaukee, and Atlanta, the board recommended Salt Lake City, Des Moines, and the Minneapolis-St. Paul area.[5] Again, in June 1941, the board raised objections to a proposed expansion at Bridgeport, Connecticut, because there was a shortage of skilled men and the supply of unskilled workers who might be trained was nearly exhausted. The federal government had already spent $8,000,000 on housing projects, and serious problems were developing in education, sewage, and water supply. The "social costs" of locating additional plant capacity in Bridgeport were so high, the board noted, that expansion could be justified only in "very exceptional cases." The Under Secretary of War circulated OPM recommendations among the chiefs of the technical services to serve as a guide for selecting sites when similar situations developed.[6] When unemployment began to appear in low-

---

[3] Memo, CofOrd for USW, 10 Mar 41, sub: Senate Resolution 71, in 00 412/2045.

[4] Expansion of Industrial Facilities Under AAF, pp. 87, 89–90.

[5] Memo for Record, E. M. Martin, Plant Site Board, 9 Sep 41, sub: Factors Involved in Selection of Sites for Small Arms Ammunition Plants, in Small Arms Ammunition: A History of an Industry, II, 138.

[6] Ltr, Martin to Patterson, 27 Jun 41, and Memo, Brig Gen Harry K. Rutherford to Chief Air Corps and CofOrd, 1 Jul 41, sub: Plant Sites in Bridgeport Area, both in OUSW Res and Prod Div 175, Labor 1941.

priority industries at the end of 1941, an attempt was made by the Plant Site Board to direct defense work to the areas affected. Lists of communities where war plants were needed to create jobs for jobless workers were given to the War Department by the Plant Site Board. Some of the communities got new plants, others did not.

In the four months immediately following the attack on Pearl Harbor, the labor supply factor was almost forgotten in the rush to get new facilities under construction. The attitude of the chief of the Air Forces' Materiel Division, whose dictum was "start building right now and justify later," was perhaps characteristic. Areas of actual labor shortage were few, and the possibility of future difficulties was not considered adequate cause for withholding plant authorizations. In fact, the need for speedy production was often a compelling reason for choosing plant sites in communities already congested with war orders. Competent plant managers and skilled labor could be found in the existing centers, although the supply was scarce.[7] Even later, when expansion was necessary, a site that fitted into the existing industrial pattern was often the only practicable location for new construction.

Communities sometimes missed the boat, because by 1943 it was becoming too late to do a thorough job of canvassing the entire situation to ensure that facilities were placed where labor was plentiful. Scranton, Pennsylvania, is an example of a city that failed to get what it considered its share of war plants. The decline of its two principal industries—anthracite mining and silk processing—during the 1930's had left Scranton with a considerable reservoir of unemployed workers, but the first rush of defense construction passed the city by. Expanding facilities in nearby cities, notably the American Car and Foundry plant in Berwick—fifty miles southwest of Scranton—drew upon Scranton's surplus, but local interests began to demand war work for their city as well. By 1943, local spokesmen claimed, there were 30,000 workers unemployed, and an additional 30,000 could be brought into war work. Housing offered no problem. But an aluminum plant that Scranton hoped to get was instead divided between Memphis, Tennessee, and Hammond, Indiana, both already crowded with war work; a rayon plant that the Pennsylvania city wanted was assigned to Front Royal, Virginia, where, according

---

[7] Expansion of Industrial Facilities Under AAF, pp. 126–28, 130, 133, 164; Edmond Kanwit, War Department Facility Allocation, Contract Placement, and Cutback Distribution From the Standpoint of Labor Supply and Labor Relations, June 1940 to May 1945, ASF IPD Monograph 11 (1946), Sec. I, p. 3, MS OCMH; Ltrs, E. M. Elliot to Maj Gen B. M. Giles, 17 Sep 43, and Giles to Elliot, 2 Oct 43, AAF 004.06, Labor Conditions.

to Scranton advocates, it would be necessary to build an entirely new city in order to house the immigrating workers. Scranton finally succeeded in getting a few war plants, including a $6 million facility for building B–29 bombers, but its share in the war program was smaller than the city believed it should have received.[8] The plight of cities like Scranton illustrated the need for carefully weighing all factors before a rigid program was adopted. Scranton had failed to make its bid for war plants early enough. By the time its appeal was made the program was set. By the end of 1942, 78 percent of the funds for Air Forces facilities for the whole war had already been allocated, and 70 percent of the War Department's entire wartime plant construction was under way. By the time the manpower shortage became critical in 1943, emphasis had shifted from expanding facilities to turning out munitions.

By the summer of 1943 most discussions of plant expansion hinged on the availability of manpower. Representatives of the War Manpower Commission attended meetings where new facilities were being discussed. At the request of the War and Navy Departments, Justice Byrnes, on 4 September 1943, laid down the special west coast manpower program, which prohibited "as far as possible" the building of new or the expansion of old plants. A month later, the War Production Board ordered that no plant expansion be allowed in critical labor areas without special recommendation from the local Area Production Urgency Committee. The War Production Board urged that these committees exercise all their "ingenuity to the end that the minimum number of recommendations for approval of new facilities is given." The board retained the right to review decisions of the Area Production Urgency Committees.[9] Policy-making officials in the War Department and the civilian production agencies continued to the end of the war to fight against placing new plants in overburdened war centers. As late as 1 March 1945, with the defeat of Germany already in sight, the Under Secretary of War asked important manufacturing concerns to move old facilities or establish new ones in areas where there was sufficient labor. On the level

---

[8] House Report 1553, 77th Congress, 1st Session, *National Defense Migration,* Second Interim Report of House Select Committee Investigating National Defense Migration, December 19, 1941, *Recommendations on Full Utilization of America's Industrial Capacity and Labor Supply in the War Effort,* pp. 82–84; *Business Week,* June 15, 1942; *Scranton Tribune,* August 28, September 7, 11, 1943; Ltrs, Elliot to Giles, 17 Sep 43, and Giles to Elliot, 2 Oct 43, AAF 004.06, Labor Conditions; Expansion of Industrial Facilities Under AAF, p. 170.

[9] Expansion of Industrial Facilities Under AAF, p. 162; WPB Adm Order 2–144, 1944, and Amendment, 25 July 1944. For the composition and functioning of these committees, on which the War Department was represented, see below, Ch. VII.

of high policy, the placing of facilities according to labor supply had become firmly established.[10]

Regardless of policy and principles, so many factors entered into locating facilities that no rigid rules were possible. Special circumstances often outweighed considerations of labor supply. The Signal Corps wanted facilities expanded in the centers of the electronic industry, which, with the exception of New York City, were generally in tight labor areas. The technical requirements of the industry were such that reviewing officials agreed to the location of facilities in regions that already specialized in electronic production. Thus the expansion of the International Resistance Company in Philadelphia was approved over the protests of labor supply officials, and later, in March 1945, the National Radio Corporation in the same region was also permitted to add facilities for making electron tubes. Battery plants in Milwaukee and Madison, Wisconsin, and in Indianapolis and Buffalo were built relatively late in the war, even though these cities had serious labor supply problems. The expansions were relatively small, and officials with the responsibility of locating the facilities believed that the availability of technical skills probably outweighed manpower supply considerations. Yet because so many Signal Corps installations were in critical labor areas, it became necessary to place batteries on a production urgency list so that the U.S. Employment Service could divert labor to the industry.[11]

To help alleviate such conditions, the Signal Corps and its contractors placed part of their operations, which required relatively simple processes, in scattered feeder plants where labor was plentiful. General Cable in Buffalo increased its production by converting an Ordnance Department facility in Lowell, Massachusetts. Crowded conditions at Point Breeze, Maryland, caused Western Electric to establish an auxiliary plant in Scranton. Hygrade-Sylvania and Raytheon built many branch plants to manufacture tubes in unindustrialized areas. Ken-Rad, another important tube producer, operated in Kentucky and southern Indiana, largely with unskilled workers, and Burgess Battery manufactured some of its output in communities in northern Illinois that had sufficient labor. In this way the skilled labor of the most congested war centers was conserved for the more difficult operations.[12]

---

[10] Memo, Brig Gen Edward S. Greenbaum for CG AAF and CG ASF, 1 Mar 45, sub: Placement of Contracts in Group IV Labor Areas, Kanwit, *op. cit.,* App. I.

[11] Kanwit, *op. cit., passim;* Henry C. C. Shute, Prod Div Philadelphia SigC Proc Dist, Industrial Summary: Signal Corps Procurement of Dry Batteries (15 Jan 46), pp. 47–48, SigC Hist Sec File.

[12] L. H. Drake and F. W. Thomas, Prod Div Philadelphia SigC Proc Dist, Industrial Summary: Signal Corps Procurement of Wire and Cable (15 Jan 46), p. 89, SigC Hist Sec File.

The Ordnance Department built the largest number of War Department facilities. Many of the plants, such as Ravenna, Sangamon, Badger, Kingsbury, Kankakee, Hoosier, and the Indiana Ordnance Works, were in areas where they competed for labor with other war industries. Production of tanks, trucks, and combat vehicles was concentrated in Detroit in spite of anticipated labor shortages. Nearly all machine gun plants were located in communities with actual or potential labor shortages. On the other hand, aside from the continuation of small arms production in some of the established New England centers, new facilities—for example, in Saint Paul, Denver, Salt Lake City, Evansville, Des Moines, St. Louis, and Milwaukee—were usually well located from the standpoint of labor supply.[13]

Late in 1944 the armies in Europe suddenly ran into an ammunition shortage, and the Ordnance Department embarked on a new program calling for a plant expansion costing about $300 million. Ordnance officials studied several locations and discussed proposed sites with labor officials in the Army Service Forces and with representatives of the War Manpower Commission. By that time there were very few labor surplus areas that could meet the specifications necessary for ordnance production, and the selections were largely based on finding the least disadvantageous spots. The fear of taking chances and the time factor proved more important than labor shortages in the approval of large new expansions at the Badger, Radford, New River, and Indiana Ordnance Works. In all these cases, manpower officials of the Army Service Forces or the War Manpower Commission protested. But the officers responsible for production carried their appeals to the highest military and civilian authorities. In the case of the $50 million Indiana expansion, for production of rocket powder, General Clay won approval by appealing to the War Production Board. Other plants, such as the American Steel Foundries in East Chicago, were approved even though they probably could not have been manned without an extraordinary immigration of workers. Between September 1944 and 15 May 1945 Ordnance sponsored 204 expansions, each costing $500,000 or more. Fifty-three of these were to be located in areas where the labor shortage was already serious. In January and February 1945, six expansions of more than $5 million were authorized, three in Detroit, one in Indianapolis, one in Rockford, Illinois, and one in Euclid, Ohio. In March 1945 a $5.5 million addition for a Ford facility at Dearborn, Michigan, was approved. None of these areas had sufficient labor. From the labor supply standpoint at least, it was fortunate that a

---

[13] Kanwit, *op. cit., passim.*

large part of the program was subsequently curtailed and some projects were abandoned completely.

Aircraft facilities were next to ordnance facilities in dollar value. Centers of airplane production were among the most congested in the United States: Buffalo, San Diego, Los Angeles, Chicago, Wichita, Hartford, and Seattle. In addition, aircraft plants were built in areas such as Detroit, which was already flooded with orders from the Ordnance Department and other procurement agencies. Willow Run was not only in the crowded Detroit area but was also inconveniently located. This was one of the reasons why the plant had tremendous difficulties in recruiting labor, and there were some experts who believed that the choice of location was a grave mistake.

Because of the growing importance of labor supply, plant processing officers at Wright Field began to furnish complete manpower data with facility proposals. Because of material and labor shortages, not many new facilities were built, but some new plants were needed to manufacture new types of planes and engines. The Air Forces tried to locate these in surplus labor areas. One of the needs was for heavy cargo planes to carry supplies to South America, to the Caribbean, and over the Hump to China; to transport key personnel and critical repair parts to the battle zones; and to evacuate the wounded. Consequently, in November 1942 Higgins Aircraft, Incorporated, was authorized to build a factory for large plywood transports in New Orleans, which had surplus labor. In July 1943 the Fairchild Aviation Corporation received a contract for a $3.5 million plant at Hagerstown, Maryland, an area with a moderate, though not excessive, labor supply.

The enlarged B–29 program called for new plants in Milwaukee, St. Paul, Scranton, and other cities, most of which had available labor. The Air Forces authorized four modification centers after 1 October 1942 in cities which, while not labor shortage areas, at least had balanced labor supply and demand.[14]

Though the Army Air Forces, perhaps to a greater extent than the Ordnance Department, had become aware of labor supply factors, its choice of sites was also limited. Thus, of twenty-five expanded facilities begun between September 1944 and the end of the war in Europe, fifteen were placed in areas of labor shortage. These fifteen expansions went to established manufacturers such as Allison Division of General Motors, Dodge Engine Plant, Bendix Aviation, and Boeing. They were for such purposes as developing jet propulsion and expediting lagging B–29 production.[15]

[14] Expansion of Industrial Facilities Under AAF, pp. 169–71.
[15] Kanwit, *op. cit.*, Sec. I, p. 19.

The apparent differences between policy and performance did not stem from a difference of opinion between procurement officers and higher officials in the ASF, in the Under Secretary's office, and in the civilian agencies.   Signal Corps, Quartermaster, Ordnance, and Air Forces contracting officers were aware of the disadvantages of building new plants and expanding old ones in congested cities like Detroit, Buffalo, Los Angeles, and Seattle, but they were responsible for getting out the work and could not take quite as broad a view as policy-making officials could.   Military needs often left them little choice in locating facilities.

The Labor Supply Factor in Contract Placement

In placing contracts, as in locating facilities, labor supply was only one of the factors to be considered.   Only when contracting officers had a choice between facilities could they consider labor supply in contract placement.   At the start of the defense effort, when production was first getting under way in selected plants, and particularly during the period at the end of the war when production was being cut back in many fields, procurement officials could pick and choose.   At the height of war production, when labor supply problems were most acute, the possibilities of placing contracts according to labor supply were most limited.

During the 1930's military procurement was so small a part of total production that from the standpoint of national economy it did not make too much difference where orders were placed, and contracting officers made awards to the lowest qualified bidders.   Even had they wanted to, under existing law they could not have considered placing orders according to labor supply.   Not until after the National Defense Act of 28 June 1940 was enacted could procuring agencies consider factors other than price and the responsibility of bidders.   The same day that the act was passed the Advisory Commission to the Council of National Defense announced that the criteria for placing orders under negotiated contracts should be, as far as possible, "the use of plants which now have excess or unused capacity and the selection of localities where there are reservoirs of unused labor." [16]   Despite this announcement most defense orders continued to be placed with customary suppliers, and an estimated 75 percent of defense contracts in 1940 were concentrated in areas containing only about one-fifth of the nation's population.

[16] Quoted in Reginald C. McGrane, *The Facilities and Construction Program of the War Production Board and Predecessor Agencies, May 1940 to May 1945*, Civilian Production Administration Special Study 19 (1946), p. 13.

The procurement pattern inevitably came under Congressional scrutiny. The Tolan Committee of the House of Representatives, which during the 1930's had been investigating the migration of poverty-stricken farm labor, now shifted the range of its inquiry to the migration of war workers. The committee was interested in the possibility of setting up a central civilian board for procurement—a project bitterly opposed by the Army—and many witnesses charged that the War Department's contracting policy was responsible for a dislocation of labor. The perennial claim was made that the War Department favored large corporations at the expense of little business, although the president of General Motors, Charles E. Wilson, pointed out to the committee that the defense program was big business. "Small plants," he testified, "can't make tanks, airplanes, or other large, complex armaments." It could be said, Wilson further told the committee, that General Motors, with 13 percent of the durable goods industry's productive capacity and only 5 percent of applicable contracts, was not getting its proportionate share of defense business.[17]

The adverse criticism, much of it grossly exaggerated, served as a stimulus for spreading the work to "distressed" areas. In July 1941 the Office of Production Management recommended a procedure by which the armed services could help solve the unemployment problem. Under this procedure, OPM would certify areas as being distressed, and the War and Navy Departments would then issue appropriate directives to insure the placing of contracts in those areas.[18]

In accordance with the OPM recommendation, Under Secretary Patterson established in the Planning Branch of his office a Contract Distribution Division to direct the spreading of work. Procurement officers were permitted to place contracts in certified areas at prices up to 15 percent above the lowest quotation received, to place trial orders on a cost-plus-fixed-fee basis, to eliminate bid and performance bonds, and in other ways make it easier for plants in communities with unemployed workers to bid for contracts. On 4 September 1941 the President issued an executive order to provide for more effective use of existing plants and to alleviate priority unemployment. To insure Army co-operation with this policy, the Under Secretary of War directed the chiefs of the supply arms and services to appoint representatives

---

[17] House Report 1553, 77th Congress, 1st Session, *National Defense Migration,* Second Interim Report, pp. 7–8, 115–18.

[18] Memo, with attachments, W. E. Levis for Knudsen and Hillman, 31 Jul 41, AAF Unemployment and Migration of Labor (1941).

to his Contract Distribution Division.[19]   But since the division "neither signed nor reviewed contracts, its functions were principally informative and exhortatory."   The supply services, faced with the problems of developing contracts everywhere, usually did not pay much attention to problems of labor supply.[20]

The War Department also asked its labor supply officers to help provide jobs for the unemployed and to direct manufacturers to government channels that could help them get orders.   As liaison officers with industry, their duties were advisory, and they were warned to avoid commitments or actions that might embarrass any other unit of the War Department.[21]   The warning was unnecessary.   The labor supply officers were too far removed from procurement officers and too deeply immersed in selective service problems to have much influence on contract placement.

Unemployment as a result of low production priorities never developed to the degree that had been predicted.   The Office of Production Management certified about twenty communities as being distressed and deserving of special consideration, but many of these, like Manitowoc, Wisconsin, rapidly changed from an area of labor surplus to one of labor shortage.   Detroit, which at the end of 1941 had a serious unemployment problem, received so many contracts that by the spring of 1942 it was on the way to being an area of acute labor shortage.   Expanded war production, rather than the efforts of procurement officers, was the major cause of the change in the employment picture.

During the first months of 1942 the newly created War Production Board attributed much of the unequal distribution of contracts to the use of competitive bidding.   Although the National Defense Expediting Act of 2 July 1940 (Public Law 703, 76th Congress) had authorized the Army to negotiate contracts, contracting officers had been reluctant to abandon the traditional method and as a result the Army had not made wide use of its authority. On 3 March 1942 the board therefore issued a basic policy directive in which authority to place contracts by negotiation was emphatically restated.   The

---

[19] USW Office Order 11–B–1, 19 Aug 41, Schedules 1 and 2 attached, ASF IPD, Maj Webber's Reading File.

[20] Memo, Rutherford for Chiefs Supply Arms and Svs, 5 Sep 41, sub: Distribution of Defense Orders, ASF IPD, Maj Webber's Reading File; Expansion of Industrial Facilities Under AAF, p. 100.

[21] Memo, Battley for OUSW Liaison Officers, 3 Oct 41, sub: Distribution of Defense Orders, and Memo, Kilbourne Johnston for OUSW Liaison Officers, 6 Nov 41, sub: Distribution of Defense Orders, both in ASF IPD, Maj Webber's Reading File.

way was opened for greater consideration of factors other than cost, although the labor factor was not specifically mentioned in the directive.[22]   With the establishment of the War Manpower Commission in April 1942, the collection and dissemination of data concerning labor shortages became more systematized and regular.   Labor supply maps showing the areas where shortages and surpluses existed were for the first time made available to procurement officers.   On these first maps there were twenty-four areas of labor shortage, fifty-one of anticipated shortage, and fifty-nine where a surplus existed.[23]

The local shortages that were developing led General Somervell to inform the chiefs of the supply arms and services that "in the interest of the most efficient use of the nation's available manpower, it is important that contracts be withheld from areas in which shortages of labor have developed or are expected to develop . . . ."[24]   A redistribution of contracts was tried in several localities with varying results.   Labor officials in the War Department recommended that as far as possible no additional contracts be placed in the Detroit area and the War Production Board made a field survey to determine which contracts could be shifted elsewhere, but managerial competence was so essential a commodity that the Detroit program did not get beyond the planning stage.[25]   By midsummer, Buffalo also had become a critical area, with a dozen different war industries all competing for the labor supply. The ASF on 22 August tried the remedy of requiring special approval from the Manpower Branch of the ASF Civilian Personnel Division for the placement of additional contracts in that locality.[26]   For similar reasons, The Quartermaster General was in late August requested by ASF labor officials to take $4 million worth of contracts out of the Seattle area.   With the exception of cold-climate clothing, contracts that could be filled in localities with a larger supply of labor were not to be placed in Seattle.[27]   Conversely, strenu-

---

[22] War Manpower Commission, History of the Mobilization of Labor for War Production During World War II, Draft MS, 1946, Ch. IV, pp. 24–25, National Archives; CPA, *Industrial Mobilization for War,* I, 422–23.

[23] Memo, Col L. J. Dillon for Chiefs Supply Svs and Field Proc Officers, 25 Apr 42, sub: Consideration of Labor Supply in Awarding Contracts, and Memo, Battley for All Liaison Officers SOS, 1 May 42, sub: Consideration of Labor Supply Information . . ., both in ASF IPD, Maj Webber's Reading File; Folder kept by W. E. Orr, Jr., ASF IPD, Labor Supply, Maps and Material.

[24] Memos cited n. 23.

[25] Memo, Mitchell for MacKeachie, May 42, sub: Action on Acute Labor Shortage, ASF IPD, Labor Supply, Maps and Material.

[26] Memo, Somers for L. J. Maloney, 26 Sep 42, ASF IPD (L–ASF Pol Nec), Labor Supply and Proc; Memo, Harrison for Chiefs Supply Arms and Svs, 20 Aug 42, sub: Placement of Contracts in Distressed Areas, copy in OCMH.

[27] Memo, Capt Boland for Lt Col J. C. O'Connell, 21 Nov 42, sub: Proc Policy—Labor Supply, ASF IPD (L–ASF Pol Nec), Labor Supply and Proc.

ous efforts were made to place more contracts in New York City, even if it meant paying higher prices for finished items than for those that could be obtained elsewhere.

Labor analysts of the War Manpower Commission and War Production Board rightly or wrongly interpreted their statistics as showing no progress in the direction of balancing contracts with labor supply. The board estimated that, from May through September 1942, 80 percent of all war supply contracts, measured in dollar value, had been placed in areas where a shortage of labor existed. Analyses made by the commission in July, September, and November 1942 were cited as indicating an upward trend in the allocations of contracts to areas already overburdened with war work.[28] As a result, the War Production Board on 10 October 1942 promulgated a "new" policy.

The War Production Board directive of 10 October recognized that primary emphasis should be placed on performance or deliveries within the time required and on the extent to which the potential contractor would need additional equipment or machinery. Once these factors had been duly considered, all procurement agencies were "to avoid" placing contracts "in communities or areas in which acute labor shortages are known to exist," if it were "practical to procure the needed items or materials elsewhere." The War Manpower Commission was to be relied upon for certification of areas with acute labor shortages. To facilitate the diversion of contracts, procurement officials were permitted to pay bonus prices.[29]

The policy did not require a radical change so far as the Army was concerned, since regulations in line with the War Production Board directive were already in effect. The move to give more emphasis to the factor of labor supply, already on foot, was perhaps quickened, and a few additional instructions were issued. A number of the supply services required their procurement officers to make a detailed explanation of contracts awarded to localities where labor was in short supply. For a time an attempt was made to allocate a specific proportion of contracts for certain types of goods to each of the twelve regions into which, on the basis of labor supply, the War Manpower Commission had divided the United States. The instructions to this effect were intricate and involved. Those received by the commanding general of the AAF Matériel Command directed him to place purchase con-

---

[28] CPA, *Industrial Mobilization for War*, I, 423; WMC, History of the Mobilization of Labor for War Production During World War II, Ch. IV, pp. 53–54.

[29] WMC, History of the Mobilization of Labor for War Production During World War II, Ch. IV, pp. 25–26.

tracts in areas of labor surplus for "a quantity of any item at least equal to
that area's proportional share of the available national labor market in the field
in which the item is manufactured . . . ." [30]   The Corps of Engineers received a list of ten standard types of items for each of which a specified
minimum of the total orders was allocated to each of the labor regions.
These complicated orders imposed such an administrative burden on contracting officers that within two months they were rescinded. [31]

Other measures, originally intended to serve other ends, were studied or
promoted as possible methods of conserving manpower.   The move within
the War Production Board to concentrate civilian production in a few companies in certain areas, although primarily intended to aid conversion to war
industry, to further the conservation of raw materials, to facilitate price stabilization, and to permit the full utilization of machinery, was encouraged by
General Somervell and Under Secretary Patterson as a possible means of dis-
tributing industrial manpower more effectively.   The concentration program,
however, disrupted traditional business relationships, interfered with brand
names and trademarks, and broke through customary distribution channels.
Business men resisted the program vigorously, and it was finally abandoned. [32]
Listings of idle plants and unused machinery, originally drawn up when
shortages of machine tools and materials developed, gradually came to be of
greatest importance in guiding the diversion of work to areas of surplus labor.
Tighter control of subcontracting, which received its first impetus from Congressional concern for small business, was urged by the War Manpower
Commission as a help in solving the labor problem.   The commission would
have wished the War Department to insert in prime contracts a clause stipu-
lating the type and amount of subcontracting, but the War Department,
when the question arose in the summer of 1943, recommended that the heads
of the interested agencies address a joint letter to prime contractors who held
orders amounting to $5 million or more each.   This was done.   A letter

[30] Memo, Col Albert J. Browning for CG Matériel Comd AAF, 28 Dec 42, AAF 004.06, Labor
Conditions.

[31] Memo, Browning for CofEngrs, 9 Jan 43, Memo, O'Connell for Purchases Div SOS, 28 Oct
42, sub: Proc Labor Supply and Shortage, Memo, Boland for O'Connell, 21 Nov 42, sub: Proc
Policy—Labor Supply, and Procurement Regulations 205.3, 205.4, 205.5 and drafts of same, 28
Nov 42, all in ASF IPD (L–ASF Pol Nec), Labor Supply and Proc.

[32] Maryclaire McCauley, *Concentration of Civilian Production by the War Production Board,
September 1941 to April 1943,* Civilian Production Administration Special Study 14 (1946); sum-
marizes the history of concentration of civilian industry.   The War Department interest in the
program is indicated in the weekly progress reports of the Manpower Branch, Civilian Personnel
Division, SOS, throughout 1942.   Typical comments are found in the reports between 14 July
and 11 August 1942.   Memo, Amberg for Browning, 23 Jan 43, sub: Truman Committee Rpt . . .,
in OUSW, War Manpower Commission.

signed by the chairman of the War Production Board, the chairman of the Maritime Commission, the director of Treasury Procurement, and the Under Secretaries of the War and Navy Departments went out to 1,000 prime contractors, requesting them to avoid placing subcontracts in areas of labor shortage and to make use of firms in communities that had a surplus of labor.[33]

The direct allocation of contracts according to the supply of manpower encountered almost as many difficulties as those raised by some of the more indirect measures. Communities that lost war orders protested vehemently even though labor might not be available to fill the orders. Charges of discrimination were hurled at the War Department. Interservice competition for labor and facilities also contributed to the problem. On one occasion, when the Army withheld a contract from a supplier in a locality where a labor shortage existed, the Navy promptly stepped in and placed a large order with the firm. When procurement officers saw other agencies placing orders with firms from which the Army withheld contracts, they became increasingly reluctant to give up reliable producers merely because other industries in the community needed workers or other communities needed the work. Furthermore, the Manpower Branch of the Civilian Personnel Division, ASF, insisted that it had neither the staff nor the information to review contracts and handle community protests intelligently. Faced with the choice of making decisions in individual cases or of expediting the placement of contracts, the Manpower Branch chose not to become a bottleneck.[34] Perhaps the greatest difficulty was the fact that manpower was only one of the elements to be considered in allocating war orders. Much of the procurement program dealt with specialized goods for the production of which special facilities were required. Once these facilities were constructed, war orders flowed into them as though by some inexorable law of physics. Aircraft contracts could not be fulfilled except at such centers as Seattle and San Diego. Ship-construction orders had to be placed where shipbuilding facilities existed, as at Norfolk and at Bath and Portland, Maine. It was impossi-

---

[33] Memo, Brig Gen Albert J. Browning for Prod Br AAF, 4 Jan 44, sub: Use of Group IV Labor Areas, AAF 004.06, Labor Conditions and Statistics, 1944; House Report 1553, 77th Congress, 1st Session, *National Defense Migration,* Second Interim Report, pp. 128–31; Memo, Maj A. E. Hewitt for Dir Purchases Div, 14 Jun 43, sub: WMC Proposal Relative to Subcontracting Policy . . . ASF IPD (L–ASF Pol Nec), Labor Supply and Proc; Memo, Maj Gen James A Ulio, 17 Aug 43, with attached Ltr, USW and Others to Prime Contractors . . ., 7 Aug 43, AAF 004.06, Labor Conditions.

[34] Ltr Mitchell to McNary, 29 Sep 43, ASF IPD; Kanwit, *op. cit.,* Sec. II; Memo, Rpts and Analysis Sec Manpower Br, CPD SOS, for Maloney, 26 Sep 42, sub: Letting of Contracts with Savery, Inc. . . ., and Memo, Somers for Maloney, 26 Sep 42, both in ASF IPD (L–ASF Pol Nec), Labor Supply and Proc.

ble to avoid placing orders in Bridgeport and other crowded cities of Connecticut for specialized items such as ball bearings. For the most part, work could be brought to the worker only when the contract involved commodities ordinarily consumed by civilians and manufactured by simple processes. The War Production Board and the Air Forces thus had legitimate grounds for complaint when orders for office forms and for easily manufactured incendiary bombs were placed in the Bridgeport area.[35] Instances of this sort, although infrequent, were facilitated by the loopholes provided by the recognition of factors other than labor supply. Contracting officers could place any orders in localities where manpower was most critical simply by asserting that established facilities existed there for which labor had been trained or that producers elsewhere could not meet the required speed of delivery.[36]

Toward the end of December 1942 the War Manpower Commission tried to plug up some of the loopholes. It proposed a board of review to pass on contracts placed in areas of labor shortage, which in reviewing the contracts would consider such matters as undue hardship, the unsuitability of workers for transfer, and whether the shortage of labor was sufficiently acute to justify barring contracts. The War Department considered the proposals an unwarranted interference with its procurement functions. Under Secretary Patterson, in a letter to Paul McNutt, pointed out that the War Production Board directive of 10 October 1942 gave the War Manpower Commission authority only to certify the facts and that it was the responsibility of the procurement agencies to place the contracts in the light of War Manpower Commission information as well as other relevant factors. "It is my feeling," Patterson concluded, "that the control of procurement by absolute directives with any factor paramount and conclusive, whether it be labor shortage or something else, is impracticable."[37] Donald Nelson, chairman of the War Production Board, upon whom Patterson had called for support, agreed with the basic position of the War Department that labor supply was only one factor governing procurement, that responsibility for awarding contracts rested with the contracting officer, and that speed of delivery was the

---

[35] Memo, AFDMA for Fairfield Air Depot, 26 Nov 43, and Memo, Volandt for CG ASF, 26 Aug 43, sub: Manpower Situation in Connecticut Valley, both in AAF 004.06, Labor Conditions.

[36] Procurement Regulations 205.3, 205.4, and 205.5 of 28 Nov 42.

[37] War Manpower Commission, Proposal for Amending the Procedures for Allocating Contracts According to Labor Supply Considerations, 22 Dec 42, and Ltr, Patterson to McNutt, 28 Dec 42, both in OUSW Miscellaneous and Subject, Contract (Re: Labor Supply); Memo, Patterson for Dorr, 23 Dec 42, and Memo, Amberg for USW, 23 Dec 42, sub: WMCs Proposed New Procedures . . ., both in OUSW, War Manpower Commission.

primary consideration.   The War Manpower Commission did not disagree, but it still insisted that no contracts should be made or renewed in "tight" labor areas if alternate facilities were available elsewhere, and it continued to urge that an interagency board of review and appeal be established.[38]

The War Department refused to concede that the War Manpower Commission had any authority over contract placement except that of laying down general policy.   In fact, one of Patterson's advisers insisted that the War Department did not have to follow "the directions of the Manpower Commission."   The chiefs of supply services were instructed to disregard instructions from the War Manpower Commission and to follow War Department procurement regulations.   Contracting officers were authorized to weigh all factors according to their best judgment, and no provision was made for clearance with or appeal to any external review board.[39]

With increasing frequency procurement officers used the very loophole the War Manpower Commission had attempted to plug.   An analysis of War Department contracts totaling $123,788,000 placed in the Buffalo district between 17 March and 15 November 1943 showed that contracts to the value of $121,000,000, or 97.7 percent, were placed in that particular locality because they required special machinery or specially trained labor.   Only a small amount of the total, to the value of $1,065,000, required no increase in labor, and the minute remainder was placed in the area for a variety of special reasons.[40]

The establishment of Area Production Urgency Committees in September 1943 promised closer control of contract placement.   These committees, originating from the west coast manpower crisis, were authorized to recommend adjustments in the military procurement program wherever labor shortages persisted, but results failed to meet the expectations of the War Production Board and War Manpower Commission officials.   The committees came to serve as hustings.   War Department representatives used them as forums for justifying contracts and generally managed to win approval

[38] Ltr, Patterson to Nelson, 28 Jan 42, Ltr, Nelson to Patterson, 6 Jan 43, Memo, Amberg for USW, 11 Jan 43, sub: WMCs Relation to Proc Policy, Ltr, Patterson to Nelson, 11 Jan 43, Memo, Amberg for USW, 13 Jan 43, sub: WMC Release of 4 Jan 43, and Ltr, Patterson to McNutt, 14 Jan 43, all in OUSW, Miscellaneous and Subject, Contract (Re: Labor Supply); Ltr, McNutt to Patterson, 8 Jan 43, OUSW, War Manpower Commission.

[39] Memo, William L. Marbury for TAG, 6 Jan 43, SPFDL–300.3, and Memo, Amberg for USW, 9 Jan 43, sub: WD Policy With Respect to Labor Shortage Areas, both in OUSW Miscellaneous and Subject, Contract (Re: Labor Supply); Memo, Amberg for USW 11 Feb 43, sub: WMC Circular . . ., OUSW, War Manpower Commission.

[40] Memo, Deputy Dir Purchases Div for Dir IPD, 17 Nov 43; other examples in AAF 004.06, Labor Conditions.

regardless of the labor supply situation.   Out of a total of 1,335 contracts
amounting to $2,221,436,500 submitted during the first four months of 1944,
the committees disallowed only 19 contracts amounting to $3,561,228, or
about .1 percent of the total amount.   Out of 682 contracts totaling
$313,000,000 submitted in October 1944, the committees rejected only 7 con-
tracts amounting to $1,454,600.[41]   By this time cutbacks and reconversion
problems were complicating the labor situation and further obscuring the
efforts that had been made to allocate orders in accordance with the labor
supply.

The statistical basis necessary for appraising the manpower program is
notoriously flimsy.   When, early in 1943, the War Manpower Commission
wished to analyze the effect of its revised policy, it could point to an increase in the proportion of War Department contracts placed in surplus
labor areas from 6 percent of the total dollar value in June and July 1942 to
27 percent in December.[42]   On the other hand, a commission report drawn
up a few months earlier showed that 43 percent of the dollar volume of 2,000
contracts, awarded during August and September 1942, for the procurement
of goods that permitted wide choice of suppliers, had gone to surplus labor
areas.[43]   Another measure of the program was the trend in the situation that
the program was designed to alleviate: the increase in the number of labor
shortages.   In December 1942 there were ninety-one areas that had a surplus of labor; at the end of the war there were twenty-five.   In March 1943
there were thirty-six localities that had a critical shortage of labor; in
November 1943 there were seventy-seven.[44]   But the standard by which
areas of labor shortage or surplus were defined was by no means constant
or exact.

A sweeping indictment of ASF and AAF procurement practices was made
in October 1944 by Col. Fred C. Foy, director of the ASF Purchases Division.   After a study of the way in which procurement officers were following the labor provisions of procurement regulations, Colonel Foy concluded
that "numerous" contracts were being placed in areas of labor shortage, that
efforts to avoid such areas were "incomplete," and that neither the War
Production Board nor the technical services had an adequate record of avail-

[41] Kanwit, *op. cit.,* Sec. II.
[42] Exec Committee WMC for WMC, 24 Mar 43 (Draft 3), sub: Effect of Amended Proc
Policy . . ., copy in OCMH.
[43] War Manpower Commission Report, 7 Nov 42, sub: Allocation of War Supply Contracts
According to Adequacy of Labor Supply, copy in OCMH.
[44] Federal Security Agency, Social Security Board, The Labor Market, December 1942, March
1943, November 1943, December 1944, and March 1945.

able facilities.   He criticized the services for their "competitive feeling," which led contracting officers to choose good suppliers in tight areas so as not to give an opening to another agency.   He further criticized the services for failing to take time to equip new facilities, for being concerned only with their own individual production, and for failing to control subcontracts in the areas of labor shortage.   Regulations designed to promote the placement of contracts in areas of surplus labor were offset, Foy charged, by pressure from price and production specialists in the services.   The Area Production Urgency Committees, according to Foy, served as a convenient "conscience" for contracting officers.[45]

Many individual cases can be cited in rebuttal.   Contracts for $20 million worth of parachute cloth were placed in labor surplus areas in the fall of 1942.   In the summer of 1943 Under Secretary Patterson ordered a reduction of procurement in the Seattle area for the purpose of saving the labor supply for bomber production and vital shipping activities.   Subcontracts for landing gear parts and other aircraft materials were shunted out of the area.   In Los Angeles the Air Forces terminated a glider contract in order to make labor available for higher-priority aircraft.   Clothing contracts were moved from Baltimore to protect the labor supply of shipbuilding and aircraft establishments.   Dayton and Akron, Ohio, lost contracts that would have required additional labor.   The Chemical Warfare Service terminated a contract for M50 bombs at Batavia, Illinois, and shell contracts were removed from the Armerican Car and Foundry plant at Buffalo which was behind on production of 14-inch Navy shells and 8-inch and 240-mm. Army shells.   The War and Navy Departments, as well as the War Production Board, surveyed the Louisville area to determine what work might be moved elsewhere so that labor would be available for expansion of the Indiana Ordnance Works, but before further action was taken the imminence of military victory made the expansion program unnecessary.[46]

The basic disagreement between critics and champions of the War Department's efforts was not, in the last analysis, on questions of fact but on the weight to be given the various elements that entered into the placing

[45] Memo, Foy for CG ASF, 5 Oct 44, summarized in Kanwit, *op. cit.,* Sec. II.

[46] Memo, Boland for O'Connell, 21 Nov 42, sub: Proc Policy—Labor Supply, ASF IPD (L–ASF Pol Nec), Labor Supply and Proc; Memo, Brig Gen A. E. Jones for Purchases Div, SOS, 28 Oct 42, sub: Placement of Contracts in Labor Shortage Areas, Ltr, Brig Gen B. E. Meyers to Senator Sheridan Downey, 27 Nov 43, Memo, USW for CG AAF, 28 Jun 43, sub: Reduction of WD Activities . . . Seattle Area, and Memo, O. P. Echols for USW, 21 Aug 44, sub: Reduction of WD Activities . . . in Seattle Area, all in AAF 004.06, Labor Conditions; Ltr, Maj Gen B. E. Meyers to Wade T. Childress, WPB, 29 May 44, AAF 004.06, Labor Conditions and Statistics, 1944; Kanwit, *op. cit.,* Sec. II.

of contracts.   No matter how closely the War Department, the War Manpower Commission, and the War Production Board agreed on what had
actually been done, on the basic question they were poles apart.   As long
as they differed on standards, it was futile to cite accomplishments, for progress cannot be measured when one of the observers counts milestones as
kilometer markers and another insists on counting them in parasangs.

Labor Supply and Cutbacks

The same labor problems that developed when facilities had to be
expanded or constructed and contracts awarded arose when the changing
demands of war made it necessary to reduce or cancel orders.   The same factors had to be considered in singling out specific contracts to be "cut back."
Labor supply, although generally considered second in importance only to
military requirements, was but one strand in a web.   To neglect it, however,
would produce unemployment, with a consequent drop in civilian morale
and in the efficient utilization of manpower.   It was, therefore, important
to make cutbacks as far as possible in areas where manpower was in short
supply and where displaced workers could easily get other jobs.

Although the problem received preliminary attention as early as October
1942, the first cutbacks involving large-scale release of workers and facilities
occurred in the spring of 1943, when the production of tanks and artillery
shells was reduced.   Some unemployment resulted in Terre Haute, Indiana,
and Carbondale, Illinois, and complaints that the "dislocation will be terrific" came from the United Steel Workers of America local at Berwick,
Pennsylvania.   "We are 9,000 employees at the American Car and Foundry
Co. Plant," the Berwick union informed Under Secretary Patterson.   "Orders
have been issued to lay off 3,000 of us . . . .   The scarcity of manpower in
other areas where tanks are being made prompts us to insist that a full
schedule of three shifts should be kept in force here where there is an excess
of manpower . . . ."[47]   President Philip Murray of the steelworkers' union
took up the cudgel and blamed poor planning on the part of the Procurement Division.   Under the pressure of criticism the cutback order was reversed and work was found for the Berwick plant.[48]   In actuality, the excess

[47] Telgm, R. C. Cashman, President Lodge 1864 United Steel Workers, to Patterson, 28 Feb
43, OUSW files.
[48] Statement of Philip Murray, Special Senate Committee Investigating the National Defense
Program, 78th Congress, 1st Session, Hearings on Senate Resolution 6, *Investigation of the National Defense Program,* Part 18, pp. 7285–86; Telgm, Mitchell to Cashman, 3 Mar 43, and Ltr,
United Steel Workers to Patterson, 10 Apr 44, both in OUSW files; Monthly Progress Reports,
Manpower, May–Jul 43, in ASF IPD, Monthly Progress Reports (1943–45).

of labor in Berwick was largely artificial.   The wartime expansion at the American Car and Foundry plant acted as a sponge, absorbing workers from surrounding farms, rural villages, and cities as far distant as Scranton.   As a result, the farming region around Berwick was unable to contribute its share to agricultural production.   Most of the workers who might have lost their jobs in Berwick at this time could have returned to their former pursuits, although at the lower agricultural income scale; some of them would possibly have added to the labor problem in Scranton and other upriver cities.

A more valid objection to the cutback in tank production was the complaint voiced not only by labor unions and the War Manpower Commission but also by employers and the Industrial Personnel Division, ASF, that they had been embarrassed by the lack of advance notice.   In order to soften the effect of sudden layoffs on the morale of the workers, the ASF on 11 May 1943 instructed the supply services and the Air Forces to notify the War Manpower Commission, management, and labor whenever a cutback was to be made.   Workers scheduled to be released were to be told about the impending layoffs and about the assistance the commission could give in finding other employment for them.   As far as security considerations permitted, they were to be informed of the reasons for the cutback.   The ASF directive did not spell out the important details of how and when the notification was to be made, and as a result it proved to be ineffective.   Security reasons and the suddenness with which cutbacks were often decided upon, on account of the exigencies of war, made it difficult to give notice in advance. Workers continued to be released without warning, and both the War Manpower Commission and the Industrial Personnel Division were in general notified after the layoffs took place.   Edmond Kanwit, an official of the Industrial Personnel Division at the time, later wrote that "by the time information reached this office it was ready for the Archives." [49]

The first major test of the ASF directive came in the fall of 1943 when the Ordnance Department closed six plants manufacturing small arms ammunition and made large reductions in force at a number of others.   In all, more than 35,000 workers were released.   Of the six plants that were shut down, two were in cities that already had a substantial surplus of labor and one was located where a slight surplus existed.   Both the War Manpower Commission and the Industrial Personnel Division again protested that they had not received adequate advance notice.   An IPD memorandum of mid-

[49] Kanwit, *op. cit.*, Sec. III, p. 7.   Kanwit's monograph provides an abundant source for details of cutback policies as seen by the Industrial Personnel Division.

November noted: "rumors have been rife for about a month that drastic reduction in the small arms ammunition program was imminent. Questions based upon these rumors have been repeatedly raised . . . [by] the War Manpower Commission and the War Production Board. Despite diligent inquiry, no definite information on cutbacks was made available to the Industrial Personnel Division until recently." [50] Further and specific complaint was made that IPD had not been officially informed about the closing of a small arms plant at Cumberland, Maryland, until three days after the news had appeared in Baltimore newspapers.[51] Unable to obtain timely and meaningful information from the field contracting officers of the technical services and the Air Forces, the Industrial Personnel Division found it impossible to discharge its own responsibility for the transmittal of such information to the War Manpower Commission.

At the urging of Mitchell, director of the Industrial Personnel Division, and partly in response to pressure from outside the War Department, the problem was lifted out of the realm of the procedural. Chiefly because of concern over the unemployment that might result from hasty, unplanned cutbacks, the Industrial Personnel Division proposed, in November 1943, that a War Department committee be established in the Under Secretary's office for the purpose of developing general policies and of reviewing the activities of the technical services and the Air Forces in cutting back production. General Clay, Director of Matériel, ASF, objected to the emphasis on unemployment at a time when a critical shortage of manpower appeared to be limiting production. Reverting to the particular, Mitchell then cited the difficulties that had arisen in connection with specific cutbacks, but Clay did not consider this a problem that could be solved "by committee action." The solution, as he saw it, was to make sure that the technical services kept the interested agencies informed of all contemplated major changes in labor requirements resulting from cutbacks. Directives to this effect were accordingly issued in late November and early December.[52]

The difficulty, though, was precisely that cutbacks had become an important issue in what Donald Nelson later called the "war within a war"— the controversy over reconversion. Reduced to its simplest terms, the issue

---

[50] Quoted in Kanwit, *op. cit.,* Sec III, p. 8.

[51] FSA, The Labor Market, Labor Supply Maps for Oct 43–44; History of Utah Ordnance, Vol. 101, p. 12, Ord Hist files.

[52] Kanwit, *op. cit.,* Sec. III, p. 10; TAG Ltr, 21 Oct 43, sub: Procedure for Reporting Information . . . on Cutback . . ., TAG Ltr, 13 Nov 43, same sub, and ASF Circular 129, 24 Nov 43, Prod Rescheduling Cutbacks, Shutdowns . . ., all in ASF Industrial Demobilization Div, Prod Advice Re Cutbacks; WD Circular 317, 7 Dec 43.

was at what point in the procurement process the specific allocation and timing of cutbacks should come under review and receive final approval. Should it be at the level of the technical services, the ASF, or the Joint Chiefs of Staff, or, should it be somewhere within the War Production Board machinery?

The War Production Board itself had been split over the extent to which the military agencies should control the scheduling of production changes. The group that insisted upon civilian control was likewise determined to obtain for the board complete responsibility for clearing cutbacks in order to use the facilities for immediate peacetime production. This group charged the Army with deliberately creating pools of unemployment for the purpose of forcing people into other war jobs, and it believed that "liberated" plants and workers should be immediately shifted to the production of coffee pots, radios, and refrigerators, or similar civilian goods.[53] On 16 December 1943 Bernard L. Gladieux, administrative assistant to the chairman of the War Production Board, proposed a plan that would have given a major role in arranging cutbacks to "the group that was at the time fostering the systematic planning of expanded nonmilitary programs, to which the Army was so violently objecting." [54] Less than a week later the Army Service Forces set up a board of review similar to that proposed by the Industrial Personnel Division a month before. Each of the technical services was directed, on 22 December, to establish a board consisting of not less than three officers of the rank of lieutenant colonel or higher for the purpose of reviewing and approving cutbacks that involved privately owned plants operating under government contracts. At the same time an ASF Headquarters Board of Review, consisting of the interested division directors, was established to review cutbacks in government-owned plants, and the technical services were instructed to notify the ASF Headquarters Board of Review of all major cutbacks in private plants.[55] The procedures recommended in November 1943 by the Industrial Personnel Division to untangle the snarled line of communications between ASF headquarters and field officers of the technical services were thus brought into being.

The results in practice were disappointing. After receiving notice from the Requirements Division, ASF, of changes made in production schedules

[53] Donald M. Nelson, *Arsenal of Democracy* (New York: Harcourt, Brace and Company, 1946), pp. 402–05; CPA, *Industrial Mobilization for War*, I, 734.

[54] CPA, *Industrial Mobilization for War*, I, 734.

[55] Memo, Maj Gen W. D. Styer for Chiefs Technical Svs, 22 Dec 43, and Memo, Clay for Dirs Prod Div, Industrial Demobilization Div, Requirements Div, and Readjustments Div, both in ASF Industrial Demobilization Div, Prod, Cutback Procedure and Policies.

by the Production Division, ASF, and after consulting with district offices, the technical services under the new procedures continued to recommend specific plants at which production was to be halted or cut back.   Field personnel of the technical services made the final decision if the recommended cutback was minor; if a major cutback was involved, the board of review of the appropriate technical service passed upon it.   If the plant was government-owned, the recommendation went to the ASF Headquarters Board of Review. No criteria were established in terms either of contract value or of workers involved that would make a cutback sufficiently large to bring it under the new procedures.   The technical services judged when cutbacks were important enough to warrant public announcement or notification to the ASF Review Board.   Even when the ASF Review Board received notice of large cutbacks in private plants, the notification frequently came, as it had in the past, after the cutback had been made.   In the opinion of some War Department labor officials the changes were largely without meaning.[56]

The Labor Branch of the Industrial Personnel Division sought to have the labor features of the procedures further modified and strengthened.   It tried to have the Air Forces brought into the arrangement.   It continued its efforts to get longer advance notice and to have a systematic procedure for notification established.   It attempted to set a definition of what constituted a "major" cutback.   In addition, the Labor Branch urged that greater attention be paid to public relations, a side of the problem that had sometimes been ineptly handled.   Finally, in an effort to give manpower officials a larger role in cutback procedures, the Labor Branch sought to have ASF labor officers appointed to the review boards of each of the technical services.[57]

Of the half dozen or so changes advocated by the Industrial Personnel Division in the early months of 1944, about half were put into effect.   Efforts of the IPD to obtain the appointment of labor officers to the technical services' review boards, to make the review of all cutbacks mandatory, and to obtain from seven to ten days' notice of cutbacks were unsuccessful.   On the other hand, the Air Forces, at Under Secretary Patterson's request, undertook to issue public announcements of cutbacks and to notify the interested agencies by procedures similar to those of the ASF.   No change was made toward co-ordinating the allocation of cutbacks, but steps were taken to improve the release of information to the press.   In a lengthy public statement

---

[56] Memo, 13 Mar 44, sub: ASF Procedures for Implementing Cutbacks in Prod, ASF Industrial Demobilization Div, Prod, Cutback Procedures and Policies; Summary of Meeting, Somervell's Staff Conference, 14 Mar 44, in Facilities Program of the Ammunition Div . . . High Explosives and Propellants, pp. 256–61, Ord Hist files.

[57] Kanwit, *op. cit.*, Sec. III, pp. 15–18, 22–24.

on 13 March 1944, Somervell described the methods of handling cutbacks and stressed the fact that they had not been as chaotic as news accounts had pictured them to be.

The major results of the Industrial Personnel Division's efforts appeared in ASF Circular 146, issued 19 May 1944. First, cutbacks involving a reduction of more than $3 million in deliveries in the three months following the cutback were made subject to review by the technical services' boards of review. As originally drafted, the circular provided for prior review by the ASF Headquarters Board of Review, but this requirement was dropped, and, as before, the only cutbacks that had to be submitted to the ASF Board of Review "prior to implementation" were those in government-owned plants. Second, the circular required contracting officers to notify all interested agencies simultaneously in the case of a cutback involving a three-month reduction of more than $200,000 in deliveries. An estimate of the number of workers to be released was required, and new standard notification forms were provided that included more information than the previous ones. In the third place, the technical services, although not required to justify allocations that were made on grounds other than the supply of labor, as the Industrial Personnel Division had suggested they should, were required to maintain a record of the reason for deciding on particular allocations.[58]

The halfway acceptance of the measures advocated by IPD can perhaps be explained by the developments that had been taking place in the realm of higher policy. A bitter factional conflict within the War Production Board had prompted Chairman Nelson to defer action on the Gladieux proposal of 16 December 1943. The Army promptly countered with an alternative that would have centered responsibility for handling cutbacks in the Production Executive Committee of the War Production Board, which had become the instrument by which the armed forces maintained control of policy with respect to their production programs. The Army and Navy representatives on the committee outnumbered the War Production Board representatives five to three. The chairman, Charles Wilson, represented the anti-Nelson faction within the board. Nelson's lack of enthusiasm for the Army's proposal is understandable. Following General Clay's presentation of the proposal, a committee consisting of Rear Adm. C. A. Jones, chief of the Production Branch of the Navy's Office of Procurement and Material, Stacy May, head of the War Production Board Bureau of Planning and Statistics, and Joseph A. Panuch, one of Clay's assistants, drew up, with Wilson's blessing, a detailed plan that gave greater representation to the War Produc-

[58] *Ibid.*

tion Board but permitted the armed services full authority to make the actual decisions with respect to the curtailment of production. Nelson was confronted with a dilemma, and the result was a stalemate that lasted until the end of May 1944.[59]

An unfortunately handled cutback of the Navy's fighter plane program forced Mr. Nelson to decide in favor of the Clay-Panuch proposals. The announcement on 22 May 1944 that Navy contracts with the Brewster Aircraft Company had been terminated raised considerable public criticism. The company had been given a week's notice, but no plans had been made to provide for the released workers, nine thousand of whom threatened to "sit in" until work was found for them. In spite of his objection to a plan that would leave the "promilitary" group of the War Production Board in control of cutbacks, Nelson on 25 May announced the creation of a Production Executive Committee Staff that would "inquire into" and "advise and recommend" on, matters pertaining to cutbacks. The Production Executive Committee Staff was to consist of representatives of the War Production Board, the War Manpower Commission, and the various procurement agencies. It was essentially what the Jones-May-Panuch committee had proposed three months earlier, but its functions were more limited. Since the Nelson directive was "notably vague" as to where authority actually resided, Director Byrnes of the Office of War Mobilization, on 5 June 1944, requested the War Production Board to adopt uniform policies for future cancellations of contracts which would insure reasonable notice to labor and management and to require the procurement agencies to "clear their proposed contract cutbacks and terminations with the Committee set up by you." Most important, the cutbacks and terminations were not to become effective until clearance had been obtained.[60]

From this time on, Byrnes was the chief architect of cutback policy. By an act of 3 October 1944, which converted the Office of War Mobilization into the Office of War Mobilization and Reconversion, his position was greatly strengthened by what has been called "probably . . . the broadest delegation of authority ever granted by Congress to an Executive agency."[61] The law specifically directed Byrnes to "determine whether any prime contract for war production, scheduled for termination, should be continued . . .

[59] CPA, *Industrial Mobilization for War*, I, 734–36; Millett, *The Organization and Role of the Army Service Forces*, pp. 227–28.

[60] The passages quoted are taken from CPA, *Industrial Mobilization for War*, I, 738. J. Carlyle Sitterson, *Development of the Reconversion Policies of the War Production Board, April 1943 to January 1945*, Civilian Production Administration Special Study 15 (1946), pp. 71–80; see also, Somers, *Presidential Agency*, pp. 196–97.

[61] Somers, *op. cit.*, p. 78.

[and] to establish policies to be followed by the contracting agencies in selecting individual contracts . . . for curtailment, nonrenewal, or termination. . . ." [62]   The War Production Board was the implementing agency.

Under the procedures worked out by the Production Executive Committee Staff, the procurement agencies furnished the War Production Board with advance notice of any cutback that would involve a reduction of $1 million or more in any one month of the next six.   "Modified information" respecting lesser cutbacks was again given to the board before final determination of the facilities to be cut back.   As detailed plans were worked out by the procurement agencies, information concerning the facilities involved, the labor area in which the facility was located, costs, past production, future requirements, capacities, and the selection of facilities to be retained or released was likewise reported to the War Production Board.   The Production Executive Committee Staff then reviewed the detailed plans and either gave them clearance or recommended changes.   When the staff did not unanimously agree, the matter went to the Production Executive Committee for final decision.   Thus the War Production Board, the War Manpower Commission, and the Smaller War Plants Corporation received notice of cutbacks before final notification was given to the contractor, and it was possible to make arrangements for the use of the facilities and manpower made available by the cutback.[63]   Certain criteria for selecting plants that were to be cut back were established.   Cutbacks were to be made "as much as possible in tight labor areas," with a view to protecting small plants, and in private plants that could readily convert to civilian production.   They were to be concentrated whenever possible in areas that would be subject to substantial reconversion after the war, and priority would be given to overloaded plants.[64]

The reconversion planning, the organizational structure, and the machinery that finally took shape were designed to serve a purpose of mammoth scope. In contrast, the actual cutbacks and reconversion that took place before the end of hostilities were lilliputian in size.   From June to December 1944, a total of 235 major cutbacks amounting to $1.65 billion were submitted to the War Production Board.   They involved the release of 138,711 employees, of whom 68,300 were in areas of acute labor shortage and 29,400 were in areas of labor "stringency."   They represented only a small fraction of the total war production.   Some of them were merely paper adjustments reduc-

---

[62] Quoted in *ibid.,* p. 79.

[63] Rpt, Dir War Mobilization to President, 7 Sep 44, quoted in Somers, *op. cit.,* pp. 197–98; CPA, *Industrial Mobilization for War,* I, 784–85.

[64] CPA, *Industrial Mobilization for War,* I, 786.

ing unattainable objectives to realistic goals.   After V–E Day there was a gradual rise in cutbacks, but again most of them were reductions in schedules for the future which did not affect current production.   Although cutbacks in the planned munitions schedules totaled about $16.5 billion from 1 April 1945 through 10 August, the actual reduction in deliveries in the four months from 1 April through July amounted to only $1.9 billion below the previously scheduled total.[65]

The mountain of planning and the time and effort consumed in devising procedures likewise brought forth only a mouse of actual achievement. According to War Production Board historians, "The great majority of proposed cutbacks were cleared without revision and in reality WPB action was with rare exceptions merely a formal clearance." [66]   Some of them were handled by procurement agencies as releases of planning schedules, which were not subject to the cutback procedures.   Many cutbacks were "nonoptional," because there were only one or two producers or because the entire output of a particular item was stopped.   There were relatively few in which the procurement agencies could exercise real choice.

During the war, procurement officials recognized that labor supply was an important factor in locating plants, placing supply orders, and cutting back contracts.   But in the case of facilities, by the time the importance of manpower became evident, the bulk of the program was already under way. Contract placement offered relatively less choice because at the peak of the production effort, when all facilities were used, the location of plants rather than the availability of labor determined the flow of work.   While procurement officials theoretically could use their discretion in cutbacks, production adjustments during the war were relatively unimportant.

Even where there had been a choice, procurement officials could not plan production according to a labor supply map.   There were too many other considerations.   Overemphasizing labor supply was placing the cart before the horse.   The paramount criterion at all times was producing and delivering supplies at the place and time they were needed.   In the long run, the balanced distribution of production according to the availability of labor was a vital element in producing for victory.   But it was only one among many elements.

With the coming of peace there was an immediate rush to halt military production and procurement.   Cutbacks were rapid and sweeping, in many cases complete, and the effect on the labor supply was tremendous.

[65] *Ibid.,* I, 786, 905.
[66] *Ibid.,* I, 888.

CHAPTER VII

The Army Makes a Frontal Attack

The year 1943 marked a change from the War Department's nebulous fear of a labor shortage to a feeling of distinct and immediate danger. Although at no time during World War II was there a general shortage of manpower in the sense that total demand exceeded the total nationwide supply, there were on occasion serious shortages in specific areas and specific plants. During 1943 these spot shortages became so widespread as to persuade the Industrial Personnel Division that the labor and manpower agencies of the government had failed to solve the manpower problem. It seemed necessary for the Army itself to make a frontal attack upon the problem. The Army thus became actively and directly involved in matters not only of contract placement according to available labor, but of industrial relations and labor supply as well. By point-blank attack on the problem the War Department tried to make sure that all available sources of labor were being used and that additional sources were tapped. The hop, skip, and jump approach gave way to a more systematic one.

The problem had already arisen where the Army was a direct employer of civilian labor—in arsenals, Quartermaster depots, Engineer construction projects, and the like—or where it had a measure of direct responsibility, as in the case of facilities that were government-owned and contractor-operated. The latter, which in the abbreviated terminology of the time came to be known as GOCO plants, were a unique product of the emergency expansion after 1940. Since almost all of them were Ordnance facilities engaged in such hazardous and classified operations as shell loading and the manufacture of high explosives, there was a security problem resembling that of the government arsenals as well as a similarity in manufacturing operations. Therefore, the Ordnance Department at first wanted the GOCO plants to be subject to the same labor policies as the arsenals, with the open shop and other limitations upon union activity. The Industrial Personnel Division objected strongly to the position taken by the Ordnance Department, and several months of argument and discussion followed. Toward the end of June 1942 a policy was finally worked out which, after receiving the approval of the CIO and the AFL, was promulgated jointly with the Navy Department on

29 July. The principle of collective bargaining and the right of employees to organize for this purpose were recognized. Discrimination in hiring on the basis of race, color, creed, or sex was prohibited. In the interest of security the Army retained the right to discharge an employee for suspicion of subversive activity or, in other security cases, to suspend the employee in question pending a formal hearing. All plant protective measures prescribed by the Army, including procedures for access to the plant, were to be binding upon management and employees. Any agreement between management and the employees that would restrict or hamper maximum production was prohibited. Finally, the War Department's contractual responsibility for approving all costs was pointed out, as well as the fact that this responsibility included the approval of proposed wage scales and of any subsequent wage adjustments.[1]

Although the contractor operating a GOCO plant was thus obliged to recruit and deal with labor in generally the same responsible fashion as a private employer, the War Department by reason of its contractual control over costs and in its own interest, as the owner of the facilities, retained the right to advise, guide, and directly assist the contractor in labor matters. The district offices of the Ordnance Department, for example, helped contractors establish grievance procedures, and, after the creation in the fall of 1942 of a War Department Wage Administration Agency, they helped contractors prepare requests for wage adjustments in order to insure favorable consideration by the wage agency. They lent counsel and assistance in such matters as training programs and the suppression of labor "pirates."[2] Possibly because of the aid received in processing requests for wage adjustments and certainly in spite of the difficulties the technical services had in establishing a field organization for labor matters, the GOCO plants throughout the war enjoyed notably smooth sailing in industrial relations.

When the War Department moved into the field of privately owned and operated plants, it discovered that the manpower battle had to be waged on many unexpected fronts. Before the battle was over it had been fought out in specific plants such as Boeing Aircraft in Seattle, over entire industrial areas such as Buffalo and Newark, and throughout whole industries whose products ranged from planes to cotton duck. It involved not only comparative

---

[1] Statement of Labor Policy, 22 June 1942, reproduced as Exhibit 30 in Office Chief of Ordnance Project Supporting Paper 59, Vol. II, Documents, Manpower and Its Utilization, Contractor and Ordnance Personnel, prepared by 1st Lt. Robert Dubin, June 1945.

[2] Office Chief of Ordnance Project Paper 59, Manpower and Its Utilization, prepared by William Voigt, Jr., July 1945, and Project Supporting Paper, Vol. I, June 1945; Hq ASF, Production and Manpower Bulletin 15, 19 Sep 44, OUSW 204.05, Prod Div ASF.

wages, working conditions, and the draft but also such seemingly incongruous factors as bus schedules, store hours in shopping centers, vitamin pills, and a host of others, any one of which could have meant defeat or victory. A "little" thing such as a child care center might release enough women to meet a labor need. Yet in arranging what on the surface appeared to be a simple matter, Army officers had to run the following obstacle course: the Federal Works Agency cleared funds for the center; the Federal Security Agency programmed the project; the Committee for Congested Areas co-ordinated the work; the War Production Board cleared material allocations; the U.S. Employment Service supplied the staff of the center; the War Manpower Commission determined manpower controls; the local school authorities ran the center; the Office of Defense Transportation provided school buses; and the Office of Price Administration controlled gasoline, tires, and the prices of items used. Numerous other agencies might have a word to say. If not disapproved or lost in this welter of agencies, child care centers could finally be built and mothers might then be able to work.[3]

Faced with these and similar problems in 1942 when it had become necessary to find workers for the transportation system in Seattle, for cotton growers in Arizona, and for the nonferrous mining industry, the Army had handled each task as a special project. Teams of officers had been organized, armed with authority to cut through red tape, and dispatched to the scene. Then, in the summer of 1943 when a manpower crisis developed in the aircraft industry on the west coast, the Army turned to the methods it had employed on these previous occasions and developed them into a standard technique.[4]

The Boeing Special Project Team

With the onset of the war the shipbuilding and aircraft industries along the Pacific coast had suddenly mushroomed, absorbing most of the available labor supply. By 1943 the shortage of workers in these two key industries was reflected in their failure to meet production schedules. Although both were affected, the aircraft industry was harder hit. Just when the U.S. Eighth Air Force was readying its bombers for a full-time pummeling of the enemy, aircraft production at home began to falter. In February 1943 the head of

---

[3] Lt. Col. Arthur Krim and Maj. Seymour Peyser, The Special Project Technique in the Handling of Critical Plan, Area and Industry Manpower Problems, ASF IPD Monograph 10, pp. 2–4, copy in OCMH.

[4] Memo, Col F. L. Furphy, Dir IPD, for CG ASF, 14 Jan 46, transmitting and attached to Krim and Peyser, *op. cit.*

the Boeing Aircraft Company warned President Roosevelt that the company's Seattle plant would not be able to meet production schedules in June or July unless drastic measures were taken to build up its labor force.   By June most of the other aircraft manufacturers were echoing the same warning, and Boeing had fallen behind schedule by thirty planes.[5]

The War Manpower Commission, which had been ordered by President Roosevelt to investigate the Boeing situation, rejected the company's complaints of a labor shortage and placed the blame on the management's personnel policies.   The executive director of the War Manpower Commission, Lawrence Appley, criticized the employment practices of the company as the cause of an excessive rate of turnover.   Further recruiting of workers for the Boeing plant would, he claimed, be nothing more than "pouring water down a rat hole."   He suggested that the appropriate remedy would not be a recruiting program but a labor utilization survey of the plant aimed at forestalling any further waste of manpower.[6]

The diagnosis made by the War Manpower Commission was at variance with the findings of the War Department, which had also investigated the situation.   The chief of the Labor Branch of the Ninth Service Command, who on instructions from the Industrial Personnel Division had conducted the investigation in Seattle, informed the IPD that a serious manpower problem existed and that the War Manpower Commission had little hope of being able to provide the necessary labor.   Conferences in Washington between representatives of the IPD, the AAF, the War Manpower Commission, and the Boeing Company confirmed the information received from the Ninth Service Command.   Although not absolving the Boeing Company of all blame, the IPD found fault with the commission for not taking the necessary action to prevent the decline in production.   The War Department decided that direct measures on its part were necessary.[7]

Under Secretary Patterson took the first step on 28 June 1943 when he ordered the commanding generals of the AAF and the ASF to withdraw all

---

[5] Krim and Peyser, *op. cit.,* p. 8; AAF Technical Sv Comd, History of AAF Activities During World War II in the Field of Industrial Manpower, *passim;* U.S. Bureau of Labor Statistics Bulletin 800, *Wartime Development of the Aircraft Industry,* by Leonard G. Levenson (Washington: Government Printing Office, 1944), *passim.*

[6] Krim and Peyser, *op. cit.,* Exhibit A, Ltr, P. G. Johnson, President Boeing Aircraft, to Maj Gen O. P. Echols, ACofAS, 22 May 43, and Exhibit B, Chronology, Summary of a Meeting, 18 Jun 43; Memo, Capt Ingles for Volandt, 18 Jun 43, sub: Labor Supply Difficulties at Boeing Aircraft, and Memo, Lt Col Belknap for Volandt, 27 Jun 43, sub: Boeing Aircraft, both in AAF, AAF Industrial Manning Board.

[7] Krim and Peyser, *op. cit.,* Exhibit A, Memo, Echols for USW, 28 May 43, Exhibit B, Chronology, and Exhibit D, Memo, Lt Col John Collins and Captain Arthur Krim for Mitchell.

contracts possible from the Seattle area and to place no further contracts requiring additional labor without prior approval of the Industrial Personnel Division. During July the ASF accordingly terminated sixteen contracts, releasing about 2,000 workmen. The dispersal of subcontracts outside the critical area was encouraged, with the result that in September the Boeing Company placed subcontracts for approximately 40 percent of its work and made plans to let out subcontracts for an additional 20 percent. The aim was to reduce the competition for workmen in the area.[8] The withdrawal of contracts and dispersal of subcontracts gave rise, however, to widespread community protests.

The complaints of manufacturers and local congressmen, who objected vociferously to taking work out of the area, could not be treated lightly. Contracting agencies of the War Department disliked to tamper with contract placements in order to release manpower, and, although they co-operated in the program, they did so without enthusiasm. They objected to it particularly because essential work, which was subject to control, could be removed, while nonessential work, which was not under control, remained and continued to operate in an expanding labor market. Among officials of the War Department the conviction was held that the cancellation of contracts should be a measure of last resort. It was, according to Assistant Secretary McCloy, a wasteful practice, one that interfered with essential procurement, caused delays in deliveries, worked severe hardship on the contractors, and all in all was one of the least effective methods of alleviating labor shortages. Nevertheless, the Seattle program had several beneficial results. Local business organized, and the community, faced with economic loss, co-operated in an attempt to find the necessary labor. A few released workers found their way into the critical industries.[9]

The mission of reducing the competition for labor in the Seattle area—of spearheading the drive to disperse contracts—had been entrusted to a team of two officers, Lt. Col. John Collins and Capt. Arthur Krim, who arrived in Seattle on 9 August. Conferring with Boeing officials, they made it clear that their job was to expedite, not investigate. They explained that their "first effort, after isolating the problems, would be to see whether the local

---

[8] Memo, O'Gara for Volandt, 17 Jul 43, sub: Boeing Aircraft Co., Memo, Ohly for Files, 11 Aug 43, same sub, and Memo, O'Gara for Dir IPD, 17 Aug 43, sub: Seattle Removal of Contracts, all in ASF IPD, Seattle Special Project; Ltr, McCloy to Byrnes, 9 Sep 43, ASF IPD, Boeing; Notes on West Coast Manpower Program, and Ltr, Col Harmon to CofOrd, 27 Mar 44, sub: Industrial Manpower on Pacific Coast, both in ASF IPD, West Coast Manpower Program; Krim and Peyser, *op. cit.,* Exhibit C, Memo, USW for CGs ASF and AAF 28 Jun 43.

[9] Ltr, USW to Nelson, 17 Aug 43, Ltr, Rear Adm Land to USW, 11 Aug 43, Ltr, USW to Asst Secy Navy, 22 Jul 43, and Ltr, McCloy to Byrnes, 9 Sep 43, all in ASF IPD, Boeing.

civilian and War Department agencies could take the necessary action." If such action were hindered by any obstacles "arising from channels or lack of authority or otherwise," they would immediately communicate with Washington, they informed the company officials, and have instructions issued to the local agencies without delay, "thus eliminating all red tape and attaining the desired objectives forthwith." [10]   The Boeing people were beginning to be exasperated at the frequent investigations that had been made without tangible result and were ready to welcome the new team with open arms provided the two officers were actually there to do the job they outlined.   Placing all its facilities at their disposal, the company promised complete co-operation.

In addition to the goal of cutting competition for labor, the Boeing Special Project Team tried to recruit as many new workers as it could and, probably most important, attempted to reduce turnover among the Boeing employees.   The question whether additional workmen were needed continued to be a matter of controversy.   The Army blamed the War Manpower Commission for the small trickle of labor into the aircraft plants; the commission placed the blame on low wages, on the high priority assigned to shipyards, and on bad personnel policies on the part of the company; Boeing, in turn, blamed subversives.   War Manpower Commission representatives continued to insist that it was a waste of manpower to recruit additional workers.   The U.S. Employment Service in Seattle claimed that it had recruited 29,000 workers for Boeing in the twenty-six months after January 1941 and that the available labor force was squeezed dry.   When the Special Project Team arrived, Boeing still needed 2,300 employees and would need an additional 8,500 within three months.[11]

Maintaining contact with the head of the War Manpower Commission in Washington, both directly and through the Industrial Personnel Division, the Boeing Special Project Team obtained authorization to recruit workers from four regions outside the Seattle area.   Actual recruiting measures were, however, delayed by the commission for several weeks.   Two of the regional directors persistently refused to advertise for workers for the Seattle area on the ground that such advertising would create shortages in their areas.   Finally, a program of regional quotas was devised.   The War Manpower

---

[10] Krim and Peyser, *op. cit.,* Exhibit D, Memo, Collins and Krim for Mitchell.

[11] Memo, Ohly for O'Gara, 14 Aug 43, sub: Boeing Aircraft, Memo, Collins for O'Gara, 6 Jul 43, Memo, Greenbaum for ACofS G–2, 19 Jul 43, sub: Alleged Subversive Activities, Ltr, Mitchell to Johnson, 22 Jul 43, and War Industries, Seattle-Bremerton Labor Market Area, all in ASF IPD, Seattle Special Project; Memo, Ingles for Volandt, 18 Jun 43, sub: Labor Supply Difficulties at Boeing, and Memo, Belknap for Volandt, 27 Jun 43, both in AAF, AAF Industrial Manning Board; Recruitment and retention of Personnel, Boeing Aircraft, WMC, Seattle, Wash.

Commission guaranteed to bring in 850 workers per week for a six-week period beginning on 7 September. If this quota were not met, advertisements for workers would be permitted outside the Seattle area. With the assistance of Colonel Collins and Captain Krim, the Boeing Company organized thirteen recruiting teams, which were sent out to enroll workers from regions other than the west coast. As an inducement to prospective employees, free transportation to Seattle was provided, and the company agreed to advance approximately ninety dollars to each recruit for subsistence en route and for subsistence and housing for three weeks after his arrival in Seattle. It was agreed that the Army would reimburse the company for the transportation allowance and for any losses incurred from making the advances against pay.[12]

The recruiting program would have been entirely fruitless if a wage adjustment had not also been made. The starting pay at the Seattle aircraft plants was sixty-seven and a half cents per hour; at the shipyards, which were competing for workers, the starting pay was ninety-five cents per hour. The average beginning rate, other than in the aircraft plants and shipyards, was eighty-eight and a half cents per hour. Furthermore, the Boeing Company had been upgrading workers slowly and had been paying a shift differential that was insufficient to attract workers to the 4:00 P.M. to midnight swing shift. After meeting with representatives of the company and the union and after discussions with the local National War Labor Board representative, the Army Special Project Team succeeded in obtaining assurances that the board would bypass normal channels and make an immediate disposition of the wage problem. At the recommendation of the War Department, the board in record time established a new starting wage of eighty-two and a half cents per hour. Although the wage increase did not bring the Boeing plant up to the level of its competitors in the labor market, it went far toward ameliorating conditions, spurred the recruiting program, and helped to hold workers once they were recruited.[13]

The rapid rate of turnover in the working force that plagued the Boeing Company, as well as all the other west coast aircraft plants, was a problem fully as urgent as and even more complicated than that of recruitment. There were many reasons why workers had to leave or chose to leave their

[12] Krim and Peyser *op. cit.*, Exhibit D, Memo, Collins and Krim for Mitchell.

[13] Interview, Boeing Aircraft Co., 4 Aug 43, Manpower Problems in West Coast Aircraft Industry, Ltr, AFL Labor Representative in Seattle to Chairman XII Region WLB, Aug 43, and Rpt, Krim, 13 Aug 43, all in ASF IPD, Seattle Special Project; Ltr, Senator Homer P. Bone to Patterson, 11 Aug 43, and reply, Lovett to Bone, 20 Aug 43, Memo, Ohly for Files, 28 Aug 43, sub: Seattle, Memo, Sufrin for Files, 1 Aug [Sep] 43, sub: Meeting With WLB Re Boeing, 30 Aug 43, and WLB Case 557, 4 Sep 43, Boeing Aircraft Co. and IAM Aeronautical Mechanics Lodge 751, copies of all in OCMH, West Coast.

jobs. In attempting to reduce the rate of turnover and absenteeism, the Boeing Special Project Team found itself involved in a variety of activities ranging from child care to the working of the Selective Service System.

The steady drain of men and women into the armed services was one of the factors least susceptible to remedial action. Thousands of Boeing employees who might have contributed more to the war effort by building airplanes enlisted or presented themselves for voluntary induction. Working at cross-purposes, recruiting officers played their part in upsetting the labor market by continuing to urge workers to join the armed forces. In this respect, Air Forces and Women's Army Corps (WAC) recruiting officers were particularly active. Although the Special Project Team managed to halt a WAC recruiting drive in the Boeing area, the situation became so bad that Under Secretary Patterson finally asked for a cessation of Army recruiting on the west coast and appealed to the Secretary of the Navy to follow his example. It was more difficult to soften the impact of the draft, for the Selective Service System was firmly entrenched in an autonomous position. Furthermore, in the fall of 1943, the Army was faced with a breakdown in its combat replacement system. In response to the rapidly mounting demands of the overseas theaters, especially for infantrymen, the Army was making severe economies and putting pressure on the Selective Service System to meet the monthly draft quotas. At the same time the Army, as the chief procurement agency, could not permit a breakdown in production schedules as a result of its demands on Selective Service. A temporary two-month stay of induction for aircraft workers, which had been granted at the request of the War Manpower Commission, was not adequate, according to the War Department, although it did alleviate the situation in Seattle. The War Department urged a six-month blanket deferment, and at the end of October the Office of War Mobilization announced that west coast aircraft workers who were certified as irreplaceable by the Army or Navy plant representatives would be deferred for a period of six months. By this time the Boeing manpower crisis had passed.[14]

[14] Memo, Mitchell for Dir WAC, 3 Aug 43, sub: WAC Recruitment Practices, ASF IPD, Seattle Special Project; Excerpt, Ltr, Richard, 18 Aug 43, and Memo, Mitchell for USW, 20 Oct 43, copies of both in OCMH, West Coast; AAF Technical Sv Comd, History of AAF Activities During World War II in the Field of Industrial Manpower, pp. 114–21; Memo, Dorr for Arnold, 18 Dec 42, sub: Discussion at War Council of Loss of Key Pers in Aircraft Industry, AAF 004.07, Labor Disputes and Strikes, Miscellaneous, 1943–44; Press Release, OWI, 24 Nov 43, and Ltr, Stimson and Knox to Workers in Essential War Industries, ASF IPD, Labor Manual 1942; Telgm, Lee to Woodhead, 9 Aug 43, in OUSW Hertz files, Gen; Memo, Hertz for USW, Draft Memo, Patterson for ACofS G–1, sub; Abolition of Recruiting Activities in Aircraft Plants, and Memo, Patterson for Under Secy Navy, all in OUSW Hertz files, Memos to Patterson and Hancock; Somers, *Presidential Agency*, pp. 162–63.

A greater number of workers left their jobs because of dissatisfaction over housing, working conditions, transportation facilities, and the like. Immediately after arriving in Seattle, Collins and Krim had called a meeting of all local agencies concerned with housing. The Boeing Special Project Team learned that housing for Boeing workers had been built, but that from four to six months would be required to obtain furniture and equipment. Within the space of three days, the team made arrangements for the immediate shipment of furniture, obtained blankets, linens, and pillows from Quartermaster stocks in Seattle, persuaded the local Building Trades Union to relax restrictions to permit completion of two reception centers within a week, arranged with local authorities for a round-the-clock reception service for incoming workers, obtained housing priorities for incoming Boeing workers, and obtained clearance for a housing project for Negro workers that had been pending for six months. The team attacked the transportation problem with equal energy. It arranged for higher priorities to be assigned to the new equipment ordered by the Seattle transportation company for use on the Boeing route. An express service was established and schedules were readjusted to reduce overcrowding. The team found also that the employment of women who had children to care for was impeded by inadequate nursery and playground facilities and by a daily fee of fifty cents per child charged for the use of the community facilities. Clearance was immediately obtained for an expansion program on which no action had been taken for some time, and an unprecedented arrangement was worked out by which the child-care fees of its employees were paid by the Boeing Company and were accepted as a reimbursable expenditure by the Army. Steps were taken to improve eating facilities in the plant, described by Collins and Krim as "abominable," and, at the urging of the Army representatives, measures were also put into effect to reduce the noise in one of the important shops. The net result, it was hoped, would be to reduce employee turnover.[15]

Labor relations were a more delicate problem. The Army Special Project Team took the view that relations between the company and its employees were "extremely bad" and that this situation was "the heart" of the company's manpower shortage. This analysis, it should be noted, was not too dissimilar from the view taken earlier by the War Manpower Commission, a view for which the commission had been criticized by the Army. The team found that the company's representative on the grievance board was "an obvious labor baiter (even though he had previously come from the

---

[15] Krim and Peyser, *op. cit.,* Exhibit D, Memo, Collins and Krim for Mitchell.

ranks of the union)," and at the urging of the team he was assigned to other work. Whenever employees committed a minor infraction of the rules, the company handed out written slips—such as, "You were caught washing your hands before closing time. For your own good, don't do this again. This is your first warning." The practice created resentment and contempt for the company, which, at the request of the Army representatives, discontinued it. The team further persuaded the company to agree to employ a labor relations executive, responsible directly to the president of the company and with full authority to establish the labor policies of the company. The importance of aircraft production and of setting aside old antagonisms toward the company was explained to the union by the team at great length and with some success. The bitter attacks against the management and the other inflammatory material that had characterized the union newspaper disappeared and were replaced by appeals for increased production.[16] In the community at large there had been a long history of ill will toward the Boeing Company. Public newspapers had added fuel to the union's criticism with stories portraying the company's poorer features. In an attempt to improve public feeling, the Army Special Project Team held meetings with the Chamber of Commerce, the Flying Fortress Committee, manufacturers' associations, and other civic groups. Advertisements emphasizing the importance of aircraft production were inserted in the newspapers and more favorable news stories about the Boeing plant began to appear. Special morale-building programs, including a large Army show, were planned in the community as well as in the plant itself.[17]

The team acted promptly. Collins and Krim did not have to worry about channels of authority. They prodded local and regional agencies into action and kept in constant touch with Washington, where one representative of the Industrial Personnel Division received all their calls. Immedi-

---

[16] *Ibid.;* see also, Memo, Ohly for Files, 8 Sep 43, sub: Boeing Developments, and Memo, Ohly for Files, 20 Aug 43, sub: Seattle Rpt of Mitchell and Brown, copies of both in OCMH, West Coast; Ltr, Harvey Brown, Former President of IAM, to Maj Leonard O. Friesz, 16 Mar 52, OCMH.

[17] Ltr, Business Representative Aeronautical Mechanics Lodge 751, 27 Mar 42, in App. to Recruitment and Retention of Personnel, Boeing Aircraft, WMC, Seattle, Wash.; Editorial, Seattle *Post Intelligencer,* September 28, 1943; Advertisement, Flying Fortress Committee, in Seattle *Times,* August 8, 1943; Memo, Collins for O'Gara, 6 Jul 43, sub: Boeing Aircraft Co., Memo, Ohly for O'Gara, 28 Aug 43, sub: Industrial Sv Div, Memo, Ohly for Files, 3 Sep 43, sub: Seattle, Boeing, Proposed Morale Program, and Memo, Chairman Program Br for Gow, 20 Aug 43, sub: Boeing Aircraft Co., all in ASF IPD, Seattle Special Project; Memo, Lt Col William J. Brennan, Jr., and Krim for McPhail, 10 Dec 43, sub: Community Program Related to Solution of Manpower, ASF IPD, West Coast Aircraft Rpts.

ately after a call, the IPD representative, in Patterson's name, advised other agencies and other persons in the War Department what they should do. Everything, down to lumber for Seattle housing, was tied in with Eighth Air Force bombing. "The wraps were off" and speed became the motto.

The immediate gains seemed high, but there were offsetting factors that could be cited. President P. G. Johnson of the Boeing Company praised the work of the War Department team. Employment rose after the first of September and production began to improve. Nevertheless, during the four-week period ending 2 October, only half the number of new workers promised by the War Manpower Commission actually arrived at the Boeing plant. By then, the demand seemed less acute and the plans for recruiting workers outside the west coast region were dropped. And, although Boeing's production in November exceeded all previous monthly figures, the company nevertheless failed to meet its original quota. The Special Project Team had brought workers to Seattle, but the problem was only temporarily eased. A year later the War Department again had to investigate a manpower shortage in Seattle.[18]

The West Coast Labor Problem

The arrival of the Boeing Special Project Team in Seattle coincided with an attack on the manpower situation at all the west coast aircraft plants. Prompted by indications that only 80,000 planes out of a total of 95,000 scheduled would be built in 1943 and convinced that the chief cause was the labor shortage, Under Secretary Patterson had ordered a complete investigation.[19]

The biggest difficulty, according to the National Aircraft War Production Council, Incorporated, was labor turnover, of which the Boeing situation was perhaps an extreme, but certainly not an isolated, case. In December 1943

---

[18] Ltr, Mitchell to Brockway, 8 Oct 43, and correspondence attached, Memo, Maj Kapp for Hertz, 4 Oct 43, Memo, Ohly for Files, sub: Seattle, Boeing Developments, and Memo, Hertz for USW, 9 Sep 43, copies of all in OCMH, West Coast; Manpower Data From West Coast, 14 Oct 43, prepared for Hertz, OUSW Hertz files, Aircraft War Prod Council; Press Release, Boeing, 2 Dec 43, in ASF IPD, Seattle Special Project; Memo, Patterson for SW, 13 Oct 43, sub: Rpt of Special Meeting at OWM, and Memo, Lovett for SW, sub: West Coast Manpower Discussion, 10 Oct 43, Stimson files, Manpower; ASF IPD, Industrial Visits, *passim;* Rpt, Boeing, Quarterly Rpt West Coast Manpower Program, Dec 43, and Ltr, Krim to Collins, 28 Dec 43, copies of all in OCMH, West Coast.

[19] Memo, Patterson, 11 Aug 43, sub: Aircraft Prod, OUSW Hertz files, Manpower Problems. For a study of aircraft production problems, see Tom Lilley *et al., Problems of Accelerating Aircraft Production During World War II* (Cambridge, Mass.: Harvard Graduate School of Business Administration, 1946), *passim.*

TABLE 1—PERCENTAGE OF JOB TERMINATIONS IN PACIFIC COAST AIRCRAFT PLANTS BY CAUSE FOR MEN AND WOMEN: JANUARY–JUNE 1943

Cause	Men	Women
Total	100.0	100.0
Military	26.3	1.4
Mandatory	17.9	0
Voluntary	8.4	1.4
Health	4.6	9.4
Working conditions	27.3	20.8
Living conditions	3.1	4.2
Personal affairs	30.7	57.8
Dismissals	8.0	6.4

the manager of the council sent a newsletter to the director of the Industrial Personnel Division in which the problem was set forth as follows:

Twenty thousand—count 'em—workers leave their jobs in the aircraft plants every month. . . .

How serious is this Turnover problem? Manhours lost in the past 11 months by Turnover are equivalent to production of 2,035 Flying Fortresses. . . .

Way to shorten war, cut casualty lists: Bomb the smithereens out of Turnover.

Cut Turnover by 50 percent, and most of the aircraft industry's manpower problem would be solved.[20]

The council bemoaned the short length of time workers remained at their jobs—45.51 percent of the women and 39.49 percent of the men turned in their badges without working a full year.[21] The causes of turnover varied among men and women workers. (*Table 1*) For the men, the three most important reasons for leaving a job—personal affairs, working conditions, and military service—were of almost equal weight. For women, personal affairs loomed almost twice as large as any other cause. Each of these classi-

---

[20] Newsletter, Gen Manager National Aircraft War Prod Council, Inc., to Mitchell, 10 Dec 43, ASF IPD, Aircraft War Prod Council.

[21] News Memo, National Aircraft War Prod Council, Inc., 31 Dec 43, ASF IPD, Aircraft War Prod Council; Extracts From Aircraft Manufacturers February 1943 Trouble Charts, 15 Mar 43, AAF 004.06, Labor Conditions; Memo, Vanaman for CG Matériel Command AAF, sub: Supplement to 16 Dec 42 Rpt entitled Mil Separations and the Trend of Female Employment . . ., AAF 00–a–Miscellaneous, 1942–44. See also reports on the San Diego area and San Francisco area by the subcommittee of the House Naval Affairs Committee appointed to investigate in critical war production areas, dated 3 and 17 May 1943, OUSW Hertz files, Committee on Congested War Prod Areas; Ltr, Victor Emanuel to Hertz, 27 Jul 43, and attachments, OUSW Hertz files, Manpower Problems; Hertz Survey.

TABLE 2—MONTHLY LABOR TURNOVER RATE PER 100 EMPLOYEES IN AIRCRAFT, MUNITIONS, AND NONMUNITIONS INDUSTRIES: 1943–44

Month	Aircraft [a]			Munitions [b]			Nonmunitions [c]		
	Separation Rate		Accession Rate	Separation Rate		Accession Rate	Separation Rate		Accession Rate
	Total	Quit		Total	Quit		Total	Quit	
1943									
January	6.1	3.9	10.3	6.5	3.9	8.7	8.2	5.3	8.2
February	5.9	3.7	9.0	6.2	3.8	7.9	8.3	6.0	8.2
March	6.8	4.8	8.6	7.0	4.6	8.6	9.0	6.7	8.3
April	6.2	4.6	7.3	6.5	4.4	7.4	9.0	6.9	7.6
May	5.6	4.2	7.3	6.0	4.1	7.0	7.6	5.9	7.6
June	6.0	4.6	8.5	6.4	4.4	8.2	8.2	6.4	8.9
July	6.7	5.2	8.3	7.0	4.9	7.6	8.5	6.7	8.3
August	7.1	5.7	7.5	7.6	5.5	7.4	9.1	7.4	8.1
September	7.1	5.6	8.1	7.6	5.4	7.6	9.3	7.7	8.1
October	6.5	4.9	7.6	6.6	4.5	6.7	7.9	6.3	8.0
November	5.9	4.2	6.3	6.0	3.9	6.0	6.9	5.3	7.7
December	5.7	3.9	3.9	6.2	3.8	4.6	7.2	5.4	6.2
1944									
January	6.2	4.3	5.3	6.3	4.0	5.8	7.3	5.6	7.5
February	5.6	3.9	4.2	6.1	3.9	5.0	7.3	5.7	6.2
March	7.0	4.6	4.0	7.0	4.3	5.2	8.0	6.2	6.6
April	6.2	4.3	3.7	6.3	4.2	5.0	7.6	6.1	6.3
May	6.7	4.6	4.7	6.6	4.5	5.6	8.1	6.7	7.5
June	7.9	5.3	5.7	6.8	4.7	6.6	7.9	6.8	9.2
July	6.6	4.8	5.3	6.1	4.3	5.6	7.2	6.1	7.3
August	8.5	6.1	4.9	7.4	5.4	5.6	8.8	7.6	7.2
September	8.3	6.0	4.8	7.4	5.4	5.3	8.4	7.3	7.1
October	6.2	4.8	4.8	6.3	4.5	5.4	7.0	6.0	6.8
November	5.6	4.2	5.2	5.7	4.0	5.4	6.8	5.7	7.0
December	4.5	3.5	4.5	5.2	3.6	4.6	6.5	5.3	5.7

[a] Includes establishments primarily engaged in manufacturing airplanes, dirigibles, gliders, balloons, and parachutes.

[b] Includes the following major industry groups: ordnance, iron and steel and their products; electrical machinery; machinery, except electrical; transportation equipment, except automobiles; nonferrous metals and their products; chemicals and allied products; products of petroleum and coal; rubber products.

[c] Includes the following groups: lumber and timber basic products; furniture and finished lumber products; stone, clay, and glass products; textile mill products; apparel and other finished textile products; leather and leather products; food and kindred products; tobacco manufactures; paper and allied products; miscellaneous industries.

Source: Monthly Labor Turnover Rates, Aircraft, Social Security Board Industry 3421, Bureau of Labor Statistics, Dept of Labor; reprint of article from the *Monthly Labor Review*, July 1945, "Labor Turnover in Munitions and Nonmunitions Industries, 1943 and 1944," Serial No. R 1757, p. 5.

fications of causes in itself was a multiple of an almost infinite number of subclassifications. Labor turnover was not one problem but a complex of problems, and to meet it a multipronged attack would be necessary.

The problem of labor turnover in the aircraft industry was not much greater than that in other industries. (*Table 2*) At the time, there was more pressure for aircraft production than for most other items, and consequently the problems of the aircraft industry attracted more attention.

Another aspect of the west coast manpower shortage was the almost equally complicated problem of production schedules. An unattainably high schedule would obviously create all kinds of problems. Some experts believed that the shortage of manpower was never really acute but only appeared to be menacing because of unfeasible schedules.

Col. William S. Volandt, who played a leading role in all attacks on manpower problems of the Army Air Forces, was dubious about the aircraft schedules and doubted strongly whether the manpower shortage on the west coast was really as acute as claimed. He cited as an example the old Army legend of the cavalry commander who, when he had to order horseshoes for his unit, had always asked for the exact number he needed and had each time received 50 percent less than his order. Finally, he decided that he would order many more than he needed in the hope that he would get enough. For the first time he got what was ordered, and the oversupply was embarrassing. Colonel Volandt believed that the large production schedules as well as the enormous demands for manpower might be the result of a supply-sergeant attitude of ordering more than was needed.[22]

Production schedules assigned to west coast aircraft plants for the first quarter of 1943 had been based on figures accepted by the Joint Chiefs of Staff and approved by the President in October 1942. The goal of 107,000 planes of all types set for the entire industry for 1943 was soon recognized as unrealistic, even by General Arnold and members of the Air Staff, but the AAF consistently opposed any attempt to whittle it down.[23] By the end of March 1943, production was far enough behind schedule to induce the War Production Board to recommend lowering the objective. The board estimated that total production for the year would be approximately 90,000

---

[22] Interview, Grossman with Volandt, 4 Apr 52, OCMH; Notes on West Coast Manpower Problem [probably by Col Witten], ASF IPD, West Coast Manpower Program; Memo, Dorr for USW, 5 Aug 43, sub: Comparison of Manpower Data, OUSW Hertz files, Gen.

[23] For an account of the debate over production schedules, see Wesley Frank Craven and James Lea Cate (eds.), *The Army Air Forces in World War II,* Vol. VI, *Men and Planes* (Chicago: The University of Chicago Press, 1955), pp. 274–87, Leighton and Coakley, *Global Logistics and Strategy: 1940–1943,* Chs. VIII, XXII, and CPA, *Industrial Mobilization for War,* I, 605.

TABLE 3—SCHEDULES OF PRODUCTION AND ACTUAL PRODUCTION OF B-17's (FLYING FORTRESSES) AT BOEING AIRCRAFT COMPANY, SEATTLE AND RENTON

Schedule	1943												1944					
	Jan	Feb	Mar	Apr	May	Jun	Jul	Aug	Sep	Oct	Nov	Dec	Jan	Feb	Mar	Apr	May	Jun
W5, 1 July 1943							240	250	260	270	270	270	270	270	270	270	270	270
W6, 12 August 1943								210	220	230	240	250	260	270	270	270	270	270
W7, 16 September 1943									200	(a)	(a)	(a)	(a)	(a)	(a)	(a)	(a)	(a)
W8, 1 October 1943										205	210	215	220	225	230	235	240	240
W9, 1 January 1944													270	270	270	270	258	258
Actual production	124	176	180	190	200	190	200	190	200	210	230	250	270	290	362	270	300	300

a Not shown on W7.

Source: W schedules in the National Archives; actual production figures from Civilian Production Administration, *Official Munitions Production of the United States By Months, July 1, 1940–August 31, 1945* (1947). p. 34.

planes, 17,000 short of the goal.   Although the Joint Chiefs of Staff refused
to approve a reduction in the official figures, the War Production Board
lowered its working schedules until in June the objective for the year had
been dropped to 95,000 planes.   When production failed to keep pace with
the revised schedule, Under Secretary Patterson, it has already been noted,
decided to investigate the manpower situation on the west coast.   That the
Boeing manpower shortage may have appeared more acute in the light of
these production schedules than it was in fact is suggested by Table 3.   By
the same token the rise in actual production after September, when the
Boeing labor problem began to ease, suggests that in the summer of 1943
the need for workers was real.

Regardless of production schedules, Patterson believed that the critical
industries on the west coast should be permitted to recruit workers from less
essential industries and that a full-fledged publicity campaign, incentive
wages, and ten-hour shifts would drive home the need for aircraft workers
and increase production.   These views he communicated to his adviser on
wheeled vehicles, John D. Hertz, whom he appointed to head the west coast
manpower investigation.[24]

Assisted by several Army officers, Hertz made a rapid survey of the west
coast during August.   Visiting the Boeing, Douglas Aircraft Company, Incorporated, Lockheed, North American, Northrop Aircraft, Incorporated, and
Consolidated Vultee Aircraft Corporation plants, he queried management,
labor union officials, and heads of government agencies in an attempt to find
the causes of the gap between schedules and actual production.[25]

Hertz made seven recommendations.   First, he wanted draft deferments
for essential workers in the aircraft industry.   Second, he suggested that the
Army release former aircraft workers to return to industry.   Third, he
believed that sixteen- and seventeen-year-old high school boys should work
after school hours.   Fourth, he favored a manpower freeze by putting teeth

[24] Memo, Patterson for Hertz, 12 Aug 43, and attached Conf Memo on Aircraft Prod by Patterson, 11 Aug 43, OUSW Hertz files, Manpower Problems; Memo, Hertz for USW, 26 Oct 43,
OUSW Hertz files, Memos to Patterson and Hancock; National Aircraft War Prod Council Minutes, 18 Oct 43 and 26 Apr 44, ASF IPD, Aircraft War Prod Council; Ltr, Baruch to Hertz, 2 Sep
43, and Ltr, Patterson to Whom It May Concern, 29 Jul 43, both in OUSW Hertz files, Gen.   For
earlier investigations of the aircraft industry see the following IPD studies, all in ASF IPD, Aircraft Instruments: Manpower Problems in Airframe Assembly Industry, 1 Mar 43; Manpower
Problems of Establishments Manufacturing Aircraft Engines, 15 Mar 43; and Manpower Problems
of Establishments Manufacturing Aircraft Instruments, Feb 43.
[25] See, for example, Interviews, North American Aviation, 6 Aug 43, OUSW Hertz files, North
American Aviation, Inc.; Consolidated Vultee Management, 3 Aug 43, and Consolidated Vultee
Labor, Aug 43, OUSW Hertz files, Consolidated Vultee; Lockheed Management, 7 Aug 43, and
Michener and Allen, UAW, 8 Aug 43, OUSW Hertz files, Lockheed.

into the procedure for "availability certificates," whereby a worker who left an essential job could not get another one until released. Fifth, he wanted the War Manpower Commission to lift its restriction against recruiting and importing labor from outside the area. Sixth, he suggested that federal agencies supervising rationing, housing, transportation, and other local problems make special provisions to attract and keep workers on the west coast. Seventh, he recommended that the War Department co-operate with industry to improve utilization of labor and reduce turnover. Hertz told Patterson that though these suggestions were "severe and politically unpopular," failure to accept them would mean failure to meet production schedules.[26]

In the meantime, other agencies had been studying the manpower situation not only on the west coast but in other areas as well. In Buffalo the regional War Manpower Commission director, Mrs. Anna Rosenberg, had developed a program whereby representatives of the War Production Board, the War Manpower Commission, and the procurement agencies, including the Army, rated plants according to their contribution to the war effort. The U.S. Employment Service then referred available labor to plants with the highest ratings.[27] The essential features of the controlled referral plan were incorporated into a manpower program for the west coast prepared by Bernard Baruch and John Hancock at the request of Director Byrnes of the Office of War Mobilization and submitted to Byrnes on 9 August 1943.

The Baruch-Hancock plan called for a "budget" approach to manpower problems. On the one hand, the War Production Board and the procurement agencies, including the Army, would balance production demands with labor supply; on the other, the War Manpower Commission would plan for the distribution of manpower on the basis of production priorities.

Baruch went on to state that the most pressing need was to halt a further loss of manpower. Like Hertz, he urged the deferment of aircraft workers. The two-month delay of induction ordered by Selective Service was not

[26] Hertz Survey; Ltr, Haber for Kapp, 16 Oct 43, and attached Memo, Haber for Kapp, sub: Use of 17-Year-Olds in Aircraft Plants, OUSW Hertz files, War Manpower Commission; Memo, Conversation With Haber, WMC, 7 Oct 43, and Memo, Kapp for Haber, 7 Oct 43, sub: Use of 17-Year-Olds in Aircraft Plants, both in OUSW Hertz files, Memos to Patterson and Hancock; Memo, Kapp for Hertz, 18 Aug 43, sub: Conversation With John C. Lee, copy in OCMH, West Coast.

[27] See Leonard P. Adams, *Wartime Manpower Mobilization: A Study of World War II Experience in the Buffalo–Niagara Area* (Ithaca, N. Y.: Cornell University Press, 1951), *passim;* Interim Rpt [probably Baruch for Byrnes], 29 Jul 43, sub: Manpower Shortage in Airplane Plants on West Coast, OUSW Hertz files, Manpower Problems; Labor Requirements Committee, Buffalo–Niagara Area, copy in OCMH, West Coast; Conference Ltr, Victor Emanuel to Hertz, 2 Aug 43, OUSW Hertz files, Emanuel, Victor.

enough and would have to be extended. Also, like Hertz, he wanted young people to be used more effectively on a part-time basis while they were still at school. Like all the others, he proposed steps that might mitigate the effects of the turnover.

Baruch optimistically believed that incentives might help increase production. Cost-plus-fixed-fee contracts hampered efficiency in that management did not benefit from improvements. Baruch proposed the ending of cost-plus-fixed-fee contracts and the institution of a wage incentive plan.[28]

The War Manpower Commission Program

The War Manpower Commission developed a plan based on the Baruch proposals. It took for itself "full responsibility" for directing and coordinating all phases of the west coast manpower program. Under its plan, no procurement agency would place a contract without War Manpower Commission certification. The War Production Board and others were to help make labor utilization surveys, while the commission was to determine employment ceilings, in part based on the effectiveness of labor utilization in the plants. The commission also called for the formation of two committees, one to deal with manpower, the other with production.

The War Department, which had been disappointed with the Baruch-Hancock proposals because they did not go far enough, objected even more strongly to the War Manpower Commission program.[29] It protested that priorities would be set and allocations of labor made by those who had no responsibility for production. The War Department believed that "all elements which are necessary in the achievement of the production schedules should be placed in the hands of the agency responsible for that production." Again, the plan seemed to transfer control of labor in the plants to an outside agency, because the War Manpower Commission, the supplier of labor, could determine working conditions. This, according to Assistant Secretary McCloy, was "contrary to fundamental principles of management" and would ruin industrial morale.[30]

---

[28] Ltr, Woodhead of Consolidated to Wilson, 19 Apr 43, copy in OCMH, West Coast. For an account of cost-plus-fixed-fee contracts, see Smith, *The Army and Economic Mobilization,* Ch. XII.

[29] Somers, *op. cit.,* pp. 310–12; Ltr, Hertz to Patterson, 16 Sep 43, and Ltr, Patterson to Baruch, 20 Sep 43, both in OUSW Hertz files, Gen; Ohly file, War Manpower Commission, West Coast Plan, *passim;* Byrnes Directive, 4 Sep 43, copy in OCMH, West Coast; AAF Technical Sv Comd, History of AAF Activities During World War II in the Field of Industrial Manpower, pp. 89–91.

[30] Ltr, McCloy to Byrnes, 1 Sep 43, cited in Somers, *op. cit.,* p. 313.

The War Department, as well as other procurement agencies, submitted its own program.   Accepting the basic organizational structure of both the Baruch-Hancock plan and the War Manpower Commission plan, the War Department proposed that the commission assign labor to plants, but only in the order of importance determined by the agencies responsible for production.   In this way the procurement agencies would control the program.

On 4 September 1943, after a short but sharp dispute, Director Byrnes of the Office of War Mobilization issued a directive that was, in effect, a compromise between the War Manpower Commission and the War Department points of view.   The commission did not receive all the power it wanted, nor did it take the back seat proposed by the War Department.[31]

In Byrnes' west coast manpower program the budget approach proposed in the Baruch-Hancock plan was used.   In each critical area along the Pacific coast, Byrnes ordered that a War Production Board representative head the newly organized Area Production Urgency Committee.   Other representatives came from the War Manpower Commission, the War and Navy Departments, the Maritime Commission, the War Food Administration, the Aircraft Resources Control Office, and the Office of Defense Transportation. The committees approved production schedules and contracts and tried to balance production with labor supply.[32]   They reviewed all contracts involving an increase in employment and recommended to the War Production Board the use of priorities for civilian production.[33]

In addition to the Area Production Urgency Committees, Byrnes ordered the formation of sister organizations, the Area Manpower Priorities Committees.   The chairman of each of these committees was to be a leading local citizen; if none was available, a representative of the War Manpower Commission would be selected.   The membership of each committee consisted of representatives of the War Production Board, the Maritime Commission, the War Food Administration, the Office of Defense Transportation,

---

[31] Somers, *op. cit.*, pp. 313–16.

[32] William J. Brennan, Jr., Urgency Production Committees and Manpower Priorities Committees Organization and Objectives, 22 Apr 44, copy in OCMH, West Coast.   For regulations concerning production committees, see Ohly file, War Manpower Commission, West Coast Plan. For a summary of the program, see U.S. Bureau of the Budget, *The United States at War* (Washington: Government Printing Office, 1946), pp. 438–44.

[33] Memo [*ca.* Oct 43], sub: Placement and Continuation of Contracts in West Coast Area, AAF, Labor, Miscellaneous; Memo, Mitchell for USW, 14 Feb 44, sub: Relaxation of Contract Placement Controls in Los Angeles, ASF Prod Div 004, West Coast; Ltr, Harmon to CofOrd, 27 Mar 44, sub: Industrial Manpower on the Pacific Coast . . ., ASF IPD, West Coast Manpower Program.

the Selective Service System, the Committee for Congested Production Areas, and the Navy and War Departments.

Each Production Committee would submit to the Manpower Committee a list of establishments selected on the basis of their importance to war production. The Manpower Committee would then study the needs for labor and fix employment ceilings for the different plants. Plants were placed in various classes. Class I plants could expand employment; those in Class II could retain their existing number of workers; whereas plants in Class III might not hire anybody and, in fact, might be asked to reduce their labor force. The Manpower Committee could in addition recommend to the Production Committee contracts that for manpower reasons might be sent elsewhere.[34]

The Byrnes directive also called for the stabilization of the labor force. Workers were referred to jobs only through the U.S. Employment Service and on the basis of priority listings. Selective Service gave special consideration to the deferment of workers in occupations in which the labor supply was critically short. Qualified registrants were transferred from low-priority to high-priority plants so that they might then be deferred.

Byrnes appears to have supported the War Manpower Commission's assertion that poor labor utilization was an important cause of the labor shortage. The War Manpower Commission, not the procurement agencies as the Army desired, was to make labor utilization studies at the request of a plant or of the War Production Board. But even after the directive was issued, the Army, supported by management, continually struggled with the commission over this question.[35]

The War Manpower Commission, with the help of the Office of War Information, was to make an intensive drive to find workers in or outside the west coast area. New workers were to be found through transfer from less essential work; by recruitment of women, part-time workers, and foreign labor; and by the use of prisoners of war and soldiers.[36]

The War Department received the Byrnes directive with mixed feelings and accepted it with reluctance.[37] Hertz criticized the dual committee or-

---

[34] For activities of both types of committees, see Progress Report of West Coast Program, Report 2, 2 October 1943, and other items in Ohly file, War Manpower Commission, West Coast Plan.

[35] Aircraft Prod Board Minutes, 1, 15, and 22 Nov 43, in AAF, Aircraft Prod Board Minutes.

[36] For the activities resulting from the west coast program, see Digest Aircraft War Prod Council, Oct 43–Jul 44, AAF files, and Rpt of Manpower Div, Aircraft War Prod Council, Sep–Oct 43, ASF IPD, Aircraft War Prod Council.

[37] WD General Council Minutes, 6 Sep 43.

ganization, one committee dominated by the War Production Board and the other by the War Manpower Commission, as being "cumbersome" and tending "to continue the conflict between WPB and WMC." There were "many pitfalls," he continued. "Industry must deal with two committees representing at least ten agencies of the Government. . . . It is the same old bureaucratic line of confused control of activities instead of a central control." [38]

Many aircraft producers voiced similar complaints, although they promised to co-operate. They also pointed to the failure to cope with turnover and the difficulty of referring workers through the already overburdened U.S. Employment Service. [39]

The plan was also unpopular with labor unions. Unions were not consulted before the directive was issued and were annoyed because they were not represented on the committees. The labor members of the War Production Board spoke for the unions when they called for the formation of management-labor aircraft production advisory committees on which both labor and management would be represented. This was done despite IPD Director Mitchell's feeling that the unions had sold Charles E. Wilson, chairman of the Aircraft Production Board, "a bill of goods." Labor might have been even colder to the plan if it had known that behind the scenes Hertz and Hancock had objected to a wage raise for west coast shipyard workers for fear that aircraft workers would also demand a wage increase. [40]

Extension of the Special Project Team Program

Irrespective of the objections, the Army worked energetically to make the directive a success. The military services promptly assigned officers to the

---

[38] Ltr, Hertz to Patterson, 16 Sep 43, OUSW Hertz files, Gen.

[39] For the Los Angeles Chamber of Commerce's views and activities, see Report of Activities, Emergency Manpower Committee, OUSW Hertz files, Manpower Problems. Notes of John Lee, OUSW Hertz files, Aircraft War Prod Council; Memo [probably Hertz] for Hancock, sub: West Coast Manpower Situation, OUSW Hertz files, Gen; Ltr, Russell to Hertz, 15 Sep 43, copy in OCMH, West Coast.

[40] Memo, Golden and Kennan for Wilson, 28 Aug 43, sub: Proposed Program; Aircraft Prod Board Minutes, 8 and 22 Nov 43, AAF, Aircraft Prod Board Minutes; Memo, Kapp for Hertz, 17 Nov 43, OUSW Hertz files, Gen; Manpower Problems in West Coast Aircraft Industry, Labor Interview with Lew Michener and Allen, UAW, 8 Aug 43, OUSW Hertz files, Lockheed; Memos, Hertz for Mitchell and Hertz for Hancock, 13 Oct 43, and Memo, Hancock for Hertz, 14 Oct 43, OUSW Hertz files, Aircraft War Prod Council; Memo, Hertz for USW, 13 Oct 43, OUSW Hertz files, Boeing; Memo, Howlett for Kietzen, 9 Oct 43, sub: West Coast Shipyard Case Before NWLB, copy in OCMH, West Coast.

Area Production Urgency Committees and to the Area Manpower Priorities Committees. As added insurance, the War Department sent another special project team to southern California.[41] Lt. Col. William J. Brennan, Jr., later to play a leading role in the Industrial Personnel Division, headed this mission. Brennan had to face problems similar to those handled by the Seattle team and he used similar tactics.[42]

The War Department again came into conflict with the War Manpower Commission. The Army considered itself above ordinary day-to-day squabbles and was certain that it could provide the leadership that up to this time had not been found. Brennan would work with "boxing gloves," while McNutt used a "powder puff."[43] The southern California team believed that the really necessary job to be done was the shifting of men from nonessential work to the aircraft plants. Since the U.S. Employment Service was overloaded with work and could not handle both essential and nonessential workers, the War Manpower Commission provided controlled referrals only for essential industries. Workers in less essential industries could not be reached by the commission. Brennan wanted the limited facilities of the U. S. Employment Service to be used instead for the nonessential workers. Brennan won out, and Los Angeles differed from other areas in the country in that the employment service handled the controlled referrals of nonessential rather than essential workers. Under this procedure, the Southern California Special Project Team was able to stimulate the transfer of workers from occupations such as waiter and gas station attendant to jobs in aircraft plants.[44]

Brennan, like Collins and Krim in Seattle, had to handle such diverse problems as adequate child care centers, improved shopping hours to lessen absenteeism, increased housing, community programs, limitation on military recruitment, and better labor relations. Brennan and his associates also

---

[41] Ltr, Witten to CofOrd, 28 Sep 43, ASF IPD, West Coast Manpower Program; Ltr, Stace to All Aircraft Facilities, sub: West Coast Manpower Program, 6 Nov 43, Memo, Stace to All Areas, 6 Nov 43, sub: West Coast Manpower, and Memo, Brig Gen Weaver for CofOrd, 10 Sep 43, sub: West Coast War Manpower Problem, copies of all in OCMH, West Coast; see also above, pp. 131–39.

[42] See ASF IPD, Southern California Program, Brennan, and Ohly file, West Coast Aircraft.

[43] Memo, Hertz for USW, 10 Nov 43, OUSW Hertz files, Memos to Hancock and Patterson; WMC role as described in Conference Progress Rpt 1, Actions Taken on the West Coast Manpower Program, 15 Sep–15 Oct, WMC, 19 Oct 43, copy in OCMH, West Coast; Memo, Lovett for SW, 14 Oct 43, sub: West Coast Manpower Discussion, Stimson files, Manpower.

[44] Aircraft Prod Board Minutes, 2 May 44, AAF, Aircraft Prod Board Minutes; Manpower and Prod Survey of Southern California Aircraft Industry, No. 43, copy in OCMH, West Coast.

visited the important plants in the region such as Lockheed and Douglas and made suggestions concerning each company's labor problems.[45]

The southern California team, like the Boeing team, played an active role in the work of the Area Production Urgency Committees and the Area Manpower Priorities Committees. Brennan asserted that the committees had four functions: first, they provided a funnel through which procurement agencies could learn the order of importance of different companies; second, procurement agencies were now placed directly between the employers and referral organizations, thereby eliminating direct pressures on the referral groups; third, the committees awakened local communities to the need for action; and fourth, they gave an impetus to the War Manpower Commission to use powers it had always had but was afraid to use.

The teams functioned until March 1944, and other officers continued to represent the Army on the various committees until the end of the west coast program.[46] Long effort on the part of many alleviated for a time the manpower shortage on the west coast. Turnover decreased and employment increased. Protest concerning the need for workers on the west coast nevertheless continued, and Brennan made another investigation in 1944. A special program and two Army special teams lessened, but could not quell, the chorus of complaints.[47]

[45] Robert D. Gray, *Systematic Wage Administration in the Southern California Aircraft Industry,* Industrial Relations Councellors, Industrial Relations Monograph 7 (1943), *passim;* Penciled Note, sub: Southern California Project—Action Required Immediately, Ohly file, West Coast Aircraft; Digest Aircraft War Prod Council, Oct 43–Jul 44, AAF files, and Rpt of Manpower Div, Aircraft War Prod Council, Sep–Oct 43, *passim,* in ASF IPD, Aircraft War Prod Council; Manpower Data for West Coast, 14 Oct 43, prepared for Hertz, OUSW Hertz files, Aircraft War Prod Council; Memo, Brennan and Krim for McPhail, sub: Community Program Related to Solution of Manpower, Rpt of Manpower and Prod Survey of Southern California Aircraft Industry, 30 Nov 43, and Memo, Wood for Brig Gen Hopkins, 19 Jan 44, sub: Follow-up on Recommendations Presented in Manpower and Prod Survey of Southern California Aircraft Industry, all in ASF IPD, West Coast Aircraft Rpts; Ohly file, West Coast Aircraft and ASF IPD, Southern California Program, Brennan.

[46] Ltr, CofOrd to Harmon, 14 Aug 44, copy in OCMH, West Coast; Memo, Patterson for Deputy ACofAS, Matériel, Maintenance, and Distribution, 27 Jan 44, sub: AAF Labor Activities in the Western Proc Dist, ASF IPD, Southern California Program, Brennan.

[47] Copy of Testimony, John Lee before House Naval Affairs Subcommittee, 19 Nov 43, and Ltr, Gen Manager, National Aircraft War Prod Council, Inc., to Lovett, 23 Nov 43, both in ASF, IPD, Southern California Program, Brennan; Memo, Brennan for Peterson, 12 Sep 44, sub: Manpower Situation in Los Angeles, Ohly file, War Manpower Commission, West Coast Plan; Quarterly Rpt, West Coast Manpower Program, 30 Dec 43, copy in OCMH, West Coast; News Memo, Aircraft War Prod Council, 21 Dec 43, ASF IPD, Aircraft War Prod Council; Memo, Hertz for USW, 14 Oct 43, OUSW Hertz files, Memos to Patterson and Hancock; Draft Ltr, Miller to All Army Contractors [after 12 Jan 44], sub: West Coast War Manpower Program, ASF IPD, San Francisco Area, Book 1; Ltr, Industrial Dept San Francisco Chamber of Commerce to Col Witten, 10 Jan 44, ASF IPD, West Coast Manpower Program; ASF IPD, Industrial Visits, describes Brennan's later investigation.

In September 1943, while the Boeing and southern California teams were still in the field, the Army organized three additional special project teams. The problems that faced the Boeing and southern California teams were confined, in the one instance, to a particular company and, in the other, to a particular area, but the conditions against which the three new teams launched their attack were industry-wide, involving the ball bearing industry, the forge and foundry industry, and the tire industry. Subsequently, twelve more special project teams were organized, of which eight were industry teams, three were area teams, and one was a company team. They ranged in size from one man for the projects involving a single plant or small area to about forty-five men for the cotton duck industry team. Although each team was patterned to fit the circumstances of the individual case, for the most part the methods and procedures of all the teams resembled those introduced by the Boeing and southern California teams.[48]

The special projects program caused considerable friction, some of which was gradually overcome. Most of the projects, particularly the industry-wide projects, fell within a realm that was technically the responsibility of the War Production Board, which at first resisted the Army's new steps as an intrusion upon the board's area of responsibility. The Army continued to make use of the special project technique in preference to the Area Production Urgency-Manpower Priorities Committee machinery, and gradually

[48] Krim and Peyser, *op. cit.,* pp. 15–19. The following is a list of special project teams organized from September 1943 to July 1945:

Date Organized	Industry or Area of Operations	Date Disbanded
September 1943	Ball bearing industry	November 1943
September 1943	Military tire industry	April 1944 [a]
September 1943	Forge and foundry industry	October 1943 [b]
April 1944	Hawaii	June 1944
August 1944	Manhattan District (atom bombs)	October 1944
October 1944	Douglas Aircraft Company, Chicago	November 1944
December 1944	Cotton duck industry	March 1945
December 1944	Newark, New Jersey	February 1945
January 1945	New Bedford, Massachusetts	February 1945
February 1945	Carbon black industry	March 1945
February 1945	Wool top industry	[c]
March 1945	Aluminum extrusion industry	May 1945
April 1945	High tenacity rayon industry	May 1945
April 1945	Cotton tire cord industry	May 1945
June 1945	Western railroads	September 1945

[a] Reactivated August–October 1944 and December 1944–May 1945.
[b] Reactivated October 1944–January 1945.
[c] Not known.

the attitude of the board changed.   In the spring of 1945 the War Production Board on several occasions unsuccessfully urged the Army to organize teams to solve the manpower problems of industries in which the Army had no interest.   The War Manpower Commission, even more directly concerned than the War Production Board, likewise objected to the Army's method of bypassing the established manpower channels by sending special teams into the field.[49]   Even within the Army itself, the teams came under fire.   The teams had no formal connection with the service command and regional labor officers.   The teams, in fact, superseded the regular field organization during the period of their operations and, not unnaturally, were resented by the regularly assigned labor officers.[50]

In July 1944 the teams were to some extent brought into the established organizational framework when the Industrial Personnel Division organized a Special Projects Section in the Labor Branch.   The function of the new section was to supervise planning for special projects and the operations of the teams and to act as the Washington contact for teams in the field.[51] The Special Projects Section thereafter designated the members of the teams and in a number of cases assigned regular labor officers to them.

Whatever anyone else might have said about the teams, members of the Industrial Personnel Division were convinced that the technique was successful and claimed the following advantages for it:

(1) There is the salutary effect of the mere formation of the project which, by the very fact of the removal of the problem from regular channels, serves notice on all concerned of the severity of the emergency.

(2) There is the concentration on the one target.

(3) There is the emphasis on speed of action.

(4) There is the follow-through, achieved by assignment of a single responsibility for the coordination of activities of many groups and agencies.

(5) There is the full capitalization of the peculiar Army position to speak for the needs of the armies abroad—the prestige of the uniform, completely divorced from local politics and partisan interests.

(6) There is the benefit of selection of the best personnel for the job—officers aware of the stress and strain of conflicting influence, experienced in the ways of getting things done quickly and effectively, placed in a direct line between field and headquarters.

(7) There is the representation of the highest echelons bringing the full weight of the War Department to the action level even for the accomplishment of the smallest detail.[52]

---

[49] Krim and Peyser, op. cit., pp. 20–21; Millet, The Organization and Role of the Army Service Forces, pp. 243–44; Memo, Styer for Dir IPD, 11 Sep 43, sub: Solution of Critical Manpower Problems, copy in OCMH, West Coast.

[50] Somers and Ohly, War Department Organization for the Handling of Labor Problems in World War II, ASF IPD Monograph 10, pp. 43–44.

[51] Krim and Peyser, op. cit., pp. 17–18.

[52] Ibid., p. 29.

Against these advantages there were, in the opinion of the Industrial Personnel Division, only two drawbacks: the possibility that the special project teams might "deflate the importance" of the Army representatives regularly assigned to the area, thus making it difficult for them to take action after the teams departed, and the danger involved in subordinating all other procurement problems in the area to the special project. The first of these, according to the IPD, could be overcome by educating labor officers to the true role of the special project teams and by making available to the labor officers "the benefits of continued capitalization of contacts and machinery created during the existence of the project." The second could be minimized by utilizing the special project technique only "in the most critical emergencies." [53]

Further analysis suggests other disadvantages. In a number of areas and industries complaints of manpower shortages continued to arise from time to time after the teams had departed, and in several cases it was necessary to reactivate the teams. The special project technique acted as a shot in the arm. Its lasting effect was questionable. Furthermore, to concentrate on one particular locality or industry was to risk the adoption of measures that could succeed only at the expense of other localities or industries.

The special project technique was admirably suited to the situation as it was in 1942 and early 1943, when the manpower shortages were few and far between and temporary in duration. By the end of 1943 and throughout 1944, the spot shortages were threatening to become a nationwide problem. Practically every major industry was complaining of a scarcity of labor. Special problems and variations among the different sections and among industries made any general formula unpractical, and no longer was it adequate to attempt to meet the problems as they arose. The situation from the end of 1943 onward called for continuous direct action on the local level under a nationwide plan of operations, and not for periodic shots in the arm.

[53] *Ibid.,* p. 30.

CHAPTER VIII

Building Up the Labor Force

During the defense emergency and for a few months after the United States entered the war, the labor problem had been for the most part a matter of preventing strikes, slowdowns, and disputes between management and labor. The problem had been one of keeping the worker at work, not primarily one of recruiting workers, for in 1940 the United States was just emerging from a decade of industrial depression and economic dislocation, a decade that had left its mark in the shape of 8,120,000 persons without jobs. Not labor supply, but equipment, machines, and materials were the problems that faced industry in 1940 and 1941. As production rose, the reservoir of unemployed workers gradually dropped, absorbed by the expanding aircraft industry, shipbuilding, and arms and ammunition plants. At the same time the build-up of the armed forces was taking an increasingly large slice of American manpower. Consequently, by 1943 there remained in the labor force only a little more than 1,000,000 persons unemployed and half of them were women.

On the other hand, a vast potential source of labor, almost as large as the total force itself, existed in the 44,000,000 persons who were not employed and were not seeking work. About 80 percent of them were women. Many of the men and women not in the labor force were too old or physically unable to work, but there were many others, particularly among the women, who might have been, and eventually were, persuaded to seek employment in industry.

Another potential source consisted of those men and women whose services were either not being used at all, or not effectively used, for reasons not of their own making. Counted as part of the existing labor force because they were willing to work, they were nevertheless barred from jobs, or severely limited in their choice because of social convention, prejudice, or considerations of security. Although women had entered the labor force in fairly sizable numbers during and after World War I, there were many types of industrial work that were considered not fit and proper for them to perform. Resistance on the part of employers and organized labor was a powerful obstacle.   Similar, but even more powerful, obstacles stood in the way of Negroes.   Another group within this same general category consisted of resident aliens, many of whom had lived and worked in the United States for years, who were excluded on grounds of military security from working in aircraft plants or on classified contracts.

The Employment of Negroes

Of that part of the population which constituted the labor force, Negro workers and job-seekers in 1940 formed a large pool of underutilized labor. Comprising about 10 percent of the total population of the United States, Negroes made up 12.5 percent of the unemployed.   Approximately 25 percent of the urban male Negroes in the labor force were without jobs as compared with only 16 percent of all male city-dwellers.   The unemployment rate among Negroes had dropped only slightly since the worst of the depression years.[1]   In April 1940 it was estimated that six and a half million Negroes were available for defense production.[2]   In certain areas they represented the greatest part of the labor supply, yet it was in precisely those areas that the most serious problems in utilizing Negroes effectively were encountered.

While the National Defense Advisory Commission was focusing its attention on discrimination in industry, the War Department had become involved in the problem in connection with military personnel.   The organization of new Negro units in the Army in the summer of 1940 and the passage of the Selective Service Act soon afterward brought forth a statement of policy that was intended to give Negroes the assurance of a "fair and equitable" place in the military effort.   Although primarily concerned with the role of the Negro in uniform, the statement also made reference to workers in arsenals and at Army posts, promising Negroes "equal opportunity" for civilian employment "at work for which they are qualified."   A few days later, on 25 October 1940, Col. Benjamin O. Davis, the senior Negro officer in the U.S. Army, was nominated for promotion to brigadier general, the first member of his race to be named to general officer rank.   On the same day Judge William H. Hastie, dean of the Howard University Law School and the first Negro

---

[1] Gunnar Myrdal, *An American Dilemma; The Negro Problem and Modern Democracy* (New York: Harper & Brothers, 1944), I, 299–301; Ulysses G. Lee, The Employment of Negro Troops, a volume in preparation for the series UNITED STATES ARMY IN WORLD WAR II, Draft MS, Ch. IV, p. 36.

[2] F. G. Davis, War Economics and Negro Labor, Table IX, ASF Director of Personnel, Negroes in War Industries.

to be appointed a federal judge, was named Secretary Stimson's special civilian aide on Negro affairs.   Although it was expected that Judge Hastie would devote most of his time to the situation regarding military personnel, Stimson expressed the hope that he would assist the War Department in connection with policies involving the employment of Negroes at Army establishments and by Army contractors.   Part of his duties, the Secretary of War wrote to Judge Hastie, would be the investigation of complaints concerning the treatment of Negro employees and job applicants of the War Department.[3]

During his first three months in office Judge Hastie received frequent complaints of discrimination in the appointment and promotion of civilian personnel.   Eligible Negroes, he reported to the Under Secretary of War, were often passed over on one pretext or another, or without an explanation. Abuses were widespread both in Washington and in field installations.[4] Out of a total of 13,000 War Department employees in Washington, there were only about 600 Negroes.   The proportion was even lower in Army arsenals, where out of a total of 38,280 employees there were only 690 Negroes.[5] Judge Hastie called the situation to the attention of the War Department Director of Civilian Personnel and Training and the heads of the bureaus and requested that investigations be made of specific cases.   Supervisory officials, according to Judge Hastie, usually explained that the situation was so difficult that they could do little about it.

The effectiveness of the office of the civilian aide on Negro affairs was sometimes weakened by lack of information concerning policy matters. Policy proposals often did not reach Judge Hastie until they had been completely formulated and had been presented for final approval.   Although a directive was issued on 17 December 1940 that all policy matters pertaining to Negroes would be referred to his office for comment or concurrence before being presented for final decision, an occasional paper continued to take a bypassing route.

Meanwhile, the NDAC had launched a program designed to improve the skills of Negro workers and to break down union restrictions against Negro members.   At the behest of the NDAC the U.S. Office of Education in July 1940 announced that federal funds for vocational training should be made

[3] Lee, The Employment of Negro Troops, Ch. IV, pp. 16, 22; ASF Hist Monograph, Negro Workers in Production Plants and Government Installations Under ASF Direction, Draft 2, ASF IPD, Race Relations.
[4] Memo, Civilian Aide to SW for USW, 7 Feb 41, sub: Rpt of Activities . . . 1 Nov 40 to 31 Jan 41, OUSW Amberg files, Employment of Aliens, Negroes, etc.
[5] Memo, Asst to Civilian Aide to SW for Amberg, 25 Jun 41, sub: Gen Information Concerning Negroes, and Incl, OUSW Amberg files, Employment of Aliens, Negroes, etc.

available without discrimination on account of race, creed, or color. Although many communities opened the doors of training centers to Negroes for the first time, many others refused to take the necessary steps that would have enabled Negroes to fit themselves for better jobs. An effort to open trade-union membership to colored workers was likewise only partially successful. Although both the AFL and the CIO agreed to make every effort to remove restrictions and a number of unions did open their ranks to Negroes, many obstacles continued to be thrown in the way of Negro applicants.[6] Impatient at the slow progress, a number of Negro groups planned a march on Washington in June 1941 to lay their grievances before the Administration.

As the result of a conference between government officials and Negro leaders, the protest march was called off and a committee, headed by Mayor Fiorello H. LaGuardia of New York, was appointed to draw up a proposal for the President that would meet the grievances. The committee recommended an executive order forbidding discrimination in war industry and requiring government contracts to bear a nondiscrimination clause. Within the War Department a number of objections to the proposals of the LaGuardia committee were voiced. Amberg summarized them for Under Secretary Patterson as follows: first, the possibility that prospective contractors, particularly in southern states, might refuse to bid or to accept orders for fear of labor trouble or litigation over enforcement; second, the insuperable difficulties in enforcing the contract clause, since cancellation of the contract would bring about the very thing the War Department was attempting to avert, namely, a drop in production; third, the predicament in which contractors would be placed if they had closed-shop agreements with unions that excluded Negroes from membership; and, finally, the apparent impossibility of meeting the complaints with a contract clause innocuous enough to avoid administrative difficulties. War Department critics of the committee's recommendation took a view similar to that of the Army toward the employment of Negro troops, that any action arousing deep-seated prejudices or placing burdens of social reform on the War Department was to be avoided.[7]

Accepting the recommendations of the LaGuardia committee, President Roosevelt issued his executive order of 25 June 1941, which established as a general rule that there should be no discrimination against workers in war

[6] Address by Robert C. Weaver, Chief Negro Employment and Tng Br OPM, at Ohio Welfare Conference, Akron, Ohio, 9 Oct 41, ASF IPD, Negro.

[7] Memo, Amberg for SW, 23 Jun 41, sub: Proposed Contract Clause Against Race Discrimination, with attached papers, and draft of Joint Memo, USW and Asst Secy Navy for President, 24 Jun 41, sub: Employment of Negroes on National Defense [probably not sent], both in OUSW Amberg files, Employment of Aliens, Negroes, etc.

industry because of their race, creed, color, or national origin and which required all government contracts to bear a clause to this effect. As to aliens, the exceptions made the rule, until June 1943. In this respect the War Department, it has been noted, faced the problem of persuading employers that they could hire aliens by special dispensation without incurring the penalties of the law and that they could reject others without running afoul of the President's executive order. With regard to Negroes, the problem was how the War Department, without means of enforcing compliance, could persuade employers to abide by the general rule. In accordance with the executive order, the War Department drafted a contract clause enjoining contractors not to follow discriminatory hiring practices. The personnel offices of contractors and government arsenals were notified to delete any mention of race or religion from job application forms. Personnel practices within the War Department were standardized, and uniform procedures in cases involving discrimination by contractors and subcontractors were established. On the local level, several states passed laws outlawing discrimination.[8] Nevertheless, until September 1943, the U.S. Employment Service continued to clear orders for workers that included discriminatory specifications. It was the policy of the U.S. Employment Service to "serve" employers by attempting to fill orders according to the employer's specifications for the jobs, even if the qualifications were discriminatory. As the labor supply was reduced and the U.S. Employment Service took on a larger role as a supplier of labor, the War Manpower Commission issued an order, on 3 September 1943, that requests for workers that included discriminatory specifications should be refused.[9]

After the reorganization of the War Department in March 1942, the ASF became the largest single employer of civilian labor in the United States.[10] Responsibility for implementing the nondiscrimination policy fell to the Industrial Personnel Division, ASF. With respect to the tens of thousands of civilians employed in arsenals and other Army installations, the responsibility was direct and authority could be directly exercised. The rate of progress was limited only by the necessity of avoiding trouble among employees. With respect to privately owned and operated plants working on government

---

[8] ASF Hist Monograph, Negro Workers in Production Plants and Government Installations Under ASF Direction, Draft 1, pp. 2, 4, ASF IPD, Race Relations; WMC, History of the Mobilization of Labor for War Production During World War II, Ch. IX, Part I, p. 23.

[9] WMC, History of the Mobilization of Labor for War Production During World War II, Ch. IX, Part I, pp. 21, 40.

[10] Annual Rpt ASF for FY 1943, pp. 234–37.

contracts, the Army had no effective direction over personnel procedures. Short of canceling a contract for breach of the nondiscrimination clause, the Army could exert only the pressure of public opinion, and success in carrying out the policies depended largely on the co-operation of all parties concerned.

It was some months after the ASF inherited the problem before progress became apparent, either in Army installations or in war industry. In June 1942 the Department of Labor estimated that more than half a million Negroes available for war production were idle because of discriminatory hiring practices, and that several million others were prevented from making a greater contribution to the war effort because they were confined to unskilled jobs. Some progress was noted in the ordnance industry. Although the majority of plants, the Department of Labor reported, were still discriminating against Negro workers, a "significant number" of arsenals were hiring all qualified applicants without regard to color.[11] In Baltimore, which had been designated by the War Manpower Commission as the first "critical labor supply area" and which had been selected in May as the first city in which to try out the government's voluntary manpower program, only 7 percent of the Negro population was employed in war industry as of 15 September.[12] An upward trend, which was country-wide but which varied widely from section to section and from industry to industry, became noticeable during the fall of 1942, extended into 1943, and continued to the end of the war. The proportion of Negroes employed in war industries rose from 4.2 percent of total employment in July 1942 to 8.6 percent in July 1945. In the War Department the number of Negro employees rose to approximately 148,600 or 11.8 percent of the total civilian employment in June 1944.[13]

The influx of Negroes into industries and localities where they had not previously been welcome aggravated tensions and led to disputes and conflicts that in some cases disrupted production and defeated the purpose of the War Department.

A thoroughly nasty and exceedingly complex situation developed in Detroit during June 1943. A tremendous immigration of workers, both Negro and white, had hopelessly taxed the city's community services. Many of the newcomers had brought their racial prejudices with them and during the winter of 1942–43 there had been a riot over housing. As the Negroes began

[11] FSA, The Labor Market, June 1942, pp. 9–10.

[12] Sanford Griffith, *Where Can We Get War Workers? (Results of a Manpower Survey in Baltimore)*, Public Affairs Pamphlet 75 (New York: Public Affairs Committee, Inc., 1942), pp. 3, 13.

[13] WMC, History of the Mobilization of Labor for War Production During World War II, Ch. IX, Part I, p. 63; ASF, Information for Hist Monographs, Negroes in ASF, in ASF IPD, Race Relations.

to make inroads into skilled jobs, further trouble and sporadic strikes had appeared. Although leaders of the labor unions encouraged on-the-job training and upgrading for Negroes, the rank and file were slow to accept the idea. In June 1943 three of the 2,500 Negroes employed by the Packard Company in the manufacture of bomber and PT boat engines were upgraded. A wildcat strike took place, led by irresponsible elements. It was put down by CIO officials and the three Negroes were promoted, but the atmosphere remained heavily charged. An argument between a Negro and a white, whose cars had collided on a Detroit bridge, developed into fisticuffs and then into a bloody riot. The rioting spread. A number of plants virtually ceased operation and war production dropped sharply. Before federal troops could be moved in to restore order, twenty-five Negroes and nine whites had been killed and six hundred people injured. The arrival of the troops stopped the disorders, and production rapidly returned to normal levels. Tensions continued, but by constant alertness on the part of the various official agencies further outbreaks were prevented.[14]

Another serious racial dispute developed in Baltimore at the Point Breeze facilities of Western Electric where about nine thousand employees produced combat communications equipment.[15] The company first employed Negroes in the autumn of 1941 and, in accordance with the Baltimore plumbing code, established separate washrooms for "every sex and color." Segregation was the community practice in Baltimore and many employees wanted segregated washrooms, showers, drinking fountains, and cafeterias. When the word "color" was dropped from the city plumbing code, the company did away with the separate Negro and white sanitation facilities. Relations between management and labor had been troubled for some time by a smoldering wage dispute and the union—the Point Breeze Employees Association—now seized upon the segregation question as an issue. In spite of the fact that all employees had to meet health standards and that the union hall itself had nonsegregated washrooms, the Employees Association protested that common toilets were a health hazard since they would expose white workers to venereal and other communicable diseases. On 4–5 October 1943 the majority of workers casting votes at a plant election authorized the union to call a strike on this issue.

[14] Memo, L. L. Foster for Collins, 10 Jun 43, sub: The Packard Strike, and Memo, Foster for Collins, 22 Jun 43, sub: Detroit Riot, both in ASF IPD, Detroit; Memo, O'Gara for Dir Civilian Pers and Tng, 29 Jun 43, ASF Director of Personnel, Hist Monograph Materials.

[15] Summary by JAG, Point Breeze Plants and Facilities of Western Electric Company, Inc., Baltimore, Md., in Ohly, History of Plant Seizures During World War II, App. A–1–a.

Not until the eve of a scheduled walkout did the Regional War Labor Board take jurisdiction. The strike was postponed pending a study of the grievances. The Fair Employment Practice Committee investigated and concluded that separate washrooms would interfere with the free transfer of workers from job to job within the plant and could not "help but lead to discriminatory employment practices." The Regional War Labor Board found the case too difficult for it to handle and passed the issue on to the National War Labor Board. This board, too, was embarrassed by social questions which could not be decided on their merits. The only alternative was to order segregation, and, in view of the findings of the Fair Employment Practice Committee, it could not do that. The carefully worded directive stated that the board would not order the company to change its policy of providing common facilities for Negroes and whites.[16]

The union promptly struck. The National War Labor Board telegraphed requesting workers to stay on the job and warning that legal sanctions would be invoked. The union acknowledged this threat but stated that it had repeatedly presented grievances and the strike would continue until the social issue was settled. The strike was effective. Except for the Negroes, most workers stayed out. Production was down to 10 to 20 percent. Emotions ran high and there were fears of violence. The National War Labor Board felt that the Army ought to intervene quickly, and the Army itself was prepared to rush troops on short notice to preserve order.[17] Within a few days, at the request of the National War Labor Board, the President issued an executive order directing the Secretary of War to take over and operate the Point Breeze facilities.[18]

The Army seized the plant on 19 December 1943. Its representatives made clear that they were not free to discuss segregation but invited talk on

[16] Memo, Foster for Maj D. Boland, 4 Nov 43, sub: Racial Problems at Western Electric, ASF Director of Personnel, Western Electric, Point Breeze, Md.; Certification by Secy of Labor to Region III NWLB, 2 Nov 43, Memo, Eli Rock, Acting Asst Dir Disputes Region III NWLB, for N. Feinsinger, Dir Disputes NWLB, 29 Nov 43, sub: Western Electric, Memo, Feinsinger for Board Members NWLB, 13 Dec 43, sub: Western Electric . . ., and Directive Order NWLB, Western Electric, all in Case 111–4733–D, Western Electric Co., NWLB, National Archives; Transcript of Executive Sessions, NWLB, National Archives.

[17] Tel Conv, Styer and Byrnes, 14 Dec 43, ASF Control Div, Western Electric; Tel Conv, Maj Long and Boland, 14 Dec 43, ASF Director of Personnel, Western Electric, Point Breeze, Md.; Exchange of Telgms, NWLB and Point Breeze Employees Association, 14 and 15 Dec 43, Case 111–4733–D Western Electric Co., NWLB, National Archives; Transcript of Executive Sessions, 13 Dec 43, pp. 208ff, NWLB, National Archives.

[18] EO 9408; Transcript Executive Sessions, 15 and 16 Dec 43, NWLB National Archives; Memo, USW for CG ASF, 19 Dec 43, sub: WD Operation . . . Western Electric . . ., and Memo, Somervell for Brig Gen A. A. Farmer, 19 Dec 43, sub: WD Operation . . . Western Electric, both in ASF Control Div, Western Electric.

other grievances.   Privately, however, many Army officials felt that in a community like Baltimore nonsegregation was untenable.   The union asserted that separate eating and sanitation facilities were the only issues, and, while it would not strike against the Army, it would do nothing to get the men back to work and would resume the walkout as soon as the Army left.[19]

It took about three weeks to get attendance and production back to normal, but the grievances still smoldered and there seemed no prospect of ending the seizure.   Various reasons were advanced for the union's implacable stand: that it was instigated by Axis agents; that the company's absentee management did not give any real power to those in charge of labor conditions at the plant; that the union was company dominated and was injecting the racial issue in an effort to maintain itself against the CIO and AFL which were active in the plant; that the Army was equivocating and encouraging defiance; that labor relations at Point Breeze were generally poor and this was only a particular manifestation; and that the strike over Negroes was an indirect way of seeking a wage increase.

Many measures were taken to meet these difficulties.   The FBI investigated strike activities.   A labor morale campaign was developed.   Interracial groups carried on an education program.   The industrial relations representative of the company and a particularly vehement leader of the union were both replaced.   The National War Labor Board considered a wage increase. The union, under advice from various government agencies not to prejudice wage concessions, withdrew its statement that its strike was only being held in abeyance during the seizure, and the National War Labor Board granted the increase.[20]

Undoubtedly these measures were of value.   But the hard core of the dispute remained; many white workers did not want to share washroom and eating facilities with Negroes.   The dispute was not settled until government agencies and plant officials, some willingly and some grudgingly, with the encouragement of a Presidential assistant, yielded in substance to the

---

[19] Memos, Maj J. S. Meyers, Emergency Protection Br Internal Security Div, for PMG, 20 and 21 Dec 43, sub: Western Electric, and Ltr, Farmer to Styer, 20 Dec 43, with clippings attached, both in ASF Control Div, Western Electric; Ltr, C. H. Dorn to NWLB, 17 Feb 44, Case 111–4773–D Western Electric Co., NWLB, National Archives.

[20] Memo, Brig Gen A. L. Lerch for CofS, 6 Jan 44, sub: Invoking Selective Service . . . Employment Date, ASF Control Div, Western Electric; Summary by JAG, Point Breeze Plants . . ., in Ohly, *op. cit.,* App. A–1–a; Baltimore *Sun,* December 30, 1943; Memos, Foster for Mitchell, 22 and 28 Dec 43, ASF Director of Personnel, Western Electric, Point Breeze, Md.; Telgm, J. E. Poulter, Representative International Association of Machinists to W. H. Davis, Chairman NWLB, 16 Dec 43, Case 111–4773–D Western Electric Co., NWLB, National Archives.

union demands. The fiction of nonsegregated facilities was maintained. Acting on a suggestion by an officer of the Industrial Personnel Division, Western Electric enlarged the locker, cafeteria, and washroom space and announced that lockers would be assigned "in a manner directed toward harmonious relationships of those involved." Those assigned to A lockers would use a toilet, drinking fountains, and cafeteria space nearby, while those assigned to B lockers would use the facilities closest to them. There were no formal arrangements, but workers tacitly agreed that one group of lockers was for whites the other for Negroes. No more significant racial incidents occurred and on 23 March 1944 the Army withdrew, after a new production record had been set.[21]

Less than five months later the Army was again called upon, this time in Philadelphia to keep the transit system running. In their effort to climb the ladder of economic opportunity, Negroes had long aspired to become conductors and motormen on trolley cars. They already held such jobs in New York, Detroit, and a few other cities, but on most traction systems they were limited to maintenance work. During the war they tried to get platform work on surface transit lines in Washington, Los Angeles, and elsewhere. The most dramatic and important conflict occurred in Philadelphia.

In 1941 both the Philadelphia Transportation Company and the Philadelphia Rapid Transit Employees Union had turned down Negro pleas for platform jobs. Then, early in 1943, the Philadelphia Transportation Company asked the War Manpower Commission for one hundred white motormen. The commission requested the company to withdraw the discriminatory request, but the Philadelphia Transportation Company explained that a clause in its contract with the union barred Negroes from these jobs.

Negro complaints had meanwhile piled up at the Philadelphia office of the Fair Employment Practice Committee. On 27 December 1943, shortly after a public hearing, the committee directed that the company and the union not interpret the contract clause as a bar to upgrading qualified Negroes. The Employees Union, with company support, denied committee jurisdiction. A petition to a special committee of Congress signed by 1776 workers (symbolic of a new Declaration of Independence) stated that "the

---

[21] Baltimore *Afro-American*, March 28, 1944; Memo for Files, Lt Col W. T. Thurman, Asst to Farmer, 24 Feb 44, sub: Conference With Jonathan Daniels, Memo, Lt Col J. S. Myers, Chief Emergency Protection Br Internal Security Div, for PMG, 18 Mar 44, sub, Western Electric . . ., SW Order Terminating Government Possession . . ., 23 Mar 44, Memo, Somervell for Farmer, 23 Mar 44, sub: Termination of WD Possession . . ., all in ASF Control Div, Western Electric.

white employees of the Philadelphia Transportation Company refuse to work with Negroes as conductors, operators, and station trainmen." [22]

The situation became even more confused when in March 1944 the CIO Transport Workers Union, which opposed discrimination, won an overwhelming election victory over the anti-Negro union and was certified as the exclusive bargaining agent for Philadelphia Transportation Company workers. But the company was reluctant to come to an agreement with the militant CIO. The defeated union tried to snatch victory from defeat by capitalizing on the failure of the CIO group to fulfill its campaign promises. It found that it could get a good deal of support among workers on the racial issue and sought to nullify the Fair Employment Practice Committee order. The company meanwhile took no action on the upgrading of Negroes until the War Manpower Commission refused to refer workers. Philadelphia Transportation Company urgently needed labor and capitulated. On 1 August 1944 eight upgraded Negro motormen were scheduled to make their trial runs. [23]

In the interval workers had met secretly and voted to strike. The night before the practice trips about seventy-five of the more rabid men met and, amid considerable excitement, urged that white motormen report as sick the following morning. If a number of men refused to take their cars out of the barns, they would block those behind them, the tracks would become clogged, and the surface system would be tied up. Most of the workers did not learn of the plan until they arrived at work the morning of 1 August. [24]

The strike was immediately effective. Workers in war plants could not get to their jobs, and absenteeism at the Philadelphia Navy Yard reached 72 percent. In some plants workers who succeeded in getting to their jobs were stranded. Race tensions mounted, there were some incidents of violence, and an ugly situation was developing. Negro and white groups appealed to the community with slogans such as "your neighbors are not your enemies," and "sit tight, keep your heads and your tempers"; municipal authorities acted vigorously. A torrential rain luckily kept people indoors. By the second day of the strike car pools were in operation and fleets of Army and Navy

---

[22] Malcolm Ross, *All Manner of Men* (New York: Reynal and Hitchcock, 1948) pp. 90–93; House Committee to Investigate Executive Agencies, 78th Congress, 1st and 2d Sessions, Hearings on HR 102, *To Investigate Executive Agencies*, Part II, pp. 1854–1926.

[23] Ltr, Davis to President, 2 Aug 44, in OWI Release N–1093.

[24] Ross, *op. cit.*, pp. 97–98; Federal Grand Jury for June, Dist Court of U.S. for Eastern Dist of Pennsylvania, Investigation of Philadelphia Transportation Co. Strike, signed C. J. Baker, Foreman (Oct 44), copy in ASF Director of Personnel, Philadelphia Transportation.

buses brought people to and from work.   Attendance in war production jobs improved greatly.   The danger of violent race riots receded, but surface transportation was effectively blocked.[25]

The walkout was a spectacular challenge to two basic wartime policies. Failure to settle it on government terms would have been a serious blow to federal antistrike policy.   The National War Labor Board took jurisdiction but found no conflict between the company and the duly elected representatives of the workers.   There was nothing for the board to settle because the issue was one of breaking the control of a group of workers acting illegally.[26] The problem was referred to the President who issued an executive order directing government seizure and designating the Army as the seizing agency.[27] Secretary of War Stimson announced that Maj. Gen. Philip Hayes of the Third Service Command would take charge of the transit properties and appealed to all loyal Americans to return to work before great damage was done to war industry.   A War Department team of specialists in labor and race relations joined General Hayes in Philadelphia.[28]

General Hayes moved into Philadelphia on 3 August and appealed to the strikers to return to work.   The anti-Negro leaders ordered the men back but changed their minds when it became clear that the War Department would not compromise on the racial issue.   On the other hand, CIO members reported to take cars out and a large number of additional men who could not make up their minds congregated at the car barns and watched developments.   During the morning part of the high speed underground system was operating, but as the day went on fewer and fewer cars went out, and by midnight movement had come to a dead stop.   The men in the barns feared the opprobrium of scabbing, doubted the adequacy of police protection, and had become wrought-up over the strike leaders' statements that the seniority rules were being thrown out and that Negroes were stealing the jobs of veterans. About three thousand men met and voted to remain on strike until they received a written guarantee that Negroes would not be upgraded.[29]

[25] Ohly, *op. cit.,* I, 297–300; Tel Conv, Capt O'Donnell and Col Boyer, 1 Aug 44.
[26] Ltr, Davis to President, 2 Aug 44, in OWI Release N–1093.
[27] Ohly, *op. cit.,* I, 300; EO 9459, 3 Aug 44.
[28] *The New York Times,* August 4, 1944; Memo, Foster and L. R. Lautier for Hayes, 10 Aug 44, in ASF Director of Personnel, Philadelphia Transportation; Memo, SW to CG ASF, 3 Aug 44, sub: WD Operation of . . . Philadelphia Transportation Co. . . ., and CG ASF to CG Third Sv Comd, 3 Aug 44, sub: WD Operation of . . . Philadelphia Transportation Co. . . ., both in Hist Rpt, Army Operation of the Philadelphia Transportation Company, in ASF Control Div, Possession and Operation of Philadelphia Transportation Company.
[29] Ohly, *op. cit.,* I, 300–305; Federal Grand Jury for June in District Court of U.S. for Eastern

On 5 August General Hayes began to bring in soldiers. Two regiments of the 102d Infantry Division, stationed at Fort Dix and ready to go overseas, were called to Philadelphia. Combat troops in battle dress were deployed at car barns and posted on operating vehicles.[30] Platoon leaders found themselves in the unfamiliar role of trolley and elevated train dispatchers. Workers were warned that those who failed to report for work on Monday, 7 August, would be fired, that if they were between eighteen and thirty-seven years of age their draft deferments would be canceled, and that they would be blacklisted for other jobs. The Department of Justice obtained warrants and the FBI took four of the strike leaders into custody. The Attorney General announced a special federal grand jury to bring indictments for criminal conspiracy against violators of the Smith-Connally Act.[31]

The threat of extensive use of government powers against individuals brought the workers back to their jobs. On Monday morning 98 percent of the employees reported, and absenteeism dropped to an all-time low. Transportation moved at above the normal rate. On the following Friday, 11 August, the troops began moving back to Fort Dix.[32]

Intelligence reports indicated that many ex-strikers were still opposed to the upgrading of Negroes and had returned to work because they were frightened.[33] Continued vigorous action prevented further incidents. The arrested strike leaders were fired, and two of them were reclassified by Selective Service for induction. About two hundred men and women had failed to report for work. Most of them had legitimate reasons, and the Army was inclined to be lenient and inflicted few penalties. But as a psychological measure each

District of Pennsylvania, Investigation of Philadelphia Transportation Co. Strike, signed C. J. Baker, Foreman (Oct 44), copy in ASF Director of Personnel, Philadelphia Transportation; Memo, Maj Gen C. P. Gross for Somervell, 4 Aug 44, sub: Philadelphia Strikes, and Memo, Brig Gen. J. F. Battley for ACofS ASF, 4 Aug 44, both in ASF Control Div, Philadelphia Strike.

[30] Philadelphia *Inquirer,* August 4, 5, 6, 1944; Hist Rpt, Army Operation of the Philadelphia Transportation Company, pp. 16–19, in ASF Control Div, Possession and Operation of Philadelphia Transportation Company.

[31] Notice, Hayes to Employees Philadelphia Transportation Co. [5 or 6 Aug 44], and Press Statement, Hayes, 5 Aug 44, both in ASF Director of Personnel, Philadelphia Transportation.

[32] Ohly, *op. cit.,* I, 309–10; *Wall Street Journal,* August 8, 1944; Maj. Allan H. Mick (ed.), *With the 102d Infantry Division Through Germany* (Washington: Infantry Journal Press, 1947), p. 31.

[33] Log, Philadelphia Strike, 14, 15, 16 August 44, in ASF Director of Personnel, Philadelphia Transportation; PMG Daily Rpts Philadelphia Transportation Strike 4 to 10 Aug 44; ASF Control Div, Philadelphia Strike. Community sentiment seems to have opposed the strike and a newspaper poll held during and shortly after the strike indicated that 63.5 percent of those interviewed disapproved of the walkout. (Clipping, Philadelphia *Bulletin,* ASF Director of Personnel, Philadelphia Transportation.)

individual had to file applications, explain, and go through the formality of being excused. Twenty-four who did not show up at all were dismissed.[34] The federal grand jury meanwhile took testimony and indicted many strike leaders. Ultimately about twenty-five of them paid fines of about $100 each.[35] A strong, positive element for racial harmony was the favorable pact made by the CIO union with the company. Its prestige enhanced by the concrete gains it brought to the workers, the union was able to allay the fears of those members who thought that Negroes in better jobs would depress wages and lower working standards.[36]

General Hayes waited until passions cooled and government and community agencies were sure of controlling the situation before restoring the Negro training program. By 17 August Negro motormen were operating cars without incident.[37] The War Department then returned transportation facilities to the Philadelphia Transportation Company, and troops were withdrawn from Philadelphia.[38] The costliest racial dispute (in terms of production loss) of World War II had been settled.[39]

The problems affecting the utilization of Negro workers were local. Thus the consequences of employing them varied widely. There was an equally wide variation among different industries. Regardless of the state of supply, an industry which before the war had employed few Negroes and which was located in a community where strong prejudices existed was not likely to increase to any great extent its proportion of Negro workers or to train them for better jobs. Practically every industry, in the North or South, that made an effort to solve its manpower problem by hiring greater numbers of Negro workers encountered new problems that were in many instances as great a threat to production as the manpower shortage.

[34] Ohly, *op. cit.,* I, 310–14; Application for Return to Work Submitted by Philadelphia Transportation Company, Application . . . by Employees, Application . . . by Philadelphia Transportation Company Employees Interviewed by Board of Officers, all in ASF Control Div.

[35] *U.S.* v. *J. H. McManamin and Twenty-Nine Others* in District Court of U.S. for Eeastern District of Pennsylvania, June Term, 1944, Violation of Public Law 89, 78th Congress . . . War Labor Disputes Act, copy in ASF Director of Personnel, Philadelphia Transportation.

[36] J. J. Fitzsimmon, Vice President Transport Workers Union of America; CIO, to Members of Transport Workers Union of Philadelphia, copy in ASF Director of Personnel, Philadelphia Transportation.

[37] The program of upgrading Negroes according to individual merit continued, and the original number of seven Negro motormen was increased, while additional Negroes were upgraded to other positions. About five months after the strike, a newspaper reporter found forty-six Negroes holding what had formerly been considered white jobs. (The Washington *Evening Star,* January 11, 1945.)

[38] Hist Rpt, Army Operations of the Philadelphia Transportation Company, in ASF Control Div, Possession and Operation of Philadelphia Transportation Company.

[39] The Final Report of the Fair Employment Practices Committee, 28 June 1946, pages 14–15, states that one million man-hours of work were lost.

Bringing Women Out of the Home

By far the largest pool of potential workers in 1940 consisted of the more than 36,000,000 women who were not in the labor force and the 2,000,000 women who were unemployed and looking for work. Throughout 1941 and during most of 1942 only sporadic efforts were made to recruit female workers for war plants. The mobilization of labor was still proceeding automatically, powered by high and rising wages and fed by an adequate, though rapidly diminishing, supply. Without much persuasion on the part of employers or the government, some 860,000 unemployed women found jobs between March 1940 and March 1942.[40]

Until 1942 most of the increased employment of women appears to have taken place in government arsenals and naval shipyards. A survey made by the Women's Bureau of the Department of Labor early in 1941 reported the extensive use of female workers in government munitions plants. Forty percent of the workers engaged in making small arms ammunition were women. In contrast, women working in aircraft plants were "so few as to be insignificant."[41] By the end of 1941 only a little over 4,000 women were employed in the aircraft industry. Practically none were working in private shipbuilding yards, and relatively few were employed in the steel industry.[42]

Reluctance of employers to hire women, not the dearth of applicants, was chiefly responsible for the inertia of private industry. New problems of health and safety had to be considered. The sickness rate was higher for women workers and their physical strength was less than that of men. They could not be assigned to jobs that required heavy lifting or constant standing. Machinery, tools, and workbenches had to be redesigned and modified. Additional washroom and rest facilities had to be provided. Furthermore, a company's training program had to be revised and additional counseling services established.[43] All this was expensive and, with materials becoming scarce, difficult. Furthermore there were statutory restrictions on the work-

[40] Based on statistics in International Labor Office, *The War and Women's Employment: The Experience of the United Kingdom and the United States*, Studies and Reports, New Series 1 (Montreal, Canada: International Labor Office, 1946), p. 167, and U.S. Bureau of the Census, *Historical Statistics of the United States, 1789–1945: A Supplement to the Statistical Abstract of the United States* (Washington: Government Printing Office, 1949), Table D11–31, p. 63.

[41] Annual Rpt of the Secy of Labor for FY Ending 30 Jun 41, p. 131.

[42] ILO, *The War and Women's Employment*, pp. 173–74; FSA, The Labor Market, May 1942, p. 8.

[43] For a discussion of these problems see, Helen Baker, *Women in War Industries*, Report Series 66 (Princeton, N. J.: Industrial Relations Section, Princeton University, 1942), Chs. III and VI, and Industrial College of the Armed Forces, Report, Women in War, SR 49–15 (1948–49), pp. 72–76.

ing hours of women. Labor unions opposed any relaxation of restrictive legislation. Some unions refused to admit women as members, and many working men objected to women moving into fields that had always been reserved for men.

In the surge of patriotism after the attack on Pearl Harbor, many girls and housewives who had never before considered taking jobs sought work in war industry. Labor agencies of the federal government attempted to check the trend, for as yet the wide-scale enlistment of women workers appeared unnecessary. On 21 April 1942 the chairman of the recently established War Manpower Commission stated publicly that there were "far more women workers who want and are available for jobs than there are job openings for them," and a few days later President Roosevelt indicated in a press conference that there was no immediate need to recruit additional women for industrial work.[44] Nevertheless, an embarrassing flood of applicants descended on employment offices. The disillusionment of some of those who were turned away early in 1942 made it more difficult to persuade them later that their services were really needed.

While the Women's Bureau of the Department of Labor insisted that "women workers are the prime source of the new labor supply now demanded," the War Manpower Commission continued to soft-pedal the idea until well into the fall of 1942. Then, with an Army of 9,000,000 men or more under discussion, the commission and the War Department agreed that vast gaps in the civilian manpower supply would appear in 1943. To fill these gaps and to keep factories and farms operating at full blast would require employing 5,000,000 women before the end of 1943, the War Manpower Commission estimated. But as long as employers refused to hire women it would, the commission apparently believed, be futile to try either to recruit them or to persuade them to register for industrial work. The Industrial Personnel Division, ASF, took a more optimistic view than had the War Manpower Commission of the first measures for mobilizing women. The voluntary registration of some 300,000 women in Detroit, of whom 181,000 indicated their availability for factory work, the agreement of AFL and CIO leaders that a national registration of women was necessary, the steps taken by some two hundred communities to provide day nurseries for the children of working mothers, and the increasing numbers of women

---

[44] WMC, History of the Mobilization of Labor for War Production During World War II, Ch. VIII, Part III, pp. 43–44.

employed in California and Connecticut were singled out as noteworthy by the Industrial Personnel Division.[45]

By the beginning of 1943 the backlog of unemployed women had all but disappeared. By March only 450,000 female workers were without jobs. In the face of what appeared to be a growing labor shortage, employer and trade union resistance to the employment of women had gradually broken down, but it was now more difficult to obtain recruits. Any substantial increase in the number of women workers would have to come from those who were not particularly interested in factory work. An effort to bring more of them into industry would have to be made, the President's special committee on manpower reported, if the country were to support an Army and Navy of 11,000,000 men.[46] Making use of filmstrips, posters, radio, and all the other paraphernalia of the advertising industry, the War Manpower Commission embarked on a series of high-pressure recruiting campaigns. The Industrial Personnel Division, ASF, assisted in producing a filmstrip, "Civilian Womanpower," and prepared a Guide to the Immediate and Maximum Utilization of Womanpower.[47] Service command officers assisted local War Manpower Commission officials in conducting the campaigns. Special recruitment centers manned by U.S. Employment Service personnel were set up in shopping districts and housing developments to cater to women. Although the commission reported in June 1943 that the recruiting of women workers had been very successful, the Production Division, ASF, found evidence indicating that the campaign was not proceeding rapidly enough to provide replacements for the men withdrawn from the labor force.[48]

At the same time American women were the target of another recruiting campaign, one that War Manpower Commission officials and ASF labor officers feared might have an adverse effect on the industrial labor program. The Women's Army Auxiliary Corps, recently brought into the Army as the Women's Army Corps, launched an all-out campaign for recruits in the fall of 1943. The quota, variously set at 10,000, 35,000, and 70,000 (ceiling strength of the WAC had been fixed at 200,000), would not seem to have

---

[45] Annual Rpt of the Secy of Labor for FY Ending 30 Jun 42; WMC, History of the Mobilization of Labor for War Production During World War II, Ch. VIII, Part III, pp. 46–47; IPD Manpower Bulletin, Vol. I, Nos. VII (11 Sep 42) and VIII (18 Sep 42), Vol. II, Nos. IV (30 Oct 42) and VIII (27 Nov 42), in ASF IPD, Labor Manual 1942.

[46] See above, pp. 47–48.

[47] ASF IPD Weekly Progress Rpt for Week Ending 9 Oct 43.

[48] ASF Labor Br Weekly Progress Rpt for Week Ending 5 Jun 43, ASF Prod Br, 205.04.

been large enough to make serious inroads into the labor supply, but the
WAC publicity certainly threatened to overshadow the War Manpower
Commission campaigns.   Although WAC officials were under the impression that their recruiting campaign had the approval of the commission,
when the campaign got under way regional directors of the commission
refused to support it.[49]   The War and Navy Departments had agreed that,
if a recruiting campaign such as that of the WAC were hurting the local
labor market, the War Manpower Commission could stop it temporarily
until a final decision was made in Washington, and the commission regional
directors were not at all diffident about exercising the power that the agreement had placed in their hands.   A proposal by the chief of WAC recruiting to stress the slogan "Join the WAC or take a War Job" in the recruiting
campaigns conducted in areas of labor shortage offered no solution because
the commission insisted that its regional directors have final decision.[50]   The
Labor Branch of the Industrial Personnel Division, ASF, was interested in
the question particularly as it affected the west coast aircraft plants and urged
a prohibition on the enlistment of any women who had been working in
those plants during the six months preceding the date of their application
for enlistment.[51]   While it is possible that some women who joined the
Women's Army Corps in late 1943 might otherwise have taken jobs in war
industry, and vice versa, there is no measurable evidence of the impact of
the two recruiting campaigns upon one another.   The employment of
women workers was fast reaching a peak, as war production itself was
beginning to level off.   In fact, at the very time when the IPD was concerned about recruiting women workers for the west coast aircraft plants,
those plants, at least in California, were releasing women employees.[52]

Thanks to the watchful regard of the Women's Bureau and other agencies
the statistics on the role of women in the war effort are more plentiful than
those on other special groups.   Even in brief summary the record is full: an
increase in the number of women in the labor force from 14,640,000 in 1941
to 19,370,000 in 1944; a decline in the number not in the labor force from
36,310,000 to 33,280,000; a shift of 1,500,000 women already employed into
new jobs in war industries; spectacular increases in the proportion of women

[49] Mattie E. Treadwell, *The Women's Army Corps,* UNITED STATES ARMY IN WORLD
WAR II (Washington: Government Printing Office, 1954), pp. 232–45.
[50] ASF Labor Br Weekly Progress Rpt for Week Ending 9 Oct 43 and 16 Oct 43, ASF Prod
Br, 205.04.
[51] *Ibid.,* 9 Oct and 6 Nov 43.
[52] ILO, *The War and Women's Employment,* pp. 167–69.

employed in specific industries—from less than a half of one percent to 10 percent in shipbuilding, from less than 7 percent to more than 18 percent in the steel industry. The aircraft industry, in which much of the work was the light precision type, found jobs for considerable numbers of women. In a year and a half, women workers in aircraft plants, not including those in office or other nonfactory work, multiplied in number from about 4,000 to more than 310,000.

One of the problems that came to light was the disparate rate of absenteeism and job turnover between men and women workers. In every industry in which the comparison was made the percentage of women who quit their jobs was higher than that of the men. The reasons were various, related to housing, transportation, child care, shopping time, and other personal welfare factors, and were impossible to eradicate completely. Establishments such as small arms ammunition plants, where a large percentage of the employees were women, therefore faced a high rate of turnover.[53]

Another problem, really a combination of two, was that involving Negro women. The trend here was not one of new workers coming in from outside the labor force but a shift in the distribution of workers and a reduction in unemployment. For example, in April 1940, 16 percent of all Negro women employed were farm workers, nearly 60 percent were domestic workers, and only 6½ percent were industrial workers. Four years later, in April 1944, the percentage of farm workers and domestic workers had dropped to 8 percent and 45 percent, respectively, while industrial workers had jumped to 18 percent. Nevertheless, many war plants that accepted female workers refused to hire Negro women.[54] Since it viewed labor problems primarily as production factors, the War Department was inclined to look with suspicion upon labor policies that were potentially disruptive, however enlightened the policies might be. When an important Signal Corps contractor in St. Louis, under pressure of the Fair Employment Practice Committee hired a few Negro women in March 1945, and, as a result, found himself with a labor dispute on his hands, the ASF, counting the cost in miles of assault wire, would have preferred to postpone the issue. One high-ranking officer, noting that the committee seemed to have a different objective, put it very bluntly: "Hold these people off until after V–E Day.

---

[53] *Ibid.*, p. 225; Manpower Conference Minutes, 17 Jun 45, ASF IPD 202.02, Manpower Reports.
[54] ILO, *The War and Women's Employment*, pp. 183–85.

Then if production goes down it will not make so much difference. . . . Wait until after V–E Day to reform the world." [55]   If the Army was not interested in social reform at the expense of production, neither would it, Secretary Stimson wrote, allow "social customs peculiar to certain sections of the country to interfere with the primary task." [56]   If additional workers were necessary and the only available workers were Negroes, a way to employ them had to be found.   But this was chiefly the task of the War Manpower Commission and other agencies, not the War Department.

Industrial Deferments as a Recruiting Measure

A means of keeping skilled, irreplaceable workers in essential jobs and of drawing additional workers into such jobs existed in the provisions and administration of the Selective Service Act. [57]   Nevertheless, during the first year and a half of the war, the occupational deferment provisions of the act were to a considerable extent neglected.   After granting deferments on grounds of dependency, age, and marital status, local draft boards, hardpressed to meet their quotas, were not inclined to be generous in the matter of occupational deferments.   The aircraft industry and the merchant marine, heavily staffed with young men, many of them unmarried, were particularly hard hit by the draft.   With war production rising rapidly, employers began to demand that something be done to halt the induction of important workers.   The Selective Service System established what were intended to be more effective procedures for deferring workers; closer liaison was maintained between Army Air Forces and ASF labor officers on the one hand and Selective Service on the other; and the number of registrants deferred for work in industry increased from less than 600,000 at the beginning of 1942 to almost 2,900,000 at the end of the year.   Well over half of the men placed in this special class because of their jobs were actually deferred because of their family status.   Although war production continued to rise sharply and steadily until the end of 1943, when it leveled off at a high rate, industrial deferments did not really begin to mount until production was almost at the peak.   (Chart 2)   The slow build-up of industrial deferments,

---

[55] Manpower Conference Minutes, 21 Mar 45, ASF IPD, 202.02, Manpower Reports.

[56] Ltr, Stimson to Representative J. E. Rankin, 8 Dec 42, OSW 351, Negroes.

[57] Unless otherwise noted, the following section is based on material in Selective Service System, *Industrial Deferment,* Special Monograph 6, 3 vols. (Washington: Government Printing Office, 1947) and Albert A. Blum, Deferment From Military Service: A War Department Approach to the Solution of Industrial Manpower Problems (unpublished doctoral dissertation submitted to Columbia University, 1953), copy in OCMH.

CHART 2—MUNITIONS PRODUCTION AND INDUSTRIAL DEFERMENTS

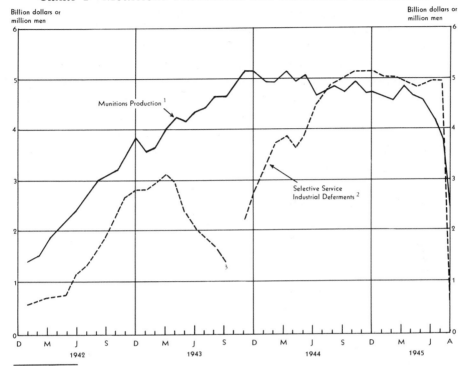

Billion dollars or
million men

Billion dollars or
million men

Munitions Production [1]

Selective Service
Industrial Deferments [2]

[1] Deliveries of selected items in month plotted multiplied by unit price in 1945; resultant index of dollar deliveries is not expenditures by or cost to government for munitions.
[2] Includes, from May 1942 through April 1944, men deferred because of both dependency and war industry occupation. After this combination class was abolished in April 1943, the majority were reclassified as dependency deferments.
[3] Data for October 1943 not reported.

Source: Selective Service System, *Industrial Deferment*, Vol. III, Tables 117 and 123, pp. 67, 86; Civilian Production Administration, *The Production Statement, United States War Program, July 1, 1940–August 31, 1945* (1947).

and their rapid increase during 1944, was conditioned by the policy of Selective Service in granting dependency deferments. As late as January 1943, out of a total of 28,800,000 registrants, 11,670,000 men, including many war workers, were deferred for dependency. By December 1943 this figure had dropped to 3,672,000; by April 1944 Selective Service was allowing only 445,000 deferments for dependency alone.[58] Until late in 1943 the granting of industrial deferments was perhaps held back by the legal requirement that deferments be based on the merits of each individual case and by interagency

[58] Information supplied by Statistics Br, Office, Comptroller of the Army.

disagreement over responsibilities for deferments.   Because of the former, blanket deferments for particular occupational groups were precluded.   Only the farmers received special treatment.

Toward the end of 1943 a new certification procedure was established, under which the procurement agencies, including the War Department, joined employers in certifying to the indispensability of particular workers and in requesting deferment for them.   Although instituted as part of the west coast plan to aid the aircraft industry, the special certification procedure was soon extended to other important industries throughout the country. During 1944, with war production beginning to drop off, the number of workers deferred because of their jobs rose sharply to more than 5,000,000. The trend appears to have been related more to the course of the fighting on the battle fronts than to the progress and needs of industry.

CHAPTER IX

Temporary Reinforcement for Industry

In addition to the workers recruited from groups which might have been counted as part of the permanent labor force but which to one extent or another and for various reasons had been excluded, temporary reinforcements were drawn from sources that were not ordinarily considered to be available. These sources included the labor forces of neighboring countries, prisoners of war, and the Army itself. The use of foreign workers and prisoners of war involved concomitant problems of discrimination, prejudice, and security similar to those raised by the employment of Negroes, resident aliens, and women workers. Drawing upon the Army for industrial workers gave rise to the same questions that were presented by deferring workers from the draft.

The Employment of Foreign Workers

Before the war, U.S. employers of seasonal labor along the Mexican and Canadian borders had frequently utilized the manpower pool on the other side of the border. Mexican agricultural workers had slipped into Texas during harvest periods, and Canadian woodsmen had been given temporary entry permits to work in the Maine pulpwood industry during peak periods. But these were special cases. In general, the practice of importing foreign workers had died with the end of the great railroad-building days of the nineteenth century.

During the spring of 1942 sugar beet and cotton growers in California, Texas, and the Southwest began requesting the importation of Mexican workers. Labor agencies of the federal government were not agreed on the extent of the need, but after consultations were held among the interested agencies the Immigration and Naturalization Service in late May or early June recommended that 3,000 sugar beet workers be admitted from Mexico. The War Department considered this preferable to deferring workers from the draft or to releasing soldiers for temporary farm work. Negotiations with the Mexican Government for a general agreement on the subject were entered into, in the course of which about 350 Mexicans were brought to

California for work in the sugar beet industry.   On receiving assurance that the Mexican workers would have the same protection afforded to corresponding American workers in the matter of pay, housing, and working conditions, the Mexican Government on 23 July 1942 agreed to permit the large-scale recruiting of Mexican nationals for farm work in the United States.   Transportation from and to Mexico was to be paid by the United States Government.   Administration of the program was assigned to the Department of Agriculture.[1]

While the negotiations with Mexico were in progress, the production of copper, zinc, and other nonferrous metals began to decline as a result of severe problems encountered in recruiting workers for the mines.   An employment stabilization order issued by the War Manpower Commission on 7 September 1942 to prevent workers from leaving their jobs made the recruiting of new workers difficult.   The remedy proposed by the War Production Board and the War Manpower Commission was the same one that had been suggested to alleviate the situation in agriculture and to which the Army had objected, namely, that soldiers be released from active duty or placed on furlough to fill the labor shortage.   Before the Army agreed to this step, it insisted that the War Production Board shut down all gold mines not engaged in producing strategic metals.   In the month after the gold mines were closed, approximately 4,300 soldiers were released from duty and were hired by the nonferrous metal mining companies.   Although some of the mines met most of their current labor requirements by hiring men released from the Army, it was anticipated that between 4,000 and 5,000 additional mineworkers would be needed to attain maximum production.   The War Department believed that it would be necessary to obtain them from Mexico and urged that an arrangement similar to the one for agricultural labor be adopted.   Mexican mines, however, were working at full capacity. Since the bulk of the output was being exported to the United States, any disruption of Mexican production as a result of the emigration of labor would have canceled any improvement in American production.   The Army therefore did not press the matter.[2]

[1] FSA, The Labor Market, May, June, and September 1942.

[2] Memo, [*ca.* 8 Nov 42], sub: Program for Importation of Mexican Nationals for Nonferrous Metal Mining Industries . . ., ASF Director of Personnel, Aliens; Memo, USW for Gen McSherry, 21 Nov 42, and Ltr, USW to Asst Secy of Commerce, 19 Nov 42, both in OUSW Res and Prod Div 470.1/129.6, Nonferrous Metals (3) Copper, October–November; Memo, Mitchell for Res Div SOS, 7 Oct 42, sub: Use of Mexican Labor in Southwest Copper Mines, OUSW Res and Prod Div 175, Labor 1942.

By far the greatest number of Mexicans joining the American battle for production were employed in agriculture and on railroad work. The peak period was reached in 1944, when 63,432 Mexicans were employed in agriculture north of the border and approximately 50,000 more were working on U.S. railroads.[3] By the terms of the agreement, no Mexicans were employed under contract in states where racial discrimination existed. Although Texas was thus excluded from the government program, large numbers of Mexicans had illegally entered and were at work in Texas.

Agreements similar to the one with Mexico were negotiated with a number of other neighboring governments. Under these arrangements, nearly 26,000 Bahamians and Jamaicans were working on U.S. farms at the end of the war. Of more direct interest to the War Department was the fact that by the end of 1944 approximately 8,700 British West Indians were employed in industry. About 2,200 of them were in food processing plants and 1,900 were employed in foundries and forges. The most important contribution to the manpower situation, in the opinion of the Industrial Personnel Division, ASF, was the employment of these workers in foundries, particularly in the Milwaukee and Racine areas, that were producing critical materials. The IPD also worked out arrangements for the employment of Bahamians and Jamaicans in War Department installations. In December 1944 about 300 Jamaicans were working at the Picatinny Arsenal, another 200 were on order by the Navajo Ordnance Depot in Arizona, and about 1,500 were employed in ordnance plants elsewhere. The successful experience at Picatinny induced the ASF to embark on a vigorous campaign designed to dissipate the reluctance of both management and labor to accept foreign workers.[4]

The War Department had no illusions as to the efficacy of the program. The recruitment of foreign workers would, the ASF recognized, solve only a few of the labor problems and would, at the same time, produce other problems. As it was, the task of feeding, housing, and clothing the Mexican and West Indian workers that were actually employed was very great indeed. Furthermore, by the time the utilization of foreign workers reached its peak, war contracts were beginning to be cut back and American workers were being released. The foreign workers made their contribution as a

---

[3] *Migratory Labor in American Agriculture: Report of the President's Commission on Migratory Labor* (Washington: Government Printing Office, 1951), p. 38; Magnusson and Poluhoff, Manpower in Industrial Mobilization, Industrial College of the Armed Forces, R 29, p. 16.

[4] ASF Study, Manpower Requirements, Part V [late Dec 44 or Jan 45], Ohly file, National Service Folder 2.

mobile reserve, particularly for agriculture, a reserve that could be used to fill temporary, spot shortages. Had the war continued much longer, with a consequent prolonging and intensifying of the industrial effort, foreign workers might have been called on to play a larger role, but it is doubtful whether the government and industry would have been prepared to utilize them more extensively and efficiently.

Workers in Uniform

The interest of the War Department in recruiting foreign labor had no doubt been stimulated by the constant barrage of requests from industry and governmental agencies that men be released from the Army to work in civilian jobs. That an enterprise as gluttonous as selective service might swallow men whose services were more valuable to industry than to the Army had been recognized soon after the Selective Service Act went into effect. A procedure, announced by Under Secretary Patterson on 23 May 1941, had been worked out under which soldiers might return to key jobs in industry. If, upon the request of an employer, a soldier indicated his willingness to return to this job immediately, the Army would study his case, and if the circumstances warranted his release from the service the soldier would then be transferred to the Enlisted Reserve Corps. Although subject to recall to active duty at any time, he was then free to re-enter his civilian job. When the ASF was organized in March 1942, a Key Personnel Unit was established in the Industrial Personnel Division for the purpose of investigating these requests with the assistance of the Selective Service System, the labor agencies of the War Department, and other interested agencies.[5]

This program was designed to rectify individual errors which had caused men whose appropriate place was in war production to be drafted into the Army. It was designed also to take care of changing industrial demands as a result of which a man might have become vitally essential to industry after he had been drafted by the Army. The program was not intended to provide reinforcements for the general manpower pool or to alleviate temporary and seasonal crises.

The first breach in the Key Personnel Program occurred in the fall of 1942 in response to the acute emergency in the production of nonferrous metals. The director of the Industrial Personnel Division, Mitchell, saw no other solution than to release men from the Army for work in the mines,

---

[5] See Maj William McFadden, The Release of Key Industrial Personnel From the Armed Forces During World War II, ASF IPD Monograph 13b, OCMH.

although the Key Personnel Unit objected to a "wholesale release" and suggested that procedures of the Key Personnel Program be utilized to the extent of having the mine operators make specific requests for former employees. This suggestion was not followed. Army installations were authorized to release a given number of enlisted men whose qualifications for work in the mines and their willingness to do so were determined through interviews with their officers. They were then released from active duty, transferred to the Enlisted Reserve Corps, and sent to the mining camps. Men who accepted the release lost their re-employment rights to jobs they had held before being drafted, a consideration that made many reluctant to volunteer for work in the mines. Although they were subject to recall to active duty if they left the jobs for which they had been released, 34 percent of the men released to work in the mines soon left for better paying, more desirable jobs.[6]

Having once permitted its manpower supply to be tapped, the Army found it difficult to resist a further drain upon its resources. During the spring and early summer of 1943 the food canning and farm equipment repair industries requested, and received, the release of a few soldiers for a three-month period to assist in training new workers. Camp commanders were persuaded to authorize their men to do part-time work when off duty. The New Jersey tomato crop was saved by soldiers from Fort Dix who were given three-day passes to work in the fields, and more than 500 men from Fort Meade helped to harvest, process, and pack the Maryland pea crop. Under public pressure, the Army also directed entire units to drop their training or other military duties and give temporary assistance to short-handed industries, particularly to agriculture. More than 5,000 soldiers in the Midwest interrupted their duties during the 1943 harvest season to help save the North Dakota grain crop.[7] The nonferrous metal mines were again facing a shortage of labor. Aircraft manufacturers and the merchant marine were in need of men. All turned to the Army.

[6] Memo, Patterson for Somervell, 28 Sep 42, Hq ASF file, USW (2); Memo, Somervell for CofS, 29 Sep 42, OUSW Res and Prod Div 470.1/129.6, Nonferrous Metals (7) Copper, September 1942; Memo, Somervell for Mitchell, 3 Oct 42, and Memo, Mitchell for Somervell, both in ASF IPD (1) Series (1) 41–3; Interview, Grossman with Thomas Kennedy, Vice President of UMWA, 15 Apr 52; Memo, Lt Hall for Col Murrell, 14 Dec 42, sub: Rpt on Examination of Western Mine Areas, ASF IPD 663, Mines; Senate Committee on Military Affairs, 78th Congress, 2d Session, Hearings on S. 1864 and S. 1870, *Manpower for War Production*, Part 3 (1944), pp. 125–33.

[7] Ltr, Chief Labor Br Third Sv Comd to Boland, 22 Jun 43, sub: Enlisted Pers Employed in Food Processing, ASF IPD, Farming Operations, May–August 1943; ASF IPD, Soldier Employment, *passim;* ASF IPD, Troop and Soldier Labor, *passim;* ASF IPD, Farm Labor, *passim.*

The labor situation in the copper industry was as critical in June 1943 as it had been twelve months before, and the Army was warned that production would fall unless more soldiers were released.[8] Under Secretary Patterson vigorously opposed releasing additional soldiers on the ground that the 1943 releases had weakened the Army without noticeably increasing production. When the War Production Board insisted that the Army was the only remaining "reservoir of skills," Patterson reluctantly agreed to a second large-scale release of men to the copper industry. This time the quota was set at 4,544 men.[9] The men were to be chosen only from the Seventh, Eighth, and Ninth Service Commands. They were to be interviewed, if possible, by a representative of the U.S. Employment Service, and, to insure their remaining at their jobs, they were to be released under supervision of the local draft boards instead of the U.S. Employment Service. Despite the closer control made possible by the new procedures, a number of untrained, unqualified workers were included among the men who were let go—one of them a man whose previous experience with nonferrous metals had been acquired as a jeweler. And, in spite of surveillance by the draft boards, some of the men again managed to give up their jobs in the mines for other kinds of work.[10]

The labor problem that faced the shipping industry was primarily the result of a tremendous wartime expansion. High wages, an intensive recruiting drive, and liberal deferment policies on the part of most draft boards were not enough to attract men in sufficient numbers to man the growing merchant fleet. In the month of December 1942 alone more ships were launched than in all of 1941, and in the spring of 1943 the monthly output of American shipyards was approaching a figure that was four times the annual production of 1939.[11] Without crews the ships would be useless. Large numbers of merchant seamen who had been thrown "on the beach" by the outbreak of the war in Europe had been caught up by the draft.

[8] *Engineering and Mining Journal,* Vol. 144 (June, 1943), p. 124; National Hq Selective Sv System, State Director Advice 217, 18 Jun 43, sub: Nonferrous Metal Mining and Milling and Lumbering and Logging Activities.

[9] *Engineering and Mining Journal,* Vol. 144 (August, 1943), p. 108.

[10] National Hq Selective Sv System, State Director Advice 217; Ltr, Patterson to King, Dir Copper Div WPB, 13 Jun 43, Hq ASF file, USW (3) 1943–45;Ltr, TAG to CG AAF *et al.,* sub: Transfer of Nonferrous Metal Miners to the ERC, ASF IPD, Release 41–3; McFadden, *op. cit.,* pp. 17–18.

[11] Samuel Eliot Morison, *History of United States Naval Operations in World War II,* Vol. I, *The Battle of the Atlantic, September 1939–May 1943* (Boston: Little, Brown and Company, 1947), p. 294. See also Frederic C. Lane, *Ships for Victory: A History of Shipbuilding Under the U.S. Maritime Commission in World War II* (Baltimore, Md.: Johns Hopkins Press, 1951), pp. 637–47.

Later, when the need for seamen became acute, the Army found itself faced with numerous requests and suggestions that these men be released. The War Shipping Administration, which recognized that its recruiting efforts were not bringing in enough men, and the unions, which took a dim and short-sighted view of the new men recruited by the War Shipping Administration, kept urging the Army to release former seamen. Although the War Department in 1943 approved the release of about 1,000 former seamen for a period of six months, the Selective Service System objected to a wholesale release. In any event, the time limitation rendered the plan unpractical. Instead, therefore, former seamen were permitted to apply individually for discharge from the Army, a procedure that gave the Selective Service System an opportunity to scrutinize and express its views on each case but did not help to solve the manpower problem.[12]

The situation in the aircraft industry was somewhat similar in that the industry underwent a tremendous expansion at a time when the armed forces were reaching into the manpower reservoir. And as a new industry, it was a young man's business. The North American Aviation company's male employees averaged twenty-four years of age, while its executives averaged only twenty-eight, and North American was no exception. Selective service hit this age group so hard, and the need for airplanes was so great, that some solution had to be found. The problem was particularly urgent at the west coast plants. As early as 1941, when a shadow of the forthcoming shortage had appeared, requests had been made for the release of workers for the west coast factories. Two years later, as part of the west coast manpower program, the Army authorized the release of 7,500 soldiers—only 1,600 of whom were actually released. The Air Forces' strict interpretation of the rules kept down the percentage released. Other branches of the armed forces announced plans to discharge men in order that they might work on the aircraft assembly lines. Although the War Department tried to release men over thirty, Selective Service objected to the number of men released to the plants who were younger. The War Department thereupon ordered the younger men back into uniform. A large part of the remainder continued at the west coast aircraft plants until June 1945, when plans were made to recall all the reservists to active duty.[13]

[12] Ltr, Marshall Dimock to Mitchell, 12 May 43, Interoffice Memo, Lt Bartell for Webber, 27 Jul 42, Form Ltr of Marshall Dimock, War Shipping Administration, and Ltr, Mitchell to Dimock, 26 May 43, all in ASF IPD, Release 41–3; McFadden, *op. cit.,* pp. 28–29; National Maritime Union, *The Pilot,* July 16, 1943.

[13] See documents in the following files: OUSW Res and Prod Div 175, Labor Supply 1941; OUSW Hertz files, North American Aviation; OUSW Hertz files, Release of Men; ASF Prod Div 049.12 Labor, 1–31 August 1941; ASF IPD Hist of Selective Sv; ASF IPD, Key Personnel; ASF IPD, Release 41–3; and ASF IPD, West Coast Aircraft Industry.

During 1944 pleas for the release of men reached the War Department in greater volume than before. Food canneries and the farm equipment industry again asked for men; this time they were refused. The aircraft industry, the tire industry, heavy artillery ammunition plants, bomb plants, the cotton duck industry, forges and foundries, meat packers, copper wire mills, and brass mills all sought to obtain men from the Army. After noting these requests and the number of men released, a study of manpower requirements made by the ASF in January or February 1945 concluded in this vein:

The signs of many additional requests are already gathering. Those men who have been released were released because the needs of the Armed Forces for the products of these industries were desperate and there appeared to be no practical immediate alternative. It is obvious that this process cannot continue if we are to have an Army with which to fight.[14]

Four industries—tire, forge and foundry, cotton duck, and heavy ammunition—were of such importance as to place their labor needs in a "must" category. Because a mechanized army moves, and an airborne army takes off and lands, on heavy tires, the War Department had early taken a special interest in the tire industry's labor problems. Beginning in September 1943, special project teams had been sent to the production centers, where they sponsored meetings and issued publicity releases aimed at convincing workers and potential workers that their jobs were necessary to the war effort. The special project teams had nevertheless failed to recruit a sufficient number of workers. Under Secretary Patterson therefore authorized the release from the Army of 1,000 experienced tire workers beginning on 7 August 1944. A similar program, subject to General Somervell's approval, was authorized at the same time for foundry and forge workers, but it was postponed for several months while attempts were made to persuade the Navy to release foundry and forge workers also. These attempts were to no avail, and early in November the Army began releasing men to the industry.[15]

The initial releases to the tire industry and to the forge and foundry industry were made under the procedure recommended by the Key Personnel Unit

---

[14] ASF Study, Manpower Requirements, Part V, Ohly file, National Service Folder 2.

[15] Memo, Chief Labor Br IPD for Chief Copper Sec Material Br IPD, 16 Sep 44, sub: Appeal for Provisions of Copper Conservation Program, ASF IPD, Furloughs, Tire Program; Memo, Patterson for Dir IPD, 7 Aug 44, sub: Transfer of Rubber Workers . . . to the ERC, Memo, Patterson for Dir IPD, 7 Aug 44, sub: Transfer of Foundry and Forge Workers to the ERC, and Memo, Somervell for Dirs Mil Pers Div, IPD, and Prod Div, 8 Nov 44, sub: Transfer of Foundry and Forge Workers to the ERC, all in ASF IPD, Release of Foundry Workers; Memo, Somervell for Dir Mil Pers Div, 8 Nov 44, sub: Transfer of Foundry and Forge Workers to the ERC, and Memo, Wolf for Bard, 5 Aug 44, sub: Release of Enlisted Men for Employment by the Foundry and Forge Industry, both in ASF Prod Div 220.711, Release of Soldiers from U.S. Army, 1 January 1943–January 1945.

in the fall of 1942, which had not been followed in providing men for the copper mines. Under this procedure, the companies were required to submit by name requests for the return of former employees. The difficulty was the companies often lacked accurate records of the men's names, their Army serial numbers, and their Army addresses, with the result that only 787 tire workers and less than 200 foundry workers were provided out of a total of 2,000 authorized. The ASF therefore reverted to the procedure that had been employed in furnishing men to the copper industry. Employers submitted a list of job titles and the number of men needed for each job. The Army combed its records for men fitted for the jobs and transferred to the Enlisted Reserve Corps all who seemed qualified. In this way most of the tire and foundry manpower quotas were provided, although complaints about the number of unqualified workers began to mount.[16]

As 1944 drew to a close it became increasingly difficult to find soldiers willing to be transferred to the Enlisted Reserve for work in industry where wages were low and working conditions poor. Hopes were growing that the war would soon be over, and soldiers were becoming reluctant to give up their rights to re-employment in their former jobs in order to transfer to less desirable employment, even if it meant getting out of the Army. The effect on the other two "must" programs—heavy ammunition and cotton duck— was becoming noticeable.

Beginning on 12 December 1944 a new method of providing industry with labor from the armed forces was adopted. Instead of transferring men to the Enlisted Reserve Corps, the War Department began to grant ninety-day furloughs to men to work in industry. The soldiers remained under Army discipline and jurisdiction and received their military as well as their industry pay. Since the men continued on active duty, did not lose their re-employment rights, and received double pay, there was considerably less difficulty finding soldiers to take jobs in those industries in which pay was low and working conditions were poor.[17] A total of 5,700 enlisted men were on requisition for the four "must" programs, in addition to the 787 tire workers that had been provided during the summer. Thanks to the new furlough system,

---

[16] Ltr. Lt Col Jensen to Mitchell, 28 Mar 44, ASF IPD, Release; Tel Dictation, Capt Peyser, 4 Dec 44, ASF Prod Div. 220.711, Release of Soldiers From U.S. Army, 1 January 1943–January 1945; Ltr, Chief Labor Br for Asst Chief, Industrial Allocations WMC, 18 Nov 44, and Ltr, Chief IPD to Companies, both in ASF IPD, Release of Foundry Workers.

[17] Memo, Styer for Dalton et al., 12 Dec 44, sub: Release of Mil Pers to Meet Manpower Shortages in Critical Programs, ASF Prod Div 220.711, Release of Soldiers From U.S. Army, 1 January 1943–January 1945; Gen Rpt of Recruitment at Camp Atterbury, Indiana, by Dir WMC, Ohio, and Memo, Styer for Dirs Mil Pers Div and IPD, 15 Dec 44, sub: Transfer of Foundry and Forge Workers to the ERC, both in ASF IPD, Release of Foundry Workers.

about 4,700 men were turned over to these industries by the end of December. At the expiration of their ninety-day furlough, all the men, except those from the Army Air Forces and Army Ground Forces, were given the choice of transferring to the Enlisted Reserve Corps and remaining at their jobs, or of returning to their stations. The Army Air Forces and the Army Ground Forces, which provided a little less than 30 percent of the men, stipulated that their men must return to active duty at the expiration of the furloughs.[18]

The continuing requests for men and the probable need for replacing those who might choose to return to active duty prompted Maj. Gen. Joseph N. Dalton, Director of Personnel for ASF, to suggest the furloughing of men eligible for separation from the Army. Between 30,000 and 40,000 men were being discharged each month, and, although efforts were made to funnel them into war industry, the same difficulties that had weakened the program of voluntary transfers to the Enlisted Reserve were encountered. General Dalton proposed that men eligible for discharge be given ninety-day furloughs instead of being immediately separated and that they be assigned to war industry during the period of their furlough. From 20,000 to 30,000 men would thus be made available for industrial work, it was estimated. Although this meant that the Army would have to include the men in computations of Army strength after their services were lost, and although Under Secretary Patterson strongly objected to the unfairness of the proposal, it was accepted and put into operation by the ASF on 13 January 1945. It came to an end eleven days later, when all discharges, except for reasons of disability, were halted. During the interval 535 soldiers had started through the furlough process and had been assigned to construction work at one of the Ordnance plants.[19]

In February the general picture appeared brighter, except for a continued small shortage of skilled workers for certain of the critical programs. The major problem was what to do when the furloughs of the men in the four "must" programs expired. They totaled about 7,700, but considerable attrition was expected. Surveys made by the Military Personnel Division of the

---

[18] ASF Study, Manpower Requirements, Table IV and App. III, Ohly file, National Service Folder 2.

[19] Memo, Brennan for Kanwit, 8 Jan 45, sub: Furlough Soldiers, Memo, Styer for CofOrd, 13 Jan 45, sub: Furlough Into Industrial Employment . . ., and Memo, Styer for CofEngrs, 24 Jan 45, sub; Recission of Plan . . ., all in ASF IPD, Industrial Furloughs of Dischargees; Memo, Dalton for CG ASF, 9 Jan 45, ASF IPD, Furlough Program, Gen; Memo, Patterson for Clay, 17 Jan 45, sub: Re-employment Rights of Veterans, ASF IPD, Separation Centers; Minutes of Meeting, 10 Jan 45, in Hq ASF file, Minutes of Meetings; ASF Conferences on Manpower Problems, 23 Jan 45, ASF IPD, Manpower Reports.

ASF indicated that about 60 percent of the soldiers working in heavy ammunition plants, 47 percent of those in forges and foundries, 44 percent of those in cotton duck plants, and 18 percent of those furloughed to the heavy tire industry desired to return to active duty. The situation was complicated by G-1's objections to increasing the Enlisted Reserve Corps and by the War Department's cautious hesitancy to take steps that might jeopardize passage of the national service bill then before Congress. The upshot was a thirty-day extension of the industrial furloughs except those of soldiers working in the foundry and forge industry.[20]

By mid-April 1945 the only manpower difficulties that remained were in a few narrow fields. The ASF headquarters conferences on manpower, presided over by Somervell and usually attended by Patterson, had in January 1945 been held every week and had lasted from two to two and a half hours. By April these conferences had been reduced to one short meeting of an hour or less every three weeks, and were being attended by colonels instead of generals. They ceased entirely after 2 May. When the furloughs of soldiers working in industrial plants expired, the men were transferred into the Enlisted Reserve and then gradually recalled to active duty. It was planned to have most of the men back in the Army by 1 August and the remainder by 1 December, but with the coming of V-J Day all of them were recalled, and the furlough programs came to a sudden halt.[21]

A backwash of the furloughing program was the release of almost 4,000 soldiers for railroad work during June and July 1945. Although the War Department successfully turned down requests from the coal industry and agricultural interests during the late spring and early summer of 1945, the important role assigned to the railroads in the redeployment of troops after V-J Day required that every effort be made to solve whatever problems the railroads faced. A special project team was organized. Selective Service was asked to give special consideration to railroad workers. Separation centers were directed to encourage discharged veterans to apply for railroad work. As a temporary stimulus, the War Department in June authorized thirty-day furloughs for 4,000 men. By the end of July, 3,050 ground troops had reported for work with the railroads. The Air Forces provided most of the remainder. As in the case of the earlier programs, it was necessary to extend

[20] Memo, Col Ralph F. Gow, Dir IPD, for CG ASF, sub: Developments in Manpower Situaation . . . as of 27 Feb 45, ASF IPD, 202.02, Manpower Reports.
[21] Memo, Dir IPD for CG ASF, 10 Jul 45, sub: Manpower Developments . . . for Two-Week Period Ending 7 July 1945, and Memo, Dir IPD for CG ASF, 7 Aug 45, sub: Manpower Developments . . . 4 Aug 45, both in ASF IPD 202.02, Manpower Reports.

the furloughs, and, along with the other programs, the railroad program ended with the victory over Japan.[22]

Both Secretary Stimson and Under Secretary Patterson opposed the furloughing of soldiers for industrial work as a matter of principle and accepted it only as expedient and palliative. The solution, as they saw it, was a national service law. The fact that the Army had had to use soldiers for functions other than those for which the men had been drafted was, in the view of Stimson and Patterson, proof that national service legislation was needed.[23]

The attitude of employers varied according to the success of the Army in sending men qualified for the jobs. When the soldiers had the requisite skills, or the aptitude and willingness to learn and work hard, there were enthusiastic reports from the industry. When unqualified men were sent to the plants, or when the soldiers did not trouble themselves to conceal their dislike of the assignment, company officials reported in appropriate vein.[24] On the whole, employers welcomed the military reinforcements. Being subject to military discipline, "furloughees" were not at liberty to quit their jobs or to protest effectively when given unpopular assignments such as the midnight shift, which in some plants became known as the military shift.[25]

Toward the furloughed soldiers, labor unions were less favorably disposed than were employers. Union leaders complained of not receiving advance notice that a release of soldiers was to take place. They were troubled not only by the fact that the soldiers received double pay and were sometimes ill-qualified for the job but also by the possibility that their presence might weaken the bargaining position of the civilian workers. The question of union membership was raised. The War Department sensibly decided not to make an issue of the question and permitted each man to choose for himself whether or not to join a union. When the Army was faced with a union

[22] Interoffice Memo, McFadden for Gow, 10 Jul 45, Interoffice Memo, Dir Mil Pers Div for ACofS G–1, 24 Jul 45, sub: Extension of Railroad Furloughs, and Memo, Dir Mil Pers Div, 23 Jul 45, same sub, all in ASF IPD, Furlough Program, Railroad Industry; Memo, Dir IPD for CG ASF, 7 Aug 45, IPD ASF 202.02, Manpower Reports.

[23] On Stimson's point of view, see Ltr, SW to President, 15 Jan 45, with attached papers, copies in OCMH, Selective Service; and Stimson and Bundy, *On Active Service in Peace and War,* pp. 480–88. The question of national service legislation is explored in Chapter XI, below.

[24] Ltr, Jensen to Mitchell, 28 Mar 44, ASF IPD, Release; Ltr, Special Truck Tire Production Team to IPD, 4 Mar 45, ASF IPD, Furloughs, Tire Program; Rpt on Use of Soldier Workers, J. B. Beaird Co. (Shreveport, La.), 21 Feb 45, ASF IPD, Heavy Artillery Ammunition Furlough Program.

[25] Ltr, 2d Lt Charles Stiles to ASF Cotton Duck Special Project Team, 14 Feb 45, sub: Screening Information on Enlisted Men at Lane Cotton Mills, ASF IPD, Transfer to ERC, Cotton Mills; Memo, Actg TQMG for CG ASF, 31 Dec 44, ASF IPD, Textiles, 1945; Somers, *Presidential Agency,* pp. 170–71.

protest over soldiers working in a closed-shop plant, the servicemen who refused to join the union were either recalled to active duty or transferred elsewhere. The War Department likewise resolved not to take a stand in advance on the question of the soldiers' position should a strike be called. After considerable discussion among War Department officials, it was decided that the Industrial Personnel Division should determine the course to be taken in each situation as it arose.[26]

The actual number of workers added to industry by the release of men from the Army was never very large. In arguing for a national service law, the War Department early in 1945 noted that over a period of three years at least 16,000 and at the most slightly more than 17,000 soldiers had been released for industrial work.[27] The number of soldiers working in industrial plants at any one time was probably less than half the cumulative total. Compared to the aggregate working force of the nation, the release of soldiers added only a drop to the labor pool—an even smaller particle than that added by the bringing in of foreign workers.

Putting Prisoners of War to Work

While the manpower pinch of 1943 was beginning to make itself felt, a large potential labor force in the form of German and Italian prisoners captured in the North African campaign had begun to take shape. Numbering fewer than 3,000 at the end of March 1943, the prisoners of war interned in the United States totaled 53,435 at the end of June 1943 and 163,706 at the end of September 1943. Their numbers grew, rising to 196,948 at the end of June 1944, and reaching a peak of 425,806 exactly a year later.[28] Not all the prisoners were available for work, and the type of work on which they could be employed was limited. According to the Geneva Prisoner of War Convention of 1929, only privates could be required to perform labor, and they could not be employed in jobs that were unhealthful, dangerous, or directly related to war operations. The use of prisoners of war in the manufacture

---

[26] See letters and memorandums in the following files: ASF Prod Div 220.711, Release of Soldiers from U.S. Army, 1 January 1943–January 1945; ASF IPD 327.22, Furloughs; ASF IPD, Cotton Duck Furlough Program; ASF IPD, Furlough Program, Gen; ASF IPD, Furloughs, Tire Program; ASF IPD, Heavy Artillery Ammunition Furlough Program; ASF IPD, Railroad Unions; ASF IPD, Transfer to ERC, Cotton Duck; and ASF IPD, Troop and Soldier Labor, See also McFadden, *op. cit.*, pp. 39–40.

[27] Statements attached to ASF Study, Manpower Requirements, Ohly file, National Service Folder 2.

[28] Lt. Col. George G. Lewis and Capt. John Mewha, *History of Prisoner of War Utilization by the United States Army, 1776–1945*, Department of Army Pamphlet 20–213 (Washington: Government Printing Office, 1955), pp. 90–91.

and transportation of arms and munitions of any kind and in the transportation of materials intended for combat units was specifically prohibited. Furthermore, the Army had established areas within which prisoner of war camps were not to be located. Although not precisely defined, these areas in general comprised, first, the blackout areas on both coasts, extending about 75 miles inland; second, a stretch 150 miles wide along the Mexican and Canadian boundaries; and third, any locality in the neighborhood of shipyards, aircraft plants, and similar establishments. The employment of prisoners outside their camps was further limited by the availability of guards. The number of military police companies allotted to guard duty in August 1943 was considered by the Office of the Provost Marshal General to be somewhat inadequate to permit full use of prisoners of war on projects outside the camps even if no transfer movements were involved.[29]

Although considerable work had been done by prisoners on their own camps and on other military installations (and this continued to be their major employment through the war), only a few small groups of prisoners had been made available to private employers before the end of 1943. When a shortage of agricultural labor again seemed to be developing in the Southwest during the spring of 1943, the Office of the Provost Marshal General directed commanders of prison camps to make prisoners of war available to private employers. Cotton growers in New Mexico wanted to use prisoners for thinning out the crop and a few seem to have been so employed. In June the president of the Association of American Railroads inquired whether prisoners of war could be employed to work on maintenance of way. After a decision by Under Secretary Patterson that this type of work was permitted by the Geneva Convention, the Chicago, Burlington & Quincy Railroad entered into a contract with the commander of the prisoner of war camp at Camp Clark, Missouri, for the employment of 250 prisoners to be used on the construction of a switching yard at Lincoln, Nebraska.

These first experiences revealed a difference of views among branches of the War Department and other agencies and pointed to the need of a set of general principles that would cover the employment of prisoners. The agencies and offices involved were the G-1 Division of the General Staff, the Office of the Provost Marshal General and the Industrial Personnel Division, both of the ASF, the Department of Agriculture, the U.S. Employment Service, and the War Manpower Commission. The major differences had to do

---

[29] Memo, Sufrin for O'Gara, 11 Aug 43, sub: Restrictions on the Employment of Prisoners of War, ASF IPD 202.02, August 1943–January 1944, Leland Reading File.

with the rates of pay for prisoner of war labor and with procedures for clearing the contracts of employment. Under instructions from the Provost Marshal General, camp commanders had been charged with responsibility for deciding whether the project on which prisoners were to be employed was essential, whether free labor was available, and what the contract price should be. Taking into account nuisance factors such as language and security problems, the Office of the Provost Marshal General had recommended that the pay rate be set considerably below the prevailing local wage scale. The Industrial Personnel Division, ASF, insisted, on the other hand, that prisoners of war should not compete with American free labor and that the contract rate should be the prevailing minimum wage. The Industrial Personnel Division objected to making prisoners of war available for thinning out the cotton crop at a rate of 15 cents an hour when the prevailing wage was 30 cents and when the local supply of free labor was more than double the demand. The War Manpower Commission agreed with the IPD on the wage question and took the further position that requests for prisoners should be submitted through the U.S. Employment Service and that the War Manpower Commission or Department of Agriculture should determine the need for such labor and the rate of pay.[30]

One of the major problems involved in the use of prisoner of war labor was revealed when the Chicago, Burlington & Quincy Railroad went ahead with its plans to use prisoners. When a temporary camp that was being built for the prisoners on the construction site was about half finished, the railroad union issued a strong statement opposing the employment of prisoners of war. There was, the union declared, a danger of sabotage, and furthermore the project, according to the union, was a violation of the Geneva Convention. The morale and efficiency of American workers, the statement continued, would be adversely affected and labor troubles would be the inevitable result. Asking the Office of War Mobilization to overrule the union's protest, the War Department pointed out that there was little likelihood of sabotage since the prisoners were to be segregated and were to be employed in a section of the yard where no opportunities for sabotage existed. All security requirements would be met. There would be no violation of the Geneva Convention since the yard was used for general traffic. The War Department further contended that, if the union's protest were upheld, the

---

[30] Memo, Sufrin for Mitchell, 28 May 43, sub: Prisoners of War, Memo, Robert M. Dinkel for Boland, 25 Jun 43, sub: Policy on Employment of POWs, and Memo, Dir IPD for G–1, 28 Jun 43, same sub, all in ASF IPD 202.02, August 1943–January 1944, Leland Reading File. See also Lewis and Mewha, *op. cit.,* pp. 102–04.

employment of prisoners for railroad work of any kind would be barred and a precedent established that might prevent the use of prisoners in any industrial employment.   The Director of War Mobilization, Mr. Byrnes, overruled the protest of the union but made it clear that his decision pertained only to the immediate case at issue.   A general policy governing future cases would have to be worked out, Byrnes stated.   Meanwhile, in order to complete the construction work before the onset of cold weather, the Chicago, Burlington & Quincy Railroad had found it necessary to drop its negotiations for the employment of prisoners and to use what other labor was available. Three months later, in November 1943, another railroad company applied for prisoner of war labor and was refused by the area director of the War Manpower Commission.   When the railroad appealed the decision with the support of the War Department, the chairman of the War Manpower Commission revealed to Secretary Stimson that the commission had adopted an "operating policy" of not certifying prisoners of war for employment in railroad work. The opposition of the powerful railroad unions continued to be strong, and the War Department ceased to press for the use of prisoners in this type of employment, particularly since large numbers of Mexicans were being hired by the railroads.[31]

The difference of opinion among the interested agencies on the matter of fundamental principles was to a large extent cleared up by the middle of August 1943.   Most nonmilitary responsibilities relating to the employment of prisoners were delegated to the War Manpower Commission.   It was agreed that the commission would investigate and, if no other labor was available, would certify the need of prisoners as requested by employers.   The conditions and terms of employment would be determined and their conformity to local conditions would be certified by the War Manpower Commission.   The War Department would be responsible for deciding whether projects conformed to the Geneva Convention and to security regulations and for determining whether the use of prisoners under the terms of the commission certification would be feasible.   In general, it was agreed that prisoners would be used only when other labor was not available, that employers should make their requests for prisoner of war labor through the U.S. Employment Service, and that they would accept the following conditions: no discrimination, the payment of prevailing wage rates, and equivalent working conditions.   An agreement embodying this understanding between the War Department and the War Manpower Commission was signed on 14 August

---

[31] Lewis and Mewha, *op. cit.,* pp. 140–43.

1943. Although changes and adjustments in procedures were made later, the basic policy remained as established by the agreement of 14 August.[32]

Italy's surrender in September 1943 and subsequent re-entry into the war as a cobelligerent of the Allied nations made it necessary to consider the status of the approximately 50,000 Italian prisoners of war. Their immediate re-patriation was not feasible, but to continue treating them on a par with the German prisoners was clearly inconsistent with the new circumstances. There were no precedents and no provisions in the Geneva Convention to serve as a guide. The solution finally adopted was the organization, early in 1944, of Italian service units into which prisoners who swore allegiance to the new Italian Government were transferred. They continued to be counted as pris-oners of war, but they were housed in separate camps, not in prison stock-ades, and were given a number of special privileges. The units were military organizations—quartermaster service companies, engineer utilities companies, and the like—intended primarily as replacements for ASF units. They were not to be employed on projects on which other prisoners of war could be used and were available.[33] By qualifying for the service units, about 34,000 Ital-ian prisoners disqualified themselves for industrial and agricultural work.

The extent to which prisoners of war were used in specific industries and in particular localities depended more upon the limitations laid down by the Geneva Convention, on community sentiment, and upon the attitude of labor unions than it did upon the available supply of civilian labor. Industries such as the railroads and the building trades that had strong unions offered little opportunity for prisoner of war employment. Prisoners of war were most extensively used in agriculture, which was not unionized and in which the prisoners could be put to work in relative isolation. In man-days of labor the work they performed in agriculture was 56 percent greater than in all other types of contract labor combined.[34] In the logging and lumbering in-dustry, prisoners of war were employed chiefly in the southeast and in Maine. Although the shortage of woodsmen was just as pronounced in the Pacific northwest and in Minnesota, there was strong opposition on the part of the unions in those two regions to the use of prisoners. The question was raised also whether lumbering might not be a hazardous occupation under the pro-visions of the Geneva Convention; pulpwood operations, which involved only

[32] Ltr, TAG to CGs Sv Comds, 14 Aug 43, sub: Labor of Prisoners of War, ASF IPD 383.6, Prisoners of War; Lewis and Mewha, *op. cit.,* pp. 107–10.

[33] WD General Council Meeting Minutes, 28 Feb and 23 Apr 44. See also OPMG Mono-graph, Headquarters, Italian Service Units, OCMH.

[34] Lewis and Mewha, *op. cit.,* table on p. 264. Contract labor represented slightly over 25 percent of the total prisoner of war labor.

small logs, were finally considered permissible. In the Buffalo–Niagara area, labor representatives on the area manpower committee consistently opposed the use of prisoners of war except in agriculture and in food processing plants. When the management of certain Buffalo feed and grain mills sought to hire additional workers in March 1944 and appeared willing to employ prisoners of war, the spokesman for the local labor union put his foot down firmly. "We don't want any part of the war prisoners . . . ," he told the Manpower Priorities Committee. "If it became absolutely necessary, and they had to work there, I wouldn't want my men to be there. The AFL and CIO have taken a definite position on the question . . . . I certainly wouldn't want to be in a position where I would overstep a policy set up by the AFL and CIO in Washington, and take it upon my own initiative to put men into those plants without consulting the members. I know what the reaction would be." [35] Community sentiment varied in unpredictable fashion, but in general people living in the large industrial centers, such as Detroit and Chicago, objected to having prisoners employed in their midst. Employers, for the most part, were anxious to obtain prisoners of war. There were some exceptions. Massachusetts farmers refused to employ Italian prisoners, although they accepted Germans; Eastman Kodak Company, in order to protect its secret manufacturing processes, would not employ German prisoners.

Of the four "must" programs, which at the end of 1944 were affected by labor shortages, the only one in which prisoners of war were employed to any extent was the forge and foundry industry. About 4,000 prisoners, of whom 75 percent were unskilled workers, were employed.[36] Early in January 1945 ASF considered the possibility of taking over a complete foundry and operating it entirely with prisoner of war labor. The experiment would have been an interesting one, but by the time the suggestion had been thoroughly discussed and approved and a foundry that was not in use had been located there was no longer a shortage of the particular type of casting produced by the foundry, and the idea was given up.[37]

The prisoners of war served to release Army service troops and civilians from work on military installations and helped to reduce the temporary or seasonal shortages of farm and industrial labor. Although their work on Army camps and other installations was by far the more extensive, it only

[35] Manpower Priorities Committee, Minutes, 8 Mar 44, quoted in Adams, *Wartime Manpower Mobilization,* pp. 70–71.
[36] Lewis and Mewha, *op. cit.,* p. 140.
[37] Manpower Conference Minutes, 17 Jan and 20 Mar 45, ASF IPD 202.02, Manpower Reports.

indirectly affected the civilian manpower situation. In respect to the work performed on farms and in industry, comparison with the similar contribution made by workers brought in from Mexico and the British West Indies is clearly called for but impossible to make. Neither the Office of the Provost Marshal General nor the Industrial Personnel Division seems to have kept a record of the exact number of prisoners at work at any one time. There was considerable concern over the productivity of prisoner of war labor, but the basis of comparison was the amount produced by free American labor and the concern was related to the wage rate. No studies were made of prisoner of war labor as compared with that of imported workers. It was enough for the Provost Marshal General to be able to point to the millions of man-days worked by the prisoners. Probably all that can be said was expressed by a New Hampshire farmer, who was quoted as follows: "They do what they are told. They don't work quite as fast as Americans or Jamaicans brought in to help solve the labor shortage, but they damage less fruit in orchards. My foreman was skeptical when we first suggested the Germans, but he is pleased now. We couldn't have harvested our apple crop up here without help and the prisoners were the best solution." [38] The few clues to the number of prisoners employed on contract work point toward the conclusion that prisoners of war were probably slightly outnumbered by the foreign workers brought in from nearby countries. In the spring of 1944 there seem to have been from 18,000 to 25,000 prisoners of war at work on farms or in private industry.[39] A year later, in May 1945, a total of 115,000 prisoners were reported working on contract, of which 70,000 were in agricultural and 45,000 in nonagricultural work.[40] If commitments made by the Office of the Provost Marshal General were fulfilled, the peak of prisoner of war employment was reached in the months immediately following V–E Day, for a total of 140,000 prisoners were then allocated to contract work to 31 July 1945.[41] Of this total, 85,000 were allocated for farm work and 55,000 for nonagricultural work.

[38] *The New York Times,* October 22, 1944.
[39] Lewis and Mewha, *op. cit.,* pages 125–26, state that 101,000 prisoners were available for work and that 72.8 percent of those available were employed. On page 116 they cite an Inspector General report, which states that one-third of the working prisoners were employed on contract labor. Use of this proportion produces the higher figure given in the text above. The lower figure is obtained by use of 25 percent derived from the statement (page 264) that slightly more than 25 percent were employed in agriculture and industry.
[40] Memo, Actg PMG for DCofS for Sv Comds ASF, 16 May 45, sub: Disposition of German Prisoners of War, ASF IPD 383.6, Prisoners of War.
[41] Memo, Actg PMG for Dir Personnel ASF, 16 May 45, sub: Allocation of POWs for ASF Priority I Work, ASF IPD 383.6, Prisoners of War.

In spite of the evident need of building up the labor force, formidable obstacles were raised to the recruiting of temporary reinforcements for industry from sources that were not ordinarily available. Labor unions opposed the employment of foreign workers and prisoners of war, and employers were reluctant to hire them. The use of prisoners of war was further restricted by the terms of the Geneva Convention. Although the Army released soldiers for work in specific industries in response to public pressure and requests from employers, a measure of adverse reaction from labor unions and management was nevertheless encountered. The principal obstacle to utilizing this source more fully was the Army's extreme reluctance to permit inroads on its supply of military manpower. Whether or not more workers could have been drawn from these three sources is uncertain. The number of reinforcements drawn from the manpower pools of neighboring countries, from prisoner of war camps, and from the armed forces that were working in American industry and agriculture at any one time probably did not exceed 250,000 or 300,000 men. Considering the total number of civilians employed, an annual average of 53,750,000 during the four war years, the temporary reinforcements from these three sources would seem to have been too few to have had much effect on the labor situation. The comparison has its dangers, for these reinforcements were in the nature of a mobile reserve. Without them, American farms would have been hard put on occasion to harvest their crops and certain industries would have had greater difficulty in meeting production schedules.

CHAPTER X

The Enforcement of Manpower Policies

Just as it had gradually come to take a more active and direct role in labor disputes, so the War Department was drawn into the position of taking direct steps to enforce compliance with policy rulings of the War Manpower Commission. The commission had been given responsibility for insuring the full mobilization and effective utilization of American manpower, but it had not been given adequate authority to discharge its responsibilities and to enforce its policies. The commission could in some measure restrict the hiring of new workers through employment ceilings, U.S. Employment Service referrals, and other regulations, but there were no legal penalties to assess against employers for noncompliance. It could exert indirect pressure on employers by withholding priorities for materials and equipment, and it could exercise direct pressure by depriving employers of U.S. Employment Service assistance in obtaining and maintaining an adequate labor force. But as a practical matter both types of pressure were inadvisable because of their effect upon production schedules. For the enforcement of manpower policies, the War Manpower Commission considered it necessary therefore to rely upon the authority and statutory powers of the other departments and agencies concerned. The Selective Service System and other agencies were brought into the picture as part of the machinery of enforcement. Various measures were adopted to force workers into essential jobs, but of these measures the two in which the War Department was most directly concerned were the use of selective service and the seizure of industrial plants and business establishments.

Selective Service as a Sanction

That the Selective Service Act might be a potent weapon to keep workers at work or to force them into certain jobs against their will had been recognized when the legislation was first under consideration. Although opposed to the use of the draft as a general antistrike weapon, the War Department was not averse to its use in specific situations. With the complete approval and co-operation of Secretary Stimson, General Hershey, Director of Selective Service, issued a directive to all local draft boards in June 1941 instructing them to cancel the draft deferments of all workers who engaged in strikes that impeded the national defense program.   The occasion for this order was the strike at the North American Aviation plant, of suspicious origin and in defiance of a mediation agreement.   Even before General Hershey issued his directive, Los Angeles draft boards had begun to reclassify the North American Aviation strikers.[1]   Again, in the fall of 1943 when the captive coal mines were closed down by strikes, the War Department made elaborate plans to induct the miners into the Army and then order them back to work. A foremen's strike in Detroit in the spring of 1944, which General Arnold characterized as "one of the most serious setbacks that the Army Air Forces program has had since its inception," prompted another threat to induct strikers into the Army, but the strike ended before any of the men were drafted.   Then, a few months later, the Philadelphia Transportation Company strike occurred.   Instructions to local draft boards to reclassify strikers for immediate induction into the armed forces were, it has already been noted, among the measures that brought an end to the strike.   In this case, the draft also provided a basis for punitive action after the strike was over.   Four of the leaders were referred by the Army to Selective Service; two of them were reclassified and ordered to report to an induction center.   All strikers who did not return were reported to their local boards for reclassification.[2]

The reclassification and induction of strikers, or the threat to do so, was in a sense a corollary of granting industrial deferments for the purpose of keeping workers at work.   If men who otherwise would have been drafted into the armed forces were deferred by reason of the work they performed, there was no basis for the deferment when they refused to perform the work. On the other hand, it was manifestly questionable to consider a worker as having lost his job status because he chose to stay home from work for a day or so.   Industrial deferments tended also to attract new workers into essential industries, but their effect in this respect was softened by the primary importance of family and marital status as a basis for deferment.   By the beginning of 1943 the War Manpower Commission had decided that greater use of the draft as a means of forcing workers into essential jobs must be made.

Under instructions from War Manpower Commission Chairman Paul McNutt, Selective Service headquarters on 30 January 1943 informed local

[1] Stimson and Bundy, *On Active Service in Peace and War,* pp. 489–90; Ohly, History of Plant Seizures During World War II, I, 32.
[2] Basic Plan, Army Operation of Coal Mines, ASF Prod Div file; Memo, Patterson for Byrnes, 16 May 44, and attachments, Stimson files, Labor, Strikes; Ohly, *op. cit.,* I, 294–311.

draft boards throughout the nation that "greater emphasis must be laid on occupation than on dependency as a basis for deferment." [3]   Manpower requirements and national interest, the local boards were informed, "will no longer permit deferment on dependency grounds of physically qualified registrants, ages 18 through 37, where such registrants are engaged in activities or occupations which are nondeferrable."   The local boards were accordingly directed to reclassify all such registrants.

Mrs. Anna M. Rosenberg, leading authority on labor relations and New York Regional Director of the War Manpower Commission, characterized the new instructions as a "major shift" in the selective service system.   The issuance of the list of nondeferrable occupations meant, according to Mrs. Rosenberg, that a new yardstick has been added.   Every able-bodied man was on "loan" from military service to civilian life, and the length of the loan depended upon the individual's contribution and worth to the war effort. [4]   Mrs. Rosenberg's view of the action taken by Selective Service headquarters was in sharp contrast to the objections raised by those who considered it a perversion of the original Selective Service Act.

Representative James Wadworth, one of the authors of the draft act, and Grenville Clark, a leader in the fight for selective service, attacked the shift in emphasis.   Wadsworth, who had recently introduced a national service bill in Congress, confessed that he was "shocked."   It was not the intention of Congress, according to Wadsworth, that the draft law should be employed "for any other purpose except recruiting the armed forces of the United States."   The act, he claimed, "never was intended to be used as a club" to compel civilians to move from one occupation to another. [5]   Clark, who supported national service legislation, was convinced that the Selective Service directive would be ineffective in pushing men into war jobs, and he opposed the action as one in which the Army would become "a sort of penal institution to be used . . . without consideration of military ends." [6]

Attacked on one flank by proponents of national service legislation, the new emphasis on occupation was hard hit on the other by the supporters of dependency deferments.   The uproar that followed the directive of 30 January 1943 was no less loud than it would have been had the mothers, not the fathers, of the United States been in danger of being drafted.   So un-

---

[3] Local Board Memo 181, 30 Jan 43, effective 1 Apr 43, Selective Service System, *Industrial Deferment,* II, 300–302.

[4] *The New York Times,* February 8, 1943.

[5] Quoted in Blum, Deferment From Military Service, p. 244.

[6] *Ibid.*

popular was the directive that local boards refused to be guided by it.   The
issue was debated in Congress during most of 1943, and on 5 December 1943
the Kilday bill prohibiting the induction of fathers, regardless of occupation,
until registrants without dependents were drafted became law.[7]   One of its
provisions was "That no individual [except physicians and certain other
specialists] shall be called for induction . . . or be inducted because of their
occupations, or by occupational groups, or by groups in any plant or in-
stitutions, . . ."[8]   Representative Paul J. Kilday, sponsor of the bill,
believed that it would prevent selective service from doing "indirectly" what
ought to be done directly.   The selective service system, he held, had not
been created to force men into industry but to raise an Army.[9]   However
favorably disposed Representative Kilday and others were to a policy of
work-or-fight, their opposition to the use of the draft as a means of enforcing such a policy and their insistence on dependency as the primary basis for
deferment forced Selective Service headquarters to scrap the directive of 30
January 1943.   It was rescinded as soon as the Kilday bill was enacted.

During the first six months of 1944 the west coast formula was extended
to most of the United States.   Employment ceilings were applied to areas of
labor shortage and "priority referral," that is, exclusive hiring through the
U.S. Employment Service, was ordered for all parts of the country.   To
ensure compliance, Justice Byrnes, head of the Office of War Mobilization,
directed that "upon application of the Chairman of the War Manpower
Commission, all interested governmental agencies will apply any and all
sanctions lawfully available to the Government. . . ."[10]   Opposition from the
War Production Board rendered the directive innocuous just as an alarming
drift of workers away from war jobs set in.

With Congress debating national service and work-or-fight legislation,
Byrnes decided to make use of the draft act once more.   One commentator
on the wartime scene in Washington has described the situation in these
words: "Because the [civilian] production and manpower authorities were
disintergrating and because the military relied on Byrnes to solve their
problems, he found himself not merely coordinating but policing the turbulent manpower front."[11]   After discussions with representatives of the

[7] Public Law 197, 78th Congress.

[8] Selective Service System, *Industrial Deferment,* I, 44–45.

[9] Blum, *op. cit.,* p. 245.

[10] Quoted in Somers, *Presidential Agency,* p. 156.

[11] Eliot Janeway, *The Struggle for Survival, A Chronicle of Economic Mobilization in World War II, The Chronicles of America Series,* Vol. 23 (New Haven, Conn.: Yale University Press, 1951), pp. 347–48.

interested departments and agencies, Byrnes announced a new drive to keep workers in war jobs. An Office of War Mobilization and Reconversion press release of 9 December 1944, a directive to local draft boards dated 12 December, and a letter from Byrnes to the Secretaries of War and the Navy a week later fixed the new policy. It called upon the Selective Service System to induct men under thirty-eight years of age who were not working in essential industries or who, without authority of the local boards, left their jobs in essential industry either for another job in war industry or for non-essential work.[12] The armed services, Byrnes suggested, might well increase the furloughing of men to war industry since some of the older men inducted under the Byrnes work-or-fight order might not be useful as combat troops. This could be done if, as the War Department insisted, such releases were not charged against the troop basis. In replying to Justice Byrnes, Secretary Stimson made note of a necessary extension in the policy, one which the public press had already assumed, namely, that IV–F's (the physically unqualified) as well as "job-jumpers" would be inducted under the order.

By direction of General Marshall, all men drafted under the Byrnes order, unless acceptable for general service, were earmarked for release to industry. They were to be sent to Camp Ellis, Illinois, for a shortened course of basic training. Then, if they were willing, they were to be transferred to the Enlisted Reserve Corps and released for work in war industry. If they were unwilling to return to industry, they were to be used as service personnel at ASF installations. Actually, the Army never carried out the plan to send the work-or-fight draftees back to industry. Col. Ralph F. Gow, then director of the Industrial Personnel Division, ASF, pointed out that it was unrealistic to expect men drafted for failure to work to be willing to go to work when the only alternative was to keep them in active military service. The head of the Labor Branch of IPD further argued that the public relations problems created by releasing the men would be far out of proportion to the number of men added to the industrial labor force. They would be more useful working on ASF projects, he declared.[13] Under Secretary Patterson had consistently opposed the release of troops to work in industry, and, as a result of War Department opposition, none of the more than 12,000 work-or-fight draftees were returned to jobs in war industry.[14]

[12] Local Board Memo 115–1, 12 Dec 44, in Selective Service System, *Industrial Deferment,* II, 258–60. See also Somers, *op. cit.,* p. 168.

[13] Blum, *op. cit.,* pp. 7–9.

[14] *Ibid.,* p. 9, citing Memo, McFadden for Gow, 8 Aug 45, Ohly file, National Service Folder 3. Somers states that "less than 50,000 men were affected" and that "most of them were sent back to industry." (Somers, *op. cit.,* p. 169.)

Few of the men drafted as a result of the Byrnes directive were physically fit for military service.   Many of them, in the words of one officer, "by no stretch of the imagination could even render any useful service either in civilian or military activities." [15]   The Army did not want them and would not by choice have taken them, but to draft the physically unfit and then discharge them for reasons of physical unfitness would have made the program a farce.   As a result, it was far more difficult for these special draftees to obtain discharges than it was for anyone else.   The doubts with which the War Department had approached the program were not dispelled when it actually got under way.

The real aim of the program was to keep workers in essential jobs and to shift more workers into such jobs.   Complaints of manpower shortages did not diminish after the promulgation of the Byrnes directive.   Nevertheless, there were some indications of a shift of workers into essential industry.   Reports received from the field seemed to the IPD to point to an increase of referrals to essential jobs, but IPD officers did not expect any improvement to be long-lasting. [16]   Mrs. Rosenberg noticed an immediate reaction to the work-or-fight order.   "There is no doubt in my mind," she wrote to Byrnes on 30 December 1944, "that psychologically it was one of the best things we have done lately, and it is unquestionably halting the exodus of many workers. . . ." [17]   On the other hand, there were many other, and perhaps even stronger, pressures operating in the same direction during the winter of 1944–45. [18]   How much of the credit can be given to the Byrnes directive is hard to say.

By April 1945 the Selective Service System was experiencing "much difficulty and some embarrassment" with the work-or-fight program as a result of inequities in treatment between agricultural workers and industrial workers.   Farmers had been placed in a special, deferred class by the Tydings Amendment to the draft act.   If a farm worker left his job, he was subject to induction only if he were qualified by age, family status, and physical fitness.   Pointing out that this "glaring inconsistency" meant that no pressure could be exerted on many farm workers, General Hershey urged the War Department to extend the Byrnes directive to agricultural labor.   The matter was the primary concern of the Office of War Mobilization and Reconversion,

---

[15] Quoted in Blum, *op. cit.*, p. 10.
[16] *Ibid.*, p. 11.
[17] Quoted in Somers, *op. cit.*, p. 169n.
[18] See Chapter IV, above.

since the work-or-fight program had originated in that office, and Secretary Stimson therefore referred Hershey's suggestion to Judge Fred Vinson, Byrnes' successor as head of the Office of War Mobilization and Reconversion. Stimson seized the opportunity to call for the ending of the program. Immediately after V–E Day a liberalized deferment policy was put into effect, and on 30 May 1945 Secretary Stimson agreed with an Office of War Mobilization and Reconversion suggestion that inductions under the work-or-fight directive be limited to men who met the physical standards of the Army. With Vinson's formal approval of this change on 29 June 1945, the work-or-fight directive lost most of its force.[19]

The War Department had accepted the work-or-fight program only as a stopgap measure and then with something less than enthusiasm. One labor expert in ASF headquarters viewed it as "a perversion of some governmental power never intended for the purpose for which it was used . . . , undemocratic, discriminatory and only partially adequate . . . , [an] emergency improvisation, . . ."[20] Another ASF officer objected that the program was "set up as a penalty or punishment, and yet the person so inducted will presumably be entitled to all the privileges and benefits of a soldier who has sacrificed a great deal in combat or otherwise."[21] Both Stimson and Patterson were stanch advocates of national service legislation as the fairest, most effective means of attacking the manpower problem. The failure of Congress to enact such legislation and the failure, in the eyes of the War Department, of the War Manpower Commission to insist upon being given the authority and means to enforce its policies compelled Stimson and the War Department to accept grudgingly a role they thought inappropriate for the Army. And as administered, the program seems to have accomplished very little. Turnover in war jobs during the early months of 1945 reached fantastic proportions. In January and February 1945, according to a Washington journalist, job controls and threats drew a record high of 2,000,000 workers into war industry, 400,000 of them into "must" jobs, but at the same time "no less than 300,000 'must' workers went prospecting for peacetime opportunities."[22]

[19] Ltr, Hershey to SW, 18 Apr 45, Ltr, Stimson to Vinson, 30 May 45, Ltr, Vinson to Stimson, 27 Jun 45, and related papers, all in AG 327.31 (27 Jun 45) (1). See also Selective Service System, *Industrial Deferment,* I, 148.
[20] Maj H. M. Somers, Manpower Controls, ASF Control Div, Labor, Manpower Reports and Statistics.
[21] Memo, Lt Kearns for Brennan, 31 Dec 44, Ohly file, National Service Folder 3.
[22] Janeway, *op. cit.,* p. 358.

Plant Seizure as an Enforcement Measure

In taking over for the government the North American Aviation and Air Associates plants in 1941, the War Department had acted primarily to maintain production of goods necessary to the defense effort. The major objective was achieved. In both cases the workers returned to their jobs, and production was resumed when the Army took over the operation of the plants. Success in achieving this primary objective nevertheless overshadowed certain aspects of the Air Associates case that were a foretaste of problems to come.[23]

Originally a small jobbing business dealing in standard airplane parts, Air Associates had branched out into certain manufacturing and assembly operations when the aircraft production program got under way. By the fall of 1941 the company had prime contracts totaling about $1,445,000 with the Army and substantial Navy contracts as well. Deliveries were being delayed by a series of strikes that followed a close union election in June 1941, which had resulted in the certification of the United Automobile Workers, CIO, as the exclusive bargaining agent. The management repeatedly challenged the certification of the union by the National Labor Relations Board and refused to co-operate with the efforts made by the National Defense Mediation Board to settle the dispute. Warnings by Air Forces representatives that the War Department would terminate its contracts unless the situation improved had no effect. The mediation board then took what action it could, that is, certification of the dispute to the President. The Air Forces now came to the unexpected conclusion that it could not transfer its orders elsewhere within any short period of time. The question whether, under these circumstances, the Army should enforce compliance with the mediation board's recommendations gave rise to an argument within the War Department that reappeared on every similar occasion during the war. Disorders and some destruction of property took place at the plant. With the local law enforcement authorities fearing that matters would get out of hand and the Air Forces urging that the plant be taken over, the War Department on 30 October 1941 recommended seizure.[24] An executive order was issued within a few hours, and on the next morning Col. Roy M. Jones, chief of the Air Forces Eastern Procurement District, took possession for the War Department.

---

[23] Except as otherwise noted, the following account of the Air Associates plant seizure is based on Ohly, *op cit.,* Vol. I. Ch. 4.

[24] The legal authority for such seizures was contained in the Selective Training and Service Act of 1940 (Public Law 783, 76th Congress).

Although production returned to normal within a short time after the War Department began operation of the plant, improvement of the labor situation took somewhat longer. The company's financial position, sufficiently weak to raise considerable doubt whether the wage demands of the union could be met, was bolstered by advance payments on the Army and Navy contracts and by a more favorable arrangement with the principal banking creditors. At the urging of the War Department, the board of directors replaced the old, intransigent management, albeit reluctantly, and only then was it possible to resume negotiations with the union over a labor contract. Although assuming responsibility for production matters and taking direct charge of operations, the Army held aloof from actively participating in labor negotiations. Its position rested partly on the desire to be an impartial instrument in labor disputes, to take no action that would give either labor or management cause to consider the Army as being on its side, and partly on the belief that a labor contract should be the complete responsibility of those who would have to maintain the arrangement after the Army's temporary role was terminated. The new president of Air Associates, Incorporated, was willing to meet with union representatives, which was what the War Department chiefly required, but he was no more inclined than his predecessor to meet the demands of the union. Although considerable progress was made, no agreement had been reached when on 19 December 1941 Secretary Stimson's special assistant, Mr. Amberg, recommended that the War Department relinquish possession of the plant by the end of the month whether or not a labor settlement had been reached. The entry of the United States into the war, Amberg noted, had created a new situation which required the War Department's full attention. Furthermore, the Air Forces again took the position that production sources other than the Air Associates company were available. On 26 December the company and the union signed a contract recognizing the union as the sole bargaining agent for the men and embodying a wage settlement satisfactory to both sides. Three days later, on 29 December, the War Department turned the plant back to the company. Although the labor situation had been taken care of to the satisfaction of the government, within three months the company had again fallen behind in production and only improved when, in April 1942, the old management regained control.[25]

In the North American Aviation company seizure, maintenance of production had been the sole objective; in the case of the Air Associates com-

[25] Memo, R. H. Gaffney for Jones, 10 Dec 41, Memo, Amberg for Patterson, 19 Dec 41, and Memo, Ohly for USW, 25 Mar 42, all in OUSW Amberg, Air Associates.

pany, it had been the primary objective.   In the latter instance, repeated failure on the part of the company to comply with decisions of the National Labor Relations Board and the National Defense Mediation Board had been a contributing factor to the labor disturbances, and the seizure of the plant was the first step toward employing the emergency powers of the President to enforce governmental decisions that were without sanctions.   Whether action would be taken when production had not been halted or when it was not essential and directly related to the war effort remained to be seen.   The question was partly answered in August 1942 when the War Department took over certain facilities of a small Massachusetts machine company—S. A. Woods Company of Boston.   What turned out to be the final step, that of seizing an establishment engaged in nonessential civilian production in which the interests of the War Department were not seriously affected, was first taken in November 1943 when a number of leather tanneries in and near Salem, Massachusetts, were seized.

The S. A. Woods Company in 1942 operated two plants in South Boston; one manufactured woodworking machinery, and the other produced shells and shot for the Army.[26]   A third plant, in Natick, Masschusetts, was being equipped to produce shells but was not yet in operation.   Negotiations leading toward a new labor contract had been going forward during the early spring of 1942 but had foundered on three demands made by the union: a maintenance of membership clause, arbitration of all matters arising from the contract, and provision for changing production rates.   After the controversy was certified to the National War Labor Board in May 1942, the company and union had agreed on a retroactive wage increase, but the three major demands continued to be unacceptable to the company.   On 1 August 1942 the National War Labor Board issued an "order" that they be granted. After receiving a reply from the company that these three demands could not be accepted and that the board order would not be complied with, the board on 18 August certified the case to the President, who on the following day issued an executive order directing the War Department to take possession of the company's properties.

There was not then, nor at any time afterward, any question of restoring production.   The union, assured by the National War Labor Board that its order of 1 August would be enforced, had taken no strike action and the South Boston shell plant was in full production when the Army took posses-

---

[26] Except as noted, the following account of the seizure of S. A. Woods Company is based on Ohly, *op. cit.,* Vol. I, Ch. 7.

sion.   It was, of course, important to maintain production.   Without doubt
the union would have called a strike and the Army's interests would have
suffered if the government had not taken steps to enforce the board order.
Patterson, then Acting Secretary of War, was convinced that, in this instance at least, such action was necessary.   "No company and no labor
organization," he declared, "can be permitted to defy the mandate of this
impartial tribunal [the National War Labor Board] with impunity." [27]

Failing to persuade the management to negotiate a settlement with the
union that would be acceptable to the National War Labor Board and unable
to obtain the company's co-operation in the operation of the plant, the
Army settled down to a siege of indefinite duration.   There was doubt
whether the Army itself could legally comply with the board ruling or even
continue in effect all the terms and conditions of employment existing at the
time the properties were seized.   Such questions, for example, as the
legality of applying maintenance of union membership to employees on a
federal payroll or of using federal funds to pay the retroactive wage increase
that had been previously agreed to by the company made the War Department's position difficult.   Since a controlling interest in the company was
held by its president and vice president, there was no hope of a change in
management as there had been with Air Associates, Incorporated.   It was
therefore decided, late in September 1942, to turn the plant over to another
private company to operate as agent for the War Department.   This was
done, and the Murray Company of Texas, a manufacturer of cotton processing machinery, continued to run the Woods establishment for the duration
of the war, after agreeing to enter into a contract with the union that would
embody the provisions of the National War Labor Board order and the wage
concessions made by the Woods management.

War Department control over operations lasted long after the Army ceased
to have any great need for the company's munitions production.   Before the
war ended the Ordnance Department was able to fill its shot and shell
requirements from sources other than the Woods plant, and at lower cost,
and on a number of occasions the Ordnance Department proposed that the
Woods contract be terminated.   At the same time a shortage of woodworking machinery of the type manufactured by the Woods Company had
developed.   The War Production Board insisted that it was of vital importance to the lumber industry that production of this machinery be maintained, which the Murray Company was reluctant to do unless the more

[27] Ohly, *op cit.*, I, 93.

profitable shell contracts were continued. Although the woodworking
machinery plant had not been connected with the labor dispute that brought
about the seizure of the properties, the Labor Branch of the Industrial Personnel Division, ASF, supported by Under Secretary Patterson, held the view
that to permit it to close as a result of closing the shell plant would be detri-
mental to the labor policy of the government. For this reason, the Ordnance
Department was instructed to continue the shell contracts and the War
Department continued in possession. After V–E Day the Ordnance Department finally stopped placing orders with the Woods plant, and at the end of
June 1945 the War Department informed the War Production Board and the
Murray Company of its intention to withdraw within two months whether
or not labor troubles in the woodworking machinery plant were the result.
The coming of V–J Day brought an end to government possession of all but
a few seized properties. Among those turned back to their owners at the
end of August 1945 was the Woods plant.

Within IPD's Labor Branch, particular significance was attached to the
Woods case, first, as a better test of government operation in the face of a
non-co-operative management than had been offered by the Air Associates
seizure, and second, as proof of the feasibility, and an illustration of the problems, of employing a private corporation to operate property seized by the
government. The latter method was never repeated. Apart from the purely
procedural or administrative significance, the Woods episode demonstrated
the willingness of the War Department to enforce upon private industry labor
regulations and policies set forth by other agencies, when to refrain from doing
so might have provoked a strike and endangered production. It indicated
also that the War Department would not necessarily withdraw from the picture as soon as the situation ceased to be of direct interest to the Army.
Before the War Department decided to continue in possession of the Woods
plant in spite of the fact that the Ordnance Department had no further need
of it, the policy had been to oppose plant seizures when the interests of the
Army were not directly involved. Accordingly, the War Department had
sought strenuously to avoid taking over the Salem tanneries in November
1943, the Fall River textile mills in February 1944, and Montgomery Ward
and Company, Incorporated, in December 1944. The fruitlessness of the
Army's objections in these three instances perhaps explains the subsequent
decision not to withdraw from the Woods plant.

These three seizures—the Salem tanneries, the Fall River mills, and the
Montgomery Ward properties—differed from one another principally in the

scope of the companies' operations and in the extent and effectiveness of the co-operation or lack of co-operation on the part of the management.[28]   In certain basic features they were alike, and any one of the three represented equally well the final stage in the use of government seizure as an instrument to enforce labor policy.   Not any of the properties taken over were engaged in producing goods directly connected with the war effort.   The Salem tanneries were not manufacturing finished products, merely processing leather that was being used for pocketbooks and other civilian goods.   Some of the textile mills in Fall River were producing military items such as insect cloth and netting, but these mills were not involved in the seizure.   The ones that were taken over by the Army were exclusively producers of articles designed for the civilian luxury trade.   Montgomery Ward and Company was not, except in a very minor way, a manufacturing concern but was a distributor of civilian goods.   In each case there was a long history of turbulent and discordant labor relations, with sporadic outbreaks of strikes.   At the time the government took possession, only thirteen of the thirty or so associated tanneries in the Salem area were on strike, seven of all textile plants in Fall River, and only a few of the numerous and widespread Montgomery Ward properties.   Thus, in each of the three instances certain plants continued in operation under their private owners, while others of the same company or closely associated with it were seized and operated under control of the government.   Whatever the ostensible grounds for taking action, the actual motive was to end a situation that constituted a threat to the effective performance of the National War Labor Board's functions.   At the time of seizure of the Salem tanneries, a member of the Labor Branch, IPD, commented as follows:

The War Department has taken over these plants for one fundamental reason—as a sanction to enforce the government's policy that there shall be no strikes for the duration of the war and that orders of the War Labor Board must be enforced.   While we talk to the outside world about the maintenance of production as such being our primary objective, the fact is that the government doesn't care about the production of these plants as such—it cares about the maintenance of this production because it is a necessary incident to the enforcement of the government's policy that production will not be interrupted pending peaceful settlement of a labor dispute.[29]

[28] The Salem tanneries and Fall River mills operations are covered in Ohly, *op cit.*, Volume I, Chapter 10, and Volume III, Appendix AA–1, Note VIII; the Montgomery Ward seizure is described in Volume I, Chapter 16.

[29] Ohly, Memo for Files, 2 Dec 43, sub: Analysis of Colonel Pratt's Proposed Recommendations Concerning the Handling of Labor Problems in the Tanneries Strike, Ohly, *op. cit.*, Vol. II, App. P–2.

In circumstances such as these the War Department argued that a civilian agency of the government, not the War Department, should be designated to take over the facilities. Its objections were overruled, except briefly in the spring of 1944, when the first steps to solve the Montgomery Ward situation were taken. On that occasion it was agreed that the Department of Commerce should act as the seizing agency for the Montgomery Ward properties, but the acceptance of the War Department's view was its own undoing, for the Department of Commerce handled the brief two-week seizure with less than complete success. When it again seemed necessary for the government to step in, at the end of the year, the unfortunate experience of the Department of Commerce was used to counter the War Department's objections to acting as the seizing agency.

The distinguishing feature of the Salem tanneries and Fall River mills seizures was that in these instances sanctions were employed against the labor unions, as in the case of the North American Aviation seizure, whereas the Montgomery Ward seizure was directed against a noncompliant management, as in the case of Air Associates, Incorporated, and the S. A. Woods Company.

The disturbances among the tannery workers at Salem and in the vicinity arose as a result of a row between the CIO union and a splinter group of skilled workers, who in August 1943 had broken away and formed an independent union. There were frequent strikes during the next two months, and on 18 September the dispute was certified to the National War Labor Board. Several weeks later two members of the independent union were discharged, or laid off (the exact nature of the action was a matter of argument), and the union immediately called a strike. When the men refused to comply with a board order to return to work, the case was referred to the President on 17 November 1943. The board was of the opinion that the continuation of the strike constituted a direct and flagrant challenge to the policy of the government and that drastic action was called for. A personal appeal from the President to the union was ignored, and on 24 November the War Department, contrary to its wishes, took possession of the strike-bound tanneries. Management gave its co-operation. The plants were reopened after the Thanksgiving Day weekend, on 26 November, with 82 percent of the working force reporting. Instead of directly entering into negotiations with the union, the War Department asked the National War Labor Board for instructions pending a final decision of the jurisdictional issues by the board. The general effect of these instructions was to prohibit the independent union from soliciting new members or collecting dues on the premises. They were

accepted by all parties as a temporary stopgap.   When the independent union
became affiliated with the AFL early in December, a step which promised to
reduce irresponsible actions on the part of the union, the War Department
grasped the opportunity to withdraw without waiting an indefinite length of
time for the board to render a final decision.   No strike followed, although
the board decision, which came in mid-January 1944, was not accepted without protest from both sides.   The two workers whose dismissal had been the
immediate occasion for the strike were ordered reinstated, a condition which
the independent union had set to its compliance with the board order of the
previous November and which the board had then rejected, and new plant
elections were ordered at the expiration of the CIO contract at the end of
1944.   By clearing the air somewhat and making it plain that prosecutions
under the Smith-Connally Act would follow a recurrence of the situation,
the seizure contributed to the settlement.

The issues and circumstances surrounding the seizure of the Montgomery
Ward properties bore a striking resemblance to those that had precipitated
the seizure of the S. A. Woods plants, and the attitude of management was
exactly the same.   The workers in the various Montgomery Ward establishments had been organized during the war into a number of AFL and CIO
unions, but recognition of the unions as bargaining agents had been extended
by the company grudgingly and only after prolonged dispute.   A controversy
lasting several months arose early in 1944, when the company refused to have
further dealings with the union in the Chicago area on the ground that it no
longer represented a majority of the workers.   A National War Labor Board
order to extend the union's contract temporarily until a new election could
be held was rejected by the company and the workers went on strike.   Seizure of the company's properties by the Department of Commerce and a new
election under National Labor Relations Board supervision followed within
two weeks.   As soon as the election was held, the government hastily withdrew.   Although the new election re-established the existing union as the
bargaining agent, the company refused to extend the old contract.   Negotiations for a new agreement foundered on the company's refusal to accept a
maintenance of membership clause, voluntary checkoff, and several other provisions that had been included in the old contract under protest.   In some
of the properties the dispute also involved such issues as retroactive wage
increases, holiday pay, and overtime.   While the unions put on pressure for
the government to intervene, the company launched a vituperative public
attack on the National War Labor Board and the whole concept of govern-

ment seizure.   Certification of the dispute to the President by the board on
20 December 1944 made seizure inevitable.   With the Ordnance Department
becoming restless over the continued S. A. Woods seizure and with no desire
to be saddled with a mail-order business, the War Department took the position that seizure by the Army would be an improper intrusion of the military
into civilian and economic fields, would seriously impair the prestige of the
Army at a time when it needed the full confidence of the public, and would
impair the morale of the Army by diverting troops from their primary mission at a time when combat needs were serious.   Nevertheless, the War
Department was chosen for the job on the practical consideration that the
failure of the Department of Commerce had demonstrated that no other
department could handle it.

On 28 December 1944 the Army therefore began taking over the Montgomery Ward properties involved in the dispute.   The action, as had been
anticipated, met with a complete lack of co-operation on the part of the
management, headed by Sewell Avery.   It became necessary to sequester the
company's records, to discharge store managers and top supervisory personnel,
and to extend the seizure to several establishments that were not directly
concerned in the labor dispute but were essential to the operations.   Slow
progress was made in putting into effect the measures ordered by the National
War Labor Board.   The Attorney General had instituted proceedings in the
District Court of Illinois to establish the legality of the seizure, and for fear
of prejudicing the case the War Department did very little toward establishing maintenance of membership and other basic demands of the union.   The
decision of the District Court that the seizure was illegal but that the *status
quo* should be maintained pending appeal stymied any progress so far as a
labor agreement was concerned until June 1945, when the Circuit Court of
Appeals reversed the ruling of the lower court.   In the meantime, the
workers had become embittered by the delay in obtaining the benefits they
sought.   Although the decision of the Circuit Court gave the War Department the right to take action on the National War Labor Board orders, a
number of problems relating chiefly to the status of company revenues made
progress almost as difficult as before.   When the war ended, the War
Department strongly recommended that the seizure be terminated immediately, but objections by the Department of Labor and the Attorney General
postponed the withdrawal for two months, until October 1945.   By then most
of the union demands had been put into effect.

Labor Problems in Plant Seizures

When the operation of business and industrial facilities by the War Department was a long-drawn-out affair, as in the case of the S. A. Woods Company and Montgomery Ward, the Army inevitably became involved in the day-to-day labor problems of the business.[30]   In the eyes of labor, management, and the public the Army had the responsibility for seeing that labor problems arising in the daily operation of an industrial establishment were disposed of in an appropriate manner.   Although the actual handling of these problems might be delegated to the former management of the plant, to a newly installed management, or to a new operating company, the Army retained ultimate responsibility for what was done.   And, when it was not feasible to delegate this part of the job, the Army utilized its own personnel to perform industrial relations functions, established policies and procedures that governed employee relations, and directly disposed of the substantive issues and grievances that are normal to the conduct of a business.   The extent to which the Army became involved in these problems depended on the nature of the business and the degree of co-operation given by the management.   The latter, in turn, depended upon the terms and conditions of work that the seizure was designed to enforce.

It was therefore incumbent upon the War Department to determine at the outset the terms and conditions that were being followed at the time of the seizure.   Not only was this desirable in order to establish a point of reference for the subsequent handling of labor problems, but it was necessary in order to fulfill the requirements of the Smith-Connally Act, which made it mandatory for the seizing agency to continue in effect the previously existing terms and conditions of employment unless they were in violation of federal law or an executive order such as the antidiscrimination order, or were a serious limitation on production.   When these terms and conditions were, as it frequently happened, involved directly in the basic controversy, it became necessary to amend them in accordance with the National War Labor Board order that the Army was directed to enforce.   Because of the ambiguities, inaccuracies, and generalities that often characterized the orders of the board, it was no easy matter to apply the orders to specific conditions of work. Lacking the power of enforcing its orders, the board drew them up in broad general terms, on the assumption that agreement could be reached by labor

[30] This section is based on Ohly, *op. cit.*, Vol. I, Ch. 21.

and management on the application of the orders to local circumstances. When this was not possible, or when one of the parties proved recalcitrant, the Army had to iron out the ambiguities and apply the orders to specific conditions. Frequently, in the interval between the issuance of the order and the seizure of the plant, the very conditions at which the order was directed had changed, and it was necessary to request further instructions of the board. When a substantive order of the board was concerned, with which management refused to comply, a written statement of the terms and conditions was then drawn up and made public.

With respect to all unsettled matters of controversy between the company and the employees, including those in the underlying substantive dispute, the Army attempted to maintain as impartial an attitude as it could, for in carrying out the government's policy and insisting on the workers staying at work while existing terms and conditions of work were observed it was imperative for the War Department to avoid being used by either party in furtherance of its own ends. The danger of this was real. In cases of labor noncompliance, management saw seizure by the War Department as an opportunity to punish the strike leaders, get rid of alleged troublemakers, introduce new plant rules, tighten up discipline generally, and eliminate union-imposed limitations on production, or even to undermine the union itself. In cases of management noncompliance, labor viewed the seizure as an opportunity to get rid of unfriendly supervisors, obtain information on production and wages that had previously been denied the union, obtain greater rights for shop stewards, dispose of accumulated grievances through direct appeal to the Army, obtain major collective bargaining concessions, and in general to pin back the ears of the management. Regardless of where the fault lay, each side attempted to turn the seizure into a victory for itself. Pressure of this sort from both sides, exerted vigorously and with cunning and subtlety, made the handling of labor relations a difficult task.

The adamant refusal of management to lend its co-operation, as in the case of Montgomery Ward, required constant policing of the instructions issued to War Department personnel at the properties and of the rules and procedures laid down for the company's supervisory personnel that were employed by the War Department. The Montgomery Ward seizure presented a number of specific and troublesome labor problems. The company had prohibited all union activity on company premises and had refused to permit the use of union bulletin boards. The union contended that the company's position was illegal under the provisions of the Wagner Act. A ruling was therefore obtained from the National Labor Relations Board and promptly placed in effect.   Montgomery Ward had likewise refused to provide the unions with information concerning individual wage rates, which the unions claimed was necessary in order to deal with wage inequities. Rulings on the subject were requested of the National Labor Relations Board, the Department of Justice, and the National War Labor Board.   The National Labor Relations Board informed the Army that furnishing such information was not required by the Wagner Act.   On the other hand, to provide the information did not, so the Department of Justice ruled, constitute changing the prevailing terms and conditions of employment and was, the National War Labor Board answered, in accordance with good industrial relations practices.   The Army therefore furnished the union with the information it desired.[31]

In the course of the Montgomery Ward operation the CIO retail union submitted a series of comprehensive demands for changes in all the basic terms and conditions of employment prevailing in certain of the establishments. These demands were of a similar nature to those which would normally be made during the collective bargaining process, but before any decision was required the seizure came to an end.   Such changes, under the Smith-Connally Act, could be made only by the National War Labor Board upon application by the operating agency or the employees.   The Army was in general reluctant to apply for a change unless both the company and the union desired it, or the company alone if there were no union, or unless production considerations required it and no serious controversy was likely to result.   When unions requested the Army to change the terms and conditions of labor, the War Department took the position that the matter was not one for the Army to decide and that a remedy should be sought directly from the National War Labor Board.   When a union filed application for changes with the board, the Army limited its comments to a statement of the pertinent facts and expressed no opinion as to what action the board should take.   In a few instances when the War Department believed that the changes by the board would be contested by management or would become the subject of litigation the War Department requested that the order be submitted to the President for approval.

Labor relations, as well as other operating problems, presented a slightly different but no less troublesome aspect when the company co-operated with the War Department and became the agent for operations.   In this situation,

[31] Ohly, *op. cit.*, I, 391–93.

which was the case in the majority of all plant seizures, the problem lay in the absence of a clear-cut demarcation of functions between the Army and its agent, the company. Through experience certain basic principles were established. When existing grievance procedures provided for mandatory arbitration of disputes as the final stage, the Army took no part in the preliminary proceedings but left negotiations to the company as the Army's representative. In the case of a contract calling for voluntary arbitration, the Army would direct the company to consent to arbitration in the event negotiations reached an impasse. If existing procedures made no provisions for arbitration, the Army participated in the final stage of negotiations, but before reaching a decision it sought and normally followed the recommendation of some impartial person selected by a civilian agency.

In the tense atmosphere that often accompanied the seizure of a plant, some arbitrary, retaliatory, and harsh disciplinary action was apt to be taken against employees. It was therefore necessary for the War Department in some cases to deviate from its policy of nonintervention in labor matters at the shop level, and to require that any proposed disciplinary action of a serious nature be first submitted to the Army for approval. This precaution was an effective restraining influence on supervisory officials, who were sometimes eager to punish strikers under the cloak of Army possession. Ordinarily, after the tensions of the first few days had disappeared, it proved possible for the War Department representatives to waive this requirement and to accept the recommendations of the management as to disciplinary action. In such cases the disciplined employee had the right to appeal through the established grievance procedures.

In the interest of maintaining peaceful labor relations and the confidence of labor and management after the termination of the seizure, it was desirable that all pending grievances be decided before the Army withdrew. In this connection a list of matters falling within the duties of the labor officer was drawn up in the Industrial Personnel Division. All union dues subject to checkoff should be turned over to the union, it was noted, and proper disposition made of all dues cards. Every effort was to be made to have the union and company reach a collective bargaining agreement before the Army withdrew. The labor officer, it was suggested, should prepare a statement of matters pending before the National War Labor Board and draw up a labor report for the War Department representative. A meeting should be held with the local officials of the union to inform them of the reasons for the withdrawal, and, if the situation permitted, they were to be notified of the actual time it was to take place. At this meeting the labor officer was to urge upon the union leaders the necessity for continued labor peace and for restraint and forbearance from disturbances. The status of any unpaid retroactive wages, the terms and conditions of employment following the withdrawal, and the desirability of a peaceful settlement were to be placed before the union officials. The labor officer was expected also to inform appropriate officials of the labor agencies of the government about the withdrawal. He was, finally, expected to recommend a time for carrying out the withdrawal. It was suggested that the withdrawal take place at the end of a shift if government funds were being used to operate the facilities. If, on the other hand, company funds were being used, then it was suggested that the withdrawal be made during a shift.[32] While the gap between what ought to be done and what actually could be done was sometimes large, every effort was made to clean up all unfinished business.

The labor policy of the government centered around the no-strike pledge made by representative leaders of labor and management in response to the entry of the United States into the war. Both labor and management agreed to abandon economic force as a means of accomplishing their ends in labor disputes and to accept the decisions of a tripartite governmental agency, which they asked the President to establish. In accord with this request the National War Labor Board was created and given responsibility over wage rates and labor disputes. To mobilize and control the flow of labor, the War Manpower Commission was established. But their decisions were not legally binding. Both agencies could do little more than exert indirect pressure or rely upon moral compulsion to persuade labor and management to accept and comply with decisions in good faith. When the growing turbulence of the labor front seemed to indicate that sterner measures were required, the board and the commission found it necessary to avail themselves of machinery and measures that had been designed for other purposes.

It was logical and practicable to employ the selective service system for the purpose of channeling workers into war jobs or preventing them from stopping work on such jobs, but under the circumstances in which it was used it proved unpractical and extremely unpopular. Drafting a physically broken-down bartender into the Army under the Byrnes work-or-fight program and inducting a strike leader represent the two approaches. The one was expected to be a deterrent, a threat which it was hoped would not have to be applied; the other was a positive sanction, punitive in intent. The

---

[32] Memo, Boland for Ohly, 23 Aug 45, in Ohly, *op. cit.,* Vol. III, App. CC–30.

former was no more than a draft of labor by indirection; the latter was akin
to punishing deserters. So far as the Army was concerned neither was a
palatable task. Congressional and public opinion, for a variety of reasons,
opposed this use of selective service. Had the results, in terms of the labor
force, been strikingly successful, the distaste within the government and
among the public might have been overcome, or perhaps disregarded. But
the very effectiveness of the draft as a means of enforcing labor policies was
a point at issue. As a threat it perhaps contributed to whatever success
other measures achieved.

When all else seemed to have failed, the government resorted to plant
seizures as a means of preventing the use of economic force in a manner inconsistent with the wartime policy for uninterrupted production. Originally
employed as a means simply of restoring and maintaining vital war production that had been halted by a strike, government seizure became also a preventive measure, a means of enforcing labor policies in situations where a
failure to do so might have interrupted war production. Eventually, as an
enforcement measure, it was extended to nonessential civilian industries. As
an expedient method of maintaining production, government seizure proved
an unqualified success. As a measure of enforcement, it was effective for
the duration of the seizure.

To the War Department, the only equitable and most promising solution
of industrial manpower problems was a national service law. All other
measures were mere makeshifts. The hope that such legislation would be
enacted and a desire to take no position that might jeopardize the passage
of a national service bill inevitably colored the War Department's attitude
toward the other measures.

CHAPTER XI

The War Department and National Service

The War Department's answer to manpower shortages that endangered the Army's supply was a national service law. Just as selective service chose men to fight, national service would put individuals to work. Most people would be expected to meet their responsibility voluntarily; those who did not would be drafted for war work.

National service had long been a controversial issue. During the 1920's there had been a highly articulate segment of opinion in favor of compulsory measures. The American Legion had sponsored "universal" service; Republican party platforms had favored conscripting workers when necessary; and President Warren G. Harding had advocated a wartime draft of "all the talent and capacity and energy of every description." Industrial mobilization planners in the War Department had likewise favored compulsory measures. But in the next decade sentiment changed. The War Policies Commission, the Nye Committee, and the War Department now opposed conscripting workers. The industrial mobilization plans of the 1930's provided for "voluntary distribution" of labor. Even after Pearl Harbor, when selective service age limits were extended, the War and Navy Departments went no further toward drafting workers than to suggest an occupational questionnaire that could serve as an inventory of skills. The idea of national service was given a back seat.

The outstanding supporter of national service at the time the United States entered the war was Grenville Clark, the "father" of selective service. As special consultant to Secretary Stimson, Clark set to work to develop a national service law for the War Department to submit to the President and the Congress. Taking as his starting point the occupational questionnaire proposed by the armed services, he outlined a plan for the use of the occupational questionnaire by a manpower board in which the controlling voices would be the Army, the Navy, and the War Production Board. At first the power of the board would be limited so that it could not assign workers to jobs. Clark believed that assignment would eventually become necessary in order to mobilize sufficient manpower to defeat the Axis. At the moment he was interested in creating machinery that could be put in motion whenever it was needed.[1]

Clark gradually changed his tactics. "I came to the conclusion that I had the cart before the horse," he explained to Stimson. Clark dropped his plan for a manpower board and instead called for a law establishing the principle of national service. In place of an immediate organization he urged "imposing a universal obligation for national service on all able-bodied men and women 18 to 65." In February 1942 Clark organized a citizens' committee whose goal was to effect the introduction of a national war service act in Congress under the "best auspices."

Both Secretary of War Stimson and Under Secretary of War Patterson warmly supported Clark. They had participated in Clark's vigorous and successful fight for selective service, and they looked upon national service as the proper companion measure. Patterson urged Stimson to use his influence with President Roosevelt. Stimson needed no urging: "Dear Grenny," he wrote to Clark, "the matter has already come up several times in Cabinet meeting, and I shall give it all the consideration that I can. As you know I am strongly in favor of your general principles." Stimson and Clark won the President's support. Roosevelt told Clark that "we are not far apart" and turned over Clark's proposals to General Hershey, Director of Selective Service.[2] Shortly afterward, Clark became critically ill and was forced to give up his work. Goldthwaite Dorr, who had taken a leading part in the recent reorganization of the War Department, now inherited the task of developing a plan for national service. Before leaving Washington Clark had suggested that the job be undertaken by a War Manpower Commission subcommittee, of which Dorr, who had been appointed War Department representative on the commission, should be chairman. This was done, and the task was thus given a measure of interdepartmental interest.

At the first meeting of the War Manpower Commission subcommittee, on 30 June 1942, Dorr suggested that the group crystallize its ideas concerning the form that legislation might take. There was no uncertainty in his mind over the need for such legislation. Recognition of the principle that

---

[1] Ltrs, Clark to Nelson and Clark to SW, 27 Jan 42, Clark, Outline of Plan, 27 Jan 42, and Clark, Memo as to the Mobilization of Manpower of the U.S. . . ., 11 Feb 42, all in Stimson files, Manpower; Ltrs, Clark to Roosevelt, 13 and 14 Feb 42, plan attached, in ASF IPD, Statements on National Service, Grenville Clark to Citizens Commission.

[2] *Ibid.*; Memo, Patterson for SW, 28 Mar 42, and Ltr, Stimson to Clark, 7 Apr 42, both in Stimson files, Manpower; Ltr, Clark to Roosevelt, 21 Mar 42, Ltr, Roosevelt to Clark, 31 Mar 42, and Ltr, Stimson to Clark, 3 Apr 42, all in Stimson files, National Service Legislation; Ltr, Dorr to Hershey, 26 Jun 42, Dorr files, National Service Legislation Correspondence, 1942.

an all-out war effort placed on the individual citizen an obligation to serve, whether in the Army or in war industry, was, Dorr believed, "morally important" and was rendered more so by the fact that Great Britain had already established national service. Dorr's colleagues on the subcommittee were in substantial agreement with him, but when it came to drafting the actual provisions of a bill differences of opinion emerged. On the one hand stood the advocates of a detailed law that would provide for most of the machinery and regulatory measures needed. On the other were those who believed, as Clark and Dorr himself did, that a brief but broad statement of policy would be more practical. A detailed bill such as had been drafted for the subcommittee by professional experts of the U.S. Employment Service would, Dorr was convinced, be unworkable. The subcommittee agreed to leave the formulation of machinery and regulations to the administrators and recommended to the War Manpower Commission a bill that was broad and general, one very much like the bill proposed by Clark's Citizens' Committee.

One or two of Dorr's own staff advisers who were cool to the whole idea of national service criticized the bill severely. They protested that it drafted workers but placed no control on employers, that it did not even compel factory owners to use workers assigned to them. The question of assignment of workers had been one of the stumbling blocks faced by Dorr's subcommittee. It was involved in the larger problem of how far the government should go in withholding one of the prime requisites of good management while holding contractors to the obligations. Dorr and the subcommittee had finally chosen not to include a provision forcing an employer to accept assigned workers, but they had done so with some doubt. Under Secretary Patterson decided that a compulsory provision should go in the bill, but he rejected the charge of the critics that the bill had every "evil" of the popular conception of a "draft labor law." Although willing to accept specific modification, Patterson supported the recommendations of Dorr's subcommittee and called upon the War Manpower Commission to take action.[3]

The War Manpower Commission submitted the Dorr recommendations to its advisory Management-Labor Policy Committee, comprised of repre-

[3] Ltr, Clark to McNutt, 20 Apr 42, Ltr, Clark to President, 22 Apr 42, and Ltr, Stimson to Clark, 25 Apr 42, all in Stimson files, Manpower; Progress Report, Management-Labor Subcommittee on National War Service Legislation, 2 Sep 42, Dorr Committee, Preliminary Report of the Commission of the WMC to the Chairman on a Proposed National War Service Act, 28 Jul 42, Memo, William Haber, 1942, and Ltr, Patterson to Dorr, 3 Aug 42, all in Dorr files, National Service Legislation Correspondence, 1942; Ltrs, Stimson to President and Stimson to Clark, 10 Jul 42, both in Stimson files, Manpower.

sentatives of management and labor and presided over by Arthur S. Flemming, Deputy Chairman of the War Manpower Commission. A subcommittee appointed by Flemming to study the proposed legislation leaned toward the type of bill recommended by Dorr, which provided for a broad policy statement obligating men between eighteen and sixty-five and women between eighteen and fifty to serve to the best of their ability in war work. Meeting jointly on several occasions, the Dorr subcommittee and the Management-Labor Policy subcommittee worked out a new draft in which certain concessions to the opponents of the Dorr recommendations were incorporated, such as travel allowances and appeal procedures and similar safeguards of individual rights. But by and large administrators were to be expected to use their discretion in applying principles to particular situations. Unlike Dorr and his subcommittee, the Management-Labor Policy subcommittee believed that the time had not yet come for the enactment of the legislation. It was a good idea, so the Management-Labor Policy subcommittee thought, to have a carefully drawn law ready in case it was needed. But with management and labor both eager to co-operate if given direction, it was hoped that further voluntary methods might be explored.

Besides this fundamental difference in approach there was considerable doubt by both subcommittees concerning the views of the President. Although the President, in a Cabinet meeting on 9 July, had given the green light to the idea of national service, he would not express an opinion on the merits of the proposed legislation. Dorr, Patterson, and Stimson therefore thought it best not to press the matter further, at least for the time being. The two subcommittees, having completed the tasks for which they had been appointed, were dissolved. There had been much discussion, some progress, but no concrete achievement.[4]

During the year 1942 advocates of national service won increasing support. Poll after poll showed that substantial majorities of the public favored compulsory assignment of workers.[5] Newspaper columnists noted that manpower shortages were lurking around the corner. For example, Walter Lippmann wrote that the honeymoon was over and that, instead of wasting

[4] Progress Report, Management-Labor Subcommittee on National War Service Legislation, 4 Sep 42, Summary of Consensus of Views Arrived at by Joint Meeting of the Commission of WMC on National Service Legislation, 10 Oct 42, Second Progress Report of the Management-Labor Subcommittee on National War Service Legislation, 10 Oct 42, Memo, Flemming for Brown, 12 Oct 42, and Ltr, Dorr to Wadsworth, 12 Jul 42, all in Dorr files, National Service Legislation Correspondence, 1942.

[5] Hadley Cantril (ed.), *Public Opinion, 1935–1946* (Princeton, N. J.: Princeton University Press, 1951), p. 1121.

time on the problem, the nation should establish the direct controls necessary for total war. Four manpower bills were introduced in Congress in the fall of 1942.[6] Paul McNutt, testifying before the Senate Committee on Military Affairs, seemed to summarize prevailing sentiment. He said that national service was "inevitable." [7]

By the middle of autumn, Grenville Clark was able to take a more active part and as a private citizen tried hard to convert sentiment into concrete action. He met with President Roosevelt and suggested several top-notch men, among them James B. Conant, William O. Douglas, and Owen J. Roberts, to direct a national service organization. But his favorite candidate was Robert Patterson. He wrote the President about Patterson, commenting that many Washington "characters" swelled without growing, while Patterson grew and did not swell. He would be the ideal director of national service.[8]

Clark believed that the groundwork had been laid and that the War Department should now bring the campaign to a successful conclusion. He taxed military spokesmen with sitting on their hands and he regretted that neither General Marshall nor Secretary Stimson spoke out. Clark repeatedly called upon them to announce that they could not carry out their program without national service. This would provide the support that was needed to secure enactment of the legislation.[9]

Stimson personally endorsed Clark's views, but he saw many drawbacks to a forthright statement endorsing national service. Opposition to compulsion in labor matters existed in the Labor Section and elsewhere in the War Department. Special adviser J. Douglas Brown noted that net results could be measured only by taking the gain from controlled manpower and subtracting from it the losses caused by compulsion. The net results, he pointed out, might well be "minus." Even more important was the apprehension on the part of Bundy, Dorr, and others that President Roosevelt had become cool to the idea of national service. Finally, Stimson feared that selective service might become entangled in political conflict over the new measure and that the flow of soldiers to the Army might, as a result, be

[6] Walter Lippmann, "Today and Tomorrow—after the Honeymoon," The Washington *Post*, July 25, 1942.

[7] Senate Committee on Military Affairs, 77th Congress, 2d Session, Hearings on S. 3297, S. 2479, S. 2788, S. 2815, and S. 2842, pp. 22–23, 45.

[8] Ltr, Clark to Roosevelt, 4 Nov 42; Telgm, Clark to President, 4 Nov 42, both in Stimson files, Manpower.

[9] Ltr, Clark to McCloy, 17 Oct 42, Stimson files, Manpower; Ltr, Clark to Patterson, 27 Jan 43, Stimson files, National Service.

hindered.   As Assistant Secretary of War McCloy advised him, "This whole manpower business is so involved at the moment that it is a little too early for you to speak about it."

While Stimson recognized that "acrimonious discussion" in wartime was dangerous, he was on the other hand plagued by the thought that there was a considerable slack left in the civilian population which could be effectively used only by a national service law.   He prepared a brief but strong statement favoring the principles of the act and turned to President Roosevelt for advice.   He explained that the time was approaching when he would have to appear before the Senate Committee on Military Affairs and express his views on manpower.   Although wanting to embark on an active campaign for national service, Stimson nevertheless hesitated to take affirmative action.[10]

President Roosevelt wavered.   He encouraged government agencies to study Clark's proposals and in general showed an interest that Clark mistook for actual support.   But for the time being the President decided to do no more than tighten administration and increase efforts for voluntary co-operation.   On 5 December 1942, he transferred the Selective Service System to the War Manpower Commission under McNutt.   McNutt was placed in the position of a "czar" over both military and civilian manpower.   Questioned by reporters about his previous statement that national service was "inevitable," McNutt parried: "Why bother talking about it?   My position is clear." President Roosevelt, on 30 December 1942, said he was not prepared to go forward with national service at any time in the near future.[11]

Stimson opposed dependence on voluntary co-operation and felt that McNutt was not the proper person to direct manpower policy.   He appointed Patterson to represent the War Department on the War Manpower Commission in the hope that the Under Secretary's firmness and resolution might influence the rest of the members, but he was most unhappy over the setback.   Stimson had been away on a short vacation when the President issued the executive order transferring the Selective Service System to the

---

[10] Memo, McCloy for Stimson, 21 Oct 42, Memo [probably by Stimson] for Justice Byrnes, 22 Oct 42, Ltr, Stimson to Roosevelt, 18 Nov 42, and Memo, Bundy for Stimson, 31 Jan 43, all in Stimson files, Manpower; Memo, Brown for Dorr, 27 Jun 42, Dorr files, National Service Legislation Correspondence, 1942; Memo, Ohly for Files, 9 Apr 42, Memo, Chairman of Legislation Br JAG for Ohly, 7 May 42, Drafts of S. 2479 and H. R. 6806, 77th Congress, all in Ohly file, Dead Bills; Memo, Draft of Statement for SW Before Senate Committee on National Service Bills, 6 Nov 42; Ltr, Douglas Arrant to SW, 4 Nov 42, Ltr, Stimson to Arrant, 7 Nov 42 [never sent], all in Dorr files, Revision of National Service Act.

[11] *The New York Times,* December 7, 8, 31, 1942; EO 9279, 5 Dec 42; The Washington *Post,* October 30, 1942; Rosenman, *Working With Roosevelt,* pp. 419–20.

War Manpower Commission.   When he returned, Roosevelt told him at a Cabinet meeting, "I've been robbing your hen roost while you were away." Stimson snapped back, "I won't go away again." [12]

In the meantime, Senator Warren R. Austin of Vermont and Representative James Wadsworth of New York had decided to sponsor a national service bill.   They conferred with Dorr, who had known Wadsworth well from the days of World War I, and, revising a first draft, the three men produced a bill that embodied the recommendations made by the Dorr and Management-Labor Policy subcommittees.   It was introduced in Congress on 8 February 1943.

The Austin-Wadsworth bill combined a broad statement of principles and policy with specific safeguards.   It stated that every person had an obligation to serve the war effort "as he or she may be deemed best fit to perform." All men between eighteen and sixty-five and women between eighteen and fifty would register under selective service.   When manpower was needed for an essential activity, workers should first be given an opportunity to volunteer.   If volunteers failed to come forward, workers would be assigned to jobs at the same pay and for the same hours as employees of the plant to which they were assigned.   The bill provided some safeguards for unions, seniority rights, traveling expenses, and other measures designed to prevent injustice or undue hardship.[13]

The Senate Committee on Military Affairs began hearings on 2 March 1943.   A few weeks later the House Committee on Military Affairs held similar hearings.   The great debate raged, and for a time public interest was keen.

Now that the issue had come before Congress, Stimson for the first time publicly expressed his views.   In his initial statement, he wrote to the chairman of the Senate Committee on Military Affairs that to wage war to the fullest the nation had to mobilize all its human resources through national service.   For the next two years he and his staff devoted a great deal of time and energy to supporting national service.[14]

---

[12] Ltr, Stimson to McNutt, 5 Jan 43, in Dorr files, WMC Correspondence, SMPC Book II; Stimson Diary, 11 Dec 42, quoted in Stimson and Bundy, *On Active Service in Peace and War*, p. 481.

[13] S. 666, A Bill to Provide for the Successful Prosecution of the War Through a System of Civilian Selective War Service with the Aid of the Selective Service System, 78th Congress, 1st Session.

[14] Ltr, Stimson to Senator Robert F. Reynolds, 26 Feb 43, Dorr files, National Service Correspondence, 1943.

Perhaps the most effective argument for national service made by Patterson, Stimson, and other War Department officials was that it would aid in winning the war. Stimson decried the "mental attitude" of seeking to win the war in some easy manner without too much sacrifice. A tough policy in which the home front would back the fighting front to the hilt was the surest way to quick and decisive victory.[15] Patterson asserted that the Austin-Wadsworth bill was bad news for the country's enemies and good news for its allies and for its fighting men, who would know that they could count on the workers back home for the utmost support. National service would save lives and shorten the war.[16]

Proponents of the Austin-Wadsworth bill argued that voluntary methods had failed, and that the experience of every principal belligerent proved the inadequacy of halfway remedies. They took the position that the United States was the only warring nation depending on a free labor market but that actually there was no genuine freedom, for manpower officials were trying to do by indirection what the Austin-Wadsworth bill would do openly. The real issue, they claimed, was not freedom versus compulsion, but what form compulsion would take.

Compulsion under national service, advocates of the Austin-Wadsworth bill stated, was democratic and proper. People were compelled to pay taxes, obey the laws, and send their children to school. Compelling citizens to aid the war effort was necessary, according to proponents of the bill, and democratic because it was based on equality of sacrifice. If it were democratic "to tap a man on the shoulder and send him to fight the Japs in a New Guinea jungle," in the words of one witness, it was similarly democratic to tell a man to load shells, to build an airplane, or to stay on the farm. In total war, so ran the argument, no man had the right to say, "I do not choose to serve." [17]

Opposition to national service was strong. For once the AFL and the CIO presented a united front, and both agreed on most points with the National Association of Manufacturers and other employer groups. A number of women's organizations opposed the measure. Spokesmen for

---

[15] Stimson and Bundy, *op. cit.,* pp. 477–80.

[16] Statement of Robert P. Patterson, 18 March 1943, Senate Committee on Military Affairs, 78th Congress, 1st Session, Hearings on S. 666, *National War Service Bill,* Part 10, pp. 405–07.

[17] Senate Committee on Military Affairs, 78th Congress, 1st Session, Hearings on S. 666. The author has extracted from and summarized statements of various witnesses including Stimson, Patterson, Wadsworth, Charles E. Hughes, Jr., President Roosevelt, Admiral Land, Col. Lewis Sanders, and others. Material was taken specifically but not inclusively from pages 4–6, 9–10, 66, 69, 72, 93, 134, 403, 405, 407, 1005, 1133, 1279–80.

minority groups feared the effects of a labor draft. Together, they presented a vigorous case against the bill.

Opponents protested that it was "particularly regrettable that the name and office of the Secretary of War be used in support of the widely propagandized Austin-Wadsworth bill" which offered no solution to wartime manpower problems.[18] National service, they argued, was undemocratic and an infringement on liberty. They revived the argument that Bernard Baruch had made during World War I that drafting a man to fight for his country was not the same as drafting him to work for an employer in business for a profit. Claiming that forced labor for a private employer was a form of slavery prohibited by the Thirteenth Amendment to the Constitution, they charged that the enactment of involuntary servitude into law would "take from millions, both on the battle and production fronts, the very essence and meaning of this war."

Trade-union leaders objected to the bill on the grounds that it failed to protect re-employment and seniority rights, made no provision for adjusting substandard wages, and undermined collective bargaining. Representatives of women's groups protested against enforced female labor. A Negro spokesman questioned the effect of the law after it percolated down to a draft board in a place like Shubuta, Mississippi, where "hapless, hopeless, and helpless" Negroes would be forced into a state of peonage. The National Association of Manufacturers warned that "production would suffer . . . because there is no substitute for the initiative and willing effort of free men."

Although everyone agreed that all-out production was necessary, opponents of the bill argued that "slave" labor would not improve the fine record already achieved by voluntary effort. They claimed that production failures had been caused more often by shortages of materials than by shortages of labor. Sending thousands of additional workers into industry might therefore only aggravate, and not solve, the problems. War Department labor advisers emphasized the difficulty of mobilizing industrial manpower on a nationwide basis. As they viewed the situation, there was no national market for industrial labor, as there was for military manpower, but rather hundreds of different local markets with varying needs. Local selective service boards, manned by volunteers and already overburdened with the task of handling occupational deferments, were, in the opinion of these labor advisers, not qualified to take on the additional task of classifying workers according to

---

[18] IPD Daily Report on Labor Problems . . ., No. 44, 3 Mar 43, pp. C-1, 2, copy in OCMH.

their capacities and fitting them into the proper slots of a complex industrial system.

Opponents of the Austin-Wadsworth bill rejected as irrelevant the fact that democratic England and its freedom-loving dominions had universal service. England, they rejoined, lived under the threat of invasion; its smaller size made migration of labor easier; and it had taken other steps of planned production in which national service was an integral part. Furthermore, they pointed out, English labor service was administered by the Ministry of Labor headed by a trade union leader of high repute.

Labor spokesmen in opposing the bill refused to accept equality of sacrifice as a valid argument for national service. American labor, they declared, recognized the sacrifice made by the men on the firing lines and was in turn ready to give up whatever was necessary to support them. But, as one spokesman said, a person does not break an arm because the other arm is broken. Because the brunt of war fell harder on some, there was no need to make it fall equally hard on others for the sake of equalizing suffering. "Yes, a national service act would increase the burden of sacrifice borne by these on the home front," William Green of the AFL said, but it would do so "without rhyme, reason or necessity." [19]

Differences of opinion were not as great as they appeared. Except for extremists, those favoring national service agreed that voluntary methods were preferable if feasible, while those opposing national service agreed that compulsion was necessary if voluntary methods would not work. The real issue was whether voluntary labor could cope with the problems of all-out production, and, if not, under what conditions and at what stages of labor shortage national service would go into effect.

Many leaders believed that even if national service proved necessary, voluntary methods should be given a further trial. They argued that

[19] Senate Committee on Military Affairs, 78th Congress, 1st Session, Hearings on S. 666. See statements by individuals and spokesmen for organizations, including William Green, AFL; Russ Nixon, United Electrical, Radio, and Machine Workers, CIO; R. J. Thomas, CIO; Van A. Bittner, United Steel Workers; Martin H. Miller, Brotherhood of Railroad Trainmen; National Association of Manufacturers; U.S. Chamber of Commerce; Women's League for Political Education; Mothers of Sons Forum; National Committee to Oppose Conscription of Women; Workers Defense League; Walter White, National Association for the Advancement of Colored People; Norman Thomas; and others. Testimony appears specifically but not inclusively on pages 88–91, 293, 369–70, 372, 375, 396, 473–74, 504–07, 522, 567–68, 570, 636, 637, 643, 647, 700–701, 774, 845, 944. William Green's statement is in Senate Committee on Military Affairs, 78th Congress, 2d Session, Hearings on S. 666, p. 184. See also, Memo, Labor Planning Sec for O'Gara, 15 Mar 43, ASF IPD, Austin-Wadsworth Bill (H. R. 1742); Memo [unsigned], 18 Jan 44, sub: Commentary on Austin-Wadsworth Bill, Ohly file, National Service.

Negroes were kept out of jobs, that aliens had difficulty getting work, that other minority groups were prevented from using their highest skills, and that in general labor was not yet being effectively used. There were other criticisms of the utilization of labor. Contracts were improperly placed in areas with tight labor markets and inadequate community facilities, while some localities had labor surpluses. Large numbers of workers were in unessential industries like the processing of tobacco, and the manufacture of toys, jewelry, and luxury goods. In spite of labor's willingness to co-operate, there was even some unemployment. In short, so ran this argument, what was needed was not forced labor but better planning and direction of voluntary methods.[20]

In the face of such arguments, even stanch supporters of national service began to waver. Secretary of the Navy Frank Knox commented that he did not think the Austin-Wadsworth bill was necessary at "the present time" but that he felt the principles of the bill were sound and it might become "necessary to legislate" later on.[21] Admiral Emory S. Land of the U.S. Maritime Commission said that he might be able to accomplish his mission without national service but that he would achieve it more efficiently with it. Since the law might become necessary eventually, "why not now?"[22]

In the War Department, much of the support for the bill was based not on immediate need but on future value. In March 1943 an Army spokesman reported that with almost a million workers engaged directly and indirectly in ordnance manufacture, there were no major manpower shortages. A War Production Board official pointed out that the aircraft industry had mobilized 1,600,000 workers without real difficulty. A further expansion would probably create problems in supporting industries, but no crisis was imminent.[23] Secretary of War Stimson, while not budging on the principle of national service, began to speak of its application as something for the future. "I think we shall have to come to your effort," he wrote to

[20] Senate Committee on Military Affairs, 78th Congress, 1st Session, Hearings on S. 666, numerous witnesses, *passim;* Management-Labor Policy Committee of WMC, Verbatim Transcript of Informal Information Conference, 19 Mar 43, pp. 2–5.

[21] Ltr, Secy Navy to Senator Reynolds, 24 Apr 43, in Senate Committee on Military Affairs, 78th Congress, 1st Session, Hearings on S. 666, pp. 1002–03.

[22] Statement of Admiral Emory S. Land, 15 April 1943, Senate Committee on Military Affairs, 78th Congress, 1st Session, Hearings on S. 666, p. 934.

[23] Statements of Col. William J. Brennan, Jr., Chief, Labor Section, Ordnance, 18 May 1943, and T. P. Wright, Director of Aircraft Resources Control Office, WPB, 1 June 1943, Senate Committee on Military Affairs, 78th Congress, 1st Session, Hearings on S. 666, pp. 959–62, 971, 1007–11.

Grenville Clark, "but there are other things which are even riper than that problem and which lie directly at my feet and in my hands." [24]

Probably the factor that discouraged Stimson most was the President's attitude. Roosevelt stated that he favored national service but, since it created problems of regimentation, the nation should use it only as a last resort. He appointed a group of high-level advisers to study the subject. This "very informal group," made up of Baruch, Byrnes, Admiral Leahy, Harry Hopkins, and Samuel Rosenman, concluded that the manpower situation was tight, a prolonged war would make national service inevitable, but at the time the Austin-Wadworth bill was not necessary. Shortly thereafter Congress buried the Austin-Wadsworth bill in committee. [25]

Stimson did not give up. First, he and his assistants worked to create a unified department-wide policy. There were those, including Maj. Gen. Wilhelm D. Styer, chief of staff of ASF, who were convinced that national service was the only effective and complete means of coping with manpower problems. On the other hand, labor experts in the Industrial Personnel Division had doubts about a broad, general national service law, but they consoled themselves with the thought that specific measures to reduce turnover, cut absenteeism, and speed transfer of workers into essential industry and other useful features might be incorporated into the law. One of these experts compared national service to a hair tonic that did little good but proved beneficial when accompanied by vigorous massage. So, too, the significance of a well-drawn, vigorously applied national service law was that it would accomplished manpower objectives that other agencies had set up but had failed to achieve. [26]

While pressing for unity within the War Department, Stimson continued to try to win over the President. "The sooner we marshal our full strength," he wrote in July 1943, "the shorter the war and the less the cost of victory." He called for immediate and forceful support of manpower legislation and begged the President to discuss the bill with Congressional leaders of both

---

[24] Ltrs, Stimson to Winthrop Aldrich and Stimson to Grenville Clark, 1 May 43, both in Stimson files, National Service Act.

[25] Leahy, *I Was There*, pp. 149–50; Rosenman, *op. cit.*, pp. 420–23; Management-Labor Policy Committee of WMC, Verbatim Transcript of Informal Information Conference, 19 Mar 43, pp. 2–5.

[26] Memo, J. E. Baron for Somers, n.d., sub: National Sv Legislation, Memo, Baron for Files, 29 Sep 43, sub: National Sv, Current Manpower Difficulties, Labor Turnover, Memo, Baron for Files, 5 Oct 43, sub: National Sv Legislation, Absenteeism, Memo, Baron for Files, 6 Oct 43, sub: National Sv Legislation vs. Improved Labor Utilization, and Memo, Baron for Files, 5 Oct 43, sub: National Sv and Our Indictment of WMC, all in ASF IPD, National Sv Legislation.

parties.   He went so far as to offer to prepare for the President an outline for a message to Congress.[27]   A few months later Roosevelt asked Stimson for a draft of a manpower bill with the possibility of making recommendations to Congress.   Stimson recapitulated his arguments for the bill, but when nearly all the Cabinet members remained unenthusiastic the President for the time being let the matter drop.[28]

In November and December 1943 Roosevelt visited the troops in battle zones and met with Stalin and Churchill at Tehran.   The "Big Three" made the final decision to open a second front on the Continent.   More than ever before Roosevelt came to feel as Stimson and Patterson did that soldiers facing death and mutilation on the fighting front deserved the all-out support of the people at home.

When Roosevelt returned, he received a request from Stimson, Knox, and Admiral Land to introduce a national service law.   Stimson also sent him a personal letter addressed "My dear Chief" pleading for full manpower utilization.[29]   Roosevelt quietly made up his mind and went out of his way to avoid further argument.   Not even Stimson or Byrnes, czar of the civilian economy, knew that the President had told Robert Sherwood and Samuel Rosenman to prepare a secret manpower insert, "The Project Q 38," for his State of the Union Message.[30]

On 11 January 1944 Roosevelt told Congress that the armed forces believed that "there can be no discrimination between the men and women who are assigned . . . at the battle front and the men and women assigned to produce the vital materials essential to successful military operations." The President spoke of the trip to Tehran, of the high resolve of American troops, and of his sense of letdown on returning to Washington.   The people at home had a faulty perspective and overemphasized lesser problems. Self-serving interests, business as usual, and luxury as usual were the influences that might undermine the brave men at the front.   Quoting the recommendation of Stimson, Knox, and Land, Roosevelt declared, "When the very life of the nation is in peril, the responsibility for service is common

---

[27] Memo, Stimson for Roosevelt, 1 Jul 43, Dorr files, National Service Legislation Correspondence, 1943.

[28] Ltr, Stimson to President, 16 Sep 43, Stimson files, National Service Act.

[29] Stimson and Bundy, *op. cit.,* pp. 482–83; Memo, Patterson for Stimson, 27 Dec 43, with attached suggested memo for President, and Memo, Dorr for Stimson, 27 Dec 43, both in Stimson files, National Service; Stimson for Roosevelt, 28 Dec 43, Dorr files, National Service Extras [probably a working draft].

[30] Rosenman, *op. cit.,* pp. 420–23.

to all men and women. A prompt enactment of a national service law would be merely an expression of the universality of this responsibility." [31]

Senator Austin immediately announced his intention of introducing a revised version of his national service bill. Within a few days after the President delivered his message to Congress, hearings on the new bill started before the Senate Committee on Military Affairs.

Roosevelt's message to Congress had caught Stimson by surprise, but he was gratified and led a strong offensive in support of the President. As in earlier debates, one of his major points was the "double standard of morality"—responsibility for the war front, irresponsibility for the home front. Testifying before the Senate Committee on Military Affairs on 19 January 1944, Stimson glowed with pride as he told of the capture of the German Army in Tunis, the conquest of Sicily and southern Italy, the air attacks on German industry, the defeat of the submarine menace, the victories in the Pacific, and the unity of Great Britain, the Soviet Union, and the United States. For the coming year the crisis of European invasion loomed ahead, but there was good reason for confidence. "Suddenly what happened?" Stimson asked. "To our troops looking over their shoulders from the battlefields of the Mediterranean and the steaming jungles of the South Seas, the American front at home suddenly seemed to be on the point of going sour. A host of what seemed to our soldiers petty controversies in industry and labor, each one of which threatened to put a check in the production of priceless weapons, arose throughout our land." A national service act was essential, he held, to lift the morale of the troops and to equalize the sacrifice of the home with that of the fighting front.[32]

Though this argument for equality of sacrifice remained the keystone of the War Department position, there were other factors which, if not entirely new, received greater emphasis in 1944. The most important of these were first, that national service was a part of a general all-out effort; second, that national service might prevent serious strikes; and third, that while there was doubt in 1943 whether a work draft was necessary, by 1944 the time had come to enact a law.

Roosevelt in his State of the Union Message to Congress had said that he "would not recommend a national service law unless other laws were

---

[31] Message, President to Congress, 11 Jan 44, reprinted in Senate Committee on Military Affairs, 78th Congress, 2d Session, Hearings on S. 666, pp. 1–8. Also reprinted in *The New York Times,* January 12, 1944.

[32] Testimony of Henry L. Stimson, 19 January 1944, Senate Committee on Military Affairs, 78th Congress, 2d Session, Hearings on S. 666, pp. 37–39; Stimson and Bundy, *op. cit.,* p. 482.

passed to keep down the cost of living, to share equitably the burdens of taxation, to hold the stabilization line, and to prevent undue profits." [33]   A year before, Patterson had expressed the War Department's position that national service was only one part of a program to overcome obstructions to the war supply program.[34]   Many congressmen challenged this view. Senator Joseph C. O'Mahoney asked Stimson whether he would accept a labor draft without the other laws the President had "tied inseparably" together.   "I do not think he used the word 'inseparably,'" Stimson replied. "If you said 'tied logically' that would be better,"   It was unfair to pass a national service law and neglect other needed legislation to increase taxes and curb profits, Stimson explained, "but I will not go so far as to say that the passage of the National Service Act would not produce some vital safety benefits now, even if there had been, to some extent, a failure on other measures." [35]

President Roosevelt in his message had spoken of the value of national service as a deterrent to strikes.   The Administration did not consider it as an antiunion weapon, but some of the sponsors of national service had recognized that it might be put to such use.   "It may amuse you to realize," Representative Wadsworth had earlier written to Grenville Clark, that "there can be no such thing as a closed shop or union dues applicable to the men who take orders and go where they are sent." [36]   Clark later wrote to Byrnes that government pleas to strikers had no effect.   The answer was national service.[37]   Secretary of the Navy Knox, who had at one time opposed national service, had swung to its support when he felt that it might curb shipyard strikes.[38]   General Somervell believed that assigning workers to jobs would end the era of appeasement in which each surrender emboldened additional unions to strike.[39]   General Marshall told the American Legion that soldiers "must not go into battle puzzled and embittered over disputes at home which adversely affect the war effort." [40]

[33] Message, President to Congress, 11 Jan. 44.

[34] Statement of Robert P. Patterson, 18 March 1943, Senate Committee on Military Affairs, 78th Congress, 1st Session, Hearings on S. 666, pp. 405–07.

[35] Senate Committee on Military Affairs, 78th Congress, 2d Session, Hearings on S. 666, p. 48.

[36] Ltr, Wadsworth to Clark, 26 Mar 42, Stimson files, Manpower.

[37] Ltr, Clark to Byrnes, 27 Dec 43, Stimson files, National Service.

[38] Ltr, Secy of Navy to President, 8 Jun 43, Stimson files, National Service.

[39] Memo, Somervell for SW, 24 Dec 43, sub: National Sv Legislation, Stimson files, National Service.

[40] Speech, Gen George C. Marshall before the American Legion, 3 Feb 44, copy in Ohly file, Statements on National Service.

Secretary Stimson and Under Secretary Patterson, though realizing the value of national service in curbing strikes, had feared that what was essentially an over-all manpower measure might be distorted into a labor-baiting law. When Knox swung to support national service in the summer of 1943, Patterson confided to Stimson that the Secretary of the Navy was under a "misapprehension" about the purpose of the bill and would change it into a strike-breaking act.[41] Stimson, in his testimony before the Senate Committee on Military Affairs in January 1944, pleaded with congressmen to "please be fair to me," as he explained that strikes by an irresponsible few did not nullify the great service labor had performed in national defense.[42] He wanted as head of a national service administration a man sympathetic to labor's needs and problems, and in his diary he noted that the best choice would be the champion of the common man, Henry Wallace. Patterson agreed that labor's record on the whole was excellent and that the voluntary no-strike pledge should continue to be the cornerstone of the antistrike program, but he was also convinced that national service, by curbing the irresponsible few, would improve the record a little more.[43]

As in previous debates, one of the major controversial issues was the need for national service. President Roosevelt in January 1944 recalled that for nearly three years he had hesitated to recommend action because he did not think the time was ripe. "Today," he said, "I am convinced of its necessity."[44]

Stimson also spoke of the overwhelming production problems of global war, which put a terrific strain on manpower. Patterson argued that proper use of manpower would speed the output of weapons and shorten the war. He cited examples of war production needs: ball bearings—essential to every tank and plane; 100-octane gas—vital to air strength; B–29 bombers—necessary to devastate enemy resources from the air; C–47's the work horses of the Army which saved the day at Salerno—required to transport cargo; the radar program, the forge and foundry industry, the copper mines—all with labor problems which national service could solve. Patterson quoted figures from the War Manpower Commission of the need for a million men in industry. These men could not be voluntarily squeezed from their jobs with

---

[41] Memo, Patterson for Stimson, 11 Jun 43, sub: Knox Proposal, Stimson files, National Service.

[42] Senate Committee on Military Affairs, 78th Congress, 2d Session, Hearings on S. 666, p. 51.

[43] *Ibid.*, pp. 78–80; Stimson and Bundy, *op. cit.*, p. 487; Memo, Stimson for President, 1 Jul 43, Dorr files, National Service Legislation Correspondence, 1943.

[44] Message, President to Congress, 11 Jan 44.

"postwar futures." For example, the prewar figure of 12,000,000 men in trades and services had been reduced hardly at all. National service would make many of these men available to industries where they were needed, and, once there, it would keep them there.[45]

Top War Department officials worked hard to marshal facts and build public support for national service. Stimson delivered a stirring broadcast over a national network. Patterson in January 1944 called on representatives of important government agencies in Washington to develop a uniform Administration position. At the same time he asked the Air Forces for a list of specific contracts that were behind schedule because of manpower shortages. James P. Mitchell, Director of the Industrial Personnel Division, asked for similar information from the supply arms and services.

War Department representatives also tried to win over labor leaders and industrialists. Patterson insisted that national service had a great deal of rank and file support among union members. General Somervell repeatedly pleaded with business groups to get behind a labor draft because "we have a hell of a lot of war left." The Secretaries of War and the Navy together with the head of the Maritime Commission issued a joint statement that the nation was not meeting the labor shortages in critical programs. A special appeal was aimed to win over the Association of American Railroads, the U.S. Chamber of Commerce, and the National Association of Manufacturers.[46]

These strong appeals notwithstanding, advocates of national service had rough going. "Leaks" from a meeting of government agencies showed a good deal of dissension within the Administration. Paul McNutt, when asked for his views, endorsed national service with the comment that "when the heads of the armed services . . . say . . . that such an act is necessary, who are we to question it?" [47] The War Department faced opposition even within its own ranks. When a long list of behind-schedule contracts was presented, labor experts in the War Department noted that these did not prevent over-all fulfillment of production goals. The Industrial Personnel Division reported that the facts "furnish a very slim basis from the procure-

---

[45] Senate Committee on Military Affairs, 78th Congress, 2d Session, Hearings on S. 666, pp. 76–78, 88–90.

[46] *The New York Times,* April 21, 1944.

[47] Memo, William Haber for Lawrence Appley, Paul McNutt, and Others, 17 Jan 44, sub: Roosevelt's Views on National Service as Reported by Judge Rosenman, Dorr files, National Service Legislation Chronology; *PM,* January 31, 1944; Testimony of Paul V. McNutt as Reported in *The New York Times,* February 1, 1944.

ment standpoint on which the case for national service legislation may be based."[48]

The efforts to win labor support were largely wasted. William Green, president of the American Federation of Labor, insisted that national service would not increase production. Philip Murray of the CIO called it "quack medicine." The only labor groups that supported the measure were those generally believed to have Communist affiliations. Joe Curran of the National Maritime Union thought it a fine idea, while Harry Bridges, the seamen's leader, told a Navy officer: "Well, by golly, I am all for a labor draft." The more conservative unions called this a "red betrayal" and compared national service to the Soviet system of conscripting labor.[49]

The War Department found similiar views among industrialists. Although many a manufacturer openly supported national service, others remained stanchly opposed. The National Association of Manufacturers reiterated its stand against the proposed law, while the U.S. Chamber of Commerce issued a statement that national service would retard rather than advance the war program.[50]

Although Stimson and Patterson had spent a great deal of time preparing testimony for Congressional hearings, congressmen were not impressed. Senator James E. Murray of Montana stressed labor's fine production record. Senator O'Mahoney of Wyoming blamed the War Department for many of the production difficulties. Even so stanch a supporter of national service as Senator Chan Gurney of South Dakota pointed out that inefficiency and waste, rather than shortages of labor, were responsible for many of the difficulties. "Suppose, for instance, Farmer Jones has a daughter who is ordered to go to Chicago or Milwaukee, or any other town," Senator Gurney said, and she writes home, "Dad, they do not need me down here. . . . You do more before breakfast than I see done by some of these workers all day."[51]

[48] Memos, Offices of the Chief of Ordnance, Chief of Chemical Warfare Service, The Quartermaster General, and Chief Signal Officer for Dir IPD, 15 Jan 44, Memos, Offices of the Chief of Engineers, Chief of Transportation, and The Surgeon General for Dir IPD, 17 Jan 44, and Memo, Hq AAF for CG ASF, 22 Jan 44, sub: Prod Failures Because of Manpower Shortages, all in ASF IPD, Miscellaneous; Memo, Dir IPD for CG ASF, sub: WD Activity and Manpower Shortages, 19 Apr 44, ASF IPD National Service Act.

[49] Memo, Patterson for Howard C. Peterson, 23 Jan 44, and Ltr, Maj. W. Burroughs to Mitchell, 22 Jan 44, both in ASF IPD, Views of Various Groups, Labor; *The Pilot,* January 21, 1944; AFL Weekly News Service, "Facing the Facts," February 1, 1944.

[50] *The New York Times,* April 21, 1944; Declaration, U.S. Chamber of Commerce, 29 Apr 43, reprinted in Senate Committee on Military Affairs, 78th Congress, 2d Session, Hearings on S. 666, pp. 292–99.

[51] Senate Committee on Military Affairs, 78th Congress, 2d Session, Hearings on S. 666, pp. 50–51, 54, 61–62.

Senator Robert R. Reynolds, Chairman of the Senate Committee on Military Affairs, afterward stated, "Stimson didn't sell me a thing." An Associated Press dispatch noted that Senator Reynolds' remark was typical of the views of the committee. Five of its eighteen members were against the bill, five more made it plain that on the basis of existing evidence they would vote no.[52] An attempt by Senator Gurney to bring the bill to the floor failed by a close margin, and it remained bottled up in the committee.

As the military situation improved, the War Department's fight for national service became even more difficult. When favorable reports filtered back from the front a wave of optimism spread throughout the country. The Joint Chiefs of Staff accepted the possibility that the war would end in October 1944. The Army canceled contracts in many areas, and thousands of workers lost their jobs. Congress debated surpluses of munitions and postwar unemployment became a major topic of discussion.

Secretary Stimson feared the psychological effect of this undue optimism both on the troops and on the home front. He hoped he would not be like Cassandra of the old myth, who predicted evil and then saw it come to pass. General Somervell presented the Army view in public statements and, while giving an optimistic picture of production, deplored the complacency that followed the successes in Europe. Each victory, he said, led to another battle, and the nation had to keep fighting and working until the last shot was fired.

The War Department continued to champion national service. Stimson went so far as to prepare another special appeal to the President. But before presenting it, he changed his mind. He was uncertain whether he could convince the President to press the measure at this time, and, regardless of what Roosevelt would or would not do, Stimson was sure that, barring a serious military setback, Congress would not pass a worthwhile law.[53]

The military setback was not long in coming. In December 1944 the Germans launched a counteroffensive in the Ardennes. The nation was

---

[52] Washington *Times-Herald,* January 12, 1944; *The New York Times,* January 16th, 1944; The Washington *Post,* January 23, 1944; WD General Council Minutes, 6 Mar 44.

[53] Summary of Meeting, Management-Labor Policy Committee, 8 Aug 44; *The New York Times,* December 5, 1944; Statement of Frederick C. Crawford, Chairman National Association of Manufacturers' Executive Committee, 17 January 1945, House Committee on Military Affairs, 79th Congress, 1st Session, Hearings on H. R. 1119, Mobilization of Civilian Manpower, pp. 353–56; Statement of Henry L. Stimson, 6 February 1945, Senate Committee on Military Affairs, 79th Congress, 1st Session, Hearings on S. 36, p. 12; Ltr, Stimson to Clark, 24 May 44, Stimson files.

alarmed. The armed services called for more men and supplies. On 21 December General Somervell wrote Stimson that there were not enough workers to produce many critical items.[54] Patterson told Stimson that the supply of the Army and Navy should not depend on coaxing people to take war jobs. The proper solution was national service.[55] Stimson prevailed upon the Secretary of the Navy, James V. Forrestal, to join him in an appeal to the President stating that the armed forces needed national service to hasten the day of final victory and to keep to a minimum the cost in lives.

In his State of the Union Message in January 1945, the President strongly endorsed a labor draft. Withdrawing from the position he had taken the year before, Roosevelt did not now make national service contingent upon the prior passage of other "hold-the-line" legislation. Pointing to shortages, he called on every American to rise to the crisis by going to or staying at his war job. "The Lord hates a quitter," he said, and the nation would have to pay for slackers with the "life's blood" of its sons. Roosevelt cited the letter of the Secretaries of War and the Navy, who were supported by General Marshall and Admiral King, to the effect that winning the war required the passage of a national service law. He called upon Congress to enact such a law for the "total mobilization of all our human resources for the prosecution of the war." The law would assure the right number of workers in the right places, prove to our fighting men that the home front was backing them, and dash the hopes of the enemy that our halfhearted efforts would enable him to snatch out of defeat a negotiated peace.[56]

The President's message notwithstanding, there was very little hope of passing a comprehensive national service law. Some officials in the War Department felt that it would be just as hard to get a partial measure as a full-scale law, but others felt that by fighting for an all-out law the War Department might prevail upon Congress to offer the advocates of national service a limited labor draft as a compromise. "Though half a loaf is better than none," one adviser wrote Stimson, any reduced request would be taken as a "clinching sign of weakness" and would ruin the chance of "even a good half." While hope of a strong law was all but abandoned, the War Department, as a matter of principle and as a matter of tactics, continued to support comprehensive national service, while at the same time conceding its

---

[54] Memo, Somervell for Stimson, 21 Dec 44, Stimson files, National Service.

[55] Memo, Patterson for Stimson, 21 Dec 44, sub: Manpower, Stimson files.

[56] President Franklin D. Roosevelt, State of the Union Message, 6 January 1945, House Document 1, 79th Congress, 1st Session.

willingness to go along with limited proposals to the extent to which they might be effective.[57]

The most popular limited proposals were those which called for forcing men classified as IV–F into essential jobs. If these men had been physically fit, they would have gone into the fighting forces. It seemed only fair that they should work at jobs that would contribute to the winning of the war. "Those qualified to fight, fight," Patterson said. Those "who are not qualified to fight, work." [58]

Congress had discussed a "IV–F bill" early in 1944. But opposition from labor and industry at a time when good news was coming back from the fighting fronts had resulted in the bill's dying in the House Committee on Military Affairs.[59] Nearly a year later, when the President delivered his State of the Union Message, he asked that, pending consideration of broader aspects of manpower legislation, Congress immediately enact a law which would be effective in using for the war effort the services of 4,000,000 men classified as IV–F.[60]

Congress paid little attention to the recommendation for broad national service legislation. But hardly had the President finished speaking when Representative Andrew J. May and Senator Josiah W. Bailey introduced bills imposing on men between eighteen and forty-five the obligation to stay on or transfer to war jobs.[61]

Although it disliked many features of the bill, the War Department gave the measure its wholehearted support. On 10 January 1945 Patterson explained to the House Committee on Military Affairs that the War Department objected to the idea that men who did not go into war work should be inducted into a special Army labor corps. The Army already had more limited service men than it could use, and besides it was wrong to use the Army as a penal institution. Patterson agreed that in order to see the bill carried out he would accept this distasteful provision, but the Committee on Military Affairs accepted his view and substituted criminal penalties for induction into the Army for labor shirkers.

[57] Memo, Peterson for USW, 25 Mar 44, Dorr files, National Service Legislation; Memo, Patterson for Stimson, 21 Dec 44, sub: Manpower, Stimson files.

[58] The Washington Post, January 23, 1944; House Committee on Military Affairs, 79th Congress, 1st Session, Hearings on H. R. 1119, 10–18 January 1945; Senate Committee on Military Affairs, 79th Congress, 1st Session, Hearings on S. 36 and H. R. 1752, 6–16 February 1945.

[59] The New York Times, April 19, 1944.

[60] President Franklin D. Roosevelt, State of the Union Message, 6 January 1945, House Document 1, 79th Congress, 1st Session.

[61] Senate Committee on Military Affairs, 79th Congress, 1st Session, Hearings on S. 36 and H. R. 1752.

Patterson also told the House Committee on Military Affairs that the only complete remedy for manpower shortages was a comprehensive national service act. But even though the proposed bill did not cover men over forty-five and women, it might help provide the 1,600,000 men needed for the Army and industry during the next six months. He regarded the bill as a genuine national service law applied to men between eighteen and forty-five.[62]

In order to back the armed services the President, on 16 January 1945, met with General Marshall, Admiral King, and key men of the House and Senate Military Affairs Committees. He then sent a letter to Chairman May of the House Committee enclosing a statement by Marshall and King. The Joint Chiefs were careful to avoid direct endorsement of any bill but stated that as agents responsible for the conduct of the war they needed 900,000 more men for the armed services and that munitions and war supporting industries would require 700,000 more.[63] On 1 February 1945, after some brief but acrimonious debate, the House of Representatives voted 246 to 165 in favor of the measure.[64]

The next step was to convince the Senate. Secretary Stimson appeared before the Senate Committee on Military Affairs and stressed again that a national service bill would assure ample munitions and aid battle morale. Patterson dwelt on actual needs and gave details of manpower shortages. Voluntary methods, he said, had failed.[65] Stimson, Patterson, and Dorr arranged to meet new Republican senators in a private room off the Senate Dining Room, and War Department officials co-operated very closely with the Citizens' Committee for a National War Service Act to win Congressional support.[66] The Purchases Division of the Army Service Forces campaigned among industrialists with whom the War Department did business, in order to wean them away from active opposition to national service. At the same time employees of the Industrial Personnel Division tried to persuade trade unionists to get behind the bill.

A major publicity campaign was undertaken. Business and labor leaders were flown to the battle fronts, in the hope that they would absorb battle-

---

[62] Statement of Robert P. Patterson, 10 January 1945, House Committee on Military Affairs, 79th Congress, 1st Session, Hearings on H. R. 1119, pp. 3–34; *The New York Times,* January 11, 1945.

[63] Ltr, President to Chairman House Military Affairs Committee, 17 Jan 45, and Ltr, Marshall and King to President, 16 Jan 45, in House Military Affairs Committee, 79th Congress, 1st Session, Hearings on H. R. 1119, pp. 436–37.

[64] *The New York Times,* January 26, February 2, 1945.

[65] Testimony of Henry L. Stimson and Robert P. Patterson, 6 February 1945, Senate Committee on Military Affairs, 79th Congress, 1st Session, Hearings on S. 36 and H. R. 1752, pp. 12–16, 26–66.

[66] Memo, Dorr for J. W. Schott, 3 Feb 45, Stimson files, Manpower.

front psychology.[67]   Patterson prepared a statement for the North American Newspaper Alliance urging Congress to pass the manpower bill.[68]   Stimson, in a major radio address, warned that the enemy would not wait while the nation struggled with "deadly shortages." [69]   News correspondent Ernie Pyle wrote from the combat zone that the people at home should accept national service so "the boys overseas won't feel so lonesome." [70]   Perhaps the best summary of the military point of view on the May-Bailey bill appeared in the Paris edition of the *Stars and Stripes,* which editorialized: "They call the proposed manpower law the May bill . . . . There can't be any May about it.   Must is the word." [71]

Yet the opposition proved strong.   Senators accused Stimson of trying to "dictate legislation" by giving "an utterly unbalanced impression" to soldiers and their families.[72]   Officers of labor unions and employers' associations again united in a savage attack on the War Department's position.   They particularly challenged War Department manpower figures.   When Marshall and Patterson claimed that they needed 900,000 draftees, no one could say them nay, though the figures were not held above suspicion.   But the demand for 700,000 additional workers because of manpower shortage was greeted with general disbelief.

The president of the National Association of Manufacturers suggested that 150,000 was probably a more likely figure, and this represented only one quarter of one percent of the working force.   Moreover, "the shortages existing today are different from those that existed last week, two weeks ago, or a month ago; and . . . the shortages we will have to face next week and a month from now will again be different." [73]

Labor's attack was even more devastating.   The War Department had given union officials a list of plants where shortages existed.   Using the list, the various unions investigated.   The International Association of Machinists reported that a Curtiss-Wright Corporation plant, where it was alleged that

---

[67] Folder of Correspondence (letters, telegrams, memos, etc.), ASF Prod Div 381, National War Service Act; ASF Manpower Conference Minutes, 17 Jan 45, Ohly file, National Service Folders 7, 8, 9.

[68] *The New York Times,* February 10, 1945.

[69] *Ibid.,* February 19, 1945.

[70] Senate Committee on Military Affairs, 79th Congress, 1st Session, Hearings on S. 36 and H. R. 1752, p. 336.

[71] *Ibid.,* p. 171.

[72] *The New York Times,* February 20, 1945.

[73] Memo Outlining Highlights of National Association of Manufacturers' Intensified Voluntary Manpower Program. . . .   [*ca.* 14 Jan 45], copy in ASF Prod Div 381, National War Service Act.

2,600 workers were needed, was getting ready to close down for nine days. The Army had reported a shortage of 1,600 men at Bell Aircraft Corporation but, on the day the CIO checked, 500 workers were laid off. Lewis G. Hines, summarizing the AFL investigations, said that the figures given the union by the Army proved in every instance to be exaggerated. President Philip Murray of the CIO told Congress that 75 percent of the cases reported to his organization were found to have no labor shortage as reported and that in 55 percent of the cases there was in fact an oversupply of labor.[74]

On more general grounds, the Army was charged with misapplying statistics. Opponents of national service pointed out that the Bureau of Labor Statistics recorded labor needs by debits and credits. In one column the bureau listed known demand for manpower, and in another column it listed known supply. Simple subtraction gave a picture of the manpower situation. But the War Department reported only demand and failed to subtract supply. The chief of the Bureau of Labor Statistics, A. F. Heinrichs, noted that the figure of 900,000 men and women for the armed forces and 700,000 for production was a gross figure, "but it is very important to *distinguish* between your *gross* and your *net* requirements." After allowing for cutbacks, military discharges, lowered retiring rate, normal growth of labor force, and so on, the figure of 1,600,000 men needed was instead 200,000.[75]

By and large labor leaders conceded that there were scattered labor shortages but that these could be taken care of by moderate, voluntary measures. The War Department solution of a labor draft, one Congressional witness with Irish friends noted, "was like using a 'shillelagh to pick your teeth.' "[76]

Many government agencies, while silenced by the President's official position, sought ways of killing strong manpower legislation. The War Manpower Commission, for instance, recommended a substitute measure for the May-Bailey bill. The War Manpower Commission bill started with a sweeping statement obligating every person to work in the job where he was most needed. It called for controlled hiring, employment ceilings, labor utilization surveys, and investigations by the armed services. But it differed most radically from the bills supported by the War Department in that it

---

[74] Memo, AFL–CIO May Committee Testimony, 25 Jan 45, ASF IPD, National Service, General; House Committee on Military Affairs, 79th Congress, 1st Session, Hearings on H. R. 1119, pp. 191, 245–50.

[75] Aaron Levenstein, *Labor Today and Tomorrow* (New York: Alfred A. Knopf, 1945), pp. 132–34.

[76] House Committee on Military Affairs, 79th Congress, 1st Session, Hearings on H. R. 1119, p. 166.

provided no real means of enforcement. It was merely a pious declaration of principle.[77]

The War Department opposed the substitute bill. "Dear Jimmie," Patterson appealed to Byrnes, "I hope that you will make vigorous opposition to the . . . substitute for the May-Bailey bill." Patterson explained that ceilings were effective only on employers. They could not mobilize lawyers, real-estate agents, brokers, taxi drivers, or other millions of self-employed workers, and as a practical administrative matter they could not touch the millions employed in small businesses. Ceilings would not get workers into essential plants, and the man displaced in a brewery would not necessarily work in a gun factory. "It does not make sense to throw three persons out of work in the hope that one of them may possibly go to a war plant . . . ." Ceilings also would cause employers to release only their most inefficient and least dependable workers. Mild as the measures were, the means of enforcement were even weaker and would, Patterson protested, render the bill "utterly useless." There were no fines, no penalties, no sanctions, but only civil suits against employees, which could have only belated effect.

Patterson attacked the other provisions saying that surveys of war plants by the War Manpower Commission would introduce a division of responsibility for war production and interfere with the activities of the procurement agencies. Similarly, an investigation of Army-Navy use of manpower would split responsibility and make an already difficult job harder. Adoption of the substitute bill, Patterson argued, would be of no value in promoting war production or in improving the morale of the troops.[78]

In spite of the strong protest of the War Department, the Senate Committee on Military Affairs favorably reported the substitute bill (O'Mahoney-Kilgore) by a vote of thirteen to four. Senators sympathetic to the War Department view tried to resubstitute the May-Bailey bill on the floor of the Senate but were able to muster only twenty-three votes. The Senate then by a vote of sixty-three to sixteen passed the "milk and water" O'Mahoney-Kilgore measure.

The fate of the bill depended on how resolutely the House would stand by the May-Bailey bill. It was buttressed in its defense of its own measure by the President, who, when asked which bill he favored, replied that anyone

---

[77] U.S. Bureau of the Budget, *The United States at War,* pp. 453, 454; Memo, Dorr for SW, 22 Feb 45, sub: Line of Attack on Senate Committee Draft of National Service Act, Stimson files, Manpower.

[78] Ltr, Patterson to Byrnes, 21 Feb 45, in Dorr files, National Service Act, 1945.

who read his State of the Union Message could tell which bill came closer to meeting his recommendations. With Presidential and War Department backing, the House, by a much narrower margin of support than in the original measure, reaffirmed its own bill.

House and Senate conferees agreed on a compromise which retained some essential features desired by the War Department. The House accepted the compromise. Again the fate of limited national service depended on Senate action. Secretary of War Stimson wrote to Senator Elbert D. Thomas of the Senate Committee on Military Affairs that "this legislation will be more useful and efficient than almost anything which could be done to assure a speedy end of the war." [79] He made a similar appeal to the House Committee. President Roosevelt also urged the Senate to accept the manpower bill. The compromise was not all that was recommended by General Marshall and Admiral King, but in controversial matters of this kind a bill could be enacted only as a result of adjusting differences. The Senate considered these appeals but, by a vote of forty-six to twenty-nine, rejected even the compromise.

Surveying the situation, Goldthwaite Dorr wrote to Stimson, "We have taken a licking after three years of hard fighting." Nevertheless, he believed that in the interest of the country the War Department should try to salvage a few crumbs, and that because of the statement of principle in the O'Mahoney-Kilgore bill, the armed services should express support of it as better than nothing.[80] But with the end of the war in sight, even this declaration of principle was not passed.

The battle for national service had been lost. No matter how strenuously the champions of national service had presented their case they had been unable to arouse sufficient Congressional support for the enactment of their program. Public opinion was mixed. If people on the whole approved the fairness and ethics of national service, at the same time they viewed with distaste any further extension of controls over the individual. Those who were genuinely persuaded that drafting workers for war industry was more palatable and no less essential than drafting men to fight were unable to overcome the opposition of influential special groups. To others it seemed incredible that there should be jobs without men to fill them, for the United States had entered the war with a vast reservoir of unemployed manpower that was not

[79] Ltr, Stimson to Thomas, 28 Mar 45, Stimson files, National Service Act.
[80] Memo, Dorr for SW and USW, 5 Apr 45, sub: Manpower Legislation, Dorr files, National Service Act.

emptied until late in the conflict, and even then no acute nationwide short-age developed.   If the advocates of national service pointed to shortages in particular industries or in particular localities, to excessive absenteeism, and to a rapidly rising turnover, their opponents in turn pointed out areas of unemployment, layoffs, and underutilization.   The very fact that the War Department vigorously supported the campaign for national service may have actually weakened the effort.   Both within and without the government a sizable body of opinion held that industrial manpower problems were the concern of the civilian agencies, and that the War Department's campaign for national service constituted an intrusion upon civilian control of the government.

   Under these circumstances, Stimson, Patterson, and other supporters of national service were unable to push their program through Congress.   But their efforts did have the effect of highlighting the urgency of the manpower situation.   Many individuals, out of patriotism, transferred to war jobs.   Bar-bers, insurance men, real-estate brokers, and others got on the production line.   Housewives went to war industries.   Many individuals not only worked on their regular jobs but also took on part-time war work.   The very talk of "work or fight" sent many able-bodied men at nonessential jobs scurrying to war industry.   The effort for national service was perhaps not a total failure.

CHAPTER XII

Looking Back: A Chronological Summary

When the war ended American industry could rightfully share in the pride of victory. Production had been pushed to unprecedented heights. Although occasional shortages of matériel on the battlefield sometimes hindered military operations, none of them could be conclusively traced to a production failure on the home front, still less to a failure on the part of labor to stay on the job. The nation's tremendous industrial accomplishment was achieved, furthermore, without any lasting or substantial disruption of the national economy and without serious infringement upon civil liberties. The men and women who labored in the factories and those who managed and directed the industrial effort merit much of the credit for the successful outcome of the war. This is not to say that industry did its job without stress and strain and the clashing of gears. There was considerable of this, notwithstanding that well over a decade of planning had preceded the emergency.

Similarly in spite of the prewar planning the War Department and labor had not always pulled together smoothly with a common will and purpose. By its responsibility for procurement and its overriding concern with getting the job done the War Department was drawn into direct clashes with labor. Nevertheless, despite indications that there may have been officers in the War Department who wished to put labor in its place and who welcomed the opportunity to do so that the war provided, the fact remains that the relations between the War Department and labor were improved by the wartime experience and moved from mutual suspicion toward mutual confidence. Although impatient of petty obstructions that appeared to reflect a reluctance on the part of organized labor to sacrifice, even temporarily, the gains it had made since 1933 and intolerant of strikes that affected military production, neither Secretary Stimson nor Under Secretary Patterson gave way to the antilabor pressures to which they were subject. Their unquestioned integrity and their wisdom in heeding the counsel of advisers like Edward McGrady and Brig. Gen. Edward S. Greenbaum played a large part in winning the co-operation and confidence of labor.   At the same time the gradual process and practical ways by which the relations of the War Department with labor evolved put the development of these relations into the hands of officials at the working level.   These officials were in the Army Service Forces, whose commander, General Somervell, had had a large and instructive experience in managing industrial relations.   His subordinate officers had to get results. Under the leadership of such men as James Mitchell and John Ohly, they found that to meet the immediate tasks realistically and effectively it was best to work actively in co-operation with labor toward the solution of problems of mutual concern, on the principle that labor should not be called upon to sacrifice its gains except when the need was real and then only under adequate safeguards against any exaggeration of the need.   The gradual growth of the War Department's direct relations with labor provided the opportunity to put this working hypothesis to pragmatic test.   As direct contacts with labor multiplied, ways of dealing with a great variety of labor problems were worked out, found workable by both parties, and were, with Patterson's approval and support, established as general policies and procedures.[1]   This process tended not only to fix the actual position of the War Department but also to convince labor of its fairness.   The mutual confidence generated on the working level played its part in bringing together Patterson on the one hand and William Green and Philip Murray on the other into a direct and effective working relationship.   As a result, the voluntary system remained in operation throughout the war with no serious impairment of the War Department's production programs.

If, in retrospect, the Army's labor planning in the interval between World War I and World War II seems unrealistic, it must be remembered that the industrial mobilization plans were not solely a product of the planners' minds but that they reflected the temper of the times, the larger issues involved in the allocation of national resources, and the state of strategic planning.

Considerable public opposition to preparations for waging war existed during much of the planning period.   Even after the outbreak of war in Europe Americans chose to rely on neutrality laws instead of mobilization plans.   The position of organized labor presented a divisive issue.   Union leaders, determined to preserve the gains won during the early 1930's and affected by the antiwar sentiment of the day, regarded the War Department

---

[1] This interpretation was suggested by a discussion of the manuscript of this volume with John Ohly, Deputy Director for Program and Planning, International Co-operation Administration, who during the war held several important policy-making positions on War Department labor matters.

labor plans with suspicion.   The plans themselves reflected a division in the
War Department between those officers who saw the task as one of safeguarding the interests of labor and those who saw it as one of protecting industry's supply of labor.   To the extent that each successive industrial mobilization plan veered in one or the other direction, either labor or industry was
dissatisfied.

A more perplexing dilemma, involving the proper spheres of the military
and civilian authorities, faced the War Department planners.   It was a fundamental principle that the basic allocation of national resources between
essential civilian needs and military requirements had to be decided by the
President acting through a high-level agency that was independent of the
War and Navy Departments and that the necessary wartime controls over
the national economy had to be exercised through civilian agencies.   In the
absence of a civilian planning agency, the War Department was obliged to
sketch out an organizational framework for industrial mobilization and to
indicate the nature of the controls that would be required.   However general
the plans were, the very fact that they had been prepared by a military agency
reacted against them.   Ferdinand Eberstadt, onetime chairman of the Army
and Navy Munitions Board, afterward gave this as a reason why, in his opinion, the 1939 Industrial Mobilization Plan was not put into effect.

Recognition that it was not primarily a War Department responsibility to
determine either the allocation of the labor force or the specific means of dis-
tributing it perhaps accounted in part for the scant attention given to the
problem of labor supply in the prewar planning.   More directly responsible
was the limited military effort envisaged by the then current strategic plans.
The pre-1939 strategic plans had not contemplated a major offensive role for
the Army against a coalition of hostile powers, and the War Department labor
planners accordingly found it almost impossible to assume that industrial
manpower would be inadequate for the task it might be called upon to perform.   As it happened, the magnitude of the effort required in World War
II was such as to bring the armed services and war industry into competition
for the nation's manpower.   Because of the policy implications it involved,
the War Department and the Joint Chiefs of Staff were reluctant to accept
the view that the size of the armed forces was limited by, and had to be tailored to, the size of the civilian labor force.

The prewar labor planners went equally far astray in their forecast of the
effect of such legislation as the Wagner and Walsh-Healey Acts.   Anticipating that the various statutes regulating hours of work, wages, and working

conditions would seriously limit production, they drafted bills to suspend these regulations in wartime. In this case, the actual problem turned out to be not one of decreased production resulting from industry's compliance with restrictive regulations but one of War Department policy in the face of noncompliance.

The surge of industrial expansion that began in 1940 and early 1941 as a result of the rush of orders from abroad, the lend-lease program, and an accelerating program of domestic rearmament produced dislocations but did not encounter shortages in the labor market. A large reservoir of unemployed workers could readily be drawn upon. A variety of growing pains nevertheless appeared. Labor unions immediately began a campaign to organize the new workers in the new and expanding aircraft, shipbuilding, and armaments plants and to consolidate their strength in industries previously organized. Minority groups likewise sought to use the opportunity to break down the job barriers that for a long time had been raised against them. Employers sought to resist the demands of labor unions and to whittle down their gains. The result was unrest expressed in the shape of strikes and slowdowns. As the principal procurement agency for military matériel, the War Department was directly interested in labor disputes when production was affected. The growing belief that some of the strikes and slowdowns were inspired by subversive elements attempting to sabotage defense production made the disruptions a further matter of direct interest to the War Department.

The rise of these problems coincided with the coming of a new team headed by Secretary Stimson and Assistant Secretary Patterson. Clothed in ability and integrity, and armed with patriotic indignation against any group that seemed to put its own interests above those of the defense effort, Stimson and Patterson gave vigorous direction to the measures taken to establish policies and procedures that would be adequate to the situation. Special advisers experienced in the different aspects of the labor problem were brought into the War Department, and Patterson's office was several times reorganized to give broader scope and greater status to the handling of labor matters.

The experiment of actively intervening as mediator in a labor dispute was tried. The initial success seemed to prove the feasibility of this approach to the problem, but the equally notable failure when the experiment was repeated a few weeks later caused the War Department to return to its established policy of nonintervention. After the failure of its attempt to negotiate a settlement of the Vultee strike, in November 1940, the War Department was content to leave the task of mediation to another agency, and for this rea-

son it supported the establishment of the National Defense Mediation Board
some months later.

In the meantime, labor unions, encouraged by the statement of policy
made by the National Defense Advisory Commission in September 1940, had
begun exerting pressure on the War Department to withhold contracts from
companies that refused to comply with federal labor laws, particularly the
Wagner Act. Within the War Department there was considerable pulling
and hauling on the question how far to go in meeting the desires of labor.
The instructions issued by the Chief of Staff in Procurement Circular 43 that
all invitations for bids must specify compliance with labor laws satisfied no
one but the labor unions and the National Defense Advisory Commission.
Coinciding with the flare-up of strikes and slowdowns at the end of 1940,
the controversy over contract labor clauses gave further impetus to the search
for an adequate method of dealing with labor disputes in war industries.
Congress turned its attention to antistrike legislation, while the War Department began giving serious consideration to government seizure of strike-bound
plants as a means of maintaining production.

Congress had not acted nor had the War Department completed its studies
of plant seizures when the North American Aviation company went on strike
in June 1941. The walkout raised a threat to essential production, posed a
problem of law and order, and presented a flagrant defiance of the government's mediation process. On the advice of his Cabinet, the President therefore directed the Army to take over the plant. The lack of policies and
procedures for conducting an operation of this kind was not considered
prohibitive, because it seemed probable at first that the Army's only task
would be to afford protection to workers who wanted to return to their jobs.
Although employment was brought up almost to normal within two days
after the seizure of the plant, the setting for negotiations between labor and
management remained as unfavorable as it had been before the seizure took
place. The Army had to stay on and, notwithstanding the co-operation of
the company officials, was almost immediately faced with a variety of operational details, a good many of which were taken to the President for decision.
The regular officials of the company continued in charge of actual plant
operations, as agents of the U.S. Government. The conduct of labor relations, including such matters as approving discharges and deciding whether
a new election for union representation should be held, was placed in the
hands of the War Department representative at the plant. Negotiations
between labor and the management of the company were resumed as soon as

the national headquarters of the union appointed new men to replace the local union officials who were responsible for the strike and who had been, by direction of the President, excluded from any further negotiations.   Under guidance of National Defense Mediation Board representatives, an acceptable settlement was reached by 1 July, and the plant was turned back to the company after three weeks of government operation.   While the strike itself had stimulated Congress into adding several antistrike riders to the Army appropriation bill, the success of the seizure in maintaining production indicated to the War Department the effectiveness of government operation as a measure for keeping the wheels of war industry moving.

The labor disputes during the first half of 1941, climaxed by the North American Aviation strike, had raised the question also of security and antisubversive measures.   The problem involved in the question was partly jurisdictional and partly one of definition and identification.   The Federal Bureau of Investigation had been given charge of investigating espionage and sabotage.   G–2, the Intelligence Division of the War Department General Staff, also had a vital interest in this field, and the distinction between legitimate labor controversies and subversive action was even more vague than the boundary between the FBI and G–2 fields of activity.   Particularly in the matters of strikes and slowdowns that might be fomented for subversive purposes, but also with respect to plant security, the War Department's primary objective was to establish preventive, precautionary measures, whereas under existing law the FBI could take counteraction only after an act of sabotage, or suspected sabotage, had taken place.   The single legal basis for excluding workers of possibly doubtful trustworthiness was a statute barring aliens from working on classified government contracts except upon written consent of the secretary of the department concerned.   New legislation to permit the weeding out of all suspicious employees in defense plants was studied, but no satisfactory solution was reached before the United States was at war.

The wide and rigid application of the restriction on the hiring of aliens had meanwhile run up against the fair employment policy of the Administration.   The President's executive order of 25 June 1941 prohibiting discrimination in defense employment by reason of race, creed, color, or national origin immediately raised the question whether it applied to aliens seeking work in defense industries.   On this point, members of Patterson's office were in disagreement.   Patterson, who was now Under Secretary of War, took the view that the order did not apply, that it protected only American citizens who might be discriminated against because of foreign birth.   This was adopted as the official position of the War Department in discussions with the President's Committee on Fair Employment Practice. As long as the question was simply one of security the War Department refused to open the door to aliens. The effect on the supply of labor was not an important consideration as yet.

At this stage of the defense effort, the availability of labor in adequate numbers assumed importance only to the extent that it was one of the factors normally considered in deciding upon the location of new plant sites. No real need for taking active measures to build up the labor force or for placing procurement contracts according to the supply of labor was seen. The early expansion of aircraft and small arms production facilities had been concentrated in a relatively few centers, and the difficulty of further expansion in those centers very soon appeared. During the summer and early autumn of 1941 the Air Forces and the Ordnance Department carefully avoided these localities when sites for new facilities were chosen, but by and large much less concern was felt over potential labor shortages than over the possibility of unemployment resulting from cutting back unessential production. Much of the pressure in 1941 was in the direction of spreading the work so as to relieve communities apparently faced with an unemployment problem.

With the number of strikes rising to a new peak, the War Department in the closing months of 1941 continued to rely on the National Defense Mediation Board and the National Labor Relations Board to settle labor disputes and chose, in the last resort, to have recourse to government seizure in order to keep production going until the dispute could be settled. The Labor Section of Under Secretary Patterson's office kept an eye on potential trouble spots, called them to the attention of the other agencies, and rode herd on them until the danger to procurement schedules was past. The imperfections of the governmental machinery were brought to light by the difficulties encountered in settling the strike at Air Associates, Incorporated, and the captive coal mine strike. The indispensability of the Air Associates output was considerably less certain than that of the North American Aviation company. War Department opinion on the question whether the Army should comply with National Labor Relations Board and National Defense Mediation Board rulings was by no means unanimous. Nevertheless, basic policies established during the seizure of the North American Aviation company were followed when the War Department took possession of the Air Associates plant, and, as in the previous case, production soon returned to its normal level. But no progress was made toward a settlement of the labor dispute.   The Mediation Board had ceased to function effectively after its CIO members walked out as a result of the coal strike; the War Department adhered to its policy of not actively participating in labor negotiations.   Not until the directors of the company installed a new management were negotiations with the union resumed.   Even then a settlement was not forthcoming until after the United States went to war and it was hinted that the Air Forces contract with the company might be transferred to another supplier.

Congressional reaction to the strike situation and particularly to the wrecking of the government's mediation machinery took the shape of new proposals for antistrike legislation.   The most stringent bill of this nature that had yet been introduced passed the House of Representatives but was sidetracked in the Senate by the Japanese attack on Pearl Harbor.

The labor problem was considerably eased by the pledge made by union leaders that there would be no strikes for the duration of the war.   By the end of February 1942 the National Labor Relations Board could even announce that work stoppages in war industry had been eliminated. Although such confidence was overly optimistic, for the most part workers did respond wholeheartedly to their leaders' pledge.   Throughout the first year of U.S. participation in the war, strikes were held down to a comparatively low level; production reached a new high.

With the onset of hostilities, tighter security measures were called for. Within a few days after war was declared, the President authorized the Army and the Navy to establish a plant security program, and on 10 January 1942 the two services jointly announced their procedures for removing workers against whom there was a "reasonable suspicion" of subversive activity.   The War Department was just then in the midst of the big reorganization of 1942 and the plant security program got off to a slow start.   In April, about a month after the War Department reorganization took place, measures for screening and investigating industrial workers were put into effect and procedures for reviewing dismissals were taken under study.   The first step toward establishing formal review and appeal machinery was the creation of a committee of officers in the Provost Marshal General's office to hear appeals.   Although the establishment of the review committee did not go as far in the direction of safeguarding the rights of the individual as labor leaders had urged, no further steps were taken until a year or so later.   The increased importance of plant security, the war-heightened suspicion of alien job seekers, and the rush to place production and procurement programs on a war footing once more brought to the fore the War Department's restrictive

procedures regarding the employment of aliens.   Neither the opposition of
the War Manpower Commission together with the President's concern for
fair employment practices nor the expiration of one of the statutory supports
of the restrictions served to relax the procedures.

One of the reactions to the attack on Pearl Harbor took the form of an
appeal for national service legislation—for registering all able-bodied men
and women and setting up the machinery and authority for their assignment
to jobs in the war effort.   The appeal for national service was not the result
of a rising ground swell of public opinion but of the efforts of some of
Stimson's War Department advisers and a relatively small, influential group
of citizens who in February 1942 organized the Citizens' Committee for a
National War Service Act.   Their advocacy of it was based upon the universal duty of citizens to the nation in a time of emergency, as a companion
measure to selective service.   Although Stimson was wholeheartedly in agreement and although the President gave sympathetic encouragement to the
appeal, for the time being neither Secretary Stimson nor the President
thought it timely to speak out officially and publicly in favor of national
service.

Production facilities were expanded so rapidly during the early months of
1942 that the supply of labor was given even less weight than in 1941.   New
facilities were often located without regard to the availability of labor.
Workers were drawn from low-paying but essential industries into new,
high-wage jobs, while the manpower intake of the armed services was increasing sharply.   Spot shortages of labor began to appear.   The War Department looked to the newly created organizations—the War Manpower
Commission and the National War Labor Board—to smooth out these
rough spots.   It supported requests by southwestern sugar beet and cotton
growers for the importation of Mexican workers, and it resisted, although
unsuccessfully, pressure for the release of soldiers to work in the nonferrous
metal mines.   In three instances—when labor shortages developed in the
Arizona cotton-growing industry, in the nonferrous mining industry, and in
the Seattle transportation system—the War Department organized special
teams of two or three officers and dispatched them to the scene to co-operate
with manpower officials.

The efforts on behalf of national service legislation had continued
throughout 1942, winning increasing support, and when the Austin-
Wadsworth bill was introduced in Congress in February 1943 both Secretary Stimson and Under Secretary Patterson spoke out in its favor.   The bill

brought together a strange assortment in the opposite camp.   Spokesmen for the AFL, CIO, and National Association of Manufacturers all came out in opposition to national service, along with various Negro organizations and women's groups.   Lacking strong Presidential support, the advocates of the bill were unable to bring it out of committee, and Congress turned to other legislation.

While the debate on national service was in progress the honeymoon that labor and management had been enjoying since the attack on Pearl Harbor showed signs of coming to an end.   The new year, 1943, had scarcely begun when 20,000 anthracite miners in eastern Pennsylvania went on strike. An industry-wide walkout of the bituminous coal miners followed.   Production of aircraft engines and motor vehicles at the Chrysler and Packard plants in Detroit was several times halted by strikes.   At Chicago, Akron, and elsewhere, strikes in defense industries were breaking out sporadically and in increasing numbers.   Most of them, except the coal strikes, were of brief duration, lasting only a few days, and were spontaneous in origin, representing rank and file dissatisfaction with the government's wage stabilization policy.   The trend was nevertheless potentially dangerous.   Again, as in 1941, the coal strikes aroused public indignation and revived Congressional interest in antistrike legislation.   This time a law was passed.   The War Department's attitude had shifted, and Secretary Stimson now joined the Secretary of the Navy in endorsing the War Labor Disputes bill, which Congress enacted on 25 June 1943 over the President's veto.   Anticipating an increase in the number of plant seizures, the War Department, on the basis of the technique it had developed so far, revised the procedures for conducting seizures and published a manual on the subject for the guidance of officers who might be assigned to such operations in the future.

Although in 1943 labor-management relations were more disturbed than they had been in the previous year, they had not profoundly deteriorated except in the coal industry.   On the other hand, the problem of labor supply for the first time had become a serious one.

The expansion of industry to a war footing had been achieved not only because a great concerted effort was made but also because there had existed at the beginning of the effort a large pool of unemployed workers.   Had the war effort come in a period of full employment, the manpower story would have been quite different indeed.   As it was, the labor reservoir began to disappear in 1943, and difficulties immediately began to multiply even though the peak of expansion had been reached.

All the additional elements that had contributed to the making of labor shortages in 1942 were of even greater effect in 1943, and the result was an increasing number of localities where the supply of industrial manpower had dwindled away.   Dissatisfaction on the part of both labor and management with the rulings of the National War Labor Board and War Manpower Commission also seemed to be growing, while at the same time Congress and manpower agencies were becoming more severe toward recalcitrants.   To the War Department, an increase in plant seizures and in the use of selective service to enforce compliance appeared likely.   Efforts to promote the employment of Negroes, up to this time a matter of social justice, were in 1943 spurred as a practical necessity.   But when industry began to recruit them in greater numbers, there were disturbances and disorders that threatened to cancel the gains.   For the first time a real effort was made to recruit women for work in war industry.   The reluctance of employers to hire women had disappeared, and the small reservoir of female job-seekers was quickly absorbed.   Now the problem was to break down the resistance of housewives and schoolgirls and all other women who did not particularly want a job. The pressure put upon the Army to release soldiers to industry continued to grow.   In the spring and early summer of 1943 the food canning and farm equipment industries requested and obtained the release of a few soldiers to help train new workers.   Eastern and Midwestern farmers received assistance in harvesting crops by the release of entire units for this purpose.   The copper industry obtained a second large-scale reinforcement.   A new potential source of labor became available during 1943 when prisoners of war captured in the North African campaign began to reach the United States. A few prisoners were made available to cotton growers in New Mexico and to one of the Midwestern railroads, but security problems, international law, public distrust, and strong opposition from the labor unions prevented widespread use of prisoners in industry.

To all these complexities, some new and some of new importance, there were added the increasing labor shortages and a desire on the part of the War Department to obtain a greater voice in the determination of manpower matters.   They all combined to impel the Army to make a frontal attack of its own on the labor problem.

The assault was carried out mainly by special project teams patterned after those that had been tried out on a few occasions in 1942.   It developed gradually, out of the success of the team sent to Seattle in the summer of 1943 to attack the labor problems of the Boeing aircraft plant.   From the

beginning of 1943, Boeing and other aviation companies on the west coast
had been complaining that production schedules could not be met because
of labor shortages. In the hope of reducing the competition for workers,
the War Department began to withdraw contracts from the localities afflicted
with labor shortages and to exercise tighter control of subcontracts. But the
extent to which this could be done was limited by community opposition to
the removal of contracts and by the necessity of using the special facilities
and trained workmen in the established centers of production. Furthermore,
although it could relieve the pressure on the labor supply in a given locality,
contract placement could not bring in additional workers. The measures
that were actually meant to build up the labor force, like the publicity campaigns for hiring women and Negroes, and the more peripheral measures,
like the reversal of War Department policy regarding the hiring of aliens,
could alleviate the general manpower situation but were not especially applicable to particular cases. What the special project teams did was to apply
all these and other measures to emergencies of a particular nature.

When the Boeing team arrived in Seattle in August 1943, it found that
action along a number of lines needed to be taken. Bearing authority to cut
through red tape, enjoying the co-operation of the management and labor,
and proceeding largely by persuasion, the team organized hiring offices, induced the National War Labor Board to take immediate action on a request
of the workers for a raise in wages, prevailed upon the local draft board to
give temporary deferments to Boeing workers, made arrangements to provide
furnishings from Quartermaster stocks for the company housing project, and
persuaded the company to adopt a new employee relations policy.

The dispatch of the team to Seattle coincided with the attack made on
the labor problem at all aircraft production centers on the west coast by a
special committee appointed by Under Secretary Patterson. On the basis
of the committee's report and the study made by Bernard Baruch and John
Hancock for the Office of War Mobilization, the War Department proposed
that procurement agencies, of which the War Department was the principal
one, establish a priorities list in accordance with which the War Manpower
Commission would allocate labor. The result was a sharp dispute between
the War Manpower Commission and the War Department and the adoption
of a compromise plan. A regional arrangement of parallel committees for
manpower and production was established, with War Department representation on each committee. The committees were given the responsibility
of fixing employment ceilings and job priorities, and the U.S. Employment
Service was assigned the task of referring workers to jobs accordingly.

To stimulate the work of the committees in the Los Angeles and San Diego areas and to reinforce the attack on the labor problem there, the War Department in September 1943 sent a special project team to southern California. It encountered the same multitude of problems that the Boeing team had faced, many of which, like housing, transportation, and recreation and welfare services, could be solved only by close co-operation with community agencies and local authorities. The tactics employed so effectively by the earlier special project teams were followed and further developed by the southern California team. With the organization of three additional teams in response to conditions in the ball bearing industry, the tire industry, and the forge and foundry industry, the procedures had become virtually standard practice by the end of 1943.

If 1943 marked a new turn in the War Department's approach to the labor situation, the next year brought a shift in the situation itself. No sooner had the Army made the adjustment to a more active and direct role than the stage was changed. On the battle fronts, the Allies seized the initiative and, although the road ahead still seemed long, during 1944 victory at last came in sight. On the production line, industrial output leveled off. The rush to expand facilities, to build up the labor force, and to raise production was over. The chief concern in 1944 was not so much that the supply of labor might dwindle away but that energies might flag as a result of rising optimism. An increasing rate of turnover and absenteeism, the rising trend in the number of strikes, and the difficulty in enforcing manpower policies were considered symptomatic. The shifting needs of production created by the changing military situation gave rise in turn to the problem of transferring labor from one plant to another. Cutbacks and reconversion loomed as knotty problems to prepare for.

The extension of the west coast manpower program to most of the United States during the winter of 1943–44 raised a difficult problem of enforcement. A directive from the Office of War Mobilization that "all interested governmental agencies" apply "any and all" sanctions lawfully available to them ran into opposition by the War Production Board. The Kilday Act, prohibiting the induction of fathers regardless of occupation until registrants without dependents were drafted, precluded for the time being the use of selective service as an enforcement measure. Although Congress resumed hearings on a revised national service bill and debated legislation designed to force IV–F's (registrants deferred because of failure to meet the physical standards of the armed services) into essential jobs, there was still not enough support to bring about action on either bill.   It was difficult to convince legislators, workers, and the public at large that manpower controls based on compulsion were needed at this time, when the peak of production had been reached and passed by efforts that were for the most part voluntary.

The steps currently taken to cut back certain production programs might have been effectively cited by the War Department as justification for enforced manpower controls, but the whole matter of cutbacks had become entangled in a bitter conflict both among and within the interested agencies. The basic elements in the conflict were whether the production agencies or the procurement agencies should decide the rate, extent, and locus of cutbacks, whether the manpower and facilities thus made available should be utilized for some other type of war production or be reconverted to civilian, peacetime production, and whether the technical services, the Army Service Forces, or the Joint Chiefs of Staff should review and approve the allocation and timing of cutbacks.   Although some of the procedural questions were cleared up during the spring of 1944, the dispute over policy lasted until June, when Director of War Mobilization Byrnes took the driver's seat.

The necessity for manpower controls in order to shift labor from industries that were cut back failed to materialize.   The actual cutbacks made before V-E Day were not large, and, as in the case of procurement, there was a considerable lead time before the effect made itself felt.   Some of them were only reductions in schedules that had been set unattainably high.   Only a small amount of manpower was therefore released as a result of cutbacks.

During the summer of 1944 the War Department decided to wage a public fight not only against strikes but also against the reconversion of industry to peacetime production.   By speeches before civic groups, motion pictures, and traveling road shows, it sought to create among workers a sense of urgency.   Appeals were made to the AFL and the CIO for workers to stay on the job in war industries and to increase production.   Business groups were warned that the time to turn to peacetime production had not yet come. Thus the War Department sought to counteract any letdown that might have been engendered by the Allied sweep across France, by the successful drives to the Philippines, and by the bomber offensive against Japan.

Whatever complacency survived the War Department's attack was rudely and abruptly shattered at the year's end by the German counteroffensive in the Ardennes and the ensuing Battle of the Bulge.   Manpower and production again assumed an aspect of critical importance.   During December 1944 and the next two months the War Department organized and put into the field five special project teams. Confronted by urgent requests to release additional soldiers for work in tire and heavy ammunition plants, in cotton duck factories, and in foundries, the War Department reluctantly fashioned a new furloughing system to provide industry with men. Another attempt was made to make use of selective service as a means of channeling workers into war jobs, this time by a directive to local draft boards calling for the induction of all men under the age of thirty-eight who either jumped jobs or were not working in essential industries. Again Congress took national service legislation under consideration.

The War Department had looked upon the selective service work-or-fight order as an inappropriate palliative, and considered it lacking in efficacy when applied. With Congress and the general public it was a more popular remedy than national service. When President Roosevelt in early January 1945 once more urged Congress to pass a national service bill, little heed was paid, but his request for stopgap legislation to force IV–F's into war jobs met an immediate response. Failing to obtain a national service bill, the War Department supported the stopgap measure introduced by Representative May and Senator Bailey. Although passed by the House, the May-Bailey bill even in a watered-down version was rejected by the Senate in early April 1945. By then the jolt caused by the Ardennes campaign had been absorbed. Germany had begun to collapse and her surrender was close at hand.

With the defeat of Germany, industrial manpower problems ceased to be a matter of pressing concern for the War Department. The special project teams were all withdrawn from the field, and no objection was interposed to the steps now made to reconvert industry to peacetime production. A partial demobilization of the Army was immediately begun. If returning soldiers sometimes proved reluctant to go back at once to their old jobs, those who did were still more than enough to fill the needs of the remaining war production programs. If strikes and labor disputes increased precipitously and if the specter of unemployment arose to haunt manpower experts, these were matters for the postwar planners. Whatever the future would be, labor had accomplished its wartime mission, and in the process a foundation of mutual confidence and understanding between the War Department and labor had been built.

Bibliographical Note

The road map to most source material for this book, like that for many volumes in the series UNITED STATES ARMY IN WORLD WAR II, is *Federal Records of World War II.* This National Archives publication describes the records of War Department agencies, most of which at the time this book was written were in the physical custody of the Departmental Records Branch, The Adjutant General's Office, Department of the Army. So abundant are these records that even if the historian limited himself to examining those documents bearing directly on his field of interest several lifetimes of research would be required. An effort is being made to sift this vast store of records and to forward those of permanent value to the National Archives. As a result, most of the War Department sources for this book are, or will become, available at the Archives.

One of the more difficult aspects of research into War Department activities in the field of industrial manpower is that, while there are numerous files dealing with this subject, for the most part records are scattered through many major War Department record collections. Because of political and economic factors involved, labor matters were often decided on the highest military levels. The files of the Secretary of War contain many documents dealing with labor matters. Stimson's own personal file has several labor folders, while that of his special assistant, Goldthwaite Dorr, has many cabinets dealing with subjects such as national service, manpower shortages, wartime strikes, and so on. Similarly, the file of the Under Secretary of War has drawers of documents dealing with labor matters. The so-called Amberg-Greenbaum-McGrady series of the Office of the Under Secretary of War file is heavily weighted with labor material as is the Hertz file. Additional labor material is found in many other subdivisions of the records of the Office of the Under Secretary of War.

An extremely useful collection of documents is that assembled by John H. Ohly while serving on the staff of Under Secretary Patterson and later of the Headquarters, Army Service Forces. Although at the time of writing it was in the custody of the Office of the Chief of Military History, the Ohly file will eventually be transferred to the Military Records Branch, Federal Records Center, General Services Administration, Region III. It consists of numerous memorandums for the record of private meetings, telephone conversations, and other events of which there would otherwise be no account, together with copies of letters, reports, and other documents dealing with many aspects of wartime labor problems.

The Army Service Forces files contain many documents on labor matters. The Headquarters, or Somervell, file of five cabinets contains a number of labor documents. The Control Division, ASF, file has some labor material. The largest single collection of source materials dealing with industrial manpower is the Industrial Personnel Division, ASF, file. While copies of some of the important policy papers are included, this file has the drawback that, while there is abundant material, much of it concerns details of operation and many important documents must be sought elsewhere. Nevertheless, this file is the best single source of original material for subjects studied in this volume. Many file folders in the records of the Resources and Production Division, which was at first a part of the Office of the Under Secretary of War, later a part of the Army Service Forces, and in 1943 was renamed the Production Division, ASF, also contain similar matter. Other ASF files with manpower materials include the Industrial Demobilization file and the Director of Personnel file.

The Army Air Forces central files, divided chronologically by date from 1939 to 1942, 1942 to 1944, and 1944 to 1946, also contain material pertinent to this study. Much useful source material is found under such headings as labor conditions, labor morale, AAF industrial manning board, and so forth.

Other primary sources in War Department files may be found under appropriate topic headings in the files of the Assistant Chief of Staff, G-2, and the technical services, particularly in those of the Offices of the Chief of Ordnance, the Chief Signal Officer, and The Quartermaster General. Brief summaries and references to some of the more important manpower matters are found in the minutes of the meetings of the War Department General Council, a set of which is filed with the records of the Office of the Chief of Staff.

In dealing with interagency relations and labor activities that cut across other government agencies the authors have generally relied on secondary sources. A minimum of exploration was nevertheless undertaken in files of the National War Labor Board, the War Production Board, the War Manpower Commission, and the U.S. Maritime Commission. The Gompers papers were examined at the American Federation of Labor offices, and some Congress of Industrial Organizations and United Mine Workers materials were perused. In addition, the authors interviewed many individuals both in and out of military service who supplemented and added information on many points.

There are several manuscripts of value dealing with War Department activities in the field of industrial manpower, most of which can be obtained through the Office of the Chief of Military History. The following manuscripts, dealing wholly or in part with topics discussed in this volume, are among the more valuable:

Anderson, Troyer S. Introduction to the History of the Under Secretary of War's Office.

Blum, Albert A. Deferment From Military Service: A War Department Approach to the Solution of Industrial Manpower Problems.

Hermes, Walter G. Manpower Limitations.

Ohly, John H. History of Plant Seizures During World War II. The appendixes to this manuscript contain one of the most valuable selections of source material in the whole field of War Department industrial relations.

War Manpower Commission. History of the Mobilization of Labor for War Production During World War II. This draft history, located in the World War II War Manpower Commission files in the National Archives, is in a very rough state but contains useful material.

Winnacker, Rudolph A. The Office of the Secretary of War Under Henry L. Stimson.

Toward the end of World War II many organizations prepared historical monographs on their activities. The Industrial Personnel Division of the Army Service Forces prepared many such monographs. A selected list of the more worthwhile items, the most valuable of which is the monograph by John H. Ohly and H. M. Somers, follows:

Monograph 2. War Department Organization for the Handling of Labor Problems in World War II, by Herman M. Somers and John H. Ohly.

Monograph 8. The War Department Role in the Shaping of Labor Standards and Related Matters During World War II.

Monograph 9. Methods of Handling Labor Supply Problems in Critical Industries and Areas, by Maj. James Doarn.

Monograph 10. The Special Project Technique in the Handling of Critical Plan, Area and Industry Manpower Problems, by Lt. Col. Arthur Krim and Maj. Seymour Peyser.

Monograph 11. War Department Facility Allocation, Contract Placement, and Cutback Distribution From the Standpoint of Labor Supply and Labor Relations, June 1940 to May 1945, by Edmond Kanwit.

Monograph 13a. War Department Role in Selective Service Inductions, by 1st Lt. Leonard J. Wechsler.

Monograph 13b. The Release of Key Industrial Personnel From the Armed Forces During World War II, by Maj. William McFadden.

Monograph 15a. War Department Wage Policies, by Lt. Col. Sidney Sufrin.

Monograph 15c. Fair Labor Standards Act, by John Fanning and Jean Flexner.

Monograph 15d. Walsh-Healey-Davis-Bacon Act, by John D. Fanning and Maj. John A. O'Donnell.

Monograph 16. The Development of a Pattern of Civilian Personnel Management Throughout the Army Service Forces, 1942–1944, by Col. Guy Wadsworth and William E. Orr, Jr.

Monograph 17. History of Classification and Wage Administration Program of Army Service Forces, by Lt. Col. Boyd Sheddan.

Monograph 18. History of Civilian Training in the Army Service Forces, 1942–1945, by Herbert Wickenheiser.

Monograph 22. Part I, The Development of a Grievance Procedure for ASF Civilian Workers and Experience in its Administration. Part II, The Development of a Procedure for Dealing With Organized Groups in ASF and Experience in its Administration.

Historical Monograph on the Employee Relations Function, IPD, Headquarters, ASF, During the Demobilization Period, 14 August 1945 to 1 January 1946.

The Policies, Plans, Problems, and Experiences of the Training Branch, IPD, During Demobilization, 15 August–31 December 1945, by Charles Eginton.

While the monographs prepared by the Industrial Personnel Division are the most important group for this volume, other military agencies also prepared historical studies which are pertinent. Most of these are in manuscript form; some are processed by mimeograph, photo-offset, or other method of preparing a relatively small edition for circulation. A very few are in printed form.

Two monographs put out by the Quartermaster Historical Section pertinent to labor matters are Harold W. Thatcher's *Planning for Industrial Mobilization, 1920–1940,* and the most excellent and thorough publication by Harry B. Yoshpe, *Labor Problems in Quartermaster Procurement.*

Useful monographs prepared in the Office of the Provost Marshal General are: Removal and Suspension of Subversives Program, Key Personnel Program, Industrial Employment Review Board, and Italian Service Units.

The following Ordnance Department monographs were consulted: Basic History of Elwood Ordnance Plant, History of Indiana Ordnance Works, History of Utah Ordnance, and Small Arms Ammunition: A History of an Industry, 1918–1944.

The Signal Corps prepared several "industrial summaries," of which the studies Signal Corps Procurement of Dry Batteries and Signal Corps Procurement of Wire and Cable contain labor materials.

Two Army Air Forces monographs provided useful information for this volume: *History of AAF Activities During World War II in the Field of Industrial Manpower,* and Expansion of Industrial Facilities Under Army Air Forces Auspices, 1940–1945.

Of the forty-one historical monographs prepared by the Civilian Production Administration, two were especially useful to the authors of this volume: Special Study 23, *Labor Policies of the National Defense Advisory Commission and the Office of Production Management, May 1940 to April 1942,* by Richard J. Purcell, and Special Study 14, *Concentration of Civilian Production by the War Production Board, September 1941 to April 1943,* by Maryclaire McCauley.

Many official documents and reports of the War Department were used in preparing this volume. Army regulations and circulars provided the basis for several statements. Progress reports and annual reports of various organizations such as the Industrial Personnel Division were also useful. Perhaps even more important were executive orders and public laws of the period dealing with manpower.

Of much greater value were the hearings and reports of Congressional committees. Among some of the more important hearings which provided valuable information were those on the National Defense Act of June 4, 1920, and of the War Policies Commission, 1931; Senate Special Committee Investigating the Munitions Industry (Nye Committee) in the mid-thirties; Senate Special Committee Investigating the National Defense Program (Truman/Mead Committee); House Special Committee to Investigate the National Labor Relations Board (Smith Committee); House Select Committee Investigating National Defense Migration (Tolan Committee); and many other hearings on manpower subjects before House and Senate Committees on Appropriations and Military Affairs.

Among the published books and pamphlets that proved to be of use were the following:

Adams, Leonard P. *Wartime Manpower Mobilization: A Study of World War II Experience in the Buffalo–Niagara Area.* Ithaca, New York: Cornell University Press, 1951.

Baker, Helen. *Women in War Industries.* Report Series 66. Princeton, New Jersey: Industrial Relations Section, Princeton University, 1942.

Civilian Production Administration. *Industrial Mobilization for War: History of the War Production Board and Predecessor Agencies, 1940–1945,* I, *Program and Administration.* Washington: Government Printing Office, 1947.

Connery, Robert H. *The Navy and the Industrial Mobilization in World War II.* Princeton: Princeton University Press, 1951.

Greenfield, Kent Roberts, Robert R. Palmer, and Bell I. Wiley. *The Organization of Ground Combat Troops.* UNITED STATES ARMY IN WORLD WAR II. Washington: Government Printing Office, 1947.

Griffith, Sanford. *Where Can We Get War Workers?* (Results of a Manpower Survey in Baltimore.) Public Affairs Pamphlet 75. New York: Public Affairs Committee, Inc., 1942.

International Labor Office. *The War and Women's Employment: The Experience of the United Kingdom and the United States.* Studies and Reports, New Series 1. Montreal, Canada: International Labor Office, 1946.

Janeway, Eliot. *The Struggle for Survival.* New Haven, Connecticut: Yale University Press, 1951.

Kreidberg, Lt. Col. Marvin A., and 1st Lt. Merton G. Henry. *History of Military Mobilization in the United States Army, 1775–1945.* Department of the Army Pamphlet 20-212. Washington: Government Printing Office, 1955.

Leahy, William D. *I Was There.* New York: Whittlesey House, 1950.

Leighton, Richard M., and Robert W. Coakley. *Global Logistics and Strategy: 1940–1943.* UNITED STATES ARMY IN WORLD WAR II. Washington: Government Printing Office, 1955.

Lewis, Lt. Col. George, and Capt. John Mewha. *History of Prisoner of War Utilization by the United States Army, 1776–1945.* Department of the Army Pamphlet 20-213. Washington: Government Printing Office, 1955.

Lilley, Tom, *et al. Problems of Accelerating Aircraft Production During World War II.* Cambridge, Massachusetts: Harvard Graduate School of Business Administration, 1946.

Millett, John D. *The Organization and Role of the Army Service Forces.* UNITED STATES ARMY IN WORLD WAR II. Washington: Government Printing Office, 1954.

Myrdal, Gunnar. *An American Dilemma; The Negro Problem and Modern Democracy.* 2 vols. New York: Harper & Brothers, 1944.

Nelson, Donald M. *Arsenal of Democracy.* New York: Harcourt, Brace and Company, 1946.

A Report of the Activities of the War Department in the Field of Industrial Relations During the War. Washington: Government Printing Office, 1919.

Richards, Allan R. *War Labor Boards in the Field.* Chapel Hill, North Carolina: University of North Carolina Press, 1953.

Rosenman, Samuel I. (compiler). *The Public Papers and Addresses of Franklin D. Roosevelt.* 13 vols. New York: Random House, 1938 (Vols. I–V); The Macmillan Company, 1941 (Vols. VI–IX); Harper & Brothers, 1950 (Vols. X–XIII).

Rosenman, Samuel I. *Working With Roosevelt.* New York: Harper & Brothers, 1952.

Seidman, Joel Isaac. *American Labor From Defense to Reconversion.* Chicago: The University of Chicago Press, 1953.

Selective Service System. *Industrial Deferment.* 3 vols. Special Monograph No. 6. Washington: Government Printing Office, 1947.

Somers, Herman M. *Presidential Agency: OWMR, the Office of War Mobilization and Reconversion.* Cambridge: Harvard University Press, 1950.

Stein, Rose M. *M-Day, The First Day of War.* New York: Harcourt, Brace and Company, 1936.

Stimson, Henry L., and McGeorge Bundy. *On Active Service in Peace and War.* New York: Harper & Brothers, 1948.

Swafford, Rosa Lee. *Wartime Record of Strikes and Lockouts: 1940–1945.* Senate Document 136, 79th Congress, 2d Session. Washington: Government Printing Office, 1946.

U.S. Bureau of the Budget. *The United States at War.* Washington: Government Printing Office, 1946.

U.S. Bureau of Labor Statistics. Bulletin 711, *Strikes in 1941 and Strikes Affecting Defense Production.* Washington: Government Printing Office, 1942.

————. Bulletin 741, *Strikes in 1942.* Washington: Government Printing Office, 1943.

————. Bulletin 782, *Strikes in 1943.* Washington: Government Printing Office, 1944.

————. Bulletin 800, *Wartime Development of the Aircraft Industry.* By Leonard G. Levenson. Washington: Government Printing Office, 1944.

U.S. Bureau of Labor Statistics.   Bulletin 833, *Strikes and Lockouts in 1944*. Washington: Government Printing Office, 1945.

————.   Bulletin 878, *Work Stoppages Caused by Labor-Management Disputes in 1945*.   Washington: Government Printing Office, 1946.

Waldman, Seymour.   *Death and Profits: A Study of the War Policies Commission*.   New York: Brewer, Warren, and Putnam, 1932.

Watson, Mark Skinner.   *Chief of Staff: Prewar Plans and Preparations*. UNITED STATES ARMY IN WORLD WAR II.   Washington: Government Printing Office, 1950.

List of Abbreviations

AAF	Army Air Forces
ACofAS	Assistant Chief of Air Staff
ACofS	Assistant Chief of Staff
Actg	Acting
Adm	Admiral, administrative
AF	Air Force
AFL	American Federation of Labor
ANMB	Joint Army and Navy Munitions Board
AQMG	Assistant Quartermaster General
AR	Army regulation
ASF	Army Service Forces
Asst	Assistant
CG	Commanding general
CIO	Congress of Industrial Organizations
CofEngrs	Chief of Engineers
CofOrd	Chief of Ordnance
Comd	Command
CPD	Civilian Personnel Division, Services of Supply
DCofS	Deputy Chief of Staff
Dept	Department
Dir	Director
Dist	District
Div	Division
EO	Executive order
ERC	Enlisted Reserve Corps
Exec	Executive
FBI	Federal Bureau of Investigation
FEPC	Fair Employment Practices Committee
FSA	Federal Security Agency
G–1	Personnel Division, War Department General Staff
G–2	Intelligence Division, War Department General Staff
GOCO	Government-owned, contractor-operated
Hist	Historical
HR	House of Representatives
IAM	International Association of Machinists
ILO	International Labor Office
IPD	Industrial Personnel Division, Army Service Forces

JAG	Judge Advocate General
JCS	Joint Chiefs of Staff
Ltr	Letter
Memo	Memorandum
Mil	Military
NDAC	Advisory Commission to the Council of National Defense
NDMB	National Defense Mediation Board
NLRA	National Labor Relations Act
NLRB	National Labor Relations Board
NWLB	National War Labor Board
NYPOE	New York Port of Embarkation
OASW	Office of the Assistant Secretary of War
OCMH	Office of the Chief of Military History
OCofOrd	Office of the Chief of Ordnance
OO	Ordnance Office
OPM	Office of Production Management
OPMG	Office of the Provost Marshal General
OQMG	Office of The Quartermaster General
Ord	Ordnance
OSW	Office of the Secretary of War
OUSW	Office of the Under Secretary of War
OWI	Office of War Information
OWM	Office of War Mobilization
OWMR	Office of War Mobilization and Reconversion
Pers	Personnel
PMG	Provost Marshal General
Proc	Procurement
Prod	Production
PT	Patrol vessel, motor torpedo boat
QM	Quartermaster
QMC	Quartermaster Corps
Res	Resources
Rpt	Report
S	Senate
Sec	Section
Secy	Secretary
Stat	Statute
Sv	Service
SW	Secretary of War

TAG	The Adjutant General
Tel Conv	Telephone conversation
Telgm	Telegram
UAW	United Automobile Workers, CIO
UMWA	United Mine Workers of America
USN	United States Navy
USW	Under Secretary of War
WAC	Women's Army Corps
WD	War Department
WLB	War Labor Board
WMC	War Manpower Commission
WPB	War Production Board

UNITED STATES ARMY IN WORLD WAR II

The multivolume series, UNITED STATES ARMY IN WORLD WAR II, consists of a number of subseries which are tentatively planned as follows: The War Department, The Army Air Forces, The Army Ground Forces, The Army Service Forces, Defense of the Western Hemisphere, The War in the Pacific, European Theater of Operations, Mediterranean Theater of Operations, The Middle East Theater, The China–Burma–India Theater, The Technical Services, Special Studies, and Pictorial Record.

The following volumes have been published or are in press:*

The War Department

Chief of Staff: Prewar Plans and Preparation
Washington Command Post: The Operations Division
Strategic Planning for Coalition Warfare: 1941–1942
Strategic Planning for Coalition Warfare: 1943–1944
Global Logistics and Strategy: 1940–1943
The Army and Economic Mobilization
The Army and Industrial Manpower

The Army Ground Forces

The Organization of Ground Combat Troops
The Procurement and Training of Ground Combat Troops

The Army Service Forces

The Organization and Role of the Army Service Forces

Defense of the Western Hemisphere

The Framework of Hemisphere Defense

The War in the Pacific

Okinawa: The Last Battle
Guadalcanal: The First Offensive
The Approach to the Philippines
The Fall of the Philippines
Leyte: The Return to the Philippines
Seizure of the Gilberts and Marshalls
Victory in Papua
CARTWHEEL: The Reduction of Rabaul

*The volumes on the Army Air Forces, published by the University of Chicago Press, are not included in this list.

European Theater of Operations
The Lorraine Campaign
Cross-Channel Attack
Logistical Support of the Armies, Volume I
Logistical Support of the Armies, Volume II
The Supreme Command
Mediterranean Theater of Operations
Northwest Africa: Seizing the Initiative in the West
The Middle East Theater
The Persian Corridor and Aid to Russia
The China–Burma–India Theater
Stilwell's Mission to China
Stilwell's Command Problems
Time Runs Out in CBI

The Technical Services
The Transportation Corps: Responsibilities, Organization, and Operations
The Transportation Corps: Movements, Training, and Supply
The Transportation Corps: Operations Overseas
The Quartermaster Corps: Organization, Supply, and Services, Volume I
The Quartermaster Corps: Organization, Supply, and Services, Volume II
The Quartermaster Corps: Operations in the War Against Japan
The Ordnance Department: Planning Munitions for War
The Signal Corps: The Emergency
The Signal Corps: The Test
The Medical Department: Hospitalization and Evacuation, Zone of Interior
The Corps of Engineers: Troops and Equipment
The Chemical Warfare Service: Organizing for War
Special Studies
Three Battles: Arnaville, Altuzzo, and Schmidt
The Women's Army Corp
Rearming the French
Chronology: 1941–1945
Military Relations Between the United States and Canada: 1939–1945
Pictorial Record
The War Against Germany and Italy: Mediterranean and Adjacent Areas
The War Against Germany: Europe and Adjacent Areas
The War Against Japan

Index

U.S. GOVERNMENT PRINTING OFFICE : 1959 OF—470151